EGYPTIAN-JEWISH
EMIGRÉS IN AUSTRALIA

EGYPTIAN-JEWISH EMIGRÉS IN AUSTRALIA

RACHELINE BARDA

CAMBRIA
PRESS

Amherst, New York

Requests for permission should be directed to:
permissions@cambriapress.com, or mailed to:
Cambria Press
20 Northpointe Parkway, Suite 188
Amherst, NY 14228

Paperback edition ISBN: 978-1-60497-796-7

**The Library of Congress has cataloged the earlier,
hardcover edition as follows:**

Library of Congress Cataloging-in-Publication Data

Barda, Racheline.
Egyptian-Jewish emigres in Australia / Racheline Barda.
p. cm.
Includes bibliographical references (p.) and index.
ISBN 978-1-60497-763-9 (perm. paper)
1. Jews, Egyptian—Autralia—History.
2. Jews— Australia—History—20th century.
3. Jews—Australia—History—21st century.
4. Jewish refugees—Autralia—History.
5. Egypt—Emigration and immigration—History—20th century.
6. Australia—Ethnic relations. I. Title.

DS135.A88B36 2011
305.892'4094—dc22

2011015787

To the memory of my beloved mother, Esther Abécassis
"A woman of worth who can find?
For her price is far above rubies..." (Proverbs 31:10)

Esther & Léon Abécassis
Alexandria, Egypt, 1934

TABLE OF CONTENTS

LIST OF CHARTS

ACKNOWLEDGMENTS

Writing this book would not have been possible without the assistance and encouragement of many people over the years, and I apologise in advance for not naming them all. I would like to thank first and foremost my friend, Lana Woolf, for initially suggesting that we record the memories of our ageing parents and compatriots and for starting me on this voyage of discovery. It was during those early interviews that we conducted together that I came to realise the importance of the task that we had undertaken and decided to give it a larger dimension.

I would like to express all my gratitude for the precious time and invaluable support Professor Suzanne Rutland provided so generously over the years and for her integrity and scholastic rigor. I am particularly grateful for her constant encouragement, as well as her patience and understanding of my problems. To Professor Konrad Kwiet, I also owe a great debt of gratitude for helping me refocus and offering a critical and fresh perspective.

To all my interviewees in Australia, France, Britain, and the United States, who opened their homes and gave generously of their time, thank you for your wonderful and interesting stories. Without these testimonies, there would have been no book.

I am greatly indebted to Australian Jewish institutions and to staff members of various libraries and archival records. The *Australian Jewish News* allowed me easy access to back issues of the *Sydney Jewish News*. The Australian Jewish Welfare Society (AJWS) facilitated access to its archives, as did the Australian Jewish Historical Society (AJHS) and its honorary archivist, Helen Bersten. Marianne Dacy, archivist at the Archive of Australian Judaica, also helped me find records pertaining to the immigration of Egyptian Jews. Kathy Buchan, librarian at Moriah College, very kindly assisted me in locating all the back copies of Jewish publications. I would also like to thank the staff at the Inter-Library Loans Department at Fisher Library of Sydney University for being so prompt in answering all my queries.

I would like to acknowledge all the organisations and individuals throughout the world who are making it their duty to research and inform others of the history and exilic experiences of the Jews of Egypt in modern times. For my research in France, I am particularly indebted to Emile Gabbay and Joseph Chalom who, through their past and present involvement with the publication of *Nahar Misraim*, the bulletin of l'Association pour la Sauvegarde du Patrimoine Culturel des Juifs d'Egypte (ASPCJE), answered all my questions and assisted me in locating sources not available through academic libraries. I would also like to thank Albert Oudiz, whose extraordinary memory of life in Egypt before the expulsion constituted an important source of information on my topic. My extended family and friends graciously provided some of the photos I have included in this book, for which I thank them.

I am particularly grateful to Paul Richardson and Toni Tan at Cambria Press for believing in the importance of publishing my book and giving a voice to all the people who enriched my research into the world of the Jews from Egypt.

Finally, I would like to thank my wonderful close and extended family and friends for their constant support during the whole period of my research, particularly my late mother, Esther, whose unconditional love, courage, and resilience were an inspiration; my daughters, Daniella and Monique, for believing in me and urging me to persist when I was ready to give up; my son David, always available at crisis time, for providing the technical expertise that I lacked—drawing the charts, setting up databases, and deciphering statistics; and finally, my longsuffering husband Joe (Giusy) for his patience with me over the last few years. I valued his assistance in every domain, whether it was transcribing, printing, photocopying, or helping during my field trips. Without the support of my family, I could not have reached the end of my journey.

ABBREVIATIONS

AAHA	Amicale Alexandrie, Hier et Aujourd'hui
AHC	Adelaide Hebrew Congregation
AIND	Association Internationale Nébi Daniel
AIU	Alliance Israélite Universelle
AJE	Association of Jews from Egypt, UK
AJOE	Association des Juifs originaires d'Égypte
AJT	Australian Jewish Times
AJHS	Australian Jewish Historical Society, Journal, & Proceedings
AJWS	Australian Jewish Welfare Society
AJW&RS	Australian Jewish Welfare and Relief Society
ALP	Australian Labor Party
ASPCJE	Association pour la Sauvegarde du Patrimoine Culturel des Juifs d'Égypte
COJASOR	Comité Juif d'Action Sociale et de Reconstruction
DP	Displaced Person
ECAJ	Executive Council of Australian Jewry

ESPCI	Ecole Supérieure de Physique et Chimie Industrielle
FSJU	Fonds Social Juif Unifié
HIAS	Hebrew Immigrant Aid Society
HLM	Habitation à loyer modéré
HSJE	Historical Society of Jews from Egypt
IAJE	International Association of Jews from Egypt
ICRC	International Committee of the Red Cross
IRO	International Refugee Organisation
JIMENA	Jews Indigenous to the Middle East and North Africa
JDC (AJDC)	American Joint Distribution Committee
JNF	Jewish National Fund
£E	Egyptian Pound (Livre Égyptienne)
LICA	Ligue Internationale Contre l'Antisémitisme
MELN	Mouvement Égyptien pour la Libération Nationale
NAAFI	Navy Army Air Force Institute
NCJW	National Council of Jewish Women
NCJWA	National Council of Jewish Women of Australia
OFPRA	Office Français de Protection des Réfugiés et Apatrides
SSJ	Service Social des Jeunes
SJN	Sydney Jewish News
SMH	Sydney Morning Herald
UNHCR	United Nations High Commissioner for Refugees
UHS	United HIAS Service
UJE	Lycée de l'Union Juive pour l'Enseignement
WCJE	World Congress of Jews from Egypt
WJC	World Jewish Congress
WIZO	Women's International Zionist Organisation

EGYPTIAN-JEWISH EMIGRÉS IN AUSTRALIA

INTRODUCTION

This book sets out to explore key aspects of the modern history of Egyptian Jews by looking at three distinct topic areas. The first part sheds light on the last three chapters of their lives in Egypt: a golden age under the protection of the colonial powers of England and France from the early 1900s until 1937; a gradual decline due to the abolition of foreigners' privileges under the Capitulations regime, the rise of Arab nationalism and increasing problems in Palestine; and finally, the crisis period that followed the outbreak of the three successive Arab-Israeli Wars of 1948, 1956, and 1967, all leading to the almost total demise of Egyptian Jewry by the early 1970s. The second part, which constitutes the core of this thesis, focuses on the migration experience of a small group of Egyptian Jews to Australian shores, including the government policies related to their immigration and integration into Australian society. The third and final part consists of a comparative case study addressing some of the more crucial themes linked to the migration experience of a select number of Egyptian Jews to France.

At first, this research project was undertaken for personal reasons—
I am also a Jew from Egypt, having arrived in Australia in 1958 and
gone through very similar experiences to most of my compatriots.
I strongly believed it was important to record the peregrinations of my
group because the Egyptian diaspora has truly come to an end, without
any sign of a return community to Egypt, even after the signing of the
1979 peace accord between Egypt and Israel.

Together with a friend and compatriot, Lana Woolf née Golliger,
I initially undertook this project as a community-minded mission and
not as an academic task.[1] At that point in time, the purpose was to create
a record of the experiences of the Egyptian Jews of Sydney. It was felt
that such a record would constitute a testimony to the richness of their
past, as well as recognition of their distinctiveness in the context of the
broader Australian Jewish community. This record was meant mainly
for the benefit of their descendants, as well as prospective researchers.
The project was based on the assumption that every personal story was
important and contributed to the development of an overall picture of the
Jews in Egypt and from Egypt, especially in view of the facts that they
were now dispersed all over the world and that the Jewish presence in
Egypt has dwindled to an insignificant number.

I gradually came to the conclusion that to do justice to the diversity and vibrancy of this particular diaspora and its exilic experiences
I needed the endorsement and the assistance of a university body. In view
of the end of a continuous and significant Jewish presence in Egypt for
the first time in twenty-five centuries and the realisation that it will probably never be revived, the importance and urgency of the undertaking
became paramount. As foreseen, once the project developed into serious academic research, under the auspices of the Department of Hebrew,
Biblical and Jewish Studies at the University of Sydney, with the supervision of Associate Professor Suzanne D. Rutland, it gained more recognition within the group of Egyptian Jews, and contacts with prospective
respondents, both in Australia and overseas, were greatly facilitated.

The first task was to contextualise the diaspora that Jews built for
themselves in Egypt and establish what happened to that diaspora after

1948. From the dawn of antiquity, Egyptian Jewry had experienced cycles of golden and dark ages, of prosperity and decline, of honour and degradation. These cycles were repeated under every known ruler of Egypt, whether Persian, Greek, Roman, Byzantine, Arab, Ottoman, or Mamluk. The relationship between the Jews and "the dominant other" was mostly one of symbiosis, and the Jewish condition often mirrored the general political, economic, and social situation prevalent at the time in that part of the world. In spite of the numerous vicissitudes it endured, the community succeeded in maintaining its Jewishness, while still espousing outward signs of the dominant culture. Under medieval Islam, in a society that was mainly defined by religion, Jews remained marginalised as *dhimmis*, protected but nevertheless second-class citizens, always at a distance from mainstream society but at the same time strengthened in their identity as Jews. Since the mid-nineteenth century, their status was greatly enhanced under the protection of the European colonial powers. However, the transformation of Egypt into a modern nation-state increasingly destabilised the foundations of Jewish life in that country. The Jews of Egypt had to respond to the dilemmas introduced by modernity with its long list of "isms", such as colonialism, liberalism, nationalism, secularism, Arabism, Islamism, Communism, and Zionism. All these ideologies pulled the fabric of their society in conflicting directions. They had to contend with a growing sense of alienation, challenges to their national identity, and political forces that eventually forced them into exile and dispersion. This study investigates every one of these issues with the objective of understanding the underlying reasons for the demise of the Jewish community in Egypt and assessing its integration and acculturation into such diverse diasporas as Australia and France.

Employing a detailed study of a sample group of Egyptian Jews who migrated to Australia and using oral history as a research tool, reinforced by historical data, I tried to construct their social profile as a migrant group, showing how and why they integrated the way they did, how successful was their integration, and how they reconstructed their identity to fit their new context. Finally, by comparing and contrasting the Australian and French migration experiences, I hoped to demonstrate that the

Jews of Egypt shared some remarkable attributes, such as an astonishing level of multilingual skills, and therefore an innate ability to accommodate a multilayered identity and to interact with people from different backgrounds. The advancing tide of an exclusivist Egyptian nationalism had or should have somewhat forewarned and prepared them for their eventual exodus. Furthermore, because the Jews of Egypt—as part of a Levantine society—had personally experienced cultural pluralism as a way of life, they already possessed the necessary skills to achieve a smooth integration into whatever country or culture they would implant themselves after their forced emigration. I have raised some pointed questions on the degree of their acculturation to the dominant culture. How did their multilingualism serve them in the monolingual Australia of the 1950s and 1960s? How did they negotiate the different layers of their plural identity in their new country, and did they retain a core identity in the process? According to my investigations, no other researcher has done a scientific study of Egyptian Jews in Australia based on those themes.

Before entering into the body of my topic, it was important to delineate the conceptual framework around which this study was constructed by clearly defining such terms as forced emigration, assimilation, integration, acculturation, and multiculturalism in order to establish their relevance to the present study. For instance, the act of forced emigration can be understood to refer to people or a group of people who are either physically expelled from their native country by authority or compelled to leave their country because of political persecution, conflicts, economic problems, or religious or ethnic discrimination, as opposed to voluntary emigration where there is an element of choice.[2] This phenomenon can also be defined as an "exodus" that, in the biblical sense, is more than just a mass departure. It is "a journey by a large group to escape from a hostile environment".[3] The people who make up this group become refugees forced to seek residence in any nation-state that will accept them within its borders.[4] My study will show that this was the case for Egyptian Jews.[5]

Once they are settled in that nation-state, the newcomers are faced with a number of different strategies destined to make them feel part of their new country, such as assimilation, integration, and acculturation.[6] It is necessary at this point to outline the differences between the three strategies.[7] In the words of historian Marion A. Kaplan's gender analysis of the Jews of Imperial Germany, assimilation is "assumed to be the process engaged in by a minority whose goal is fusion with the majority".[8] In the Jewish context, Kaplan uses the term assimilation "to indicate the loss of a Jewish ethnic and religious identity", the discarding of Jewish ties:[9]

> "Assimilation" is an appropriate description for a small group of consciously and totally "Germanised" Jews (many of whom were baptised or had intermarried) who lived in total estrangement from anything Jewish and who sought relationships only with Christians and other Jews like themselves.[10]

Kaplan's concept can apply to any Jewish diaspora, whether in Egypt, France, or Australia. For instance, assimilation was the policy of conformity advocated by the Australian government towards its non-British migrants of the immediate postwar period.[11] The understanding was that those migrants were to shed their cultures, traditions, and languages and, through socialisation away from their own ethnic group and eventually intermarriage, become undistinguishable from the host population.

Integration is also a social process engaged in by a minority—that of entering a host society, but on a more egalitarian basis. The Oxford Dictionary defines integration as "the bringing into equal membership of a common society those groups or persons previously discriminated against on racial or cultural grounds".[12] From the mid-1960s to 1973, the Australian government policy in respect to its non-British migrant population gradually abandoned a failing assimilation strategy for the concept of integration. This new policy recognised the diverse needs of the migrant population and did not advocate the necessary loss of "any individual's original language and customs but nevertheless, saw their principal value in their utility as a means to full participation in an integrated Australian culture".[13]

From 1973, the notion of "multiculturalism" was introduced to foster full integration whilst allowing each ethnic group to retain its unique cultural identity. Thus, the term has come to describe the cultural and linguistic diversity of Australian society. As noted by Suzanne Rutland, in a multicultural society "newcomers are encouraged to maintain and promote their ethnic heritage" because "a pluralistic approach will enrich the Australian way of life and cultural heritage".[14] For migrants such as the Jews from Egypt, considering the intrinsic multicultural and multi-layered aspect of their identity, it is clear that this new policy promoted an even greater sense of comfort and belonging in Australian society. The acceptance of diversity leads to the next step in the process of socialisa-tion of minority groups, which is acculturation. Acculturation refers to the concept of mutual contribution of both minority migrant groups and the dominant host society to the makeup of a common national identity.[15] Kaplan defined acculturation as:

> the acceptance of many of the customs and cultural patterns of the majority of society and the simultaneous commitment (conscious or unconscious) to the preservation of ethnic and/or religious distinctiveness.[16]

Thus, Jews in Imperial Germany acculturated by accepting the standards of the dominant culture while recognising and maintaining ethnic separ-ateness. It is the same process by which Egyptian Jews became Austra-lian or French or Brazilian and remained Jewish at the same time.

This research and the subsequent evaluation of the collected data have been conducted keeping in mind those definitions of the conceptual framework. The themes of assimilation, integration, multiculturalism, and acculturation are central to postwar Australian history. This book aims to shed more light on the macrosituation through a microstudy of Egyptian Jews in Australia.

The first chapter reviews the various publications referring to Egyp-tian Jews after their dispersion throughout the Western world, particu-larly Australia and France. Although their "second exodus" has been the subject of a number of academic monographs and theses in Israel, Europe, and the Americas, the specific character of their dispersion after 1948 has interested only a handful of scholars of Jewish history.

The body of literature covering this topic is not extensive.[17] The state of research on Egyptian Jews in Australia is understandably even more restricted, due to their small number and low profile. The few historians who have dealt with this issue did so briefly, in the context of a broader study of Sephardim in Australia. In France, where the size of the Egyptian diaspora is more significant, personal migration stories have been the object of several memoirs, but even there it seems that only a few researchers engaged in a serious and systematic study of the Egyptian Jews as a distinct migrant group.

Chapter 2 outlines the methodological strategies, including a description of the different approaches to the evaluation of the data, bearing in mind the basic social concepts that have just been outlined. Oral history as a research tool is discussed with the intention of identifying its inherent strengths and weaknesses, as well as explaining why it was particularly appropriate for this study. The use of archival records and secondary sources was also essential for comparing and contrasting the results of the collected data.

Based on primary and secondary sources, chapter 3 proceeds to establish the history of the Jews of Egypt in the modern period, starting with the landing of Napoleon Bonaparte in 1798. Following a thematic approach, this section concentrates on the rise and fall of Egyptian Jewry, looking at the way the Jews of Egypt responded to the clashing ideologies of the interwar period, focusing on the chain of events that led to their mass exodus starting from 1948, and ending with the near-total demise of a viable Jewish community in Egypt.

Both Chapters 4 and 5 deal with the oral history data, using a quantitative and qualitative approach by linking the questions to the findings. Chapter 4 compares and contrasts elements of the Australian participants' stories and their personal perspective of the events that so dramatically changed their lives, to the official version of those same events. The analysis of their demographic, ethnic, socioeconomic, and cultural characteristics leads to a reconstruction of their experience as Jews in Egypt, evoking both the privileges they enjoyed earlier and the discrimination they suffered later. It also helps to define their identity as a pluralistic, multicultural, and multilingual group. Chapter 5 examines the religious divisions of the sample group into Sephardim, Ashkenazim, and Karaites, again comparing and contrasting their differences and similarities. It also looks at the themes of inclusion versus exclusion and allegiance versus alienation, in terms of the participants' perception of their place in an independent Egyptian nation and their level of involvement in the political scene.

In Chapter 6, the events of the three successive wars that triggered the exodus of Egyptian Jews are evaluated in relation to the participants' personal experiences, clearly showing that the majority was more or less coerced into leaving the country, either through direct expulsion or economic strangulation. Some of the questions raised in this chapter are: Did the participants expect that rejection? Was it justified? And how prepared were they for emigration?

Chapter 7 explores the process of migration of the sample group and the different stages of the journey to Australia. It outlines the impact of the restrictive "White Australia" Policy and the various difficulties it imposed on Jews of Middle Eastern origin. It also sheds light on the crucial role played by Jewish institutions and their leaders in securing landing permits for Egyptian Jews. It evaluates their difficult beginnings in Australia and their gradual integration and contribution to both mainstream society and Jewish community. Chapter 8 discusses the crucial concept of plural identities, revealing how Egyptian-Jewish migrants negotiated the various layers of their identity in Australia. It also assesses their interaction with other Jewish ethnic groups and their commitment to Jewish communal issues, linking up with the broad concepts of forced emigration, integration, acculturation, and identity.

The analysis of all those aspects of migration led me to widen the scope of my research in Australia with a comparative study of the immigration experience of a select number of Egyptian Jews in France, contrasting the two geographical, social, and cultural contexts, again using oral history as a research tool. The differences and similarities between the two experiences are assessed, taking into consideration the difficult socioeconomic conditions in both Australia and France in the 1950s and 1960s, and the critical role played by international and local Jewish organisations in the migration and integration process of the Jewish refugees from Egypt. The crucial themes of culture, integration, and acceptance by the host society are central to this chapter, as well as the themes of memory and transmission of the group's cultural heritage to the next generation.

In Australia, the Jews of Egypt have not particularly attracted the attention of sociologists as a migrant group. Within the context of Australian Jewry, their story is largely unknown. Therefore, my in-depth analysis of their migration experience in Australia, looking at their demographics; ethnic, national, and religious profile; Western education; multilingualism; and other facets of their multilayered identity, covers an area of the rich Australian history of migration that has remained unexplored.

Apart from the personal aim of preserving historical data and memories of a community that has almost disappeared, the objective of this book is to evaluate the Australian migration experience of a particular ethno-religious group, by looking into the history of the Jews of Egypt, past and present, and comparing certain aspects of their experience with that of a similar group in France. At the same time, my research intends to illuminate certain key issues of Australian immigration. The topics of forced emigration, memory, resettlement, and reconstruction of identity of a minority migrant group into the dominant society all fit into the realm of important concepts of social sciences. Through the use of my two sample groups as successful examples of "second-time-around" acculturation, I hope to contribute to the body of research into the exile and migration of minorities and into the policies that regulate the process of assimilation and integration of those minorities into the host society.

CHAPTER 1

STATE OF RESEARCH

The modern history of the Jews of Egypt and their dispersion after 1948 has only recently started to attract the attention of scholars. Although serious research on this topic has made significant progress since the 1980s, the amount of published material dealing with the topic is still not extensive. Even less has been written on their migration experience to Australia owing to their small numbers and low profile. However, the study of Jews in the Islamic world has generated several publications from a number of scholars. The Orientalist historian Bernard Lewis delved into the complex and often-paradoxical history of Jewish-Muslim relations from the late medieval to the early modern periods in his book *The Jews of Islam*.[18] Bat-Ye'or (pseudonym of Giselle Littman née Orébi), an independent and controversial historian and émigrée from Egypt living in Switzerland since 1956, published *The Dhimmi: Jews and Christians under Islam* (1985) in which she re-evaluated the meaning of the dhimmi status for Jews and Christians living under Islamic rule from the time of the prophet Muhammad until the establishment of the State of Israel in 1948. She argued that the protection the "People of the Book" were supposed to enjoy according to *shari'a* law[19] was far from idyllic and that, on the contrary, persecution was endemic in Muslim countries. To illustrate her point, she detailed numerous incidents of antidhimmi riots, forced conversion, and oppression due to the restrictive legislation that regulated the religious and economic activities of nonbelievers in the Muslim world. However, she seemed to overlook the long periods when Christians and Jews flourished under Muslim rule and discriminatory provisions were regularly flouted. Her conclusions are construed by a number of scholars as too one-sided and polemical.[20] The American historian Mark R. Cohen called this style of gloomy representation of Jewish life under Islam "a neo-lachrymose conception of Jewish-Arab history", arguing that both this pessimistic interpretation and its opposite, an inflated vision of an interfaith utopia, are but a myth and countermyth rooted in the current political discourse of Arab and Israeli historiography.[21] Other scholars, such as Harvey E. Goldberg and Michel Abitbol, tend to agree that, with the winds of a new pan-Arabic nationalism blowing since the late 1930s and the identification of Jews as agents of the hated British and French colonialists, the discrimination against the Jews of Arab lands in the hands of their respective governments grew significantly worse.[22] The argument as to whether they were genuine victims of persecution in their own land is at the heart of the issue of identification and feelings of belonging that I investigated in the course of my interviews.

The Jews of Arab Lands in Modern Times, a book by Professor Norman A. Stillman—whose special area of interest is Jewish and Islamic history and culture—was particularly relevant to my study because of its time frame. It focused on the far-reaching consequences of the sudden and brutal penetration of Europe into the Middle East, with the landing of Napoleon Bonaparte in Egypt in July 1798, and its impact on all the peoples of the Middle East and North Africa, particularly the non-Muslim minorities.[23] Whereas the Muslims perceived that impact to be a threat to their civilisation, the Jews saw it as a way out of their subordinate status of dhimmis. In fact, Stillman pointed out that before the Europeans' arrival in the area, apart from a very small prosperous minority, the vast majority of Jews were not only poor and oppressed like most of the population but also "had to bear the burden of social isolation, inferiority, and general opprobrium".[24] Whereas France had been the traditional protector of Catholics in the Levant since the sixteenth century, the Jews of the region had no Western protection until the 1830s when England started to take "a protective interest in the welfare of Ottoman Jews as a group".[25] In addition, Stillman portrayed the conflicts faced by traditional Jewish communities in response to the challenges of modernity and the contending forces of Zionism, European colonialism, and Arab nationalism. He discussed the darkening shadows of the interwar period, the trouble brewing in Palestine, the rise of Nazism, and Jewish responses to the problem of anti-Semitism. He examined the increase of anti-Zionist agitation in the Arab world after 1943, which translated into anti-Jewish riots throughout several Arab countries. He presented the case of Egypt where mass demonstrations, accompanied by looting and ransacking of the Jewish quarter and Jewish businesses, occurred on the anniversary of the Balfour Declaration, November 2, 1945.[26] According to Stillman, by the time the State of Israel was established in 1948, the status of Jewish minorities in Arab lands was already considerably weakened, and their faith in a secure future in those countries significantly eroded. Therefore, one of his main contentions was that, although the question of Palestine was certainly "a major contributing factor in all of this…it was by no means the only one".[27]

Stillman pointed to the strong ethnic and religious component of Arab nationalism, which was gradually excluding Jewish minorities from the national project, and to the first Arab-Israeli War, which led to the beginning of a mass exodus of Jewish populations from the Arab world.[28] That exodus was resumed in force after the October 1956 Arab-Israeli War, which is considered to have been the *coup de grâce* (the final blow) for an Egyptian Jewry already destabilised by the 1954 discovery of a spy and sabotage ring composed of eleven young Egyptian Jews working for Israel.[29] Stillman also provided an invaluable collection of primary sources, selected from various archives, particularly from the records of the *Alliance Israélite Universelle* (AIU), as well as from newspapers, correspondence, and diaries. These documents bear testimony to the past vibrancy and diversity of the Jewish communities of the Arab world and their responses to the challenges of modernity. They speak for themselves by bringing to life the historical upheavals of the period and their impact on the local Jewish populations, providing the researcher with the opportunity to make an assessment of the situation based on these primary sources.[30]

Specific study of modern Egyptian Jewry includes the works of scholars such as Joel Beinin, Maurice Fargeon, Jacques Hassoun, Gudrun Krämer, Jacob Landau, Michael Laskier, and Shimon Shamir, all of which were found to be invaluable tools for my own research. The 1938 monograph of Maurice Fargeon, *Les Juifs en Égypte: Depuis les origines jusqu'à ce jour*, was interesting because, as its title states, it strove to cover the whole period of Jewish history in Egypt from biblical times until the onset of World War II.[31] The section that was relevant to my research dealt with the ethnic characteristics and the demography of Egyptian Jewry, from the time of Mohammed Ali, Viceroy of Egypt (1805–1848), to the beginning of King Farouk's reign (1937–1952). The book endeavoured to paint a total picture by including both urban and rural Jewish communities, noting their religious, philanthropic, and cultural institutions, their communal leaders, their schools, their synagogues, and the individual rabbis who served the different congregations. It also presented interesting statistics, listing Jews according to place of residence, gender, and personal status. The importance of this book as a social document lay mainly in its perspective of a particularly golden era in the history of Egyptian Jewry. However, there are a number of problems associated with Fargeon's study. Modern-day scholars have challenged some of his estimates, especially in regard to the Napoleonic period.[32] In addition, Fargeon did not offer any critical evaluation of the situation of Egyptian Jewry. He painted an idealised picture of a community very much in command of its own destiny, very comfortable in its Egyptian home, and without a hint of the rising tensions in the political and social arenas. It is obvious that this picture reflected the world view of the author, as well as the general feeling of security and supreme confidence in which most Egyptian Jews basked pre-1948.

Jacob M. Landau's monograph, *Jews in Nineteenth-Century Egypt*, was found to be much more precise and scholarly in its study of demography, place of residence, and occupation that was based on solid literary sources and official censuses. These elements attested to the inferior social, economic, and political status of Egyptian Jews in those days and shed light on the reasons why the Jews actively sought foreign protection. Landau meticulously outlined the community structure and its institutions, as well as the intercommunal relations. He also reviewed the domain of intellectual and religious life, pointing out the paucity of literary works written by Jews and published in Egypt until the end of World War I, apart from a number of religious studies and didactic publications. Nevertheless, Landau noted the high level of literacy within the community and listed the different schools attended by Jewish children, highlighting the critical role played by the AIU in the realm of Jewish and secular education. He also commented on the gradual decline in religious observance among the young with the advent of modernity and the growing attraction of European culture. In addition, he looked into the initial struggle of an organised Zionist movement in Egypt up to World War I, attributing this struggle to the apolitical nature of most Egyptian Jews and their deep sense of security in the country. Like Stillman, Landau included in his work a number of original documents in Arabic, English, French, or Hebrew—collected from various archives— that vividly illustrated the general situation of Jews in Egypt and their activities from about 1750 to 1916. In addition, Landau's book titled *Middle Eastern Themes*, published in 1973, brought together a series of journal articles he had previously written. This collection included a number of chapters that concerned Egyptian Jewry. One particular chapter provided a review of the ritual murder accusations—mostly from the Greek Orthodox community—that occurred in Egypt during the last thirty years of the nineteenth century, based on archival records of the Foreign Ministries in London and Rome.[33] Another chapter evaluated the part played by the Jewish community in the modernisation of education in nineteenth-century Egypt.[34] The story of the most interesting figure among the leading Jewish supporters of Egyptian nationalism, Yacub Sanua, known as Abu Naddara (1839–1912), was outlined. Landau highlighted Naddara's importance in the literary and journalistic fields and in the Egyptian theatre, where he introduced political satire using for the first time colloquial Arabic.[35] By exposing the social and political context of the environment of Egyptian Jews in the pre-1914 period, Landau's work contributed significantly to the understanding of the whole period and therefore was found to be extremely useful.

Another important study that dealt with different aspects of the Jewish society in modern Egypt was Shimon Shamir's book, *The Jews of Egypt: A Mediterranean Society in Modern Times*, published in 1987. This publication incorporated a collection of papers by a number of Israeli and international scholars, such as Aryeh Schmuelevitz, Jacob M. Landau, Shamir himself, Gudrun Krämer, Jacques Hassoun, Sasson Somekh, and others, which were presented at a conference titled "The Jews of Egypt in Modern Times", convened at Tel Aviv University in June 1984. These authors each selected topics within their sphere of interest, such as the Ottoman background of the Jews in Egypt, the extent of their political participation in Egyptian society, their contribution to the economy and to the Egyptian-Arabic culture, their diversity, and finally "the self-view of Egyptian Jews and the ways these Jews were viewed by the Egyptian majority and by the founders of Israeli society".[36] Shamir dealt with the complicated issue of Egyptian nationality by looking at the evolution of Egyptian nationality laws and how they were applied to the Jews, a topic that concerned quite a number of my respondents. The book also includes an array of impressive primary sources related to the respective subject of each section.[37]

One of the most comprehensive studies of the history of Egyptian Jewry in the first half of the twentieth century can be found in *The Jews in Modern Egypt, 1914–1952*, by Gudrun Krämer, published in 1989.[38] Krämer chose to focus on the social and economic position of the Jews in Egyptian society, as well as on their political activities, compared to the position of other non-Muslim minorities. Drawing on a number of primary and secondary sources, Krämer painted an extremely informative picture of the Jewish community with its diverse ethnic composition, its multiplicity of languages, its distinctive rites and regional origins, and its occupational and social structure. Krämer also pointed to the stability and efficiency of the communal organisation despite the diversity of the Jewish population and looked at the complex issues of nationality and the privileged status of foreigners. Furthermore, Krämer reviewed the socio-economic and political changes that occurred between 1915 and 1948 and their negative impact on the relations between the Muslim majority and the local Jewish minority from the late 1930s on. She argued—as is also my contention—that this was really the beginning of the end for the Jews in Egypt, "not so much caused by new conditions or behaviour within the Jewish minority itself as by a gradual shift in the political climate in Egyptian society at large".[39] She raised the critical issues of integration and acculturation of Jews into Egyptian society in view of the inevitable alienation caused by their wholesale adoption of European languages and education. However, she still suggested that even if, from the 1930s, the bulk of Egyptian Jews had opted for the Arabic language and culture and had actively participated in Egyptian life and politics, it was probably already too late for them as non-Muslims and non-Arabs to be accepted as full members of Egyptian society. Although she rejected Bat Ye'or's thesis that Jews were consistently subjected to discrimination in Egypt, as in all Arab countries, she also argued against the postulation that it was mainly Zionism that created problems between the Muslim majority and the Jewish minority. Rather, she was of the opinion that there were periods of acceptance and rejection, and although Zionism played a part in the latter it was not the only factor. It is regrettable that Krämer's book touched only briefly on the mass departure of the Jews after the Arab-Israeli Wars of 1956 and 1967 and thus did not add anything new to our understanding of the events after the 1948 war and their consequences for Egyptian Jewry.

The historian Michael Laskier provided a different perspective in his book, *The Jews of Egypt, 1920–1970*, published in 1992.[40] He focused on the last decades of Jewish life in Egypt, particularly on the Zionist

activities of the community and the gradual disintegration and dispersal
of the Jewish community in the wake of the first three Arab-Israeli Wars.
Laskier argued that previous studies failed to examine the relationship
between the Jews of Egypt and the Yishuv since the time of the granting of the Palestinian Mandate to Great Britain in 1920. He also maintained that the critical role of the French-language Jewish press had
been largely overlooked. Laskier ended his study in 1970, the year of
President Gamal Abdel Nasser's death, when Jewish communal life in
Egypt had virtually come to an end. His main sources were the archives
of the American Joint Distribution Committee (JDC) in Jerusalem and
New York, the Israel State Archives for the period 1948–1958, and the
Egyptian, Israeli, and European press. Oral history methodology was
used to gather the testimonies of former Israeli emissaries and members of Zionist youth movements. Laskier's examination of the issue of
illegal immigration to Palestine prior to the establishment of the Jewish
State in 1948, and the crucial role of the Yishuv's emissaries to Egypt,
was particularly interesting because it authenticated the testimonies of
some of my interviewees who reported having been involved in some
of the covert operations mentioned by Laskier.[41] Even more relevant
to my own work was Laskier's research on the aftermath of the 1948
Arab-Israeli War, with the arbitrary sequestration of the largest Jewish enterprises and the internment conditions of Zionist suspects at the
Huckstep prison camp. Once again, the details he provided confirmed
my own interviewees' testimonies.[42] The most interesting section of the
book dealt with the previously mentioned Lavon Affair—also known as
The Mishap—when Egyptian authorities arrested and tried a group of
young Egyptian Jews in 1954 on charges of espionage and sabotage on
behalf of Israel. Laskier provided transcripts of the interrogation of the
accused during the trial, as well as reports on the political manoeuvr-
ings of Israel and major Jewish and international organisations, once the
individual verdicts were delivered.[43] Laskier was very critical of Israeli
military intelligence handling of the whole matter, especially considering the tragic outcome for the accused, calling it "an irresponsible act
politically".[44] By providing such extensive primary sources relating to

that highly embarrassing episode for the Israeli government, Laskier demonstrated that in spite of his empathy with the Zionist State he was not an apologist, and his coverage of the Lavon Affair was extensive and balanced. The last chapter of his book examined the deteriorating situation of Egyptian Jewry after the Suez War in 1956, highlighting the crucial role played by the Jewish Agency, the JDC, the Hebrew Immigrant Aid Society (HIAS), and the International Committee of the Red Cross (ICRC) in the exodus and resettlement of the Jewish refugees from Egypt. One of the valuable aspects of Laskier's work was his analysis of the role of the ICRC, which acted as the intermediary for the Jewish organisations, "as no Jewish organization—Zionist or non-Zionist— could function in Egypt itself", and it was "the cooperation between the UHS and ICRC that made it possible to accomplish movements of population".[45] The crucial part played by HIAS, with the complicity of the Spanish Embassy in Cairo, in securing the release from jail of nearly all the Jews imprisoned by Nasser in the wake of the 1967 Six-Day War, was documented by Tad Szulc, an award-winning journalist and author, in his book *The Secret Alliance*, published in 1991.[46]

The most incisive and provocative piece of scholarly work on the subject is undoubtedly Joel Beinin's book, *The Dispersion of Egyptian Jewry: Culture, Politics and the Formation of a Modern Diaspora*, published in 1998.[47] This book focused on two critical periods in the life of the Jewish community in Egypt: the period immediately preceding 1948 until the 1956 Suez War and its aftermath, and the period from 1957 with the community's gradual deterioration until its nearly total disintegration after the 1967 Arab-Israeli War. The focus then shifted to the dispersion and re-establishment of Egyptian Jewish diasporas in Israel, France, and the United States. Beinin also discussed the crucial question of identity, either reconstructed or retrieved, based on what he called the contested memories of life in Egypt obtained through oral history. He sketched out the diverse ethnic, linguistic, ideological, and socio-economic background of Egyptian Jews and their multiple identities. He pointed out the complex divisions among Sephardim, Ashkenazim, and Karaites, between the Egyptianised and the Europeanised, and between the rich and the poor. He raised the conflicting themes of nationalism versus colonialism, demonstrating why most Egyptian Jews had difficulty obtaining Egyptian citizenship and how a privileged few bought the security of European nationalities, whereas the majority remained stateless. He argued that a large proportion of young middle-class Jews, imbued in French education and socialist ideology, were highly politicised. However, only a small minority turned to Zionism, even as a more significant number embraced Marxist ideology, which somewhat explains his focus on the Egyptian graduates of the leftist Zionist youth movement *ha-Shomer ha-Tza'ir* in Israel and on the Communist émigrés in France.[48] According to Beinin's basic thesis, most Egyptian Jews were sympathetic to the idea of a Zionist State as a haven for European Jews after the Holocaust, but they did not believe they were in need of such a haven because of their own secure situation in Egypt. It was only after the 1948 Arab-Israeli War and more so after the 1956 Suez crisis, when their security was fatally compromised, that some reconsidered the option of immigrating to Israel.

Beinin was, therefore, highly critical of the overly negative representation of Jewish-Arab history promoted by Zionist historiography and adopted by writers such as Bat Ye'or, one of the earliest exponents of this perspective.[49] He also pointed to other historians—Norman Stillman, Bernard Lewis, and Martin Gilbert—who, in his opinion, all tended to take the same view.[50] He claimed that prior to 1948 most leaders of the Jewish community, even those who considered themselves Zionists, were proud of the long and peaceful history of the Jews in Egypt. Although he rightly argued against the contention that Jewish life in Muslim countries was a story of continuous persecution,[51] it is also undeniable that, since the decline of the Ottoman Empire and by the time of the French invasion of Egypt, Jewish life in those places was in a state of significant degradation. One has only to read Edward William Lane, who lived in Cairo in the 1830s, depicting the Jews as being "held in the utmost contempt and abhorrence by the Mooslims [sic] in general" and their condition, apart from a privileged few, as "wretched" and depending on alms.[52] One could just as rightly argue that the gradual improvement of their social and legal position from the 1840s was facilitated by the intrusion and growing influence of Europe in the Middle East and that their personal welfare and economic security were insured by the presence of European governments.[53] Once these governments were removed or removed themselves from the area, that protection was no longer effective and the status of Jews plummeted. Beinin's proposition that "the neo-lachrymose interpretation of Jewish Arab history distracted attention from Palestinian claims by construct- ing a narrative focusing on the eternal suffering of Jews under Islam"[54] could be construed to emanate from Beinin's personal ideological views rather than from solid evidence.[55] Conversely, Beinin's own historical account validates the claims that the Jews of Egypt were encountering increasing difficulties in obtaining citizenship and in being recognised as "real Egyptians", and they were specifically targeted after each of the three wars between Egypt and Israel.[56] In the last chapter of his book he even rejected, although not as vehemently, the claims of innocence and fairness of the Egyptian nationalist discourse regarding the fate of the Jews of the Arab world. Like Krämer, he tended to conclude that the truth probably lies somewhere in the middle. It is, therefore, difficult to understand his rationalisation that because those "occasional instances of socially structured discrimination against Jews in Egypt" were linked to the contextual political climate, they were not significant.[57] Even if in the second half of the twentieth century the Jews of Egypt were not dis- criminated against for being Jewish but for being "others" in the midst of an Arab Muslim world, the fact remains that they were forcibly driven out of that world and suffered considerably in the process.[58] My book addresses that issue through in-depth analysis of the various experiences of my interviewees.

The other controversial issue raised by Beinin is his retelling of the Israeli intelligence operation of July 1954, known as the Lavon Affair, already discussed in relation to Laskier's work. Beinin stated that it was "the most salient symbol of the transformation of the status of the Jews in Egypt".[59] Again, from Beinin's own account of the so-called Affair, the official Egyptian representation tried to minimise the seriousness of the conspiracy—calling it child's play —and to stress that the accused were not on trial as Jews.[60] It is again difficult to see how this could be construed to represent the defining moment for Egyptian Jewry. I would argue that, although this particular episode was certainly embarrassing and somewhat destabilising for the Jews of Egypt at the time, their future in the country was already sealed after the signing of the Treaty of Montreux in 1937, which abolished the privileges granted to foreign nationals and their protégés under the Capitulations regime. The first cracks started to appear immediately after World War II, with the riots in the streets of Cairo organised by the fundamentalist Muslim Brotherhood and the violent reaction aimed at the local Jewish population after the establishment of the State of Israel in 1948. The last straw was the tripartite attack on Egypt by England, France, and Israel in 1956.

The most interesting part of Beinin's work was his discussion of the crucial themes of identity, dispersion, and struggle over the retrieval of identity, these themes being at the centre of my own research. He claimed that, as far as the Jews of Egypt were concerned, there was no single, authentic Egyptian Jewish identity, and that "the Jews of Egypt were always already a heterogeneous community of cosmopolitan hybrids. This was both the strength of the community and one of the factors in its ultimate demise".[61] He tried to represent that heterogeneity through his selection of case studies: the graduates of the socialist Zionist movement *ha-Shomer ha-Tza'ir* in Israel, the Communist émigrés in France, and the small community of Karaites in San Francisco. However, seeing as all three case studies represented very marginal subgroups within Egyptian Jewry, one is left to wonder about the identity of the bulk of Jewish Egyptian émigrés, their destinations, and their diverse post-exodus experiences, particularly because the title of Beinin's book promised the readers a history of "The Dispersion of Egyptian Jewry".[62] The present book intends to fill part of that void by listening to the stories of some of the more common types of émigrés from Egypt.

Nevertheless, Beinin did present an argument based on a critical assessment of a variety of sources and texts. His knowledge of Hebrew and Arabic allowed him to delve extensively into Egyptian and Israeli, as well as American and British, archival collections. In addition to published and unpublished works, he examined articles that appeared in the Egyptian and Israeli press, as well as films and television programs. He made extensive use of oral history as an additional investigative research tool and demonstrated impressive insight, particularly on the fundamental issue of identity conflict and resolution in minority groups. Beinin also offered an original perspective of the Levantine identity, which in his opinion typified Egyptian Jews. Beinin argued that they represented a model of how people handle multiple identities and loyalties in a turbulent political and cultural context, although he recognised the drawbacks of marginal identities. Thus, his work constitutes an essential tool for researchers interested in the topic of Egyptian Jews and their recent dispersion, and I heavily relied on some of the data he provided. It is also critically important to the study of the formation of culture and identities and to the understanding of the complexities of the modern Middle East.

Any serious research into the profile of Egyptian Jews as a migrant group in Australia had to start with the examination of official records, namely the National Archives of Australia, which houses the records of their landing permit applications and entry into the country, as well as all related correspondence. Turnbull's *Safe Haven: Records of the Jewish Experience in Australia* (1999) greatly facilitated my access to those records. That publication is part of a series of research guides published by the National Archives with that specific aim.[63] For example, chapter 2 of that guide provides an overview of government policy regarding the entry of Jews into Australia from the beginning of the twentieth century to 1974, with a listing of correspondence files, their reference numbers, their origin, their present location, and their contents. The files A445, 325/5/9 include information on the "Alleged discrimination against admission of Jews...Question of Jewish or Not on departmental forms, 1939–54"; the files A446, 1972/77857 refer to the "Admission of Jews of Middle East Origin, 1949–74". Chapter 3 lists immigration case files that contain correspondence between individual migrants and the Department of Immigration "on a range of issues, including the initial application to migrate, security and other assessments, travel arrangements, etc.".[64] Chapter 4 offers a representative sampling of series related to the naturalisation records of non-British Jewish immigrants, and other sections dealt with different aspects of Jewish life in Australia, including a select bibliography and a list of Jewish research sites on the Internet.

Australian scholarship directly related to the topic of Egyptian Jewry was found to be very limited. Because of the tragic circumstances that befell European Jewry pre- and post-World War II, any study of Jewish migration has largely focused on the Jewish refugees from Europe. Small subgroups, such as the Jews from Egypt, have not attracted the attention of migration researchers, although they were also refugees when they arrived in this country. Their numbers were too small and their migration appeared too uneventful to attract the attention of people outside a restricted inner circle. Nevertheless, their immigration experience is a part, however small, of the broader picture of the history of postwar migration to Australia.

POSTWAR MIGRATION TO AUSTRALIA

The consultation of specific publications by historians—for instance, Janis Wilton, Richard Bosworth,[65] and James Jupp, all eminent experts on Australian immigration history—was critical in providing understanding of the implementation of the White Australia Policy in the postwar period and how it applied to non-British migrants, particularly non-Europeans.[66] For instance, in his book *Immigration*, Jupp reminded his readers that it was the Chifley Labor Government that introduced for the first time "mass non-British immigration in 1947 and began the process that changed Australia from a monocultural to a multicultural society".[67] The extensive recruiting program from the Displaced Persons (DP) camps of Europe, which were full of refugees looking for new homes, was not inclusive of all ethnic groups; Jupp stated that Jewish refugees "were actively discouraged in the early postwar stages, reflecting a fear of anti-Semitism in Australia".[68] Suzanne Rutland, a specialist historian on Australian Jewish migration, pointed out in *The Edge of the Diaspora* (1988) that Calwell imposed a quota system limiting the number of Jews permitted to immigrate.[69] It was clear, therefore, according to Jupp, that the DP program—while allowing into Australia for the first time "large numbers of non-British aliens" —remained essentially true to the principles of the White Australia Policy.[70]

Nevertheless, it would be wrong to minimise the important part played by Australia in the DP resettlement scheme by welcoming over 170,000 refugees between 1947 and 1954, followed by British, Dutch, German, Italian, and Greek migrants. Catherine Panich's publication, *Sanctuary? Remembering Post-War Immigration*, analysed the problems of transportation and reception of such a large intake of newcomers. While most of the expenses for transporting these refugees were covered by the IRO (International Refugee Organization), supplemented by an *ex gratis* payment of £10 per head by Australia—and British migrants enjoyed the privilege of the 1946 "U.K. Free and Assisted Passage Agreement" for which they paid £10—this was not the case for the fifteen thousand Jewish refugees who came to Australia by 1949, as noted by Panich:

> Because Calwell did not wish to be seen to discriminate in favour of Jews, the Australian government did not give assisted passages to Jewish immigrants. Instead, two American-Jewish organizations, JOINT (American Jewish Joint Distribution Committee) and HIAS (Hebrew Sheltering and Immigrant Society), financed the shipping charters and were repaid by Australian sponsors.[71]

Using oral history, photographs, original documents, and general memorabilia, Panich recorded the early experiences of over one hundred refugees/migrants who were seeking to restart their lives in Australia. The very personal accounts of their voyages in "refugee class" and the living conditions in the reception and holding centres where they were first settled provided a fascinating insight into a unique era in the history of Australian immigration.

The issues raised by Panich were applicable to all non-British migrants of the postwar period and, therefore, her study of European refugees in the immediate postwar period was just as relevant for the Egyptian Jews who arrived in Australia beginning in 1948. The issue of assimilation, which dominated the postwar immigration program and "demanded that all previous allegiances be relinquished, along with traditions and languages", was very much at the heart of Egyptian Jews' early experience.[72] Panich pointed to the fundamental differences between the mindset of a refugee and that of an economic migrant and how the different motivations impacted on the way they adapted to their new environment and on their sense of identity, which was also relevant to my own research.

Through the oral testimonies of "New Australians", Panich recorded the culture shock they experienced when confronted with the mentality, habits, and customs of "Old Australians", an experience that was very similar to that of the Egyptian refugees. Conversely, many Old Australians, faced with such an intense immigrant influx from vastly differing backgrounds, saw the newcomers as a threat to their British way of life and therefore harboured feelings of resentment and suspicion. Another crucial issue raised by Panich was the problem of language: "Many Europeans who had a poor command of English or who spoke with a heavy accent were treated unsympathetically" and discriminated against in the workplace.[73]

Being the daughter of postwar migrants herself, Panich's connection with the subject matter was deeply personal as well as scholarly. Her examples were varied, interesting, and clear. She identified succinctly the problems raised by such an intense immigration scheme, which makes her book extremely valuable for researchers interested in the history of Australian migration policies. As she stated in her conclusion, "unless closely associated with someone who did come to Australia after the war, one can have little understanding of the conditions and experiences shared by these immigrants".[74]

Those conditions and experiences were also the object of a detailed and comprehensive study of Bonegilla, one of the most important reception and training centres, as part of a series of historical monographs promoted by the Department of History at the University of Melbourne. Glenda Sluga's *Bonegilla: A Place of No Hope*, published in 1988, was based largely on oral sources—such as formal and informal interviews, conversations, and personal letters—complemented by research into government archives.[75] Three hundred thousand people from all over Europe passed through Bonegilla from its opening in 1947 to its closure in 1971. The monograph clearly illustrates how integral the role of a reception centre such as Bonegilla was to the overall postwar immigration program. It was run according to the principles upon which the program was implemented. For instance, its geographical isolation from metropolitan centres—eight miles from Albury, the nearest town—was considered essential to maximise "the immigrants' potential as a directable and controllable pool of labour".[76] It was a place where, within a period of six weeks, the newcomers would be taught English, familiarised with the Australian way of life, and then placed in "suitable" jobs.[77]

Jewish Migration

In her book, *The Edge of the Diaspora*, Rutland discussed at length the issue of postwar Jewish migration to Australia. She outlined the negative reactions to Calwell's initially generous policy on Jewish refugee migration by politicians, members of the press, and the general public. As previously indicated, Calwell imposed a quota system "which limited the number of Jews permitted to travel on any boat to twenty-five percent" and made travel to Australia from Europe "almost an impossibility".[78] Furthermore, in her 1990 doctoral dissertation Rutland pointed out that the Australian government, "both Labor and Liberal, insisted that the reception and integration of Jewish refugees was the sole responsibility of the Jewish community".[79] In fact, very few Jewish refugees went through the government-run migrant reception centres. Assistance came from their families in Australia and the Jewish American refugee agencies, such as HIAS and JDC, together with the Australian Jewish Welfare Society (AJWS).[80] A network was developed to welcome and help the newcomers acclimatise to their new life. Migrant hostels, such as Camberwell House in Melbourne, the Chip Chase Hostel—later Komlos—in Sydney, and Welfare House in Brisbane, were quickly established and played a crucial role in the reception and accommodation of refugees.[81]

Some of my respondents confirmed being welcomed by representatives of Jewish institutions as soon as they landed on Australian soil, and others were offered low-interest loans by the Jewish Welfare Building Society when the time came for them to buy their first homes. The history of the AJWS, Sydney, was researched by Anne Andgel and published in 1988.[82]

In her study of Jewish settlement in Australia, Rutland also dealt briefly with the question of the migration of Sephardi Jews, pointing out that after 1948 and throughout the early 1950s the official policy of the Australian Government was to prohibit entry to all Jews of Middle Eastern background on the presumption that many were "non-European in appearance".[83] Egyptian Jews who sought to migrate to Australia in 1956 fell in that category, and it has been suggested that it was only on humanitarian grounds that the admission of relatives was allowed. Rodney Gouttman published an interesting article on that very issue in which he analysed the rationale behind the 1949 secret decision by the Australian Department of Immigration to prohibit entry into Australia to Jews of Middle Eastern origin.[84] This decision was based on a warning in 1948 emanating from an Australian immigration officer in India that a large number of "coloured" Jews from the Middle East were considering immigrating to Australia. As late as 1954 this policy of exclusion was still being implemented.[85] The question "Are you Jewish?", which appeared on immigration forms No. 40 and No. 47, was not deleted until 1954.[86] Gouttman pointed out that the question of the admission of the Jews from Egypt arose at a time when the Department of Immigration was unable "to maintain its traditional stand" on a preferred migration from Great Britain and had to look to other sources of migrants. Because a significant number of the applicants from Egypt held Italian or Spanish passports, they could not be classified as being of Middle Eastern origin and on that basis were granted landing permits. Gouttman recognised that intense lobbying, mainly by the small Jewish community of Adelaide on behalf of family and friends in Egypt, could have contributed to their admission to Australia. However, his contention was that the failure of the exclusionist policy was inevitable once the religious question was removed from application forms Nos. 40 and 47 and the Jews of Middle Eastern origin "blended into the common pool of potential immigrants".[87] Gouttman's paper succinctly and clearly analysed the restrictive aspects of the White Australia Policy on the postwar immigration of Jews in general and particularly those suspected to be coloured, but it did not touch upon other critical issues related to the settlement of minorities, such as acceptance by and acculturation to the host society.

MIGRATION OF EGYPTIAN JEWS

In 1984, Rutland was the first Australian scholar to conduct a case study of a relatively large group of Egyptian Jews who settled in Adelaide, where they made a significant impact on the existing Jewish community. Based on oral testimonies by a number of key individuals and an examination of the records of various communal institutions—such as Adelaide Masada College, the South Australia branch of the Australian Jewish Historical Society (AJHS), the South Australia Jewish Board of Deputies, and the AJWS—Rutland briefly related the intense lobbying by Adelaide Egyptian Jewry to facilitate the admission of their relatives into Australia and the significant help provided by Patrick Galvin, a Labour Member of Parliament, in that respect. Rutland reported on their smooth integration within the ranks of the South Australian Jewish community, in spite of some initial tensions. Rutland also discussed the value of oral history as an investigative tool, showing how it helped to better understand "the adjustment and interaction of the immigrant culture with the host society", while still recognising its limitations.[88]

The topic of the settlement of a numerically significant group of Egyptian Jews in Adelaide was taken up again only in 1998 as part of a study of Adelaide Jewry and its institutions by Bernard Hyams. He reported that in spite of their difficult beginnings the Egyptian Jews "maintained a degree of internal social solidarity" because of their emphasis on family hospitality. He also indicated that, according to the records of the local Jewish Welfare Society, that institution provided a lot of support to the Egyptian refugees when they first arrived.[89] However, given the numerical importance of Egyptian Jews in Adelaide, Hyams' discussion of their contribution was superficial, and he did not add anything new to the existing scholarship.

It is mainly through the study of Sephardim in Australia that the specific case of Egyptian Jews, as a major Sephardi group, came to be investigated. Aaron Aaron, founder of the New South Wales (NSW) Association of Sephardim, published *The Sephardim of Australia & New Zealand* in 1979, in which he retraced their early steps in Australasia from 1788. He briefly noted the influx of Egyptian Jews to Adelaide since 1956 and their active contribution to the Jewish life of the community, but most of his study concentrated on the Sydney Sephardim and the events that led to the formation of the association in 1954 and the subsequent building of the Sephardi synagogue in 1962. Although this section was obviously based on personal experience, Aaron made extensive use of primary sources, such as correspondence, brochures, minutes, and articles in the Jewish press. He acknowledged the important parts played by Max D. Friedman, General Secretary of the Zionist Organisation, and Rabbi Dr. Israel Porush, Chief Minister of the Great Synagogue, in organising the Sydney Sephardim. He also acknowledged the vital role of Sydney D. Einfeld in overcoming the initial reluctance of the Executive Council of Australian Jewry (ECAJ) to approach the Federal Government on the matter of Sephardi immigration and in securing landing permits for Sephardim from Egypt and Asia. However, when it came to relating the various inner conflicts and rifts that occurred in the late 1960s and 1970s within the association's membership and among the association and other communal bodies, such as ECAJ and the NSW Jewish Board of Deputies, Aaron chose to deal with these controversial issues by reproducing editorials or articles that appeared in the Jewish press at the time or through copies of related correspondence among the various communal bodies, without further comment or evaluation on his part. He demonstrated that the association had to fight for the right of a representative to sit on the board of ECAJ and the NSW Jewish Board of Deputies. He revealed the association's grievances about the lack of action by those institutions regarding the freedom of Syrian

Jewry, suggesting a climate of discrimination by the Ashkenazi majority against the Sephardi sections of the community. The same methodology was used to report on the various activities of the Sydney Sephardi community through brochures, invitations, and photos.

The merit of Aaron's book relates largely to its collection of these invaluable primary sources, which succeeded in painting a fascinating picture of a man who worked tirelessly to bring to the predominantly Ashkenazi Jewish community an awareness of a different but worthy Jewish tradition. In his conclusion, the author stated that he hoped that his book, in addition to recording the past and present history of the Sephardi community, would intensify "the historical consciousness of many Sephardim in Australia, inspiring them...to preserve the continuity of their noble customs and traditions by establishing Sephardi institutions in Australia".[90]

It was in the context of an extensive academic study of the Sephardim of Sydney that Naomi Gale's doctoral research also dealt with some of the issues relating to the immigration of the Jews of Egypt who settled in Sydney.[91] Gale reviewed the racially motivated Australian immigration policy vis-à-vis Sephardim of Middle Eastern origin, labelled "an undesirable class of Jews" because of their dark complexion. She explored their history and experiences as new immigrants in an Anglo-Australian society. According to their oral testimonies, apart from the help provided by prominent Ashkenazim, such as Sydney D. Einfeld and Abram Landa, there was a general lack of enthusiasm shown by Jewish philanthropic institutions towards the Sephardi newcomers, whether they were from Egypt, India, or Iraq. This attitude caused some lingering bitterness among a number of Sephardim who arrived in Australia after 1956, especially when they compared it to the seemingly preferential treatment granted to the Hungarian refugees around the same period.

Gale raised the complex issue of Sephardi identity as a combination of self-identification and identification by others. She argued that the Sephardim themselves often viewed their ethnicity as an obstacle to acceptance by the dominant Ashkenazi community, resulting in a negative ethnic identity and self-rejection. Gale also noted that the process of acculturation—or "Ashkenization", as she called it—of the young was accelerated through attendance at Jewish day schools, which I also found to be true in the sample group I interviewed. However, it seems that the Ashkenazim, who considered themselves a part of White Australia and feared an anti-Semitic backlash, displayed a superior attitude towards Afro-Asian Sephardi Jews, based on cultural and racial criteria. Linked to the problem of retrieval of identity, Gale looked into the fundamental reasons for the emergence of tension between Sephardim of Iraqi or Indian origin and those of Egyptian origin, pointing to the lack of a common past between the two subgroups, some variation in their rituals, and different levels of religiosity. Gale deduced that the tension was rooted in the perception that the Egyptians considered themselves superior, more cultured, and generally more Westernised than the Iraqi/Indian Sephardim. The major reasons for her concern were the lack of productive communication, a general climate of apathy, and the continual process of assimilation to Ashkenazi and Australian societies, particularly within the younger group. Gale's conclusions were not optimistic regarding the viability of the Sephardi community and the maintenance of a distinctive Sephardi identity in the next generation. She also pointed to the Sephardi leadership's failure to develop "strong social and cultural strategies to permit them [the Sephardim] to implement their distinctiveness either formally or informally within the general Jewish community".[92]

Although Gale's research focused on the Sydney Sephardi community, and most of her findings referred mainly to the Iraqi/Indian component, her perceptive and informative views on the many facets of Sephardi identity and her inferences seemed just as valid for the other Sephardi communities in Melbourne and Adelaide, and therefore constituted an essential tool for an in-depth study of these communities, including the Egyptian one.

Another important doctoral dissertation on the topic of Sephardi Jewry of NSW is Myer Samra's "Yisrael Rhammana: Constructions of Identity among Iraqi Jews in Sydney, Australia", which recorded "the experience of the [Iraqi] community during its first generations in Australia" from the point of view of an insider and addressed the question of Sephardi identity and the problems of cross-cultural communication between minority and dominant groups.[93] Although the focus of Samra's study was his own community, he included some comparative research on the group of Egyptian Jews. He found that the interaction between Iraqi and Egyptian Jews, apart from their common involvement in the synagogue, was limited due to "differences in cultural taste and education", particularly the common use of French in the Egyptian milieu.[94]

Like Gale, Samra discussed the Australian immigration policy pertaining to its discrimination against Sephardi Jews and the various representations that were made to the government to allow them into the country on the basis that they were not "coloured".[95] He tried to establish a profile of the Sephardi community of NSW based on its ethnic background and demographic features, as well as the analysis of the residential distribution of Sephardi households, including the Egyptian component, within the metropolitan regions of Sydney.[96] According to his research, there were around three thousand Sephardi Jews in NSW, and the Egyptian Jews were the second-largest segment of this category after the Iraqis, although he did not provide exact figures pertaining to the relative size of the two groups.

In his examination of the issues of identity and identification, Samra argued that, in order to be better accepted by the dominant Australian/ Ashkenazi Jewish community as European Jews and not as Arab Jews, the Iraqi Jews—who were ethnically a very homogeneous group—constructed for themselves a new identity as Sephardim, strictly meaning from Spain, although they were not of Spanish ancestry. The Egyptian Sephardim—who claimed a variety of ethnic origins but still considered themselves authentic Sephardim, unlike their Iraqi brethren—did not look favourably at this reconstructed identity. As for the issue of identification with Israel, Samra's research has shown that, whereas Israel was important to "Sydney's Sephardi Jews at virtually all levels and phases of their identity", the fact that it was central to the identity of all Jews, whether Sephardi or Ashkenazi, created a bond between the two groups.[97]

The split within the Sephardi community into two different institutions, the NSW Association of Sephardim (NAS) and the Eastern Jewish
Association (EJA), as well as the political features of their relationship
and the often-strained relationship with the wider Jewish community,
was also extensively dealt with in the course of Samra's work. He raised
other issues at the heart of the community's concerns, namely Sephardi
prestige and education, involvement in communal institutions at an
executive level, and the plight of Jews in Arab lands.

As noted earlier, the focus of Samra's study was mainly on the Iraqi
community, and the Egyptian Jews were mentioned only in the context
of their relationship with the Iraqis, as fellow Sephardim. Nevertheless,
Samra's incisive analysis of his community was extremely useful for my
own research, given that the two communities shared important cultural
and religious similarities, in spite of their ethnic differences. His conclusions about the future of Sephardim in Australia appear more optimistic
than Gale's predictions.[98]

AUSTRALIA AND THE 1956 SUEZ CRISIS

What was the Australian political context around the time of the arrival
of Egyptian Jews, mainly in the wake of the Suez crisis of 1956? Again,
the study of official documents and correspondence files of the Department of External Affairs, held at the National Archives, revealed Australia's close monitoring of the situation and its firm agreement with
Great Britain in the matter of the nationalisation of the Suez Canal in
July 1956 by Egyptian president Gamal Abdel Nasser. For example,
Series A1209/23, Item 57/5736 PT2 contained a confidential report
addressed to the Prime Minister, R. G. Menzies, briefing him on the
personality of Gamal Abdel Nasser before his official meeting with
the latter in August 1956. This file also included a message from the
president of Egypt to the Australian Prime Minister, agreeing to meet
with him and other representatives of the eighteen user countries of the
canal, and the subsequent exchanges between the Australian Legation
in Cairo and Canberra about the failure of the talks between Nasser and

that committee. W. J. Hudson's work, *Blind Loyalty*, revealed the leading part taken by Australia through Menzies' mission to Cairo and his
seemingly blind and extraordinary loyalty to the British cause, despite
dissenting opinions within the ranks of his own government—notably
from his Foreign Minister, Richard Casey, and his Defence Minister,
Philip MacBride.[99] Hudson argued that this kind of devotion to the
mother country was symptomatic of:

> the generation born late in Victoria's reign and educated in
> Edward's...at the end of several decades of prodigious devel-
> opment in the colonies and when the British Empire reigned
> supreme. The major figures in the Australian cabinet of 1956 were
> men of that generation.[100]

A further proof of this unswerving devotion to the mother country by
the Menzies government was provided in the recent work of Chanan
Reich, *Australia and Israel: An Ambiguous Relationship*. Reich coun-
tered the commonly held belief that "Australia, in contrast with Britain,
sympathised with Jewish national aspirations in Palestine before 1948",
particularly in view of the active role of H. V. Evatt, as chairman of
the United Nations (UN) Ad Hoc Committee on Palestine, "in bringing
about the partition resolution of 29 November 1947".[101] Reich's examination of recently declassified documents in both Israel and Australia
revealed that the United Australia Party (UAP)—predecessor of the Liberal Party—headed by Menzies in 1939–1941, unequivocally supported
British policy in Palestine, including its opposition to the migration of
Jewish refugees to Palestine. It was, therefore, very hostile to the Yishuv
because of its anti-British feelings. The records showed that Menzies
had even opposed the partition of Palestine in 1947 and "vehemently
resisted the establishment of the State of Israel".[102] This harsh attitude
from the Menzies government of 1939–1941 was reflected in its restrictive immigration policy concerning European Jewish refugees seeking
entry into Australia before 1939.[103] In the early 1950s, Australia's Middle East policy continued to mirror that of Britain and the United States,
regardless of Israel's interests and in spite of a number of representations

by leaders of Australian Jewry asking their government for more support of the Israeli position.

At the time of the 1956 Suez campaign and in its aftermath, the familiar pattern of "Menzies agreeing, often uncritically, with the policies of the British Government" was again obvious, except that this time Britain and France were allies of Israel and the three acted in collusion. In spite of the fact that Menzies had been left largely in the dark about the whole operation, and although he found himself almost isolated, he immediately declared his support of those three countries at the UN and even "expressed in Parliament an understanding of Israeli position".[104] In fact, as pointed out by Reich, "Canberra's support for Israel coincided with Egypt's decision to break off diplomatic relations with Australia".[105] The stand taken by Australia in this instance could be considered a watershed event in the relations between Australia and Israel as they entered a more cordial phase.

Reich produced a comprehensive and important study of the early history of the Liberal Party's relationship with Israel before and after its inception, its reaction to the conflict in the Middle East, and the role of the Australian Jewish leadership. Although this book did not deal specifically with the issue of Egyptian Jews, I found particularly interesting the fact that the Suez crisis of 1956—the event that actually triggered the second exodus from Egypt and the arrival in Australia of most of the Egyptian refugees—marked the beginning of close and warm bilateral relations between the Liberal Party and Israel.

OTHER EGYPTIAN DIASPORAS

In Australia, the Jews of Egypt were perceived as part of the broader Sephardi group, although a substantial minority among them was Ashkenazi. The circumstances surrounding their migration to Australia in this time period were not considered striking enough to generate a large volume of publications, as compared to what happened beginning in the 1980s in the various diasporas where Jews from Egypt settled after their exodus, particularly France, the United States, Brazil, and of course Israel.

When I delved into the state of research on Egyptian Jews in France, I discovered that some of them were actively involved in promoting their specificity as Jews in and from Egypt. The name of Jacques Hassoun emerged as one of the most significant amongst the many expatriate Egyptian Jews who have written about their past history or given oral testimonies. Hassoun was one of the founding members of the Association pour la Sauvegarde du Patrimoine Culturel des Juifs d'Égypte (ASPCJE), created in Paris in 1979.[106] His contribution to the publication of the association's quarterly bulletin, *Nahar Misraim* (River of Egypt), remained constant for the nine years of its existence, from 1980 to 1989.[107] All the issues covered in the bulletin—whether historical, religious, political, or personal—concerned the Jews of Egypt before and after their so-called second exodus.

In 1984, Hassoun also collaborated with other members of the association in the publication of a popular coffee-table book, *Juifs d'Égypte, Images et Textes*, which traced the long history of the Jews in Egypt through an impressive collection of photographs, images, and accompanying texts.[108] As the editor of *Histoire des Juifs du Nil* (1990), a book that included a collection of scholarly articles referring to the various stages of Jewish life in Egypt from antiquity to modern times, Hassoun wanted to demonstrate the continuity of a Jewish presence in the land of Egypt going back to the sixth century BCE and up to the mid-twentieth century.[109] The Islamic period was covered by the Egyptian-born historian Alfred Morabia in a chapter called "A l'ombre protectrice de l'Islam: les Juifs d'Égypte, de la conquête arabe à l'expédition de Bonaparte (641–1798)", in which he discussed the varying fortunes of Jews in Egypt under Islamic rule until the arrival of the French expedition in 1798, asserting the fluctuation between the good and bad times.[110] Morabia also collaborated with Gudrun Krämer in covering the modern period. In the chapter "Face à la modernité: les Juifs d'Égypte aux XIXè et XXè siècles", the two historians assessed the responses of Egyptian Jewry to the challenges of modernity and to the social and political changes that transformed the face of Egypt from the period of Mohammed Ali (1805–1849) to the Six-Day War of 1967. Hassoun's noteworthy contribution, "Chroniques de la vie quotidienne", presents a picture of Jewish life in Egypt in the first half of the twentieth century, looking at the occupations, customs, and religious traditions of ordinary Jews, Rabbanites, and Karaites in their urban or rural environment, while revealing the dichotomy between their primary Egyptian dimension and their emerging Western dimension. The last chapter of the book fittingly symbolises the end for the Jews in Egypt after a continuous presence of more than twenty-five centuries. It reproduces the personal testimony of an Egyptian Jew as it appeared in the French weekly *L'Express*, in December 1967, relating a story of torture, suffering, and humiliations reminiscent of Holocaust survivors' narratives. Like most Jewish males over the age of fifteen, he had been arbitrarily arrested a few weeks after the Six-Day War in June 1967 and spent four difficult months in the notorious Abu Zaabal prison camp in Cairo before being simultaneously released and expelled from the country.

Another Egyptian Jew, Maurice Mizrahi, who saw himself as a committed Jew and an Egyptian citizen, published a book titled *L'Égypte et ses Juifs: Le Temps Révolu* in 1977, as a testimony to the vital role played by leading Jewish families in the modernisation of Egypt, the development of the sugar and textile industries, the banking and transport systems, housing projects, and international trade. Mizrahi's main argument was that, through all these economic initiatives the Jewish contribution to the welfare of Egypt was out of proportion relative to their percentage of the total population, and therefore the Jews had more than repaid Egypt's hospitality.[111] Nearly twenty years later, an Egyptian social historian, Samir W. Raafat, who wrote extensively on different aspects of Cairo's history, seemed to share Mizrahi's perspective in his book *Maadi 1904–1962: Society and History in a Cairo Suburb* (1994), relating how that "suburban paradise" was the result of meticulous planning by British and Jewish companies in the heydays of the British protectorate and free entrepreneurial initiatives by privileged minorities. Raafat also wrote several articles that appeared in the Egyptian press, evoking the lives and achievements of famous Jewish families, the history of Egyptian synagogues, and the current status of the few remaining Jews in Egypt.[112]

The Israeli Academic Centre in Cairo, which is the representative in Egypt of the major Israeli universities, has published its own bulletin since 1982. In 1998, a special issue of that bulletin was dedicated to the history of the Jews of modern Egypt.[113] Professor Shimon Shamir, who was the centre's founder and first director, has written widely on the topic of modern Egypt, as indicated earlier.[114] In that particular bulletin, Shamir contributed the introductory article, in which he examined major trends in current research of that history, highlighting the difficulty of studying a community that is dispersed, and thus the crucial importance of oral history projects.

The Centre for Studies of the Jewish Egyptian Heritage, which was founded by Egyptian-born Professor Arie Schlosberg in 1999 and is based in Tel Aviv, publishes a bulletin reporting on scholarly and cultural activities in the area of modern Egyptian Jewish history, such as weekly meetings, monthly lectures, films, plays, and related publications.[115] One of the most important aspects of the centre's function is to grant scholarships to students interested in postgraduate research into the history of modern Egyptian Jewry. Its Bulletin No. 4 (Autumn 2004) reported on the "International Research Conference on the Jews of Egypt in Modern Times" held in January 2004, organised by the Department of Jewish Studies of Bar-Ilan University in Tel Aviv, and opened by Professor Shamir. Most of the speakers were either directly or indirectly connected to the Jewish experience in modern Egypt, and their papers covered a variety of social, political, cultural, and religious topics.[116]

The International Association of Jews from Egypt (IAJE), based in New York, also produced a newsletter—edited by Dr. Victor D. Sanua, its founder and president, now deceased—with the specific objective of placing "the Jews from Egypt on the map" and documenting the history of Egyptian Jewry in modern times.[117] In addition, a number of articles on the various emigration experiences and memories of Egyptian Jews have appeared in the Jewish press wherever Egyptian Jews have settled after their exodus. *Nahar Misraïm*, the revived newsletter of the French ASPCJE;[118] the periodical *Los Muestros—the Sephardic Voice*, edited by the author Moise Rahmani[119] in Brussels and published in three languages: Ladino, French, and English; and the *Jewish Renaissance*[120] in London have all published oral testimonies of ex-Egyptian Jews or provided primary or secondary sources illustrating Egyptian Jewish history.

It is significant to note that, notwithstanding the revived interest in the story of Egyptian Jews, a formal and systematic study of Egyptian Jews as a migrant group in France seems to have attracted the attention of only a small number of researchers, although the original size of the Egyptian community in that country—over ten thousand—was relatively important. In 1982, Egyptian-born Ethel Carasso, now living in Paris, presented a Master's thesis on the Jewish community of Egypt from 1948 to 1957.[121] Her quest was not only scholarly but personal—she was only two years old when her parents left Egypt in 1957, and her connection with Egypt belonged more to the mythical realm. She tried to uncover the fundamental reasons for the liquidation of Egyptian Jewry, besides the obvious and direct link with the 1948 and 1956 Arab-Israeli conflicts.

Carasso first examined the demographic, socioeconomic, and legal status of the Jewish community before the outbreak of the 1948 war with Israel, using primary sources such as government census and community year books (*l'Annuaire du judaïsme égyptien*, Le Caire, 1943) that provided useful information on the professions, nationalities, and levels of education of the Jewish *haute bourgeoisie* (upper middle class). She looked at the *Bottin Mondain du Proche-Orient* (Le Caire, 1954), which was a general directory listing all Egyptian notables, both Jews and non-Jews. Finally, she examined the British Foreign Office archives regarding the Zionist activities of the Jewish community in Egypt. For the second part of her thesis, which traced the gradual decline of the community after 1948, she examined official Egyptian government sources, as well as the Arab, international, and Jewish press. She studied the various laws enacted by the Egyptian government of the time and their implications for Egyptian Jewry, such as the abolition of the Mixed Tribunals, the Martial Law of May 1948, the Nationality Law of 1950, and the text of the Egyptian Constitution of 1956. She particularly noted the creation in

1955 of a special department within the Ministry of Interior in charge of
Jewish affairs that implied an official intention to regulate the process
of specifically targeting Jews. To document the mass arrival of Egyptian
Jews in France in 1957, she consulted the French Jewish press—mainly
the *Arche*, a monthly publication sponsored by the umbrella Jewish
institution called Fonds Social Juif Unifié (FSJU)—as well as the Egyptian and the world press. To collect the data concerning the reasons for
their mass exodus and their choice of destination, Carasso used a brief
questionnaire divided into two sections. One was quantitative, addressing the demographic details, and the other was qualitative, addressing
the subjective issues of integration, degree of involvement in Zionism,
reason for departure, and others. This questionnaire was sent to Egyptian
Jews who had settled mainly in France, but also in Israel, Switzerland,
Great Britain, Italy, Belgium, the United States, and Australia. Out of
one hundred questionnaires, thirty-five were returned, including twenty
from France. The responses demonstrated that the majority of respondents migrated to their host country mainly for family reasons. As far as
France was concerned, the reason was primarily cultural affinity, which
somewhat confirmed my own study of Egyptian Jews in France. There
were no follow-up interviews, and Carasso's whole thesis was largely
based on the examination of official records, government edicts, and the
general press, with a very brief section dealing with the questionnaire
responses. It would have been interesting to have a more comprehensive
analysis of that particular data. Nevertheless, the selection of primary
sources was broad and instructive. It objectively exposed the political
situation in Egypt during the period under examination and the mindset
of its leaders regarding the Jewish minority.

Alain Lévy, sociologist, presented an interesting doctoral thesis on
the itinerary of an Alexandrian family between 1920 and 1962 in Egypt,
North Africa, Western Europe, and Brazil, in the sociopolitical context of that period.[122] Using what he called *l'approche biographique*,
Lévy's main primary sources were eight members of that family. In the
course of several meetings and over a period of several months, alter-
nating between formal, recorded sessions and informal discussions, the

interviewees were asked to help reconstruct the history of their family through their personal memories.[123] Lévy's aim was to depict, through those individual stories, the migration process in its totality by exploring the fundamental reasons for their sudden exile from Alexandria. He argued that the growing feeling of insecurity experienced by the community around them prepared them for the idea of migrating long before they were forced to do so. Lévy's impressive work is a reflection on the conditions of cultural pluralism in the different socioeconomic and political contexts in which this family gravitated, such as cosmopolitan Alexandria, the colonial circles of Upper Egypt, and Algeria in the last years of French rule. In his view, the experience of living in these diverse milieus engendered a special way of behaving and of looking at the world. The notion that Alexandria as a social environment created an exemplary society capable of co-existing and functioning in harmony with heterogeneous ethnic, religious, cultural, and national groups anywhere in the world was raised by some of the participants of my own research.[124]

In 2004–2006, Sophie Saunut presented a brief but well-documented study titled "L'Immigration des Juifs d'Égypte vers la France entre 1948 et 1970". She based her research on French government archival records, as well as the archives of COJASOR, the Red Cross, the general press, and the Jewish community press. Her research was complemented by a small number of interviews. These seem to be the only three formal studies to date on the general topic of the immigration of the Jews of Egypt to France. This paucity of academic research in that area could be due to the fact that the migration of Egyptian Jews to France was often identified with the much broader North African Jewish migration with which they shared a number of features, such as languages—French and Arabic—Western education, and lifestyle, as well as religious and ethnic traditions. From Algeria alone, 120,000 Jews fled to France. It is understandable that the ten to twelve thousand Jews from Egypt who settled in France—although not a negligible number—were somewhat overlooked as a distinct group. For instance, when discussing their impact on French Jewry, the historian Michael Laskier, who, as previously mentioned, researched extensively the fate of Egyptian Jewry post-1948, included them in his research paper on the immigration and integration of North African Jews into France.[125] Another reason could be their low profile and tendency to adapt and quietly blend into their new environment without attracting attention, which was very much the case in Australia.

An interesting thesis on the emigration of Egyptian Jews to Brazil titled *Nuits d'été au parfum de jasmin: Souvenirs des Juifs d'Égypte à Rio de Janeiro—1956/57*, translated into French, was presented by an Alexandrian-born journalist and researcher, Joëlle Rouchou from Brazil. Although the study of Egyptian Jews in Brazil was not meant to be a part of my research, a brief examination of Rouchou's research and methodology was deemed important in view of the fact that the thesis was based on the oral testimonies of a small number of émigrés and some of their children.[126] It looked at the construction of identity and memory by the exiled Jews of Egypt and the process of transmission of these memories to the first generation born in Brazil.[127] The author focused on the subjective reactions of her respondents, who lived through political and social upheavals that had a determining effect on their future. She found that the shock of being more or less forced to leave one's familiar surroundings was still remembered with a high degree of distress after more than forty years, although the Egypt that was evoked did not exist anymore. Contrary to the immigration policy of Australia, the Brazilian government of Juscelino Kubitschek opened the doors of Brazil to the Jews from Egypt without restriction. However, the cost of transporting and settling the refugees was entirely undertaken by HIAS, without the Brazilian government bearing any of the related costs, as was the case for Australia. This study also contributed to the understanding of how the Egyptian group interrelated with the diverse ethnic communities that co-existed in Brazilian society, and presented an informed and remarkable study of the themes of loss, exile, identity, and memory.[128]

Several novels, written in French and English by expatriate Egyptian Jews, have provided further insight and colour to the life of the community, both in Egypt and in their adopted countries. In France, Paula Jacques, who left Egypt as a little girl, was one of the first to write in that genre, evoking the modern exodus of Egyptian Jews in her semi-autobiographical novels *Lumière de l'oeil* (1980) and *Baiser froid comme la lune* (1983). These novels painted a critical but sympathetic picture of Jewish society in Egypt prior to the Suez crisis of 1956, based on the personal and often collective memories of the author. In a tragicomical style, using a particular form of Egyptian-French that often borrowed literally from Arabic or from other surrounding cultures, Jacques exposed the problems of forced emigration to France of a typically Westernised Jewish family, the unforeseen difficulties of integration in what was presumed to be a friendly and culturally familiar environment, particularly for the older generation, and the identity crisis experienced by such émigrés.[129]

Alexandria-born André Aciman, who left Egypt in the early 1960s as a teenager and currently teaches comparative literature at the City University of New York Graduate Centre, wrote a highly acclaimed book on the subject of memory and exile, titled *Out of Egypt: A Memoir* (1994).[130] Set in cosmopolitan Alexandria, a city "teeming with people of a dozen ethnic groups, creeds, rules and habits", Aciman's book told the story of his eccentric and flamboyant Sephardic family from the time of their arrival from Turkey at the beginning of the twentieth century to their expulsion in 1964. Mixing memory and imagination in a style reminiscent of Marcel Proust, Aciman strove to recapture the charm of a now-vanished world while revealing the permanent sense of loss and dislocation that exile often brings. The characters are larger than life, the tone of the narration witty and humorous because the narrator is now an adult exploring his memories as a young boy, "who even as he longs for the wider world, does not want to be led, forever, out of Egypt". Through this very personal perspective and a continuous back-and-forth in time and space, the book succeeds in recreating the haunting atmosphere of that last period of Jewish life in Egypt after the Suez War.

A growing number of similar semi-autobiographical novels in Hebrew, French, and English have been published in Israel, France, the United States, and Great Britain. Some have been well received by the literary press.[131] The common themes of most of these novels, as illustrated by the following examples, are memory, dislocation, and loss, the inevitable consequences of any forced emigration. *The One Facing Us* (1995), by Ronit Matalon from Israel, is about a young girl who, in the context of postcolonial Africa, through old photographs and scraps of letters, tried to reconstruct the story of her Egyptian-Jewish family and their displacement in the 1950s from Cairo to Israel, Cameroon, and New York.[132] *Apricots on the Nile* (2001), by Colette Rossant from New York, is a mosaic of mouth-watering recipes and the memories of Colette as a young girl in Cairo and her afternoons with her grandmother in the kitchen or in the bazaar.[133]

In fact, the traditional cuisine of Egyptian Jews, an integral part of their cultural heritage, occupies an important place in the collection of Sephardi recipes gathered by the celebrated food writer, Claudia Roden, in *The Book of Jewish Food*, published in 1997. Roden described her work as "a celebration of roots: of generations past, vanished worlds and identity".[134] Based in London, Roden was born and raised in Cairo in a privileged Jewish family from Aleppo, but the Suez War marked the end of that period of her life.

Victor Teboul from Canada wrote *La Lente Découverte de l'Etrangeté* (2002), based on the author's painful memories of his family's expulsion from Egypt. Seen through the prism of the main character's childhood diary, the book is a recollection of life in cosmopolitan Alexandria leading up to the events of 1956, which resulted in the child's tragic removal from the only home he had ever known. The voyage from Alexandria to Montreal via France became a personal voyage of discovery of a multiple and complex identity or, as the title indicates, "the slow discovery of being a stranger".[135]

In 2008, Cairo-born Lucette Lagnado, an investigative reporter for the New York *Wall Street Journal*, won the prestigious Sami Rohr Prize for Jewish Literature for her autobiographical novel, *The Man in the White Sharkskin Suit*, which relates the story of a failed immigration experience. Through the palpable and vivid memories of Lagnado as six-year-old "Loulou", the narrative, set in Cairo in its cosmopolitan heyday, unfolds around the charismatic figure of the father she adored—"the Captain", "the man in the white sharkskin suit". In 1963, the Lagnado family was forced to leave their home and abandon all their possessions and privileges. They faced a precarious and impoverished future. For the first time, Loulou's proud father Leon could not provide for his wife and four children while they waited in a dingy Paris hotel for a visa to the United States and had to depend on charity from Jewish relief agencies to survive. Unfortunately, the family's exodus to the "Golden Medina" proved to be a source of deep pain and disappointment for Lagnado's ageing and disoriented father. Always longing for Cairo, he could never abandon the patriarchal mentality and conservatism of his Levantine world and missed the warmth and compassion of Egyptian society. Desperately ill, "stripped of any identity", he was eventually admitted to a nursing home and died in 1992. The book is Lagnado's poignant testimony to the anguish of her uprooted parents, but it also pays tribute to a long-lost world of tolerant and harmonious coexistence among Muslims, Jews, and Christians.

In Australia, I came across only one semi-autobiographical book, written by Alexandria-born Victoria Thompson, *Losing Alexandria: A Memoir* (1998), which dealt with the cosmopolitan world of Alexandria in the 1950s—but not specifically the Jewish world—, as well as a short autobiography, *Second Exodus*, by Cairo-born Melburnian Meyer Harari, published in 1999 as part of a Jewish community project.[136] I was also given two unpublished autobiographical manuscripts written by another Jew from Egypt, the late Freddy E. Dayan, who was professor of French Literature at the University of Hobart.[137] Furthermore, Australian-born Andrew Strum, whose mother came from Cairo and who is particularly interested in the history of the Jews in Egypt, has published a few articles originating from his research into his ancestry, such as "The Livro de Cantares de Baruch Bentata",[138] and others specifically addressing Egyptian religious customs, such as "Wheat, Chickens and the Expiation of Sin, or Vegetarian *Kapparot*: The Ancient Origins of an Obscure Egyptian Jewish High Holy Day Custom", but nothing on the Jews from Egypt after emigration.[139] All of these publications were valuable personal recollections, but none of these writers addressed systematically the wider issues of forced emigration and acculturation.

Non-Jewish Egyptian émigrés have written extensively on the peregrinations of their own communities in modern Egypt and their particular exodus experiences, evoking the same themes of memory and loss as Aciman, Matalon, and Teboul. One of the most prolific and popular writers in that category is Robert Solé, who won a French literary prize, Prix Méditerranée, for his novel *Le Tarbouche* (1992). It is a nostalgic and tender tale of a Syrian Christian family who immigrated to Egypt in the nineteenth century and became prosperous by manufacturing a type of head covering that was popular throughout the Ottoman empire, the fez, or *tarbouche* in French. However, like the Jews, even after four generations in the country Syrian Christians were not considered true Egyptians, and when the military came to power they were ruined and left the country. For Solé, the fez became the symbol of those happy days and the sweet memories of an Egypt that was no more. Solé also published reference books on modern Egyptian history. *L'Égypte, passion française* (1997) documents the special relationship between Egypt and France since Napoleon's military expedition to Egypt in 1798; *Les Savants de Bonaparte* (1998) brings to mind the great achievements of the prominent scholars and scientists, artists and technicians who accompanied Napoleon's army on that expedition; and *La Pierre de Rosette* (1999), written in collaboration with Dominique Valbelle, recounts the remarkable story of the deciphering of the hieroglyphs by the Frenchman Jean-François Champollion.[140]

It is clear from the study of this corpus of writings that research on the history of modern Egyptian Jewry has attracted renewed interest recently, particularly as part of the bigger picture of the history of Jews from Arab lands. Besides the scholarly research, associations of ex-Egyptian Jews have been created in different parts of the world—publishing newsletters, organising cultural events and social activities, writing about their migration experiences, trying to reconnect with their memories of the past, and giving a voice to their stories. However, this was not the case in Australia for a number of reasons, including the small size of the group and its low profile, but mainly because of a self-perception that their immigration experience as Jews from Egypt was not special enough to warrant being represented in written form. This book tries to reconstruct their history through the memories of a cross-section of Jews from Egypt, to assess their level of integration into and contribution to their host country and to their ethnic and religious community, and to demonstrate the critical value of their multilayered and multifaceted identity.

CHAPTER 2

UNDERSTANDING THE HISTORY OF THE EGYPTIAN JEWS

Consultation of primary sources, such as archives and memoirs, gathering of critical literature, evaluation of data, and comparative analysis of oral testimonies were all part of the methodology used in this study to reconstruct the history of the group of Egyptian Jewish émigrés, with the ultimate aim of shedding light on their specific characteristics.

This book seeks to understand the socio-historical background of Egyptian Jews and how this background affected their migration to Australia. My research focused on their experiences and lifestyle in Egypt before their forced emigration, as well as their experiences of integrating into their new life in Australia. By exploring the multicultural dimension of their identity in Egypt, I have tried to assess their level of acculturation both in Egypt and Australia. Because Egyptian Jews in Australia constituted a fairly small group, their experiences were compared and contrasted with the larger Egyptian Jewish community of France.

I approached the socio-historical topic thematically—through examination of a number of concepts related to the experience of forced exile, migration, and acculturation—with the aim of enriching understanding of those general concepts. For instance, I looked at those concepts in terms of binary oppositions, such as exclusion versus acceptance, liberalism versus exclusivism, alienation versus acculturation, integration versus assimilation, and multiculturalism versus monoculturalism. I examined the issue of construction and reconstruction of identity faced by migrants from minority groups, differentiating between self-identity and identification by others, and I looked at the issue of cultural heritage and its transmission to the next generation.

My primary form of research was verbal data obtained in the course of both random and selective interviews with Egyptian Jewish émigrés, mainly in Australia and France, using them as "oral historians". Thus, it was important to take a critical look at oral history as a tool for the social researcher, defining precisely its meaning and usefulness in relation to the present study, appreciating its importance, and recognising its limitations. In her *Oral History Handbook*, Beth M. Robertson recommended a step-by-step *modus operandi* for that method of investigation and suggested a basic and practical definition:

- a recorded interview in question-and-answer format,
- conducted by an interviewer who has some knowledge of the subject to be discussed
- with a knowledgeable interviewee speaking from personal participation,
- on subjects of historical interest, and
- which is made accessible to other researchers.[141]

Another definition offered by the British historian, David Lance, regarding the use of this methodology as a primary source in the sociology of ethnic relations, seemed particularly appropriate:

> Oral history is formed from the personal reminiscences of people who were participants in or witnesses of the events or experiences

they recount and—by present conventions—information is obtained by interviewing methods and recorded verbatim by one means or another.[142]

The utilisation of oral history as a scientific tool is a fairly recent phenomenon. The use of verbal data is considered to be one of the keystones of contemporary social science and was crucial to the accomplishment of my study.[143] Seeing as the number of Jewish migrants from Egypt was very small compared to the overall Jewish population and the written sources were scarce, the choice of an oral methodology was determined to be the best way to bring to the fore their past history, personal experiences, cultural diversity, and feelings of identity. The British historian, Paul Thompson, who is regarded as one of the pioneers of oral history as a research methodology, stated why this methodology is so valuable:

> Oral history is a history built around people. It thrusts life into history itself and it widens its scope. It allows heroes not just from the leaders, but from the unknown majority of the people… It helps the less privileged, and especially the old, towards dignity and self-confidence.[144]

The use of oral history and interviewing techniques has been central for developing a picture of many ethnic groups in Australia. For example, research in the field of ethnic relations conducted by Lois Foster and Anne Seitz on German migrants in Victoria illustrates the fact that "only intensive interviewing could obtain data on aspects such as the use of standard or dialect German, use of English, reasons for emigrating, reactions to a new place and culture, retention of German culture, and not least, information regarding German culture".[145] It is clear that the contribution of oral testimonies remains crucial to the development of a history of postwar immigration and to a wider understanding of the fabric of the Australian nation.

As a first step, I looked at the use of oral history as a tool in the context of my own research in order to identify its inherent strengths and weaknesses, as well as to explain why it was particularly appropriate for this study. I addressed the structural side of the research, its technical difficulties, and how they were handled. The value of a preliminary questionnaire, both as a selection tool and as a guide for the interview, was assessed together with other factors, such as the structure and the nature of the questions, whether those questions were qualitative or quantitative, and how they helped to construct the respondent's profile and define his or her world view. The differences between the field conditions in Australia and those in France, regarding the building of a database of potential respondents and the mode of selection of suitable interviewees, were evaluated in regard to the time factor and accessibility of the target group. Problems that occurred mid-stream and necessitated changes were reviewed because it was not always possible to strictly adhere to the chosen methodological path. The various methods of processing the raw material—such as tape recording, note taking, and telephone interviewing—were also assessed as to their advantages and disadvantages.

The next step was to deal with the actual data provided by the various oral testimonies, the type of analysis to which the data was subjected, and how it was checked against government archives material and other primary and secondary socio-historical and literary sources. The aim was to detect elements of distortion and understand the motivations of the interviewees in relation to these distortions.

One of the initial tasks was to acquire appropriate interviewing skills—thanks to a special training course provided by the Oral History Association of Australia at the State Library of New South Wales—in order to learn how to extract the best possible results from a single interview. Different methods were empirically demonstrated, illustrating the importance of body language, eye contact, and proximity to the interviewee. Concerns about asking questions that move the interview along, allowing the respondent to answer without interruption or comment, refraining from making moral judgments, and putting forward one's own opinion or version of the facts were all raised during the sessions. The technique of narrowing the focus of the interview, without making the interviewee uncomfortable about answering pointed questions, was also practised during group exercises. These acquired skills were very helpful and were built upon as the interviews progressed. They allowed early detection and subsequent avoidance of common mistakes, such as interrupting the flow of information too soon by asking a new question or commenting at length with one's own interpretation. As argued by Robertson in her *Oral History Handbook*, interviewers "who talk too much, or impose their own ideas or opinions, will inhibit communication and miss out on important information".[146] At the same time, an interviewer must not fall into the trap of allowing a more verbose interviewee to wander from the focus of the interview by providing tangential and superfluous details, thus overlooking more important information.

Following the guidelines of ethical practice established by the Oral History Association in 1978, at the beginning of every session a clarification of the purposes of the interview was provided to reassure the interviewee and dispel any misapprehension. Each participant was assured that a copy of the tape would be available on request. The identity and privacy of each respondent was protected by way of a signed agreement, which also allowed the interviewer to use the information for research purposes.[147] Generally the response to those guidelines was positive and encouraging. Each meeting was briefly evaluated at the end of the meeting until the interview could be transcribed using a copy of the tape while the original was secured elsewhere.

The study was divided into two phases: an initial questionnaire that was sent by mail, followed by a personal interview. The questionnaire was accompanied by a cover letter outlining the goal of the project and its importance, then asking for the cooperation of the recipient in the form of a personal interview at a time to be determined and in the language of choice—English, French, or Italian (see Appendix 1). It was presumed that such a questionnaire would facilitate identification of those interested in granting a meaningful interview to the researcher. Once the questionnaire was returned, an appointment was arranged. If the questionnaire was not answered within a reasonable amount of time, a discreet reminder was made over the telephone or via common contacts, given that age, idiosyncrasies, and other sensitivities of the potential interviewees had to be taken into account. Some addressees never answered. Some answered the questions very minimally and sent back the questionnaire indicating they did not wish to be interviewed. A few stated they were totally uninterested in reviving the past. Others even considered the project an intrusion into their private lives by well-meaning but meddling "amateurs". Others refused to participate, arguing, for example, that the questions relating to their departure from Egypt—such as: "Did you leave all your possessions behind or did you manage to salvage your money and belongings?"— were too intrusive. Sometimes they could not see the cultural relevance of the questions about their lifestyle in Egypt, for instance: "Type of cooking at home: Western or Middle Eastern; mode of dress: Western or Middle Eastern". In light of those objections, a few of the more confronting questions were slightly revised and assurances were given that there was no obligation to answer all questions if one did not wish to do so and that any contribution was valuable.

Apart from those few negative reactions, the mailing of the preliminary questionnaire was generally favourably received. As the initial project progressed, it revealed an unsuspected depth and wealth of information, apart from the human-interest angle. Each interview brought in a fresh perspective or a unique element, with the added realisation that this method of gathering information gave a voice to those who were never able or willing to tell their story outside the immediate family circle. By acquiring a voice as well as a sympathetic and empathetic listener, the interviewees felt suddenly empowered by the fact that outsiders could be interested in their memories. As a consequence, it made them more eager to share those memories with the interviewer. It validated their cultural heritage as something worth imparting to others without it being perceived as incompatible with the new culture they had more or less adopted.

In addition, the interview method constituted an undeniable asset as far as immediacy of information and interaction with the interviewees. This mode of gathering people's memories proved especially valuable when compared with data obtained via other more "objective" primary and secondary sources, such as media and government archives and literary material, history books, journals, and novels. This comparative exercise allowed me to check for any possible distortion conveyed by interviewees and to recognise that even distorted reminiscences could add another perspective to the overall research. The goal was to paint a picture of a pre- and postmigration experience as it was lived by the individuals concerned, not only as it was recorded in history books, keeping in mind that the results of such an investigation could never be totally conclusive.

In fact, when one adopts the oral history approach, one has to take into consideration the notoriously selective nature of memory and the difference between reality and perception. The issue of distortion, whether conscious or unconscious, can be considered a possible clue in itself, but it is still an element of misinformation that has to be taken into account. Although it is debatable whether any absolute truth exists, distortion of strictly historical truth is a common problem with oral history. The limitations of human memory are well documented, as stressed by William Foddy: "Even when respondents have been exposed to a particular event, there is no guarantee that they will have taken in much information about it or, if they have, that they will have remembered it".[148] People generally remember things they understand or things they are interested in. They might remember places, events, feelings, or attitudes, but not facts or dates or even chronology. They will remember more if they played an active role in the event under scrutiny. Charles Thompson pointed out the role of involvement in event recollection:

> One of the…ways to explore personal memory is to look at the relation between memory and the subject's level of involvement in the event…One can actually play in it, one can watch it, or one can read about it in the newspaper. These three methods of information again vary on at least two dimensions, the level of mental involvement in the event and the level of physical involvement in the event.[149]

The determining impact of active involvement was clearly demonstrated by the nature of the various testimonies gathered in the course of my research. For instance, one of the questions I asked related to a specific event—the burning of Cairo on 26 January 1952 by an out-of-control mob—to try and establish if that particular incident played a seminal role in the decision to leave Egypt.[150] It was found that when the interviewee had witnessed the event personally or suffered some direct trauma resulting from the rioting, the memory was not only clear and precise but it also revived the fear experienced on that day. One such witness was able to recall, even after forty-five years, the exact details of what he saw and what he was doing on that particular date, at that particular time. Because he lived across from the British Turf Club in Cairo, on that "Black Saturday" he reported watching with horror from the rooftop of his apartment building as British soldiers were thrown out of windows, amidst the burning and the looting. He had seen the devastation first-hand and therefore was able to describe it graphically.[151] In contrast, other interviewees who lived away from the centre of Cairo and had not personally witnessed the scenes of destruction could only relate, at best, a mediated account of the day based on what they heard or read after the event. The same principle applied to interviewees who had been imprisoned or expelled in 1948 and/or 1956 by Egyptian authorities for reasons of national security. These reasons included suspected involvement in a Zionist or Communist group, or simply, as was the case in the wake of the 1956 Suez War, being a French or British national, or being Jewish and at the head of a large enterprise. The victims inevitably conveyed a different perspective of the period than those who did not personally experience the trauma associated with arbitrary arrest or immediate expulsion, although the whole Jewish community of Egypt would have suffered some level of trauma by being forced into exile either overtly or covertly.

There is always a problem when interviewees are asked to recall events many years after they happened. Some level of distortion will naturally occur when the period between the actual event and its reporting is too great. To cover up a lapse in memory or confusion about details, an interviewee might subconsciously overcompensate by inflating or deflating certain aspects, according to how much he or she remembers. Then again, with the passage of time subsequent events often colour the memory of a particularly salient period in one's life and cloud the earlier experience or perception. In the present study, it was found that the telescoping phenomenon, as described by Sudman and Bradburn, was common, in view of the fact that the events in question had taken place over forty years earlier.[152] This phenomenon refers to a distortion of the time frame within which a certain event has occurred by setting it either earlier or later in the past. To try to overcome this problem, my questions had to be very specific, focusing on a particular issue or event, such as: When was emigration from Egypt envisaged and why?; What was your date of arrival?; Did you travel alone or with family and/or friends?; To what city did you first come and where did you stay?; What was your occupation then and what do you do now? The method of aided recall, also discussed by Sudman and Bradburn, was used sparingly and only when necessary to prompt the interviewee's failing memory by providing easy clues to the topic under investigation, so as not to unduly influence his or her response.[153] The problem with this type of approach is that it could suggest to the interviewee a quick and easy response, thus missing interesting and significant details.

Distortion can also be caused by different perceptions of self among interviewees. For example, when asked about their sense of identity while in Egypt, depending on their ethnic background and social standing, some interviewees saw themselves as foreigners living in Egypt and felt alienated from their Middle Eastern milieu. Others felt closer to their Egyptian roots and were more likely to consider Egypt their home. In spite of the gap between the two perspectives, it is not impossible that the interviewees, in hindsight, were subconsciously reinterpreting their position in Egyptian society because the new interpretation would currently be more politically correct. Therefore, in the final evaluation of those responses, the psychological factors of denial and projection had to be kept in mind.

I also took into consideration the fact that the interviewees were aware that I was part of their "in group" and their answers might have been somewhat different if solicited by an outsider. Upon reflection, I concluded that, on the contrary, it was more likely that they would not be as candid about their true feelings of identity to an outsider for fear of being adversely judged, whereas an insider would be deemed more understanding of any sign of ambivalence in this respect.

Suppression could also be considered a form of distortion. It might be deliberate or self-protecting, with the aim of repressing uncomfortable memories. For instance, one interviewee happily related all about his early life in Egypt, but when it came to the crucial time of the 1956 Suez War, he became agitated and refused outright to discuss his personal experience during that period. He claimed it was still too painful for him to evoke. In another instance, a woman apologised for not participating in the project, although she understood the motivation behind it. She explained that she could never talk about her past life in Egypt because of the suffering she had endured there. She only wanted to forget her memories of that time. The challenge facing me was to identify the various modes of distortion and suppression, understand the underlying reasons, and subsequently reassess them in the wider historical context.

At the onset, as previously mentioned, the choice of oral history as my research method was not the result of theoretical studies and abstract notions based on formal sociological models. Rather, it was conceived as a practical, user-friendly exercise, in order not to frighten away participants. Development of the questionnaire was based on personal experience and familiarity with the Egyptian Jewish community. Sharing the same ethnic background, the same migrant status, and the same languages as the interviewees created a climate of complicity between interviewer and interviewee, very similar to the findings of Foster and Seitz in reference to their 1985 study of German migrants in Victoria:

> The researcher's ethnicity (evidenced in language and cultural knowledge), status (being a migrant, identification with and perceived sponsorship by a university, experience of adjusting to Australian life over a lengthy period of time) and gender facilitated initial contact with interviewees and rapidly established a situation in which the interviewees were at ease, offering many reminiscences quite spontaneously.[154]

For instance, my fluency in French and Italian and my understanding of Arabic often broke down any linguistic and psychological barriers when interviewees did not feel confident enough to express themselves in English or when they borrowed an expression from one of those languages to make a particular point. In fact, some of the interviews in Australia, particularly with older participants, and obviously all the interviews in France were conducted in French, the *lingua franca*[155] of the minorities in Egypt, at least until the late 1950s. Italian was sometimes used in conjunction with French, depending on the specific ethnic background of the interviewee, whereas the use of Arabic was restricted to a few comments. The underlying reasons for the multilingualism of the Jews of Egypt and the privileged status enjoyed by the French language in that context are discussed at length in the historical section of this book.[156] Furthermore, the issue of gender was important in view of the fact that male respondents saw a female interviewer as less confronting, and female respondents found female interviewers more reassuring, especially the older respondents.

In planning this research, there were a number of keys issues to consider. The first issue was identifying and then reaching the target group. The project was initiated in Sydney because it was my and Lana Woolf's hometown. An advertisement was placed in the Jewish press explaining the aim of the project and asking for volunteers. An initial list of sixty-eight names was established from personal contact; we intended to connect with additional respondents by word of mouth. When the project was combined with my doctoral research, the two Egyptian-Jewish communities in Adelaide and Melbourne were also targeted. Assisted by a network of friends and active members of the Sephardi Association of Victoria, the Sassoon Yehuda Sephardi Synagogue in Melbourne, the Adelaide Hebrew Congregation (AHC), and the Adelaide Progressive Jewish Congregation, I developed several relationships, which led to a full program of formal interviews and informal meetings with Egyptian émigrés in those communities. By the end of the Australian component of the study, a total of ninety-two people participated, as well as another twenty to thirty who did not wish to be interviewed at length but were willing to answer a few questions in a more casual conversation. Selection of the French sample was planned and the interviews conducted over two visits to Paris, three years apart. A short trip to Egypt was also undertaken to contact the few remaining members of a dying Jewish community, as well as a tour of other Jewish diasporas from Egypt in the United States and Great Britain, to complement the overall data.

Priority was given to older interviewees, who had migrated to Australia around 1956, in their late thirties or early forties. They were in their eighties by the time this research began; haste was essential before their memories became too faded or distorted due to age or ill health. Such was the sad case of one respondent interviewed in Montefiore Home, a Jewish retirement home on the outskirts of Sydney. The interviewee, who usually displayed a relatively clear recollection of the past without prompting, was disorientated by revisiting her past—brought on by my questions—and kept confusing herself with her mother and sister. She unfortunately died not long after our meeting. The interview in itself was not very useful at the time but was ultimately salvaged by her son, who was able to fill in the gaps and clarify some of the confusion. It also reinforced the urgency of the situation as far as older respondents were concerned. They were gradually disappearing, along with their memories of the vanished Jewish world in which they had been born and raised. In fact, by 2009 at least twelve of the interviewees had died. Obtaining data from the second generation had many inherent limitations.

The overall aim of the written questionnaire was to cover the relevant issues quantitatively and qualitatively in chronological order, with an underlying thematic and conceptual thread. For example, the questionnaire was first divided into two broad sections: (1) life in Egypt; and (2) life in Australia. Within those sections, several fundamental concepts were raised, such as acculturation, alienation, inclusion, identity and identification, importance of memory, and transmission of memory. Whenever possible, questions were closed rather than open-ended in order to keep the survey simple and not confuse the respondents. The procedure of aided recall mentioned earlier proved to be very effective. For instance, a list of eight possibilities was offered in response to the question of what languages were spoken at home. For the question about domestic help in Egypt, five options were offered. The questionnaire was only used as a guide during the actual interview, which allowed for the addition of more complex questions. The interviewee could then elaborate on or clarify issues brought up in the written questionnaire, such as the extent of communal involvement in Egypt and Australia, personal experiences of anti-Semitic incidents, and feelings of identity.

The main concern was that the respondent understood each question and was encouraged to provide as much information as possible. Therefore, the questionnaire had to be concise, simple, and direct, but it also had to be sensitive because it was directed at individuals who had gone through the trauma of forced emigration, loss, and displacement. An area that needed to be treated with special care was the recounting of events immediately preceding their departure from Egypt. As mentioned earlier, the questionnaire was constructed chronologically and thematically. The section on life in Egypt included standard demographic questions— name, age, socioeconomic status, ethnic origin, level of education, and culture. It then focused on what it meant being Jewish in Egypt before and after 1948; the degree of involvement in Jewish communal affairs and/or in the Egyptian political arena; the sense of belonging; and the circumstances surrounding their final departure—whether it was imposed by government policy, by loss of livelihood, or just by the realisation that Jews had no place left for them in Egypt.

The next section dealt mainly with the issue of transit in Europe for eventual immigration to Australia; the reason that Australia was chosen as a destination; and the hurdles that had to be overcome as far as housing, work, language, and culture were concerned. The concluding section inquired about the respondents' present sense of identity—the way they saw themselves, as well as the way others saw them. This issue was crucial for the final analysis of the integration, acculturation, and contribution of Egyptian Jews at the level of both the Jewish social microcosm and the broader Australian macrocosm.

For the comparative research in France, the second section of the questionnaire was modified to fit the different national context. Also, as opposed to the Australian approach, in France the two procedures— questionnaire and interview—were fused into a single process, whereby I, as interviewer, controlled both the written and oral sections. Although early contacts were made from Australia, the actual list of potential respondents was finalised and appointments were made only after arrival in Paris. Therefore, I could not afford the delay required to mail the questionnaires ahead of the interview. This procedure extended the whole exercise by about an hour compared to the interviews conducted in Sydney, which usually took from one and one-half to two hours. It also meant that respondents did not have the flexibility to reflect on or come back to problem questions at their own pace, which could have affected the nature of the answers provided. Nevertheless, this method was judged the most appropriate given the limited time available to spend in Paris. When a contact was made, the interview was immediately scheduled, giving the respondent no opportunity to back out. I had used that particular methodology for the Melbourne and Adelaide interviews—where time was also of the essence—and found it to be effective

Considering the much larger migration of Egyptian Jews to France, as well as the unavoidable restrictions imposed by geographical distance and the time necessary for locating and interviewing a proportionate number of respondents, my objectives were not to reproduce the quantitative and qualitative research already undertaken in Australia. Only that exact study could have led to an equitable and sustainable comparison.[157] Nevertheless, I believed that the introduction of a comparative group would enrich and give more substance to the Australian side of the research. Therefore, the research in France focused mainly on the primary themes of any migration experience—culture, identity, integration, and contribution to the host society—through the case study of an elite group of individuals, located in Paris for the most part, although some had moved from France to England or to the United States. The French sample, although much smaller in size, was particularly interesting. Not only was it representative of the characteristics specific to the Jews of Egypt as revealed by the study of the Australian sample, but it was also singularly committed to the preservation and transmission of their cultural heritage and actively promoted these issues.

My work was based on twenty-one formal interviews conducted in 1999 and 2003, as well as numerous informal meetings and personal discussions with Egyptian Jews in France, England, and the United States. The three-year gap between interviews was particularly significant; the second lot of interviews reflected the change of climate in France, with the rise of anti-Semitic incidents following the start of the *al-Aqsa Intifada* (the second Palestinian Uprising), often disguised as legitimate expressions of anti-Zionism. For the first time, a French interviewee admitted pessimism regarding his future as a Jew in France, a reaction somewhat similar to what some of my respondents had said about Egypt after 1948. It was, therefore, deemed necessary to reassess some of the earlier responses by revisiting the first group of interviewees whenever possible.

The interview itself was basically on a one-to-one basis although a third party was often present, either a co-interviewer or the interviewee's spouse. The latter case was found to be disruptive at times and helpful at others, depending on the relationship between the spouses. As argued by Bradburn and Sudman, "response effects are more likely to occur when the third party knows the respondent".[158] This was found to be true in cases when both spouses were interviewed in succession and one would interrupt the other to correct a statement or provide more information.

Regarding the value of the questionnaire versus the interview, generally the two procedures were found to be complementary. For example, the more open type of questions asked during the interview brought to the surface experiences that were totally buried in the subject's memory and therefore never mentioned in the written response. In some situations, the respondent considered filling in the questionnaire a tedious exercise and preferred the interview method, whereas in other cases the respondent would shy away from talking to a stranger and just filled in the questionnaire. By using both the written and oral approaches, the collated data was maximised.

Telephone interviews were sometimes conducted when the respondent was unable to meet personally with the interviewer. This method yielded rather unsatisfactory results because the interviewee often sounded distracted or rushed, which in turn inhibited the exchange of information. It was only adopted in special cases, such as the occasion when I finally convinced a reluctant respondent to relate her experience in a Jewish hostel, or when I could not arrange a face-to-face interview with an interstate respondent.[159]

The various stages of processing the raw material included assessment of the completed questionnaire followed by tape recording the subsequent interview. The interview was then either transcribed verbatim if the information was considered too sensitive to be edited simultaneously or summarised in a succinct account of the more relevant issues raised in the course of the meeting. The information was then grouped under different titles and according to themes. When recording was not possible because the interviewee refused to be taped, or if it was impractical to do so because of the location of the actual interview, the note-taking method was adopted. This last procedure somewhat inhibited the flow of information by giving the interview a more formal structure. However, it had the advantage of greatly facilitating the transcription process. This method was more frequently used on field trips overseas, particularly in the case of impromptu encounters with prospective respondents.

As the work progressed, new elements surfaced from experience in the field. Some issues were initially missed, such as the effects of migration on the interviewees' children and their own integration into Australian society. This was difficult to rectify as far as the completed interviews, but in the course of subsequent sessions those topics were introduced to try to compensate for the earlier omissions.

All the data gathered through the questionnaires and interviews was entered into a database using a special computer program.[160] It was then imported onto an Excel chart and organised into categories, resulting in a multidimensional, polyvariable analysis. For instance, it enabled me to connect at a glance the predominant reason for migrating to Australia, the ages of the migrants, their date and place of arrival, and whether they received any assistance. This chart also allowed me to verify whether there was a connection between linguistic skills, occupation, and positive feelings of identity, thus combining both the quantitative and qualitative approaches. This type of analysis helped me to outline a tentative profile of the Jew "in" Egypt based on gender, age, occupation, social class, education, and ideology, and compare it to the profile of the same Jew "from" Egypt now living in Australia, using the same criteria.

Accessing other major primary sources—such as Australian government archives, Jewish institutional archives, and records of the Jewish and general press—complemented the oral history methodology. Official government records were invaluable because they provided backbone to the data gathered through other means. Whether archival material validated the personal data or discredited it was not the core issue; what mattered most was the fact that by presenting their version of the facts, both sources gave me as the researcher the ability to distinguish between reality and myth, without discounting people's perceptions of a particular occurrence. Reading the transcripts of Australian ministers' memos at the time of the Suez crisis of 1956 was particularly enlightening; they opened a window into the official Australian politics of the time, a perspective that would have been inaccessible to the people directly affected by those policies.[161]

Concurrently, the records of Australian Jewish institutions uncovered details of the immediate reaction of the local community to the events in faraway Egypt and the proactive stand adopted by those institutions. At the time of the Suez War in particular, both the general press and the Jewish press covered the events in the Middle East extensively. Considering the usual hyperbolism and inaccuracies often found in such reports, their representation of the plight of Egyptian Jews during that period closely reflected the testimonies of the interviewees.

For the comparative study of the French sample group, I used the same thematic approach, but I did not attempt to delve extensively into primary sources and archives; that would have been the subject of another dissertation. I primarily consulted secondary sources, such as books and journal articles, to obtain background information on the contextual conditions in France after World War II and the implementation of its social and immigration policies. As mentioned previously, the two postgraduate theses on the topic of the Jews in modern Egypt pre- and postemigration—which were submitted in Paris—also relied heavily on oral history. Nevertheless, I was able to add considerably to my knowledge and understanding of French conditions and learn about interactions among members of this uprooted community, and their diverse interests and preoccupations, through various contributions to *Nahar Misraïm*, the bulletin of the ASPCJE. This bulletin also conveyed valuable information on the past and present achievements of the Jews of Egypt in the socioeconomic, literary, political, and religious domains, both in Egypt and in France.[162] The works of Michael Laskier and Michel Abitbol on the integration of North African Jews into France added another dimension to my research by revealing a migration story that was both contemporary and comparable to the Egyptian story. In addition, the numerous published testimonies, memoirs, and novels written by Egyptian-Jewish émigrés in France, Switzerland, Belgium, and the Americas contributed by constructing a picture of a difficult beginning, then satisfactory achievement—on both an individual and a collective basis—in preserving and transmitting the heritage of the Jews of Egypt.[163] The availability of this material helped consolidate the findings from the small French sample. In contrast, all the material published in Israel or Egypt on the topic of Egyptian Jews was virtually inaccessible unless it was translated into English or French, due to my very basic Hebrew reading skills and my poor knowledge of literary Arabic. Thus, the inevitable gaps that resulted had to be taken into account.

Looking at the outline of the strategies used in my research, it is clear that thematic and conceptual perspectives constitute the backbone of my work. Oral history was the primary tool, and the strength of this methodology has been highlighted as far as its economy, direct approach, immediacy, and ability to maximise the flow of information. Its weaknesses, such as distortion, omission, and telescoping, have been taken into consideration and turned into positive input. My insider's knowledge has proven fundamental to the understanding of the cultural behaviour of the group. The procedure adopted to check this information against government and community archives, the press, and literary sources was obviously crucial to drawing any authoritative conclusion. It had its limitations, given that the list of publications can never be exhaustive. The distance in time and space was also an impediment in the collating of relevant data, and I had to contend with what was available and accessible. While taking into consideration the limitations of the methodology I adopted, I have tried to construct—through a socio-historical thematic approach backed by personal testimonies and primary and secondary sources—a clear and informed summary of the subject matter, allowing for more valid conclusions.

CHAPTER 3

THE JEWS OF EGYPT
IN THE MODERN AGE

A CHEQUERED HISTORY

The documented history of Jewish settlement in Egypt stretches back
twenty-five centuries without interruption. However, this study does not
claim that today's Egyptian Jews are the descendants of those ancient
Israelites, and the gap between the mythical history and the historical
reality is not disputed. As recognised by most specialists in the subject,
such as the historian Shimon Shamir, "the majority of modern Egyptian
Jewry was the product of waves of immigration…when Egypt became
a land of opportunity" in the 1860s.[164] Nevertheless, in the collective
memory of Jews from Egypt now dispersed throughout the world, the
feeling of continuity between them and their forebears, whether justified or not, constitutes an integral part of their perception of self, of their
identity. Thus, both the mythical and historical forces have contributed
to the shaping of the Egyptian Jewish identity.

THE 1798 FRENCH EXPEDITION AND ITS CONSEQUENCES

According to convention, the modern history of Egypt begins in 1798, with the landing of a French expeditionary force led by Napoleon Bonaparte. Historians have traditionally considered this invasion the catalyst that first exposed Egypt to modernity and Western influence. Obviously this exposure has had a profound socioeconomic impact on the various population groups. I have therefore chosen this period as a starting point for the modern experience of Egyptian Jewry.

By the end of the eighteenth century, Egypt stood ravaged by internecine wars among the local Mamluk rulers, trying to throw off the yoke of the Ottoman Sultan. Inefficiency and disorder were widespread and the country was plunged into anarchy. From about 1780, "a state of quasi-permanent civil war" reigned, which led to a severe financial crisis.[165] Epidemics and famine decimated an already destitute general population. Economically and culturally, Egypt was in a state of total disintegration. Various sources mention a depleted Jewish community of about six or seven thousand, subjected "to the whim of the local rulers, who maltreated them and confiscated their property".[166] For the most part, the Jews lived in extreme poverty, confined to restricted quarters, working as small artisans, pawnbrokers, and moneychangers.

This was the situation Napoleon Bonaparte was confronted with when he landed in Egypt in 1798 wearing the mantle of liberator of the oppressed. There is historical debate about the aims of the young French Republic in launching this expedition. Some have claimed that it was politically motivated by Franco-British rivalry and by the desire to impact on Britain's trade with India.[167] Others have argued that the object was both commercial and scientific, seeing as Bonaparte "devoted a great deal of his attention to the means of developing the commerce and agriculture of that rich country".[168] Another rather spurious reason was the avenging of the honour of France because of the constant harassment and humiliation imposed by the Mamluk *beys* on resident French merchants.[169] Whatever the real reasons were—underlying the political and economic pragmatism—the young Republic, self-appointed champion of human rights, needed to invoke a much nobler ideal to justify its occupation of Egypt, the republican ideal of a *mission civilisatrice et régénatrice*.[170]

This imported idea of civilising and regenerating Egypt proved to be the cornerstone of Egypt's future from then on. An array of scientists—167 altogether—joined the French army of fifty-four thousand men embarking from the port of Toulon on May 19, 1798. They included Orientalist scholars, engineers, administrators, mathematicians, zoologists, astronomers, draughtsmen, architects, printers, interpreters, health officers, and even musicians.[171] The French forces landed in Alexandria with great fanfare, after successfully escaping British naval surveillance. In spite of an initial military victory against the Mamluks at the Pyramids, the French army was left stranded in Egypt when the entire French fleet was destroyed by the British at the Bay of Aboukir on August 1, 1798. A year later, because of the urgency of the political situation back in France, Napoleon was forced to flee the country secretly, leaving behind the bulk of his forces under the command of General Kléber. The new commander tried in vain to negotiate with the Ottomans and the British command an honourable repatriation of his men. His successor, General Jacques Menou, a French convert to Islam and an able administrator, attempted to focus on some of the early objectives of the expedition, such as instituting land and tax reforms.[172] However, his plans did not come to fruition due to the surrender of the French forces after the Anglo-Ottoman invasion of 1801. He ended up overseeing the evacuation of the humiliated French troops on board British ships, as well as the confiscation by the British of most of the treasures gathered by the French scientists. Among those treasures was the famous Rosetta Stone, which proved to be the key to the deciphering of the hieroglyphs by the French Orientalist Jean-François Champollion in 1822.[173]

In spite of the military setback, the French scholars and scientists pursued their avowed task of discovering Egypt and revealing it to Europe while bringing Western *savoir-faire* and civilisation to what they considered a backward part of the world. Their achievements were numerous. The French were responsible for introducing in the Middle East the first printing press with fonts in Arabic as well as Latin and Greek.[174] As stated by the Orientalist professor Timothy Mitchell, "the absence of printing over the preceding centuries has often been cited as evidence of the backwardness and isolation of the Arab world that the French occupation was to shatter".[175] The Institut d'Égypte was created in August 1798, modelled on the famous Institut de France.[176] In 1809, Napoleon's *corps des savants* (group of scholars) produced the encyclopaedic work *Description de l'Égypte*, based on their comprehensive study of contemporary and ancient Egypt. Undeniably, the most important French contribution was in the field of archaeology with the deciphering of the hieroglyphs.

Apart from all the achievements of the scientists and the scholars, one might ask if the French Expedition had any other significant impact on Egypt, after a presence of a mere three years and three months. Although Al-Sayyid Marsot claimed there was nothing of substance, she acknowledged that the importance of the expedition lay elsewhere and was not to be discounted:

> It broke the last links between Mamluk beys and the indigenous population when the former showed that they were incapable of saving Egypt from invasion. It also brought French technocrats to the country, many of whom were St Simonians, and inspired them to offer their services to Muhammad Ali after 1815...Lastly, it brought the British into the Mediterranean...This last factor was to have more enduring effects on Egypt than anything else.[177]

From the British perspective, analysts also seem to agree that, in spite of the utter failure of the French expedition, it had far-reaching consequences both for the future of Egypt and for the penetration of European influence and trade in that part of the world, as stated by the British historian Henry Dodwell:

> French occupation of Egypt came to an inglorious end. But it had been far from fruitless. It had shaken Mamluk power; it had fully awakened English minds to the strategic importance of a country placed midway between East and West; it had illustrated

Turkish incompetence; and incidentally it had brought to Egypt an Albanian adventurer, Muhammad Ali.[178]

In fact, this so-called Albanian adventurer, who first set foot in Egypt in 1801 with the Anglo-Ottoman expeditionary forces and who had "no cultural identity other than the Ottoman one", ended up ruling the country and founding a dynasty that would endure until 1954.

As far as the Egyptian Jews were concerned, their first contact with modernity embodied by the French invaders was not altogether positive. In his usual autocratic way, Bonaparte ordered them to organise themselves like the Jews of France, in an institution called the *Consistoire*, headed by two rabbis (*Grands Prêtres de la Nation Juive*) and seven councillors (*Conseillers*). This body would be responsible for the whole of the Jewish community, in case of any disturbance or reprehensible behaviour.[179] There is no evidence that this order was followed after Bonaparte's departure. One document, dated September 17, 1854, written in Arabic, outlined the statutes of the Alexandria Jewish community, which did not appear to follow the Napoleonic model.[180]

Bonaparte was also reputed to have ruthlessly bombarded a synagogue that stood on the present site of the Eliahou Hannavi Synagogue in Alexandria, on the pretext that it was obstructing the operation of his cannons. The real reason is thought to have been one of retaliation for the nonpayment of a heavy monetary imposition on an impecunious Jewish community.[181] Nevertheless, in spite of the initial victimisation of Egyptian Jews by the French invaders, and considering the privileged role French culture played in Egypt from that time on—especially vis-à-vis the non-Muslim minorities—it is clear that the French Expedition deeply affected the future destinies of Egyptian Jewry, albeit indirectly.

MUHAMMAD ALI AND THE MODERNISATION OF EGYPT

Muhammad Ali's reign over Egypt spanned nearly half a century, from 1805 to 1849, and proved crucial for the development of the country. During the first years of his rule, he established his authority by ruthlessly eliminating any opposition and massacring his sworn enemies, the Mamluk beys. He was then free to occupy himself fully with his plans of modernising Egypt's socioeconomic base. According to Al-Sayyid Marsot, he firmly believed "in the value of specialists. He searched them out, learned from them and made use of that knowledge".[182] He found them initially among ethno-religious minority groups, such as the Armenians, who served as "translators, interpreters and high officials in the bureaucracy", or the Syrian Christians, regarded as experts at tax levying and as astute merchants.[183] However, it was mostly towards France that Muhammad Ali turned for financial and technical expertise to help him realise his ambitious plans of administrative and economic reforms. As early as 1805 the French had recognised that he was the only possible ruler for Egypt, and their local agents cultivated privileged relations with the Pasha.[184] He used the skills of the French technocrats who had come to Egypt with the French army or others "who flocked to Egypt in search of jobs when Napoleon's Empire collapsed and the army disbanded".[185] For instance, in 1825, in an effort to raise the dismal standard of public health, Muhammad Ali sought the services of a French physician, Antoine Barthélemy Clot, who became known as Clot-Bey, and set out to establish a military hospital in conjunction with a medical school. It was the first time that the study of a language other than Arabic—in this case French—was introduced as part of the official curriculum of a government institution.[186]

The Pasha's reforms also targeted the military, due to his obvious need for a strong army. By enrolling the services of French and British officers, he transformed his troops from an unruly and potentially dangerous amalgamation of mercenaries and foreigners into a professional army "following European discipline, formed on the European mode of organisation".[187] The new, drafted, regular army was called *nizam jadid*. Muhammad Ali created barracks, training camps, and training schools for military cadres. From 1844 to 1849, Egyptian students from the social elite were sent to Paris to attend a school set up by the Egyptian government and run by the French Ministry of War, where the motto was order and obedience.[188] Egypt became the first province of the Ottoman

Empire to have an army trained and organised along these lines. The objective of Muhammad Ali was obviously not only to train the bodies of his subjects, but also to shape their minds into a Western mould.

Equally, Muhammad Ali again did not hesitate to send to France, at his expense, a number of handpicked young Egyptians to be trained in the domain of public administration. His ultimate aim was to displace the Turks, who had a monopoly in that sector of government. In addition, a number of technical schools were created locally under French and Italian initiative, and Egypt was reputed to have been "the first oriental country in which anything like a regular system of westernised education was established".[189]

THE JEWISH MINORITY IN NINETEENTH-CENTURY EGYPT

How did this political, cultural, and institutional upheaval affect the indigenous non-Muslim minorities? Eventually, and inevitably, the wide programs of reform and Westernisation instituted by Muhammad Ali impacted very significantly and very favourably on those minorities. However, as far as the Jews were concerned, their lot did not improve dramatically during the early part of Muhammad Ali's reign, although the new laws provided them with better protection than under the previous administration.[190] Contemporary observers, such as Edward William Lane, who wrote extensively on that period of Egyptian history, noted the oppression to which Jews were still subjected and how both Muslims and Copts hated them and treated them with great contempt. Lane added that Jews could still be "arbitrarily arrested and only released upon payment of a heavy fine", which explains why they were apparently very careful not to show any exterior sign of wealth.[191] They were still bearing the burden of the *jizya* tax—which was only abolished in 1855—plus a community tax, in addition to the other heavy taxes imposed on the general population.

Although undistinguishable from the rest of the indigenous population except for the colour of their turbans, most Jews remained very devout and close to their traditions.[192] Their occupations varied from hawkers, small traders, artisans, and shopkeepers to moneychangers (*sarrāf*) and general merchants. As with all dhimmi communities, the division between Jews and other ethnic groups was drawn on religious lines, and they lived segregated and alienated from the Muslim majority.[193]

The Jewish community of those days consisted mainly of two religious groups: a minority of Karaites who only accepted the authority of the Written Law,[194] and a majority of Rabbanites, who followed the rabbinical tradition, which included both the Oral and the Written Law.[195] As a testimony to the ancient origins of Karaite Jews in Egypt, the Karaite Jewish historian Mourad El Kodsi, claimed that:

> The Karaite community in Egypt had in its possession, until the end of the nineteenth century, a legal document stamped by the palm of Amr Ibn al-As, the first Islamic governor of Egypt, in which he ordered the leaders of the Rabbanite community not to interfere in the way of life of the Karaites nor with the way they celebrate their holidays. This document is dated 20 AH (641 CE), more than one hundred years before Anan.[196]

However, recent historical scholarship invalidates this claim and most scholars do not support the existence of a seventh-century document that mentioned the Karaites. Similar documents, such as, for example, the Geniza letter of privileges to the Jews of Kaybar, were well-known forgeries.[197]

According to Landau, the exact size of the Jewish community in the first half of the nineteenth century is very difficult to ascertain because no censuses were taken at the time.[198] From local accounts or those made by travellers, it is assumed to hover around six or seven thousand. The Karaites had been living in Egypt for over one thousand years and, except for their religious practices, were significantly assimilated into their Muslim environment as far as language and lifestyle were concerned.[199]

Until the beginning of the twentieth century, the Karaites and the Rabbanites lived and functioned separately from one another, although their differences were more on issues of religious practices and calendar rather than dogma and faith.[200] However, according to Laskier, European colonial penetration and the influx of Jews from Europe "made the Karaites even less significant than before, compelling them to cooperate ever more intensely with the Rabbanites".[201] A definite rapprochement occurred between the two communities under British rule because of its policy of "recognising only the Sephardi Rabbanite community as the sole representative of all the Jews of Egypt vis-à-vis the authorities", a policy which more or less forced the Karaites under the umbrella of the Rabbanites.[202]

As for the Sephardim, they came to Egypt in the aftermath of the Christian *Reconquista* of Muslim Spain and their subsequent expulsion from Spain and Portugal in 1492 and 1497, respectively.[203] They were only marginally integrated in their Muslim context and had retained their particular language—Judeo-Spanish or Ladino—as well as a number of traditions they had brought with them from their country of origin. There was also a small group of Ashkenazim who had been in Egypt since the sixteenth century; their numbers were reinforced by the arrival of refugees from the Ukraine, escaping persecution by the Chmielnicki Cossacks in 1648.[204]

The living conditions of the minorities gradually improved as Muhammad Ali's successors continued to display even more partiality to the West, wishing "to direct the country's economy towards the European world market", as noted by Marsot.[205] Their *laissez-faire* policy opened the door to an increasing number of foreign nationals who started to flock to Egypt, set up shop, form colonies, and gain influence.[206] They were particularly encouraged by the special status granted to foreigners under the Capitulations regime.[207] Originally intended to protect foreign merchants residing in the Ottoman Empire, this regime had grown to allow all foreign nationals to enjoy special economic and legal privileges. Apart from guaranteeing their lives and property, freedom of religion, and exemption from the *jizya*, it also exempted them from local taxation and placed them under the jurisdiction of their own local consuls and out of reach of Muslim courts.[208]

Under the Mamluk regime, these privileges had not always been respected, and foreign merchants were often attacked and held for ransom in spite of protests by their governments. As mentioned earlier, this was one of the reasons for Napoleon Bonaparte's ill-fated expedition to Egypt. Muhammad Ali, however, with a view of attracting foreign trade and investments, decreed that all outward manifestations of xenophobia towards non-Muslims were to be suppressed. Distinctive clothing and social restrictions were abolished. Foreigners were to be protected in the spirit of the Capitulations, which was further reinforced by the clout of the Mixed Courts, established in 1875.[209] This new institution completely shielded foreign nationals from the local powers of law and order.[210] Not only did the Egyptian police not have the right to arrest Europeans, they could not even interfere in altercations between them and indigenous Egyptians.[211] It is obvious that, for reasons of personal safety, economic privileges, and social standing, status as a foreigner became a very desirable commodity, and Jews and non-Jews alike sought it actively.

THE GOLDEN AGE OF EGYPTIAN JEWRY

With Western powers gaining more and more of a foothold in the country, Egypt had gradually become a very attractive destination for Greek, Italian, Syrian, North African, and Armenian migrants. According to Landau's figures, a large proportion of the immigrants were Jewish, coming from the rest of the ailing Ottoman Empire and the Mediterranean basin on the outbreak of the Greek-Turkish War in 1821. In 1840, Muhammad Ali had even encouraged such Jews to settle in the country. It is important to realise that at the time, "the Ottoman authorities did not prevent travel within their empire, and Jews from Iraq and elsewhere emigrated to Egypt to benefit from a government that ruled more leniently than those in other parts of the empire".[212] They came from places such as Corfu, Salonika, the Aegean Archipelago, and Italy. Krämer also mentions the Ashkenazi Jews from Russia, Rumania, and Poland, who came in the hundreds in the late nineteenth and early twentieth centuries, particularly after the Kishinev pogrom of 1903, "almost all of them young and without means of support".[213]

COLONIAL RULE

Underlying the previously mentioned conditions were three key elements that transformed Egypt into a new Eldorado and brought her into the international market economy: the building of the Suez Canal in 1869; the British occupation of the country in 1882; and the development of the cotton industry, a result of modern methods of agriculture.

The opening of the Suez Canal proved to be critical to the expansion of modern Egypt seeing as it introduced the country to the world and created fresh opportunities for local and foreign entrepreneurs. In 1854, the Viceroy Muhammad Said Pasha—son of Muhammad Ali—awarded the construction of the canal to the French Saint-Simonist engineer Ferdinand de Lesseps. Initially France provided about half the capital, together with the technical expertise, even as Egypt contributed the remainder of the funding and the necessary manpower. The construction proceeded under conditions described as being very close to slave labour and is said to have cost the lives of between 100,000 and 125,000 Egyptian workers. The two governments agreed that the Compagnie Universelle du Canal maritime de Suez was to run the canal for ninety-nine years, after which time its ownership would revert to Egypt. The inauguration of the canal in 1869 by the Empress Eugenie of France was a lavish affair, organised on a grand scale by the extravagant Khedive Ismail and attended by numerous European heads of state as well as the elite of Egyptian society. As part of the celebrations, Ismail engaged in an extensive building program. Luxurious hotels, such as the Gezira Palace Hotel—operating today as the Marriott Hotel—were raised to host the prestigious guests and their retinue.[214] A new road between Cairo and the Pyramids was constructed especially for the visitors. Furthermore, Ismail—who saw himself as a great patron of the arts—announced plans to build a new eight hundred and fifty-seat opera theatre in Cairo. He even commissioned Verdi to compose the opera Aida for its opening but, due to various delays, the opera's premiere in Cairo did not occur until December 1871, in front of a predominantly European audience.[215]

In fact, the Khedive Ismail, a fervent Francophile steeped in Western culture, wanted his country to become part of Europe at all costs.[216] Due to his extravagant lifestyle, he squandered Egypt's reserves in the process and was forced to sell all his shares in the Compagnie du Canal to the British in 1875.[217] On the edge of bankruptcy, Egypt was compelled to hand over control of its treasury to a Franco-British Commission. In 1882, on the pretext of protecting the interests and safety of foreign nationals, British troops landed in Egypt to squash a military rebellion led by Colonel Orabi Pasha. The colonel was trying to impose a nationalist government on the Khedive, free from foreign interference, under the slogan "Egypt for the Egyptians".[218] Great Britain effectively ruled Egypt up to the end of World War II, and its presence on Egyptian soil was maintained until the Suez War of 1956.[219] Under the British Protectorate, Egypt entered an era of political stability and economic growth. The climate of economic liberalism and legal privilege fostered by British rule, while favouring the Egyptian elite, also raised considerably the status of the non-Muslim minorities who, as noted by Laskier, "welcomed with considerable enthusiasm French and British colonial penetration".[220]

The third element of the equation was the development of the cotton industry by Muhammad Ali in 1820 and the introduction, towards the end of the nineteenth century, of long-staple cotton, the finest variety of that commodity.[221] Britain needed an adequate supply of that particular type of cotton for the textile factories of Manchester and Leeds. Because the American Civil War had interrupted cotton exports from the Confederacy, high demand for that raw material brought Egypt into the world commodity markets after 1860.[222] A number of experimental farms were established, and much research went into cotton selection, fertilisation, and irrigation. Agriculture was transformed, infrastructure was widely expanded, and demand for credit and capital soared.[223] Egyptian revenue from cotton rose dramatically, and by 1914 cotton exports accounted for 92 percent of the total export sector.[224] According to the testimony of Maurice Mizrahi, the contribution of the Jews to the development of the cotton industry was disproportionate to their number:

> Avant la nationalisation, on trouvait à Alexandrie quelque
> quarante-cinq sociétés d'exportation de coton, vingt-cinq d'entre
> elles appartenaient à des Juifs, sans compter les compagnies dont
> le personnel et le directeur étaient juifs.[225]

At the same time, political and social upheavals occurring in different parts of the Jewish diaspora impacted the ethnic makeup of Egyptian Jewry. Widespread pogroms and persecution of Jews in Eastern Europe and Morocco in the second half of the nineteenth century had already brought to Egypt a significant number of refugees in need of asylum.[226] As noted by the historian Shimon Shamir, "Egypt was for the Jews a veritable 'Land of Goshen'—a safe abode for the local community and a haven for Jews from neighboring countries".[227] Additionally, Laskier indicated that between 1914 and 1916, on the pretext that they were enemy subjects, "over eleven thousand Ashkenazi Jews expelled from Palestine by Jemal Pasha, the Ottoman commander of Syria and Palestine, fled to Alexandria, Cairo and Suez".[228] The number of Jews in Egypt reached thirty thousand by 1882 and doubled by 1918. The last census conducted by the British in 1947 indicated a Jewish population of about seventy to seventy-five thousand, which constituted 0.4 percent of a total Egyptian population of nineteen million.[229] Laskier's study found that "there were approximately six thousand Ashkenazim, at least thirty-five hundred Karaites, and ten thousand indigenous Jews, the rest being Orientals and Sephardim who were recent emigrants, or their descendants".[230]

The newcomers' diverse ethnic backgrounds dramatically altered the face of the indigenous Jewish community, which emerged as a multicultural and multilingual mosaic. The Sephardim, who constituted the majority group, were often conversant in Ladino, French, and Italian, as well as Turkish and Greek. It is from their ranks that the social elite of Egyptian Jewry rose to occupy all the leadership positions until 1956. The Greek Jews, or *Romaniot*, spoke Greek, and the Ashkenazim spoke Yiddish, Polish, and/or Russian. Egyptian Arabic remained the language used at home by the Karaites and the underprivileged section of the community, but immigrants from other Arab countries spoke their own Arabic dialect. Krämer called it a linguistic chaos. It was only after World War I that Jews gradually dropped the use of their native tongue outside the home context in favour of adopted European languages, first Italian and then overwhelmingly French.[231] Although English was favoured by the Egyptian Muslim elite educated in British schools, Jewish middle- and upper-class families used it only for business or on official occasions. Jewish community records were kept in French and, with some exceptions, the use of Arabic sank to the level of the language of the poor and uneducated Jews. A basic knowledge of colloquial Egyptian Arabic was sufficient to get by in everyday situations. French became the lingua franca for all. This Levantine cosmopolitanism was widely practised and accepted, serving the Jews well under British rule, and even up to 1947.

THE NATIONALITY ISSUE

The population of Egypt was traditionally defined along religious lines. In the new world order ushered in by Muhammad Ali's reforms, religious minorities saw the potential to forge a better future for themselves. After having been subjected for generations to the inferior status of dhimmis and the various restrictions it entailed, they suddenly found a way of ensuring their physical and financial security while promoting their social and economic advancement. Although the Jews' situation had somewhat improved by the mid-nineteenth century, they still suffered periodically from blood libel accusations or attacks from sections of the Greek or Muslim population, as revealed by Landau's research.[232] Then again, by adopting the citizenship of countries such as Austria-Hungary, Italy, France, and to some extent Great Britain, Jews could acquire a new national identity, even though most of them had never set foot in any one of those countries. Evidently, the point of the exercise was to enjoy the privileges of the Capitulations and the protection of the Mixed Courts.[233] In view of the fact that the distribution of the judges' posts in the Tribunals was done on a pro-rata basis, depending on the size of the foreign colonies, the countries concerned were often more than willing to grant protection to those who asked for it.

Great Britain, being the dominant power in the country, "could afford to impose strict limits in granting any kind of British protection" and was therefore more selective than others.[234] Only families originally from Gibraltar, Malta, or Cyprus were considered eligible. As a general rule, it seems that the British granted passports mainly to leading Jewish families who could serve them politically by acting as intermediaries between them and the local rulers. Alternatively, the Austro-Hungarian Empire, France, and Italy, keen to inflate the size of their respective colonies, acceded to the demand for protection more readily. In fact, on the basis of the Crémieux Decree of 1870, the French welcomed into their ranks any Jew who could prove even a loose Algerian descent.[235] The French Prime Minister went as far as declaring in 1930 that "the Jewish community is one of the most important and most French groups in Egypt; a possible reduction in our influence on them could not leave the government indifferent".[236] Italian citizenship was also relatively easy to obtain, especially if one was prepared to pay for it. The fact that all the municipal records of the town of Livorno had been destroyed in a fire at the end of the nineteenth century significantly facilitated the procedure. "There was hardly a prominent Jewish family in Egypt whose head was not a foreign national", noted Landau. Leading families, such as the Suarez and Mosseri families, were Italian subjects, whereas the Cattaoui[237] and Menasce families were Austro-Hungarian.[238] Some were even granted titles of nobility for services rendered to foreign legations, such as the Baron de Menasce.[239] However, the ambiguity of their official foreign status did not prevent these Jews from considering themselves an integral part of Egypt.

This must not lead one to believe that all the Jews of Egypt held a foreign nationality. In fact, only 25 percent did. Over 40 percent were stateless (*sujets locaux*), and 25 to 30 percent were Egyptian subjects. In spite of the reality of these figures, the issue of nationality eventually led—in the rising nationalistic and pan-Arabist discourse of the 1950s—to the stigmatisation of the whole of Egyptian Jewry as a foreign and alien element.[240]

WESTERN EDUCATION

With the longing for a foreign national identity came the longing for Western culture and its perceived superiority over the local culture. In the prevailing climate of Westernisation from 1840 onwards, the Egyptian authorities encouraged the establishment of foreign language and missionary schools. Elite schools, founded by foreign nationals for their respective colonies, provided Western-style education to whoever could afford it. From 1844 in Alexandria, and later in Cairo and some provincial towns, Christian schools for boys run by French missionaries dispensed an excellent education in both French and Arabic.[241] In 1845, the nuns belonging to the Mission des Sœurs de Saint-Vincent de Paul undertook girls' education, the languages of tuition being mostly French and Italian. Upper- and middle-class Jews from Alexandria and Cairo began sending their children to French, British, German, or American missionary schools. Landau pointed out that, throughout the first half of the nineteenth century, Jewish boys were traditionally educated in the *heder*, a religious elementary school, whereas girls were not given any formal education.[242]

For the Jewish community, the desire to acquire French culture did not rise solely from within. It was reinforced from without, through the action of the Jews of France, imbued with the principle of the superiority of Western civilisation. Their aim was to educate and "regenerate" their Eastern brethren by promoting French culture, which would usher them into modernity. The Jews of the Middle East had captured the attention of French Jewry on the occasion of the so-called Damascus Affair of 1840, a blood libel accusation levelled against the Jewish notables of that town. The leaders of the community had been arrested and tortured into confessing their alleged crime. Adolphe Crémieux—the French Jewish politician later responsible for granting French nationality to the Algerian Jews—together with the great British philanthropist, Sir Moses Montefiore, came on a mission to Egypt to meet with Muhammad Ali, then ruler of Syria, and plead for the release of the prisoners and their full exoneration.[243]

During that visit, Crémieux was appalled by the state of Jewish education and called on Egyptian and French Jewry to help establish a school for boys and one for girls in Cairo and later in Alexandria. Due mainly to lack of funds, those schools were closed two years later, but this endeavour was not to be a total failure.[244] It motivated local Jewish philanthropists to found community and vocational training schools in Alexandria and Cairo. Beginning in 1854, free Jewish community schools were established in Alexandria to provide a more modern education to the underprivileged, thanks to the concerted efforts of a number of prominent families, such as the Aghions and the de Menasces. The syllabus of the Aghion schools—as they were popularly referred to—included the teaching of Hebrew, Arabic, French, and Italian simultaneously.[245] Girls were also catered to in those schools.[246] The language of instruction was at first Italian because of its popularity amongst the Jewish community, and later switched to French when the latter displaced the former as the lingua franca of most of the religious minorities in Egypt. Crémieux's initiative also paved the way for the AIU to come to Egypt in 1868 and open new schools in the cities and the countryside.

The AIU's *mission civilisatrice* was to bring French culture to the uneducated Jewish masses in the Middle East and North Africa. The situation in Algeria, under French rule since 1830, was somewhat different. As discussed previously, thanks to the Crémieux Decree of 1870, the Jews of Algeria had become full citizens of the secular Republic of France. Stillman pointed out that the change of status had the following result:

> After 1870, Jewish schools all but disappeared in Algeria, as the new Jewish citizens went to state and private French schools. Jewish education was so thoroughly neglected that by the beginning of the twentieth century the Alliance Israélite Universelle, which had not felt the need to establish any schools in Algeria previously, opened large schools in Algiers (1900) and Constantine (1902) and organised courses in religious education throughout the country.[247]

In Egypt, the situation was again different. The decision to open AIU schools in Egypt was apparently taken "to halt the flow of Jewish children to non-Jewish and, in many cases, to Christian missionary schools... [as these] schools tried to convert their Jewish pupils".[248] Stillman noted one particular case that scandalised the Jewish community in 1914 and "galvanised it into action", when "twenty-two boys then enrolled or recently graduated from Catholic institutions in Cairo and Alexandria secretly converted to Christianity".[249] Furthermore, as late as 1911 the AIU was still reporting to its central office in Paris anti-Semitic incidents and blood libel accusations in Egypt.[250] However, the Jewish community possessed enough clout with the local authorities to obtain justice in nearly every case. In 1919, the AIU considered its mission accomplished and transferred back to the community all its schools of Cairo and Alexandria—except for one in the small town of Tantah, which continued to function until World War II. By 1947, the rate of literacy reached by the Jews of Egypt was as high as 82.2 percent overall, but illustrating a gender gap, with males at 89.7 percent and females at 75.9 percent.[251]

Most of the Jewish community schools provided only primary education and some vocational training. To the Jewish urban middle and upper classes that resented the missionary activities of some Christian schools,[252] the new French schools, known as Lycées de la Mission Laïque Française, offered an excellent secular education, complete from kindergarten to matriculation—*baccalauréat*—in both Alexandria and Cairo.[253] Furthermore, a Jewish primary and secondary day school called Lycée de l'Union Juive pour l'Enseignement (UJE), established in 1925, provided a nonsectarian education along the lines of the French secular schools under the stimulus of Maître Félix Benzakein, a leading member of the B'nai B'rith Lodge of Alexandria, together with the philanthropist Baron Alfred de Menasce. They were both outraged by the latest blood libel accusation emanating from a Catholic school in Alexandria. In the course of his Easter sermon, a priest of the Collège Sainte Catherine, Brother Léonce, accused the Jews of killing Christian children at the time of Passover, giving credence to the libel that Jews had to mix the blood of a Christian child into unleavened bread.[254]

Conversely, under British rule English was the language of power, and its teaching was promoted as the ultimate key to Western culture, in both government and private schools. Anxious to ensure an even better future for their children, some Anglophile Jewish families enrolled them in prestigious British private schools, such as Victoria College, where they sat on the same benches as Egypt's elite.[255] This elite included members of Egypt's royal family and royalty from other Arab countries, such as the future King Hussein of Jordan, as well as members of upper-crust Egyptian society.

In spite of the prestige associated with English culture, especially amongst the minorities, English never succeeded in dislodging French as the preferred language of the Westernised urban centres of Egypt, and French remained the second official language of Egypt after Arabic until the late 1950s. A good knowledge of French was essential in the legal, professional, and business sectors, as well as in all social situations. It was also the nominated language at the Mixed Courts, which followed in part the Napoleonic Code. This phenomenon was a true representation of the world view of the Egyptian elite minorities. It had created a milieu, within a Middle Eastern context, where a major section of the literate population communicated in a European language, such as French, with different degrees of proficiency, across the barriers of ethnicity, religion, and nationality.

Until 1945, all private and communal scholastic institutions, whether French or English, Jewish or Christian, secular or religious, operated independently of local government interference and could, therefore, establish their own curricula and pursue their own agendas.[256] The type of education they promoted was fundamental in the shaping of a new generation of Jewish and Christian Egyptian-born young men and women. As for their tertiary education, the more privileged amongst them were sent to universities in France, Britain, or Italy and then returned home to practise their chosen profession.

This up-and-coming generation—proficient in many languages except perhaps Arabic, inculcated with Western culture, and equipped with Western values—inevitably looked at the world through Western eyes. As a consequence, it experienced a growing sense of alienation from its Middle Eastern background. Furthermore, in the atmosphere of relative liberalism prevalent in the interwar period, young Jews were exposed to other ideologies, such as socialism, Communism, and Zionism. Some even joined the Egyptian Communist Party, which was illegal at the time.[257] They started to distance themselves from the strict religious adherence of their parents. Nevertheless, Jewish festivals were still scrupulously observed by most of the Jewish community, and this observance often affected the non-Jewish population. For instance, on Jewish festivals the stock exchange was closed, in addition to the numerous Jewish-owned businesses and department stores.

THE LIBERAL AGE

In 1914, the British declared Egypt a British protectorate, thereby officially ending Ottoman sovereignty over Egypt. As noted by Krämer, "the tensions underlying a highly uneven distribution of power, wealth, and prestige…grew considerably during the war".[258] On November 13, 1918, two days after the signing of the armistice, a group of Egyptian politicians led by the nationalist Saad Zaghloul (1860–1927) informed the British High Commissioner, Sir Reginald Wingate, that they wished to represent Egypt as a delegation (*wafd*) at the Versailles Peace Conference, intending to claim independence in the name of the Egyptian people.[259] Permission was refused, and Saad Zaghloul and his companions were arrested and deported to Malta. Students, workers, peasants, and even women took to the streets, and the month-long uprising of April 1919 forced the British not only to liberate Saad Zaghloul but also to unilaterally declare the end of the protectorate and grant independence to Egypt in 1922. The Sultan Fuad became the new ruler and ascended the throne as King of Egypt (1922–1936). However, as noted by Krämer:

> the British reserved for themselves four spheres of control, which were to be excluded from Egyptian sovereignty: imperial connections, that is, the Suez Canal; defense; the Sudan; and, last—but highly important in the context of the position

of the Jewish minority—the protection of foreigners and local minorities.[260]

The Anglo-Egyptian Treaty of Alliance of 1936 secured more concessions from the British but did not mean the end of their presence on Egyptian soil. Britain retained much of its influence on Egyptian politics, and the national aspirations of the various Egyptian interest groups remained unfulfilled. According to Krämer, although nationalism continued to be the major concern of Egypt's political scene during the whole of the interwar period and beyond, "the rising class of Egyptian entrepreneurs was gradually forced to abandon the aim of full independence as they entered into ever closer cooperation with the foreigners and minorities dominating the local economy".[261]

Under British rule, Egyptian Jewry reached a highly privileged social and economic rank. Symptomatic of the new socioeconomic conditions arising from European penetration, a Jewish upwardly mobile middle class was emerging, entering the workforce in great numbers to fill the new administrative positions as clerks and bank employees. As in other countries, Jews were prominent in the textile trade and the free professions of law, medicine, and journalism.[262] The more fortunate ones were engaged in banking, industry, export, and property development. The new national bank, Bank Misr, established in 1920 in an attempt to create an independent banking system and industry, had amongst its founders two prominent Jews of Egyptian nationality: Joseph Aslan Cattaoui and Joseph Cicurel. Writers, such as Maurice Mizrahi and Samir W. Raafat, who wrote from different perspectives, agreed on the considerable contribution of "Egypt's leading Jewish families in the development of the sugar and textile industries, the banking system, railway lines, public utilities, international trade, and housing projects".[263] Jews gradually left their traditional neighbourhoods for more exclusive suburbs in Cairo and Alexandria.[264] Thanks to the generosity of its more affluent members, the Jewish community was able to establish its own institutions, which—apart from the various schools already mentioned—included hospitals, sports clubs, retirement homes, dowry funds, and shelters for the underprivileged.[265]

On the political front, "the documentary evidence suggests that until well into the 1930s, little interest in the local political scene was shown by the vast majority of the Jews living in Egypt", reported Krämer.[266] Nevertheless, a number of Egyptian Jews were attracted to the Egyptian nationalist movement[267] because of its inclusive and liberal orientation, and joined the political party of the Wafd at an early date.[268] Given that the Egyptian constitution of 1923 embodied "the principle of national unity over and above all ethnic and religious boundaries", a small number of Jews belonging to the elite sought and gained representation in the various parliamentary institutions.[269] The heads of the leading Jewish families enjoyed very close relations with the royal family. In 1925, the president of the Jewish community of Cairo, Joseph Aslan Cattaoui Pacha, was named Minister of Finance and later Minister of Communications. He was appointed to the Senate in 1927.[270] His wife held the prestigious post of Chief Lady-in-Waiting to the Queen Nazli, wife of King Fuad I.[271]

However, in the context of an emerging independent Egypt the issue of nationality took on a new dimension. There was a growing debate on who was and who was not an Egyptian national, essentially meaning who belonged and who did not. Initially, the decree law number 19 of 1929 very liberally recognised as Egyptian nationals: (1) those whose families had resided in the country without interruption since 1 January 1848; and (2) those former subjects of the Ottoman Empire who made their "habitual residence" in Egypt on November 5, 1914, (when Great Britain declared war on the Ottoman Empire and Egypt officially ceased to be a province of the Empire) and had stayed there since.[272] Also eligible were the children of foreigners—born and residing in Egypt provided they gave up their foreign citizenship—and anybody who had resided in the country for ten years, knew Arabic adequately, and had no criminal record.

The scene seemed set for Jews to be counted as equal citizens of the modern state of Egypt. Again, opposing forces were at play and, as always, the reality on the ground was different from theoretical and well-meaning principles. On the one hand, most of the Jews did not react immediately to the offer of Egyptian citizenship, the reason for their reticence being either apathy or convenience. Until the Convention of Montreux of 1937, which stipulated the end of the Capitulations regime, and the abolition of the Mixed Courts to take effect from 1949, most upper- and middle-class Jews, like other minorities, preferred to retain the special privileges of a foreign passport. On the other hand, after 1937 the balance of power shifted; foreign protections were being phased out while the process of Egyptianisation was intensified. Egyptian nationality became essential for employment in banking and for any business dealings with government institutions. At the same time, the Egyptian administration was gradually making it exceedingly difficult for non-Muslims, especially Jews, to gain citizenship, presumably due to the rise of an Arab/Islamic type of nationalism. There were several cases of Jews who complied with the new laws and renounced their foreign nationality to achieve naturalisation, but were ultimately rejected.[273] This was true in particular for the poorer and less-educated Egyptian Jews; even though in principle they were legally eligible, they remained for the most part stateless.

Another possible reason for the apathy of Jews toward officially claiming their Egyptian citizenship could have been economically based. As Laskier pointed out, for the underprivileged "the fee of five Egyptian pounds that had to be paid in order to obtain a certificate attesting to their new nationality was an inhibiting factor" in itself.[274] Additionally, in those days such a certificate would not have been considered essential, seeing as Jews were still living under the control of their autonomous communal courts as far as their personal status was concerned. In his work on Egyptian Jewry, historian Joel Beinin argued that the "legal autonomy of non-Muslims was not solely a product of colonialism" and that the secular nationalism reflected by the nationality law of 1929 was undermined by the preservation of that zone of religious legal separatism.[275] The regime of religious autonomy applied to all religious communities in Egypt, including the majority Muslim population, based on the Ottoman *millet* system. The Muslims shari'a courts filled the same functions for their co-religionists as the rabbinical tribunals, similarly free of state intervention until their closure by Gamal Abdel Nasser in 1955.[276]

The new Anglo-Egyptian Treaty of 1936 constituted a watershed for Egyptian Jewry and brought them to a crossroad. As a minority group in a predominantly Arab-Muslim country, the Jews faced an identity crisis. Who were they, where did they belong, and how did the majority perceive them? These fundamental issues call for pause and reflection on the main features of the Jewish population at that particular point in time, before further discussing the main focus of this book— the period between 1936 and 1956.

It has been demonstrated how culturally, socially, and ethnically diverse and fragmented the Egyptian Jewish community was. In the nineteenth century there were several communities living away from the two main metropolises, in the Delta region and Upper Egypt. From the beginning of the twentieth century, Egyptian Jews became more and more urbanised and concentrated in Cairo and Alexandria, the centres of economic and administrative activities. The level of their religious observance was, for the most part, inversely proportionate to their socio-economic status and access to Western-style education. Although Jewish identity was strong in both cases, the less-privileged Jews were closer to their Jewish roots and to the Arabic culture, whereas the more affluent Jews adopted a more secular European lifestyle and grew less observant in their religious practice. The Ottoman regime of the millet continued to regulate their communal lives, their lay leaders being their sole representatives vis-à-vis the government and their rabbis engaging in religious duties only. Most of the time, Egyptian Jews used the languages of power—English and French—and sent their children to European schools if they could afford it. The issue of foreign nationality has also been raised to explain why only one-quarter of the Jewish population had managed to obtain Egyptian citizenship, whereas another quarter held foreign passports and half remained stateless.

In the prevalent climate of a secular brand of territorial nationalism and under the protection of the British, Egyptian Jewry thrived in the socioeconomic sphere, as well as in the political arena. Apart from a few blood libel accusations, the relationship with the dominant Muslim and Coptic majority was generally harmonious, especially between members of the upper echelons of society.[277] Furthermore, the acquisition and wholesale adoption of foreign culture reinforced the privileged status of the Jews while at the same time multiplying the degrees of separation between them and the Egyptian culture and milieu. This is where the Jews in Egypt stood before 1936, at their apex, astonishingly comfortable in their multicoloured coat, their eyes turned towards the West, but their feet firmly planted in the East.

The Decline and Final Demise of Egyptian Jewry (1937–1967)

With the benefit of hindsight, if one were to pinpoint the start of the downhill process for Egyptian Jewry, it would have to be the period from the late 1930s onward, even if that change was imperceptible to the people concerned. The chain of events put into motion at that time gathered its own speed, which could only signify the end of the road for the Jews of Egypt, long before the end actually happened. Notwithstanding measures such as the abrogation of the Capitulations at the Montreux Convention of 1937 and the planned closure of the Mixed Courts in 1949, new elements were being keyed into the emerging political picture. Ideologies—such as pan-Arabic nationalism, Islamic fundamentalism, Communism, political Zionism, and Fascism—were fighting for a significant place under the Middle Eastern sun. Egyptian Jewry was fundamentally affected by the clashing agendas of those rising ideologies, as history has demonstrated. The aim of the next section is to show how the Jews of Egypt responded when confronted with new challenges, how the evolving political climate impacted upon them, and whether they were actors or merely "extras" in the chain of events that brought about their final demise.

As previously stated, the main concern of the nationalist leaders of 1919 was "to abolish British rule and to create a sovereign Egyptian state", free from foreign control and influence.[278] The emphasis being on unity irrespective of religion or ethnicity, leading members of the Jewish community, such as Yusuf Cicurel Bey and Yusuf Aslan Cattaoui Pasha, like many of their Muslim and Coptic compatriots, identified with and supported the Egyptian nationalist movement, as confirmed by both Krämer and Beinin.[279] Reciprocally, the dominant trend among the liberal Egyptian intelligentsia was to regard Egyptian Jews as "full members of the nation".[280] Some prominent Jewish figures, such as the journalist Leon Castro and Maître Felix Benzakein, did not see any contradiction in equally supporting both the Egyptian nationalist movement and the Zionist movement.[281] In those early days, the national struggle overrode any involvement in foreign affairs, including the Palestinian conflict, and the British were perceived as the common obstacle to the fulfilment of both nationalist dreams.

By the late 1930s, the limited national independence achieved in 1922 was increasingly eroding the secular and strictly territorial concept of nationalism, promoted by the liberal nationalists. This erosion was the consequence of a number of underlying factors, both from within, such as the considerable power still exerted by the British in collusion with the monarchy, and from without, such as the intensifying Arab-Zionist conflict in Palestine and the rise of Fascism and Communism in Europe.

The combination of all these elements led to the rearticulation of a more militant and more xenophobic form of nationalism embracing an exclusively Arab-Islamic world view. New players, such as paramilitary youth groups and Islamic movements, appeared on Egypt's political stage in opposition to the traditional power triangle of the monarchy, the British, and the Wafd Party. The radical Society of the Muslim Brothers, founded in 1928 by Hasan al-Banna, gradually overshadowed other Islamic groups and developed into a major political force. The Muslim Brothers believed in a fundamentalist view of Islam as the basis and guide for all aspects of life. They "did not see national liberation as an end in itself, but only as a first step on the way to the restoration of the Islamic *umma* (nation) transcending all boundaries of nation, state and ethnicity".[282] Therefore, they embraced and promoted the Palestinian cause as a Muslim and Arab cause. On the home front, they were also highly critical of what they considered a corrupt political establishment and were actively pushing for economic and social reforms. Their stance gained them widespread respect and popularity among the urban lower and middle classes. This brand of nationalism, based on the restoration of an ideal Islamic society and a deep hatred of the British occupiers and their lackeys, advocated a new political reality. Both the Muslim Brothers and the paramilitary movement Young Egypt (*Misr-al-Fatat*) excluded Jews from membership, either because they were not Muslims or because they did not consider them "real Egyptians".[283] By definition, the makeup of the new Egypt, as they saw it, would provide fewer chances of integration and participation for non-Muslim minorities, particularly the Jewish one.

After King Fuad's death on April 28, 1936, the advent to the throne of his sixteen-year-old son Faruk (1920–1965) was perceived as a new beginning in Egyptian politics. The new Anglo-British Treaty of Alliance of August 1936 granted more independence to Egypt. It was followed by the Convention of Montreux of May 1937, which signified the end of the privileged regime enjoyed by foreign nationals. Consequently, local minorities lost the protection of the colonial powers and, for the first time, Egypt was free to involve itself in foreign affairs. It was inevitable that the growing Palestinian conflict between the Arabs and the Yishuv,[284] resulting in the outbreak of the Arab revolt in 1936, would attract the Egyptian public's attention and dramatically affect the status of the local Jewish community.[285] According to Krämer's research, "as a result of this growing involvement in the Palestine question, the second half of the 1930s witnessed the first attacks on local Jewry as the fifth column of Zionism".[286]

During the aforementioned Arab revolt of 1936–1939, attacks in the Egyptian Islamist and pan-Arab press were not only anti-Zionist but also vehemently anti-Jewish. These attacks had a very distinct racial flavour, consistent with the Fascist discourse of those days. Led by the Muslim Brothers and the Fascist-style group Young Egypt, violent student demonstrations broke out in May 1938 against Jewish residents in Cairo, Alexandria, and Tantah, and the police had to intervene to protect the threatened Jewish population. Anti-Semitic publications, such as Arabic translations of *Mein Kampf* and the *Protocols of the Elders of Zion*, were distributed at various political gatherings where "Egyptian Jews were denounced as sympathisers with Zionism, exploiters of the Egyptian masses, and elements dangerous to their host peoples".[287]

The leaders of Egyptian Jewry did not underestimate the potential gravity of the situation and reacted by using their extensive network of contacts with the Egyptian hierarchy and foreign diplomats to try and stop the wave of anti-Zionist and anti-Jewish propaganda. As duly pointed out by Krämer, they also pressured the "local Jewish associations, notably the Zionist ones, to end all overt activities that might cast doubt on the loyalty of the Jewish citizens of the state of Egypt".[288] The *mot d'ordre*—the watchword—from the top down was "to remain as inconspicuous as possible, keeping a low profile in order not to draw attention to the existence of a Jewish minority in the country, let alone a national movement in its midst".[289]

Not all Egyptian Jews advocated a "lie-low" attitude in the face of such attacks. The Jewish press—and principally the leading pro-Zionist newspaper *Israël*, which appeared in three languages: French, Arabic, and Hebrew—not only reported meticulously the events in Palestine but was also very vocal in its criticism of the British mandatory administration in Palestine and of Palestine's radical Arab leaders. The mere fact that *Israël*'s editorials were allowed to voice their criticism and appeal for solidarity with the Yishuv is proof enough of the extraordinary freedom of expression Egyptian Jews still enjoyed in the 1930s, as opposed to the strict censorship of the 1950s.

Another example of Jewish communal activism manifested itself in 1933 when, in reaction to the Nazi takeover of Germany, Jewish leaders lobbied extensively to enlist the support of non-Jewish minorities in expressions of protest against German anti-Semitism. An association of all the Jewish institutions of Egypt created the Ligue contre l'Antisémitisme Allemand to defend itself against pro-Nazi activities on Egyptian soil. It later joined the international branch of that same organisation (LICA), with the prominent lawyer and journalist Leon Castro as its vice president. Its goal was to put pressure on the local press against publishing Nazi propaganda material, as well as to promote the boycott of German goods and films. According to Maurice Mizrahi, LICA provided useful information to the Allies during the war years about any breaches of the maritime blockade.[290] One respondent recalled that, when Fascist Italy declared itself an ally of Germany, a number of prominent Italian Jews in Egypt, who had fought for their country in World War I, returned their passports in protest and wrote outraged open letters to the newspapers. Young members of LICA even formed picket lines to prevent opera aficionados from attending the performances of the visiting Italian Opera Company.

It is important to remember that at the time the sympathies of the intellectual and nationalist Egyptian circles were strongly anti-British and therefore pro-Nazi. Furthermore, anti-Jewish propaganda was being promoted by Palestinian-Arab political exiles, such as the Mufti of Jerusalem, Haj Mohammed Amin al Husseini, a Nazi collaborator and rabid anti-Semite, who was inciting youth groups and university students to carry out anti-Jewish demonstrations.[291]

Whereas Egyptian Jewry's response to the spread of Fascist ideology was unified and decisive, its response to Zionism was much more fragmented. As pointed out by Joel Beinin, such response was "inflected by differences of class, ethnic origin, religious rite, educational formation, political outlook, and personal accident".[292] Zionist activity in Egypt was no different from what was happening in most other Jewish communities in the Islamic world. At first it was mainly confined to philanthropic fundraising on behalf of the Keren Kayemet le-Ysra'el (henceforth, the Jewish National Fund [JNF]) and the Keren Hayesod (henceforth, the Palestine Foundation Fund). Laskier reported that, after the Balfour Declaration of 1917, "Zionist federations were created in Cairo and Alexandria as an initiative of Ashkenazi emigrants and several local Sephardim".[293] It has been argued that the reason the Ashkenazim were more involved in the Zionist cause than their Sephardi counterparts was because most of them were relatively recent arrivals in Egypt from Palestine after their expulsion on the eve of World War I. The assumption was that they had not yet formed a deep attachment to Egypt and thus never intended to stay on.

During World War II, Zionist activities were stepped up with the arrival of emissaries from Palestine, promoting emigration and youth education through various pioneer youth movements. The movement *he-Halutz ha-Tsa'ir* was founded in Cairo in 1933 and in Alexandria in 1934. The Kibbutz movements *ha-Shomer ha-Tsa'ir* and *B'nei Akiva* were founded in 1932. As indicated by Laskier, "the Zionist pioneer movements in Egypt enjoyed a legal or semilegal status as scouting organisations" until the establishment of the State of Israel in 1948 and the outbreak of hostilities.[294] Revisionist Zionists also operated in Egypt but were banned after November 1944 when two members of the Stern/Lehi Gang assassinated Lord Moyne—the Minister Resident in the Middle East—in Cairo, in protest against British rule in Palestine and the implementation of the White Paper Policy.[295]

However, Zionist activism was not predominant in the community, and it is true that in the interwar period the Jewish establishment in Egypt displayed a lukewarm reception to Zionism as a political and national movement. Most of the influential economic elite of Egyptian Jewry remained opposed to Zionism for various reasons. First, they did not think the whole issue of a homeland for the Jews concerned them, in view of the fact that their own situation in Egypt seemed so secure. It was more of a solution for European Jews because of their suffering from Nazi persecution and later the horrors of the Holocaust. Secondly, and most importantly, the Jewish leaders did not wish to stir any anti-Jewish feelings or be accused of dual loyalty. They were still hoping for a negotiated settlement of the Palestinian conflict with the Yishuv. Krämer gave an account of a dialogue among Egyptian politicians, Zionist representatives, and local Jews during the interwar period, and even during World War II, in an effort to mediate the Arab-Zionist conflict. However, it seems that the British discouraged those initiatives because they were not prepared "to welcome an Egyptian role in the search for a comprehensive settlement of the Palestine conflict".[296]

At the onset of World War II in September 1939, the Egyptian government had to honour its obligations under the Anglo-Egyptian Treaty of Alliance of 1936, in spite of the secret sympathies of both the King and the nationalist parties for the Axis powers. It imposed strict press censorship and declared a state of siege. On the political level, the British were pulling nearly all the strings by controlling the nomination of political and military leaders. Egypt was the regional base for the British army and allied troops. Nevertheless, although the Egyptian government interned or expelled all residing German citizens except German Jews and interned a great number of its Italian citizens—except Italian Jews and known anti-Fascists—it did not formally declare war on the Axis powers until February 1945.[297]

In contrast, the Jewish community openly sided with the Allies in the looming conflict. Not only did local Jews of British, French, and Greek nationality join the fight on various fronts, but also "wealthy members of the community donated large sums of money to the British war effort and established clubs for Jewish soldiers in the British army stationed in Egypt. Some Jews collaborated in the Egyptian branch of the *France Libre* movement led by General de Gaulle".[298] Therefore, Egyptian Jewry felt very threatened in 1942 when the victorious Germans were advancing in North Africa.[299] According to Jewish Agency reports, thousands fled Alexandria for Cairo and further south. Others tried desperately to obtain entrance visas to places such as Chad, Congo, or Syria. By June 29, 1942, cash withdrawals from banks in Alexandria were reported to have exceeded two million pounds. Many Jewish merchants who had invested heavily in merchandise found themselves trapped, due to a shortage of funds. The lower-middle-class Jews who did not have the financial means to go anywhere felt even more vulnerable than their more-privileged co-religionists.[300] Anxiety subsided only when the British defeated the Germans at El-Alamein—one hundred kilometres from Alexandria—in November 1942. The Jewish community as a whole rejoiced in the final victory of the Allies in 1945.

Actually, not everybody in Egypt was rejoicing. The effects of the war on Egyptian society were manifold. The multitude of industries and companies that had employed between 200,000 and 245,000 employees in wartime had to dismiss them when the war ended. As a result, the gap between the privileged and the disadvantaged grew considerably, creating even more resentment against the foreign presence on Egyptian soil and the privileged supporters of that presence.

For Egyptian Jewry, problems rose again toward the end of 1945. On November 2 and 3, 1945, the date of the twenty-eighth anniversary of the Balfour Declaration, a number of Islamic associations called for a general strike. After being riled by the leader of the Muslim Brothers near the royal palace of Abdin in Cairo, the demonstrators were so impassioned that they marched on the Jewish quarter and attacked bystanders, shops, and synagogues. Jewish youth, who had been trained in self-defense in Zionist youth groups, managed to repel the assaults by setting up barricades. However, the rioting and looting continued and spread to European sections of Cairo and Alexandria. According to Beinin's research, "six people were killed, several hundred were injured, and dozens of Jewish, Coptic, and Muslim-owned stores were looted". The only Ashkenazi synagogue in Cairo was set afire. As pointed out by Beinin, this was "the first indication that there might be a popular base in Egypt for militant anti-Zionism spilling over anti-Semitism", and the riots of November 2 and 3 exposed "the vulnerability of the Jewish community to the consequences of the conflict over Palestine".[301]

POLICY OF EGYPTIANISATION

As previously indicated, the privileged status of the Jewish community had already been weakened by the Montreux Convention of 1937 because of its planned phasing out of the privileges enjoyed by foreigners and non-Muslim minorities. Furthermore, a deliberate policy of Egyptianisation, long advocated by both nationalists and Islamists, was implemented. It inevitably affected the business activities of European businessmen and their agents. For instance, from the early 1940s, in an effort to alleviate growing unemployment among the highly politicised educated youth and to counteract the predominant role of foreign languages in business dealings, the use of Arabic was made compulsory. This measure forced merchants and businessmen, who because of their European education could not read and write Arabic, to hire Arabic-speaking employees.

The process of Egyptianisation also targeted the education system in foreign schools where the teaching of Arabic was made compulsory. Egypt-related subjects, such as Egyptian history and geography, were introduced into the curriculum. It is important to remember that until the Suez War of 1956, ninety-seven thousand students were enrolled mainly in French and British elitist schools.[302] As pointed out earlier, until 1945 these various scholastic institutions operated independently of local government interference.[303] After the Suez War of 1956 their importance waned considerably as the government sequestered private foreign schools and expelled all British and French teachers. By 1960, the number of students had declined by more than half.[304] The subsequent nationalisation of foreign schools led to a sharp drop in the quality of education due to overcrowding and the paucity of funds devoted to education by Gamal Abdel Nasser's government.

Another blow to the status of foreign nationals and stateless minorities was the enactment of the Company Law of July 29, 1947. It required all companies and subsidiaries of foreign companies to maintain a staff of Egyptian nationals comprising 75 percent of total salaries and that 40 percent of their Boards of Directors be Egyptian nationals. The new law also "obliged all firms concerned to submit detailed lists specifying the nationality and the salary of their employees".[305] Clearly, these measures were meant to favour Egyptian nationals, and applications for naturalisation rose dramatically, especially from a Jewish lower and lower-middle class fearing a massive loss of jobs.[306] However, as previously mentioned, the authorities showed a growing reluctance to deal with these applications, especially those coming from Jews and, as pointed out by Krämer, "by 1948–49, hundreds of decisions were still pending, with many applications having already been rejected".[307]

Upon the birth of the State of Israel on May 14, 1948, and the start of hostilities between the new state and its Arab neighbours, the whole

Jewish population of Egypt was implicitly implicated. Martial law was declared and censorship established. No one, not even foreign nationals, could leave the country without a special exit visa. The official reason was to prevent Jews from flocking to Israel. At the same time, Zionist youth movements were declared illegal and some went underground, while emissaries from Israel fled to avoid being caught. In May 1948, hundreds of Jews were arrested as suspected Zionists or Communists and thrown into prison; the maximum number of Jewish detainees at any one time was seven hundred to eight hundred.[308] Although hostilities ceased in January 1949 followed by a cease-fire agreement between Egypt and Israel on February 24, 1949, there were still throughout the various detainment centres two hundred and fifty Zionist and sixty Jewish Communists interned in July 1949.[309] The interviews conducted in the course of my research confirmed that most of the detainees ended up being expelled after a period of incarceration of six to twelve months. Their families were given a few days to settle their affairs in order to be ready to join the prisoners directly on the departing ship. The majority of those departures were bound for Israel, via Europe, with the help of the Jewish Agency and the JDC. It has been estimated that about sixteen thousand Jews immigrated to Israel between 1949 and 1951.[310]

In addition, during the summer and autumn of 1948, Jews and their property were attacked repeatedly in retaliation for the bombing of a Cairo suburb by the Israelis.[311] The main suspects were the Muslim Brothers. It has been suggested that, although the authorities did not actually encourage such attacks, they did not wish to undermine their tenuous hold on power by defending the Jewish community against the powerful Muslim Brotherhood.[312] Therefore, their response was often inept and disingenuous. Thanks to the prevailing censorship, no mention of excessive violence perpetrated against Jews was allowed to appear in the press.

The enactment of emergency decrees enabled the Egyptian government to sequester indiscriminately the property of any person, or take over the assets of any enterprise, deemed prejudicial to the safety and security of the state. Wholesale sequestrations of the assets of prominent

Jewish individuals and companies active in vital sectors of the Egyptian economy were carried out until the spring of 1949.

As an obvious consequence to the arbitrary detentions, sequestrations, and attacks to which Egyptian Jewry was subjected, a feeling of insecurity permeated the whole community, from the humble employee to the successful businessman. The Wafd return to power in January 1950, and the lifting of martial law somewhat improved the community's predicament. Laskier reported that gradually the sequestration of Jewish assets was halted, and most of the Jews' possessions were returned. Many Jews were released on condition they agreed to leave the country immediately. Some interpreted the change as a return to normalcy and were lulled into believing they could resume their comfortable and privileged lives as before. For others, emigration became for the first time a viable option.

Apart from Israel, approximately six thousand Jews went to Europe or other destinations. Beinin's study of the dispersion of Egyptian Jewry charted the various trends of this population movement. For instance, committed Zionists, as well as less-privileged families, tended to go to Israel, whereas the wealthier and more educated chose to go elsewhere. The younger members of the community were more inclined to emigrate than the older ones. The Ashkenazim, who were more likely to have connections in Israel or the West, emigrated more readily than the Sephardim, who had closer ties with Egypt.[313] Some of those trends were replicated in the course of the next exodus in 1956. They were also apparent in the exodus pattern of my sample group.

As a general rule, the community emerged from that difficult period somewhat diminished in stature and numbers but superficially mended, contrary to the dramatic decline Egyptian Jewry experienced after the 1956 and 1967 wars with Israel. Although their public presence was more subdued, the remaining fifty thousand Jews continued to work in their chosen professions and conduct their social and religious activities relatively freely. Jewish community institutions, such as hospitals, schools, and sports clubs, functioned normally, although the communal schools were placed under close supervision of the Ministry of Public Education.

In spite of the appearance of normalcy, the signs of alienation were growing between the Jews and the Muslim majority. According to Laskier, after 1948 and perhaps even earlier, "it had become quite difficult for Jews to attend local universities in significant numbers. Very few were accepted in 1949 into the universities of Fuad I and Faruq".[314] In addition, the increasing difficulty for Jews in obtaining citizenship papers highlighted the vulnerability of their legal and political status. The historian Shimon Shamir looked into the evolution of the Egyptian nationality laws and how these laws were applied to the Jewish population:

> The main problem was evidence. The law left it to the discretion of the Minister of the Interior to decide what proofs would be required to establish nationality (Art.21)...In particular, autochthonous Jews found it difficult to prove (for the requirements of Art. 1[2]) that their families had been living in Egypt since before 1848...Difficulties were also encountered by families originating from Ottoman territories. In the pre-1914 realities, travel between provinces of the empire was free and hardly accompanied by traceable documentation.[315]

In the emerging social and political climate of radical nationalism and fundamentalist Islam, the label Egyptians, "in common or even legal parlance, came to signify in fact Muslims, or possibly Muslims and Copts, to the exclusion of all others".[316] When the 1947 Company Law was promulgated, demanding that Egyptian nationals be given a majority share in large companies, a great number of stateless and even foreign Jews tried to secure their jobs by applying for Egyptian nationality. It was already too late and "some forty thousand stateless Jews were declared foreigners".[317]

After the 1948 war with Israel it became practically impossible for Jews to acquire Egyptian citizenship. The first amendment, in September 1950, to the 1929 Nationality Law, dealing with the withdrawal of Egyptian nationality "from any person involved in actions in favour of states that were at war with Egypt", was clearly aimed at the Jewish minority.[318] The new Nationality Law (No. 392) of November 1956 was even more blunt, specifically defining them as Zionists. As testified by the majority of my respondents who held Egyptian nationality, they were subjected to automatic denaturalisation upon their departure from Egypt, particularly after 1956.

To the nationalists and critics of the regime, the Egyptian defeat of 1948 revealed the rampant incompetence and the extent of corruption among political and military leadership. Furthermore, the struggle against the British military presence was intensifying and developed into guerrilla-like warfare in the canal region. A mass demonstration against the British in reaction to their indiscriminate killing of forty local policemen in the course of a bloody confrontation in the small canal town of Ismailyia developed into full-scale rioting. On what has since been labelled Black Saturday—January 26, 1952—an enraged mob burned and looted, unabated, large parts of modern Cairo. The riots were mainly directed against British, Jewish, Greek, and Armenian establishments, as well as the ruling elite. It is evident that, once more, the local Jews felt targeted and vulnerable as a non-Muslim minority, having benefited from British rule and protection. Some of the interviewees witnessed the rioting, the burning, and the brutality of the event and were quite traumatised by its sheer horror. The fire of Cairo was seen as forerunner to the overthrow of the monarchy by the Free Officers six months later, on July 23, 1952.

It was only natural for Jews to feel even more insecure under the new regime, with which they had no social or political connection and vice-versa, in spite of the show of goodwill toward non-Muslim minorities expressed by Muhammed Naguib, the first president and prime minister of Egypt. As pointed out by Beinin, "several of the Free Officers had backgrounds in the society of Muslim Brothers or Young Egypt, organisations that did not view Jews as authentic Egyptians", and they were very embittered by their humiliating defeat at the hands of the new fledgling State of Israel.[319] Naguib's demise in March 1954, in favour of the hardliner nationalist Gamal Abdel Nasser, marked a further downturn for the Jews, who felt more insecure and alienated. With the deterioration of the economic situation in Egypt from 1953 on, the Jewish community's position grew even more precarious. Although it is true that most Jews faced no special restrictions, the Egyptian secret police kept a close tab on their activities. They were arrested in increasing numbers during the second half of 1954, accused of involvement in both Communist and Zionist activities and of plotting against the regime.

Another critical blow to the standing of the whole Jewish community was the Lavon Affair, which resulted in the arrest in July 1954 of an underground network of Egyptian Jews, accused of spying on behalf of Israel. Their mission was to launch acts of sabotage against British and American institutions, which would be blamed on religious fundamentalists and/or Egyptian nationalists. The ultimate aim was to "discredit the new regime and impair Egypt's relations with the USA and Britain".[320] According to Beinin, the whole unfortunate affair "provided an excuse to treat the entire Jewish community as potential subversives".[321]

The situation between Egypt and Israel was becoming increasingly volatile, and Egyptian Jews were again caught in the middle of the turmoil. The *coup de grâce* to their security and to their livelihood was the outbreak of the Suez War in October 1956. In light of the concerted British-French-Israeli attack on Egypt, the Jews were made to bear the brunt of the government's anger. A series of government decrees established a state of siege and strict censorship, allowing expulsion, mass arrests, confiscation of property, sequestration, and denaturalisation.[322] Although these measures also affected foreign residents and other minority communities, the worst hit were the Jews, whether they were citizens, stateless, or foreign nationals. The exit visa issued to them upon leaving Egypt, either "voluntarily" or under expulsion orders, stated prominently that they would not be permitted to return and that they renounced all claims against Egypt. The bleak picture painted by Beinin in his analysis of the situation reinforced the testimonies of my oral historians:

> About 1,000 Jews were detained, more than half of them Egyptian citizens. Thirteen thousand French and British citizens were expelled from Egypt in retaliation for the tripartite attack, among them many Jews. In addition, 500 Jews not holding French or British citizenship were expelled. Some 460 Jewish-owned businesses were sequestered. Many Jews lost their jobs.

> The government nationalised the assets of all British and French citizens, and Jews holding those nationalities were affected in that capacity…When the hostilities were over, Jews were subjected to unofficial pressures to leave Egypt and renounce their citizenship. According to the World Jewish Congress, between November 22, 1956, and March 15, 1957, 14,102 Jews left Egypt…Most of them abandoned the great bulk of their assets in Egypt and came to Israel as impoverished refugees.[323]

According to the respondents who were imprisoned after both the 1948 and the 1956 Arab-Israeli Wars, living conditions inside their camps—which the majority called concentration camps—were just bearable, especially after overcoming the initial shock of being arrested, interrogated, and deprived of their liberty, often without any specific charges brought against them. There were few cases of systematic physical mistreatment, contrary to the conditions following the Six-Day War in 1967.[324]

Nevertheless, as stated by Laskier, the Egyptian government seems to have pursued a systematic policy of ridding the country of its Jewish population "by expulsion and through 'voluntary' emigration".[325] What was left of Egyptian Jewry was subjected to the usual humiliation, intimidation, and harassment techniques not always reported in history books. For instance, as revealed in my interviews, entire families were consigned to house arrest and suffered continuous surveillance, false denunciations, or arbitrary midnight visits by the Egyptian Secret Service. A typical example was the testimony related by Interviewee #9:

> The authorities had called on the British and the French to register at the police station. Fifteen days after that notice, we were put in forced residence, my mother and myself, no radio, no telephone. After another fifteen days, they came at midnight and took us to the police station, my parents, my husband and I, and the baby. When they called us in, we were given twenty-four hours to leave the country.

It is, therefore, easy to understand how the combination of official government policy, economic hardship due to loss of jobs, and inability to regain employment caused a flight hysteria amongst the Jews, which was later referred to as the second exodus. Thousands of people flocked to the offices of the Rabbinate and various consulates and embassies, seeking assistance and means of escape. Laskier reported that by 1958, twenty-three to twenty-five thousand Jews had emigrated, "including six thousand (until June 1957) who left on ships chartered by the ICRC... with funds provided by the United Jewish Appeal".[326] The Jewish Agency directed the immigration to Israel via European ports, even as the United HIAS Service handled the immigration to Brazil, Argentina, the United States, Canada, Australia, and other regions, again via European centres of transit.[327]

By mid-1957, the dust had started to settle in Egypt, and there was evidence of a relaxation of the pressure exerted upon the Jewish community. Some Jews, who had been expropriated at the height of the crisis—although they were not British or French—and were still in Egypt, had their property returned to them.[328] Nevertheless, it was all too late for the viability of Jewish communal life in such an unstable political climate and without the community's lay and religious leaders.[329] The emigration of the Jews continued, albeit at a slower pace. The emigrants of the later wave were economically better off than the earlier ones and preferred other destinations, such as Europe or the Americas, rather than Israel, which was considered a harder option. The following years saw a growing degradation of a dramatically shrunken Jewish community. According to Laskier, on the eve of the Six-Day War in June 1967 there were twenty-five hundred Jews left in Egypt out of the eighty thousand before 1948.[330] It is important to point out that by then the other religious minorities, such as the Greeks, Armenians, Lebanese, and Syrians, had also been hit hard by various nationalisation decrees as the Nasser regime seized the assets of some eight hundred and twenty "capitalist reactionaries".[331] Therefore, these communities were also feeling excluded and undesirable and were looking for new shores to settle on.

The outbreak of the third Arab-Israeli War in June 1967 and the subsequent defeat of the Arab coalition sealed the fate of the few remaining Jews in Egypt. Most of the male Jewish population was rounded up and imprisoned. The Egyptian nationals remained incarcerated until May or June 1970. Instigated by HIAS, the Spanish Embassy intervened and issued temporary Spanish passports to most of the remaining detainees. The rest were gradually allowed to leave on condition that they renounce their Egyptian nationality, leave all their assets behind, and pledge never to return.[332] Laskier estimated that, by the end of July 1970, there were about three hundred Jews in Cairo and two hundred and fifty in Alexandria.[333] These numbers could only have dwindled since then, seeing as there is no evidence of any Jews migrating back to Egypt, even after the signing of the peace accord between Israel and Egypt in 1979.[334] One can assume that this era marked the closing chapter of the long and rich history of the Jews of Egypt.

As one can see, in twenty-odd years a vibrant, established, and respected community suffered a complete reversal of fortune. The Jews of Egypt responded with a diversity of voices to the challenges that modernity and its long list of "isms" brought in its wake: capitalism, imperialism, colonialism, Fascism, anti-Semitism, nationalism, pan-Arabism, pan-Islamism, and Zionism. They embraced some and fought for them, rejected others and fought against them, but were indifferent to most. By the 1950s, whether they were Egyptian, foreign nationals, or stateless; Zionists or anti-Zionists; orthodox or liberal; Francophone or Arabophone, their status was fatally compromised. In an Egypt where they were not perceived as real Egyptians, they were seen as having actively or passively profited from colonialism. They were therefore implicated as agents and collaborators of the hated British and Zionists. They were considered potential enemies of the state and, in Joel Beinin's words, "were transformed from a national asset into a fifth column overnight". They were expelled or "willingly" left their native land because they felt they had no other option. Apart from a privileged few, most were unable to take any of their material possessions and were destitute when they left Egypt with the help of international Jewish charity organisations.

The question that has been regularly raised by many historians is whether the creation of the State of Israel was the catalyst in the final demise of the Jewish communities of the Arab world, or whether this demise was inevitable. I agree that Israel was a determining factor in the disintegration of all the Jewish communities of the Arab world, but it remains only one of the factors. It is also true that, by distancing themselves from their cultural and national roots, by sending their children to foreign-language schools, and by preferring French to Arabic, the Jews of Egypt had already heavily mortgaged their future in that country. However, the "inevitability" thesis would be just as valid because one cannot deny that—even if Jews had remained politically and culturally close to their Middle Eastern milieu, even if the Palestinian conflict had not erupted when it did—one element of the equation remained unchanged. Their primary condition as Jews in an Arab-Muslim world, with nationalism and fundamentalism on the rise, would have sooner or later become untenable. Whatever the answer to the initial question, it is not the main issue here. Conjectures about what would or could have happened if history had taken a different turn are seldom conclusive or productive. The purpose of my study is to understand how the Jews of Egypt navigated in the midst of the political upheavals of the times, by trying to define what made them who they were, both as a community and as individuals.

To sum up, one can say that, beginning in the late 1930s, the situation on the ground for the Jews of Egypt gradually deteriorated—for a number of internal and external reasons—until they became *persona non grata* in their own land. Transformed into refugees, they dispersed all over the world in search of a new home and a fresh start. Did their intellectual, cultural, and ethical baggage help them respond to the difficult challenges of expulsion, exile, and separation on the one hand and integration, re-acculturation, and redefinition of self on the other? Constrained by the inevitable limitations of my research, I could only study in depth the Australian experience and compare it somewhat succinctly to the French one. I have tried to assess the value of that Egyptian background assuming that, in essence, it would have been similar for the whole group of Jews from Egypt, wherever they settled, even when they were confronted with different cultural contexts. All these elements had not been extensively documented previously, and oral history gave me as a researcher the tool to gather and evaluate these elements through testimonies and personal interviews, and to compare and contrast them to official historical records, with the backing of primary and secondary sources.

CHAPTER 4

THE AUSTRALIAN
SAMPLE GROUP

SOCIOECONOMIC AND
CULTURAL CONFIGURATION

As I have pointed out earlier, oral history methodology allowed me to hear the voices of ordinary members of the Egyptian Jewish community, retelling the history of Egyptian Jewry the way they remembered it and the way it impacted them, from their own perspectives as opposed to the "objective" versions recorded in history books. I looked at the case histories of ninety-two Egyptian Jews who settled in Australia. I studied their demographic details, such as gender, age, place of birth, and place of residence. Using a thematic approach, I tried to identify differences and commonalities to see if there was such a thing as a typical profile of the Egyptian Jew as a migrant. Before dealing with their actual migration experience in Australia, I raised questions about various aspects of their lives in Egypt, touching on the themes of ethnic origin, socioeconomic status, education, language, identity, ideology, and connection with Egypt as the "mother country". Finally, I analysed the events that triggered their second exodus to try and determine if that exodus was already foreseeable before the final break, and how prepared they were for that break.

DEMOGRAPHICS

The group of interviewees was virtually equally divided as far as gender was concerned—47 percent male and 53 percent female. All except one[335] were born in Egypt, mostly in Cairo (fifty-three) and Alexandria (thirty-one), with a few (seven) in smaller rural towns, such as Tantah and Mansourah, in the Delta of the Nile,[336] and even in Upper Egypt.[337] At the time they were interviewed, their ages ranged from around the mid-fifties to the late eighties. Almost half the respondents (about 48 percent) had lived in Egypt for two generations, which meant both interviewee and parents were born there; over one-third (37.5 percent) were first-generation immigrants, and the rest (15 percent) had been there for three or more generations. These percentages, although confirming the relatively recent migration of Egyptian Jewry in the modern period, attested nevertheless to a physical presence in the land of over two generations on average.

As noted earlier, due to favourable economic opportunities created by the government's program of reform and modernisation and its welcoming attitude to entrepreneurial foreigners, Egypt had attracted large numbers of migrants beginning in the mid-nineteenth century. The migration pattern of Jewish populations from the Ottoman Empire, the Mediterranean region, and Eastern Europe has been the object of studies by a number of historians.[338] Krämer looked closely at the immigration pattern of nineteenth-century Jews to Egypt and commented on the diversity of the various migrant groups:

> The immigration of Jews from the Ottoman Empire, Greece, the Balkans, Corfu, and Italy, who were mainly of Sephardi (i.e., Spanish) origin, began in the early nineteenth century and continued until the 1920s. Sephardi and Oriental Jews from North Africa migrated to Egypt chiefly between 1897 and 1907, when

their home country experienced a stock market crash brought on by speculation. They settled mostly in Cairo, and in certain trading centres in the Delta, notably Tantah. On their way to Palestine, Jews from Yemen and Aden often got no further than Egypt, as their funds ran out. Most of them arrived between 1900 and 1914 and settled in the Suez Canal Zone or in Cairo. Ashkenazi Jews from Russia, Rumania, and Poland arrived in the late nineteenth and early twentieth centuries, and, for the most part, went to Cairo. In 1914–15, over 11,000 Ashkenazi Jews expelled from the district of Jaffa by the local Ottoman commander fled to Alexandria, Cairo, and Suez, but returned to Palestine or Eastern Europe after the end of the war.[339]

As illustrated in the following chart, the Australian sample group was not only a typical representation of the inherent diversity of Egyptian Jewry, but its inner composition also reflected the size of the internal categories: a dominant Sephardi component originally from the Old Ottoman Empire (Turkey, Syria, and Greece) and from North Africa (Morocco and Algeria); a smaller but still significant Ashkenazi group from Eastern Europe (Russia, Rumania, Bulgaria, Austria, and Hungary)[340]; with the rest consisting of a few respondents from both Western and Eastern Europe, of mixed Sephardi and Ashkenazi parentage, to which was added belatedly a single Karaite Jew.[341]

The interviewees' narratives confirmed that economic, social, and political reasons underpinned the migration of Jews to Egypt in that period. Typical of any migration story, they had been attracted to Egypt by the strong economic climate, work opportunities, political stability, family reunion, and security in a welcoming and tolerant society. The mobility of prospective migrants was further facilitated by the fact that, technically speaking, Egypt was still a province of the Ottoman Empire—and this was the case until 1914 when it became a British Protectorate—whose subjects were relatively free to move from one region to the other.

The only interviewee (#14) who was not born in Egypt relates the story of his mother—widowed with seven children—who decided to leave Turkey, a country where Jews had lived for hundreds of years, to settle in Egypt. The interviewee never forgot that they used to be

Chart 1. Dominant ethnic origin.

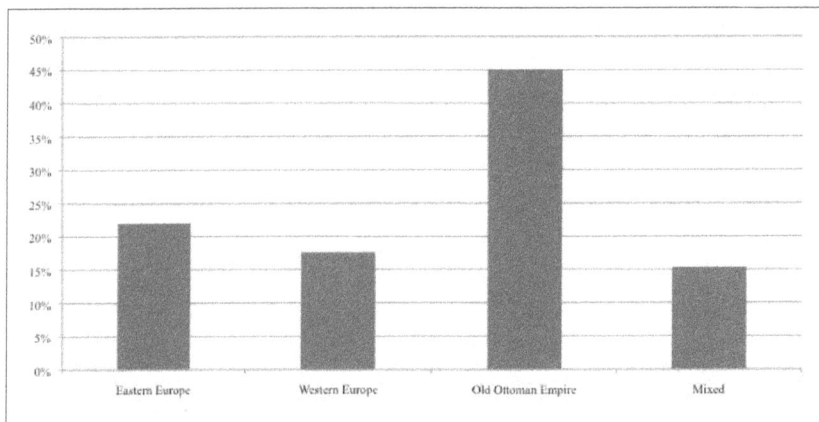

Spanish before their expulsion from Spain: "Nous étions espagnols mais avec Isabelle la Catholique et Ferdinand d'Aragon, tous les Juifs ont été expulsés". His ancestors first found refuge in Leghorn (Italy), and then Turkey opened her doors: "Les Turcs ont voulu nous prendre, ils ont été très bien pour les Juifs". He was born in a small village near Smyrna (modern-day Izmir), a town that used to be a vibrant Jewish centre of the Old Ottoman Empire before it went into rapid decline after World War I. His father was a grower of sultana grapes, which he used to sell every-where. After the father died, the family decided to leave the country in 1921 because of the ongoing conflict between Turkey and Greece. The Jews were often caught in the middle, hated by the Greeks in particular for their closeness to the Turks. In comparison, Muhammad Ali's Egypt offered an envied political stability, as well as promising opportunities for enterprising migrants. The family travelled by boat to Alexandria and settled there because they found employment. Communal help was more readily available for newcomers in an urban environment, and the respondent, who was six at the time, was sent to the Jewish community school, where he received a European education free of charge.[342]

Apart from the socioeconomic motivation, political unrest was another factor that pushed Jews to leave their native countries and seek a safe haven in Egypt. Three Corfiot respondents reported that their parents had left their homes in Corfu in the wake of blood libel accusations by the Greek majority and chose Egypt because of its reputation for tolerance.[343]

Other interviewees related how their families also found refuge in Egypt after fleeing pogroms and persecution in Russia and Rumania. Interviewee #38 remembered hearing stories about saving the young boys of the family from conscription in the Russian army from the age of eight and for a minimum of twenty-five years, as was customary in those days:[344]

> My father was born in Bessarabia, and my mother in Sofia en route to Constantinople from Odessa. The family had left Odessa because they had sons and they didn't want them to go into the Russian army. They arrived in Alexandria by ship towards the end of the nineteenth century but decided to settle in Cairo because there were more opportunities for work. [345]

Other respondents came from Salonika, Istanbul, and Smyrna (Izmir) between mid-nineteenth century and the beginning of the twentieth century. However, they still considered themselves literally from Spain, over five hundred years after the Expulsion of 1492, as related by Interviewee #16, whose ancestors had lived in the Ottoman Empire for centuries:

> Originally we were from Majorca. The family left Majorca at the time of the Expulsion from Spain in 1492, and went to Salonika. In Salonika, there was a congregation from Majorca. We ended up being called the children of Majorca, which is "Ben Mayor". We can trace our name back to a rabbi called Solomon Ben Mayor who was buried in 1562. My father's family came from Smyrna. The family must have moved from Salonika to Smyrna sometime in the 1800s.

Interviewee #3 also pointed to the Spanish origin of his family, whose original name, Ha-Eleon, meant from the province of Leon and Castile before it was changed to the more modern form, Aghion. Subsequent genealogical research confirmed that his ancestors left Spain after the Expulsion Edict of 1492 and settled in Baden-Baden, where they remained for ninety years before moving to Amsterdam. Around 1841, they were invited to move to Egypt because of their financial expertise. As stated earlier, Muhammad Ali's program of modernisation of Egypt needed the help of Europeans.[346] This particular narrative showed a direct link between the opening up of Egypt to modernity and the transfer of a Jewish family from Europe to Egypt.

Italy was another prestigious origin claimed by some of the interviewees. Interviewee #33 stated that her grandfather came to Egypt from Leghorn to sell trains to the Khedive Ismail, Muhammad Ali's grandson, who ruled between 1863 and 1879. The role played by Jewish families in the construction of several railway lines has been documented in both Krämer and Raafat's research on the contribution of Jewish notables to Egypt's modernisation. In fact, the Suares family, who also came to Egypt from Leghorn in the early part of the nineteenth century, established in Cairo "the first public transport company, the horse-drawn carriages of the Omnibus Company…which, until 1940, serviced the busy Muski Street". [347] Those carriages were popularly known as *Arabiyat Suwaris* after their founders. The Suares brothers also built the railway line from Cairo to Helwan and several other lines in the rural areas of both Upper and Lower Egypt.[348]

The majority of my respondents were urban dwellers; over one-half (56.8 percent) were born in Cairo and one-third (34.1 percent) in Alexandria. Again, these figures reflected the findings of Landau and Krämer in the Egyptian censuses of 1897 to 1947.[349] According to Landau, the attraction towards urban living was already prevalent in the nineteenth century, due to such obvious factors as settling in the first place of arrival, usually the port of Alexandria, the need for a communal life, and better work prospects as shopkeepers, brokers, and clerks.

The traditional rivalry among the inhabitants of two capital cities survived transplantation to the "Edge of the Diaspora", and the interviewees still saw themselves as distinctively Alexandrians or Cairenes.[350]

The Alexandrians expressed a special attachment to their city, claiming that the lifestyle, the people, and even the sense of humour were particular to the place.[351] Nineteenth-century Alexandria, with its harbour opening onto the West, was already considered a more European city than Cairo. The number of foreigners in Alexandria exceeded one-third of the total population, which engendered a very cosmopolitan atmosphere.[352] A French historian, Robert Ilbert, called Alexandria "le symbole d'une Méditerranée ouverte au monde."[353] Furthermore, the Alexandrian Jewish community was more Mediterranean in its composition and outlook, and less exposed than its Cairene counterpart to the autochthonous Egyptian environment. Until the early 1940s it was also considered to be better organised and more united than the Cairo community because "all Jews living in the city regardless of rite and origin were considered part of the community", whereas in Cairo, the Sephardim, the Ashkenazim, and the Karaites functioned separately.[354] However, by the late 1940s Krämer stated that "Cairo finally assumed the leading role among Egyptian Jewry", displacing the predominance of Alexandria.[355]

The issue of lesser or greater exposure to the indigenous atmosphere was a determining factor in the feelings of security and inclusion articulated by respondents in the course of their interviews. Being closer to the political nerve centre of the country, Cairo-born respondents often personally witnessed some of the seminal moments of Egypt's recent history, such as the riots in 1948, the burning of Cairo in January 1952, and the Free Officers' Revolution of July 1952. They often expressed a stronger attachment to the land, had a better knowledge of the native language, and also displayed a more personal understanding of the events leading to the general demise of Egyptian Jewry.

Did the self-perceived differences between Alexandrians and Cairenes carry any special significance for the current study, or were they just anecdotal? It is true that those differences had their roots in the socio-historical context that determined the posturing of the two communities. In the psyche of its European inhabitants, Alexandria—"the capital of memory", to quote Lawrence Durrell—was not at the time truly representative of Egypt, whereas Cairo was always an integral part of Egypt.

As a result, the Alexandrian Jews saw themselves as more cosmopolitan and more detached from their Egyptian environment, whereas the Cairene Jews, who lived in a city popularly known as *Om el-Donya* (Mother of the World), considered their Alexandrian brethren provincial and pseudo-Europeans. Whatever the significance of these differences, when the end of Egyptian Jewry was spelled out they did not affect the final outcome.

According to Krämer, "in the interwar period, there were still several small Jewish communities in the major trading centres of the Delta and the Suez Canal Zone".[356] Only a small percentage (about 7 to 8 percent) of my respondents came from the smaller rural towns, but they did not remain there beyond their school years. As the attraction of urban centres grew, most of them moved as young adults to Cairo or Alexandria for the traditional reasons: better education, more work opportunities, and stronger communal institutions. One notable exception was the case of the rabbi of Port Said, who remained there until the war with Israel in 1948, when he was arrested as a Zionist sympathiser. His daughter (#82), who now lives in Sydney, related that event: "my father was kept in solitary confinement for forty-four days because he was a rabbi. The other Jews that were picked up remained together, only my father was segregated".[357]

In 1938, Maurice Fargeon looked at the Jewish population of the villages in Upper Egypt, quoting a total figure of 962 Jews.[358] Interviewee #5 claimed his birthplace as Assiut, a village situated halfway between Cairo and Aswan in Upper Egypt, where there was very little record of a significant Jewish population and no organised community. According to his recollection, "there were only about five Jewish families". His father immigrated to Egypt in 1889 from Istanbul:

> Business was very bad in Turkey and the situation in Egypt was good so he came. He was an electrician and opened a shop of electrical appliances and later added spare parts for cars. He named the shop Samuel Levy [although it was not his name] because at that time, Jewish people were very respected and trusted.

This example clearly demonstrates the high regard in which Jews were held, even in a remote little village such as Assiut. Despite the fact that his father's shop was financially very successful, my respondent only dreamt of leaving his native village to study pharmacy at the university in Cairo. He eventually followed his dream, operating his own pharmacy in Cairo until the events of 1956 forced him to leave.

Interviewee #6 was a third-generation rural dweller. Like her father and grandfather, she was born and raised in the small country town of Mansurah, situated on the Nile Delta. Her father was the accountant for the local branch of Barclays Bank. The family remained there until 1948 and left for Cairo because of her father's early death. The interviewee described their lifestyle in the country town as privileged:

> It was a small town. All the farmers sold their cotton crop to the Barclays Bank and conducted all their business transactions with the same bank. We lived in an apartment. My mother had a lot of servants. She was busy supervising them, cooking, and socialising. My parents had friends coming over on Saturday and Sunday. There was even a Jewish club. Before World War II, there was a very big Jewish population and, during the war, a lot more came to Mansurah when they started bombarding Alexandria. After the war, most of them went back to Alexandria. Others, born and raised in Mansurah, also left.[359]

The Egyptian census of 1917, as well as records of the AIU, confirmed that there were about eighty Jewish families in Mansurah at the time, which made the Jewish community one of the largest outside Cairo and Alexandria. Fargeon claimed that there could have been around one hundred and fifty families at the beginning of the twentieth century. This number dwindled to about five hundred individuals by 1927 and two hundred on the eve of World War II. Their main activities revolved around the cotton and manufacturing industries.[360]

The only other case of a Mansurah-born interviewee (#27) was not significant because his parents, originally from Alexandria and Cairo, settled in that town for professional reasons. They were offered positions as French teachers during the war years by the Mansurah Greek community school and by the Egyptian local school.[361] The interviewee was only seven years old when he left Egypt with his family. What was interesting was the fact that, in such a small town, French would be included in the curriculum of both the Greek school and the local public school, further evidence of the high status of French culture.

Of all the provincial towns of Egypt, Tantah seemed to have a special resonance for a number of interviewees, either as their own or their parents' birthplace.[362] Situated between Cairo and Alexandria in the centre of the Delta region, Tantah was, at the turn of the twentieth century, "the major marketplace of a large cotton growing area and was linked to all centres of the country by a close network of railway lines", reported Krämer.[363] He also pointed out that, in 1909, the population of seventy-five thousand inhabitants included a considerable number of Greeks and Jews. The Jewish migrants came mainly from Morocco, Syria, Algeria, and Iraq. Before the economic crisis of 1907, the local Jewish community was very prosperous. An AIU school was established in 1905, catering for boys and girls of the community, as well as for some Muslim pupils.[364] One Tantah-born interviewee (#29) testified to having attended that school at the primary level, where he was exposed to French culture for the first time. By the eve of World War II, the Tantah community had gone into decline due to a change of economic conditions and the departure of its wealthier members. However, according to a report from the AIU, poor Oriental and Ashkenazi immigrants—attracted by the social services and other advantages offered by the local community, such as free education for their children—filled the vacuum left by the rural exodus of the middle and upper classes.[365] Tantah's Jewish population remained relatively well organised, with four synagogues, three bearing the names of their founders, Louna Botton, Chamla, and Eskanderany, and the fourth reserved for the Moroccan Jews, *Kenisset el-Mogharba*.[366] Interviewee #53 was very proud of his family's Tantah origin, and he considered himself an authentic Egyptian. He could trace his roots back to the eighteenth century; leading a modest life on the land and probably from the land: "we were *fellaheen* [peasants]", he said without inhibition. He even boasted, "we had seventeen synagogues in Tantah".[367]

Another significant rural centre, al-Mehalla al-Kubra, considered the centre of the cotton industry, was the birthplace of the father of Victor

Aghion (Interviewee #3, now deceased). His family came to Egypt around 1840 from Amsterdam, in response to Mohammed Ali's invitation to Europeans. At first they settled in Alexandria because, as this interviewee explained: "Alexandria was where all the activities were, where you had the harbour, the bankers, where all the cotton was gathered and shipped overseas—and you know what cotton meant to Egypt". Later, the family moved to al-Mehalla al-Kubra:

> My grandfather was a banker and a cotton merchant. He had all sorts of properties in the centre of the cotton industry in al-Mehalla al-Kubra. This is where my father was born. My grandfather was the *gabbai*[368] of the synagogue. There was a very large [Jewish] community in Mehalla, which was on the way to Cairo, before Tantah...It was an important locality. A lot of Europeans, Jewish and other, lived there, the proof being the size of the synagogue. There were five hotels in the city of Mehalla, and my grandfather owned four of them. The schools in Mehalla were government schools. There were no French or English schools. My father and his sister had a private tutor who was coming from Alexandria, and I know they were fluent in Arabic, French, and Italian.

The importance of al-Mehalla al-Kubra as a Jewish centre was particularly stressed by Fargeon, who claimed that a Jewish presence in that town went back six hundred years. In the modern era—around the 1900s—the community was very prosperous, before many of its members moved either to Tantah or to the cities of Alexandria and Cairo, leaving behind the poorer members. By 1937, there were only ten Jewish families left.[369]

In his chronicle of Jewish life in the villages, the historian Jacques Hassoun evoked with nostalgia the faces of the last Jewish peasants, who looked and lived exactly like their Coptic and Muslim neighbours. He also brought to mind the Jewish commercial travellers coming from Cairo and Alexandria, rushing from one village to the other, trying to sell their wares, staying whenever possible at inns owned by fellow Jews and sharing the latest news from the city with them.[370]

Gradually, as income prospects grew and city lifestyle became more attractive, the general exodus of the commercial middle class and the younger generation towards Cairo and Alexandria gained momentum and, in parallel, made "life in the provinces even less attractive and migration to the big cities even more alluring".[371] As confirmed by the findings of Fargeon, Landau, Krämer, Hassoun, and others, most of the Jews left the rural centres in search of better economic opportunities in the big city centres of Cairo and Alexandria.[372] The respondents' testimonies reflected that strong pull towards an urban lifestyle. By the time of their departure from Egypt, all the respondents were living almost exclusively in Cairo or Alexandria.

The Nationality Issue

Given the fact that the entire sample group was of diverse ethnic origins but still native to Egypt for at least two generations, one would have expected the majority to be Egyptian nationals. However, as seen in the following chart, nearly one-half of the group (46.5 percent) held a foreign passport and less than one-quarter (20.5 percent) held Egyptian nationality. The rest (33 percent) were stateless, or *sujets locaux*, which usually meant that they were considered Ottoman subjects before Egypt gained independence in 1922 and somehow did not obtain either an Egyptian or a foreign nationality. It is interesting to see how these figures compared with the overall statistics for Egyptian Jewry.[373]

Since enactment of the Nationality Law of 1947, the stateless were under the same obligations as foreign nationals and had to obtain a resident permit to be renewed every ten years. The late Alex Golliger (#37) recounted the difficulties he faced in this respect:

> I was stateless but I tried to become Egyptian. I applied to the Ministry of Interior and was asked: where was your father born? I replied, he was born in Egypt, I was born in Egypt, and I want to be Egyptian. I was told: I am sorry, we can only give you a *carte de séjour* (resident permit), which must be renewed every

CHART 2. Nationality of interviewees.

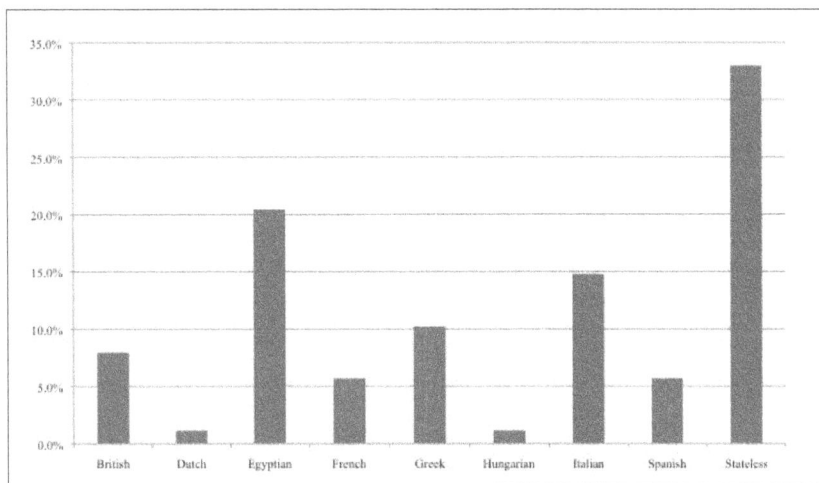

ten years…I bought an Italian passport in 1956, six months before leaving. A man called M…said all I had to do was to make a statutory declaration that my grandmother was Italian and was born in Sienna. There had been a big fire in Sienna and all the municipal records of Sienna had burned down. I agreed, provided I would also get passports for my wife, my three children, my sister, my niece, and myself.[374]

After the opening of the Suez Canal in 1869 and the British occupation of Egypt in 1882, the issue of nationality became a major area of concern for non-Muslim minorities. According to Krämer, the problem was compounded after the Montreux Convention of 1937:

Nationality gradually began to assume a relevance it never had before. Formal citizenship, as opposed to religious affiliation, gained further importance when, in the late 1930s, the Egyptian government started to Egyptianize the economy and the administration by reserving a growing number of positions for Egyptian citizens.[375]

Historians do not always agree on the demographics of the Jews in Egypt, and some discrepancies exist between the numbers given. For instance, whereas the 1947 Egyptian Census listed 65,639 Jews, Fargeon claimed they were 59,184 in 1937; Hassoun quoted an approximate figure of ninety thousand by 1946, whereas Beinin's estimate was seventy-five to eighty thousand by 1948.[376] As for their nationality, the picture is even more confused. Laskier claimed that about one-quarter of the Jewish population had a foreign passport, another quarter had Egyptian nationality, and the remaining 50 percent were stateless, or *sujets locaux*.[377] Beinin argued that by 1948, only 12.5 percent were Egyptians, and 37.5 percent were foreign nationals, which also left half the Jewish population as stateless:

> At the turn of the twentieth century, autochthonous Jews who would be entitled to Egyptian citizenship by the 1929 nationality law and its successors made up at least half of the Jewish community. But in 1948, only 5,000–10,000 of Egypt's 75,000–80,000 Jews held Egyptian citizenship. Some 40,000 were stateless, and 30,000 were foreign nationals. Many of the 10,000 poor, Arabic-speaking residents of the Rabbanite and Karaite Jewish quarters… of Cairo or the 15,000 residents of the port district…of Alexandria were among the stateless.[378]

Krämer pointed out that the Egyptian censuses of 1937 and 1947 did not list stateless persons separately. The last official census of that grouping was conducted in 1927, revealing that 33 percent were Egyptian, 22 percent were European, and the remaining 45 percent were listed as "others", which could have meant stateless. According to the next Egyptian census of 1937, the proportion had changed to 35 percent foreigners and 65 percent Egyptians, and in 1947 it had reached 80 percent Egyptians compared to 20 percent foreign nationals. Because those censuses did not treat the stateless group as a separate category, the assumption is that they were included in the Egyptian category, which would then explain the discrepancy. Taking this conclusion into consideration, Krämer extrapolated that "all evidence suggests that the majority of those who lost, or gave up, their foreign nationality, as well as of the indigenous

Egyptian and the Oriental Jews (mostly former Ottoman subjects) in fact did not obtain Egyptian passports", which would explain the high proportion of stateless Jews reported by Beinin.[379]

Assuming that the three historians more or less agreed on the high percentage of stateless Jews, the discrepancy in their respective estimates was in the categories of Egyptian and foreign nationals. What seems more relevant here was the notable size of the "stateless" category in Krämer, Laskier, and Beinin's research compared to the other two categories. This phenomenon was confirmed by the data I gathered from the Australian sample group, where the stateless counted for one-third of the total. However, the higher proportion of foreign nationals in that group—nearly one-half (46.6 percent) compared to the 20.5 percent of Egyptian nationals—is a reversal of the general trend. The reason for this reversal is probably due to the privileged socioeconomic composition of my sample group, particularly when one takes into account the findings of a 1922 statistical study of the nationality of the Jewish upper class, revealing that it was "mostly the affluent and educated middle and upper classes, which were able to obtain either foreign or Egyptian passports".[380] It appears that a significant proportion of the Egyptian Jews who migrated to Australia came from the educated middle and upper-middle classes.

The circumstances in which the Jews of Egypt obtained foreign citizenship or protection have already been discussed. It is important to remember that a large percentage of them did not have direct connections with their assumed mother countries, whether Great Britain, France, or Italy. Their connections were more with regions under the political control or protection of those countries, such as French North Africa, Malta, Gibraltar, Syria, Iraq, Libya, and Lebanon, and sometimes even those connections were tenuous.[381] In my evaluation of this aspect of the data, it was essential to differentiate between ethnic origin and nationality because they seldom corresponded. For instance, Interviewee #34, who claimed Italian and Algerian descent, had a French passport thanks to the Crémieux Law of 1870, which granted French nationality to all the Jews of Algeria. Another interviewee (#71) explained that her parents

fortuitously acquired French citizenship, whereas her uncle acquired
Italian nationality:

> My uncle was a *"Gaulliste"*. He had paid some kind of mem-
> bership during the war. Also, because we were Polish, we were
> *"protégés français"* [protected subjects]. The French government
> needed money for the war effort during World War II and they
> offered us French nationality. My uncle did not go through with
> it…but he bought the Italian nationality. It was much cheaper than
> the French.

Conversely, Interviewee #31 reported that he had no problem in obtaining Egyptian citizenship in 1929, although his father came from Crete
and his mother from Leghorn. The late Ziza Lester née de Botton (#20)
also claimed that she had obtained the Egyptian nationality without difficulty because her maternal grandfather was born in Turkey: "By law,
anyone who was a descendant of a Turkish subject could automatically
apply for Egyptian citizenship".[382] She was obviously referring to the
Nationality Law of 1929, which recognised as Egyptian nationals "those
former subjects of the Ottoman Empire who made their 'habitual residence' in Egypt on 5 November 1914". [383] Interviewee #46 related that
his father, who came from Turkey in the 1900s, originally from Bessara-
bia, somehow obtained Egyptian nationality, although strictly speaking
he was not eligible. Apparently he was registered on his birth certificate
as *raeya*, code word for stateless. All these examples illustrate how arbitrary and haphazard the granting of Egyptian nationality was when it
came to Jews.

Obtaining a foreign nationality was not always straightforward either.
My data showed that 42.9 percent of the interviewees holding British
passports were originally from the Old Ottoman Empire, and the connection with Britain was again fortuitous. For example, Interviewee
#43, originally from Damascus, was granted British nationality because
a member of his family had given sanctuary to the British consul in
Damascus during anti-Western riots, and was thus recompensed by Her
Majesty's government. In another case, the interviewee's husband was

Maltese, which automatically made him a British subject. A further example was Interviewee #88, whose grandfather came from Gibraltar and therefore enjoyed British protection. In only two cases was the connection with England direct, through one set of grandparents who were from Lancaster.[384]

It is clear that the various nationalities were as diverse as the ethnic origins themselves. For the purpose of this study, the nationalities of the respondents have been grouped into three general categories, Egyptian, stateless, and foreigner. The last category incorporated a variety of different passports: British (8 percent), Dutch (1.1 percent), French (5.7 percent), Greek (10.2 percent), Hungarian (1.1 percent), Italian (14.8 percent), and Spanish (5.7 percent).

The reason for the high proportion of Italian nationals was probably due to the fact that the Italian passport was the easiest to obtain, after a fire at the Leghorn municipality destroyed all the communal records. However, not all of those respondents were *Italiens de passeport* (Italians in name only), as they used to be called. Traditionally, from the early days of Egypt's opening to European influence, Italy had developed strong trade links with Egypt, and Italian Jews had forged themselves an important niche in the life of the Jewish community of Egypt. Interviewee #8 found the proof of his family's direct link with Italy when he leafed through the old registers of the Alexandrian community and found the entry related to his great-grandfather, dating back to 1840:

> The official records of the Alexandria Jewish community showed that my family originated in Tuscany. My grandparents spoke Italian at home. They distanced themselves from any Egyptian traditions and customs. They even sent their children to boarding schools in Lausanne.

Even the records of the community in Alexandria were kept in Italian before the switch to French at the beginning of the twentieth century.

It was also interesting to note the surprisingly high number of Greek nationals within the sample group, most of them originally from Corfu.[385] The reason for their immigration to Egypt has already been discussed.

It is evident that, in view of their own or their parents' past experiences in Corfu, they did not have a strong bond with Greece. They hardly ever considered settling there after leaving Egypt in the 1950s, in spite of their Greek passports. In fact, Interviewee #24 reported that he had been repatriated to Greece after being imprisoned in 1956 for Zionist activities and then expelled from Egypt. The Jewish community of Athens, keen to try and rebuild the community of Rhodes that had been exterminated by the Nazis during the Second World War, promised to pay both his and his brother's fare, assuring them of a livelihood if they agreed to settle on the island. The respondent, then an adventurous young man, preferred the lure of the much bigger island of Australia and integrated very well in his new country. Despite a strong Australian accent, he still admitted to speaking the Venetian dialect of Corfu with the older members of his family.

Taking into consideration the ethnic origins and various nationalities of the sample group, it became clear that its demographic profile was urban-based, multinational, and multiethnic, regardless of a single birthplace. Study of other facets of its identity, such as socioeconomic status, level of education, and linguistic skills, was necessary to complete the picture of the Jew from Egypt in Australia.

SOCIOECONOMIC STATUS

To establish the socioeconomic status of the respondents, I had to assess their responses to some key questions regarding housing, lifestyle, occupation, and schooling against their own rating of their position on the social scale. Based on the data they provided, the interviewees' evaluation did not always correspond to the social reality as it was described. However, seeing as oral history is often more about perceptions than scientific truth, any disparity was never openly challenged but was reassessed as objectively as possible once matched with the rest of the data. Any readjustment had to take into account the comparative issues of location, lifestyle, schooling, and leisure, while keeping in mind that, in most of the cases discussed in this book, the category of lower-middle class referred to a *petite bourgeoisie* rather than a true working class.[386]

The main discrepancies were found in the middle- and upper-middle-class categories. For instance, two members of the same family had different assessments of their social standing. The brother saw himself as a member of the upper class whereas the sister maintained that the family was middle class. A ruling had to be made, bearing in mind certain criteria. The occupations of the father and the mother, a schoolteacher and a secretary respectively, plus the fact that the sister—despite her high intellectual and academic abilities and unlike her brothers—could not pursue her tertiary education because of financial constraints, tipped the scale in favour of middle-class rather than upper-middle-class status.

To illustrate the three class divisions as they were represented in the sample group, I have chosen the stories of three women, each belonging to a different social stratum, but all sharing the same family values and work ethics acquired in their formative years in Egypt.

The lower-middle class or petite bourgeoisie is represented by Esther Abécassis (#1), my late mother—one of the oldest participants, well into her eighties at the time of the interview. She preferred to tell her story in French as her level of English, adequate for simple everyday communication, was not sufficient for a more complex narrative. She was born in Alexandria of Syrian parents (Aleppo). Her father's death at the age of thirty-six left the family nearly destitute. She attended the Jewish community school, l'Ecole Aghion, where she was taught the basics in French, Arabic, and Hebrew, some rudiments of English, as well as sewing and embroidery. She also learned Italian and Greek from relatives and friends. She left school at thirteen to join the workforce and help support her mother and two younger siblings. She even taught herself dressmaking to supplement her meagre earnings. She had very little formal education, but was fluent in the Egyptian Arabic vernacular as well as French because these were the languages used at home with her mother, who was probably illiterate. In her youth, she lived in the modest Jewish neighbourhoods of Muharram Bey and Attarine in Alexandria. Although she led a very Jewish life, she always lived in harmony with members of the different ethnic groups that made up Alexandrine society, including the autochthonous population. After marrying my father, she continued to work as a telephone receptionist for the first few years because the family needed the double income. The household could afford only one live-in servant, which was a minimum in those days. Leisure time consisted of a weekly movie, family gatherings, and outings with friends to the beach or to the municipal gardens. In accordance with Jewish tradition, her life ambition was for her children to become professionals, and with her husband she ensured that their four children gained a solid French education at the Lycée de la Mission Laïque Française. Because they could not afford tertiary education for all of their children, the boys were given priority over the girls. The eldest son was preparing to go to France to study medicine in Montpellier when the 1956 Suez War erupted. The youngest son eventually became a civil engineer in Montreal, Canada. My mother made certain through sheer hard work and determination that all her children were given the educational tools necessary to move up the socioeconomic ladder. It is particularly exceptional for a woman of her background, in the Middle Eastern patriarchal context of the interwar period, to display the independence and the courage that characterised her life story:

> Avant tout j'ai travaillé dans une teinturerie à l'âge de douze ans. A treize ans, je me suis présentée à la Compagnie de Téléphone mais ils m'ont dit, nous engageons seulement à quinze ans. Moi j'avais besoin, je faisais de la couture…pour apporter de l'argent à la maison…Parfois on n'avait pas à manger…Comment j'ai appris à coudre, toute seule, depuis que j'étais petite. Une artiste du Casino Alhambra m'a apporté une robe à réparer à la teinturerie où je travaillais et elle m'a demandé si je connaissais une couturière. Je me suis proposée comme ça…C'était ma première cliente.[387]

Her immigration experience, first in Canada and then Australia, illustrated the particular ability Egyptian Jews seemed to have to uproot themselves, integrate into their new surroundings, and interact smoothly with people of different backgrounds.

The second case (#17) was a younger woman from a comfortably middle-class family in Alexandria, where she attended a private non-denominational English school. She arrived in Australia at the age of thirteen. Her father was Greek, originally from Corfu, but he also spoke French, Italian, Arabic, and English. He had studied law in Egypt and worked at the Mixed Courts before joining the family menswear business. Her mother was Ashkenazi, originally from Germany, educated in French schools, with a very poor command of Arabic. She was therefore totally alienated from the local population because she could barely even communicate with the servants. Socialisation was mainly among fellow Jews and members of other ethnic groups. Despite a strong sense of Jewish identity in the family, religious observance at home was not strict and the atmosphere was rather liberal. The family's leisure time was divided between visits to the exclusive Alexandria Sporting Club, having tea with friends while doing embroidery or *petits points*, playing cards, or going to the movies. The interviewee described that most genteel lifestyle:

> My mother was a grand lady in Alexandria and never worked. We lived with my grandparents in this big apartment and my aunt, her husband, and two kids. We all lived there. It was a really big apartment.

However, once the family arrived in Australia with very modest funds, the mother did not shy away from seeking employment as an office clerk, despite her total lack of work experience. She learned to love the independence it gave her and remained in the workforce until the age of retirement, without ever losing her "grand lady" style. She showed the same resilience demonstrated by many of the women of a similar background that I encountered who, somehow, managed a quiet and dignified adjustment to their change of circumstances and drop in social status.

The third case (#20) was the previously mentioned Ziza Lester, who was seventy-three years old at the time of the interview. She was an educated and independent woman, whose family was part of the Sephardi aristocracy of Egypt. She believed her family roots could be traced back to the times of the Inquisition. Both Ladino (Judeo-Spanish or *judesmo*) and French were spoken at home, as well as Italian and Greek. Arabic was reserved for communication with the numerous servants who worked for the family. The grandfather was educated in a private Catholic school run by the Jesuits. He had cotton plantations, and his son eventually became "one of the pillars of the textile industry". The family also entertained close relations with the Egyptian establishment before 1948, which was apparently the reason they succeeded in acquiring Egyptian nationality. "My father dealt with people in government on a daily basis", said Ziza. She demonstrated her independent spirit by joining the workforce as soon as she left school, although her father was against it. It was not proper for the daughter of such a prominent man to go out to work. Because of her excellent English skills, she worked at the American Embassy during the war years. The family was also very active in philanthropic work for the community. She remembered that her grandfather was awarded the prestigious Légion d'Honneur for his role in founding a French Jewish school in the new suburb of Heliopolis, northeast of Cairo:

> My grandfather S. F. wanted to create a Jewish day school and he did. He called it l'Ecole Abraham B'tesh. Abraham B'tesh was a very rich man who did not have any children and a very good friend of my grandfather. My grandfather had collected most of the money for the school, but he needed another £5,000, so he went to Abraham B'tesh and told him: if you give me that sum, I will name the school after you and because you have no children, your name will remain known from generation to generation. The first children to go to that school were us, the grandchildren of S. F. We spent a year there to show the people that the rich and the poor can go there. I remember the caretakers were Ya'ub and Rachel. The teachers were French from France. At first the school went to the Certificat d'études and later up to the Baccalauréat. It was free for the poor, but those who could afford it paid school fees and the community subsidised it.[388]

Both father and grandfather headed the Jewish community, in turn as president and vice president, and led a very traditional Jewish life. Ziza recalled that "the Chief Rabbi of Egypt, Rabbi Nahum Effendi [1872–1960], used to come and spend the weekend" with her grandparents.

Their interests were mainly intellectual and consisted of cultural *soirées prolongées* (extended evening parties), attended by writers, artists, and musicians. All the family fortune was sequestrated after 1948, and Ziza arrived in Australia penniless, together with her parents and brothers. Using her multilingual skills in Arabic, French, Italian, and Spanish, she worked for international organisations as a simultaneous interpreter and later as a medical interpreter. As an integral part of her privileged upbringing, she had been instilled with high principles of work and moral ethics, and diligently pursued her activities well into her retirement years, again without fuss or fanfare.[389]

Although these three examples were representative of the different cultural, ethnic, and class divisions that made up Egyptian Jewry, these divisions were not represented in the same proportion in the Australian sample, where a strong middle class predominated overall by nearly two-thirds.[390] As shown in the following chart, one-fifth of the respondents belonged to the upper-middle class. The Western Europeans had the highest representative proportion, with about 40 percent; the Levantines were second with 21 percent; the Eastern Europeans together with the "mixed" group were equal at 15.8 percent. As for the lower-middle-class grouping, because of its minuscule size—seven respondents in all—the statistical results could not be considered a true representation of the social reality. Nevertheless, they revealed a relatively even spread between the Eastern Europeans (15.8 percent) and the "mixed" respondents (14.3 percent), even as the Levantine grouping stood at 7.3 percent. Western Europeans were not represented at all in the lower category, which was significant in itself.

One possible interpretation could be that the Jews of Egypt who were of a lower socioeconomic status did not usually end up in Australia but rather in Israel, as claimed by both Laskier and Beinin.[391] Another possibility is that those who migrated to Australia were better equipped financially and culturally to deal with the cost of relocating in such a faraway country, the unfamiliarity of the Anglo-Celtic culture, and the restrictive immigration policy of Australia.

The statistics that emerged from the combination of birthplace and social status reinforced the previous findings, with some variations

CHART 3. Socioeconomic composition according to ethnic origin.

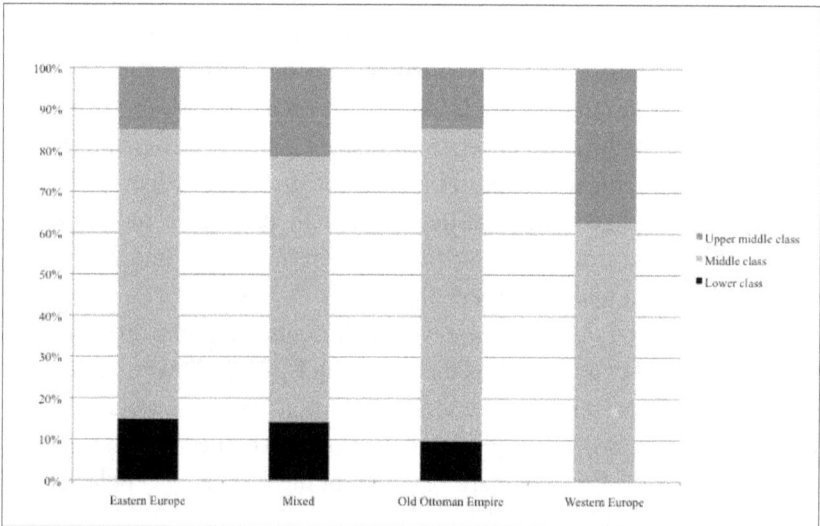

between the urban and rural centres, as seen in chart 4. The Alexandrians were divided as follows: 10 percent in the lower-middle class, 70 percent in the middle class, and 20 percent in the upper-middle class. The Cairenes had only 4 percent in the lower category, 74 percent in the middle, and 22 percent in the upper section. The rural dwellers had the highest percentage (57 percent) in the lower class, 43 percent in the middle and, not surprisingly, were absent in the upper echelon.

Again the overall picture of a large urban middle class—with a broader disparity in the upper and lower echelons between the urban and the rural dwellers—was validated.

A similar pattern emerged from the statistical analysis of the relationship between class and nationality, as demonstrated in chart 5. In each national group the size of the middle class was predominant, with, nevertheless, a strong upper class. Twenty-one percent of the stateless respondents placed themselves in the lower strata, 69 percent in the middle strata, and 10 percent in the upper strata, whereas the French,

CHART 4. Socioeconomic composition according to birthplace.

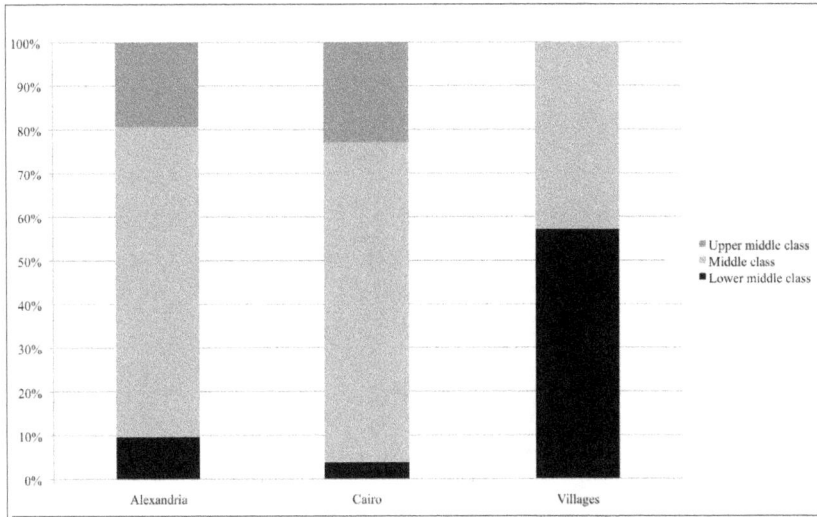

Greeks, Italians, and Spanish were not represented in the lower category. The French interviewees constituted 40 percent of the middle class and 60 percent of the upper-middle class; the Greek and Spanish intervie-wees were all middle class, whereas two-thirds of the Italians were in the middle class and one-third in the upper class. The British represented 14 percent of the lower class, 71 percent of the middle class, and 14 percent of the upper class. As for the Egyptians, a mere 6 percent declared themselves in the lower class, 61 percent in the middle, and 33 percent in the upper-middle class. Most of the lower-middle class came from the group of stateless, which again was to be expected, given that they would not have been in a position to bribe any officials in high places and, thus, acquire either the Egyptian nationality or a foreign passport.

Based on these statistics, one can deduce that the class structure of the sample group consisted of a dominant middle class, a significant upper-middle class, and a small lower-middle class. These figures reflect the

CHART 5. Class structure of each nationality.

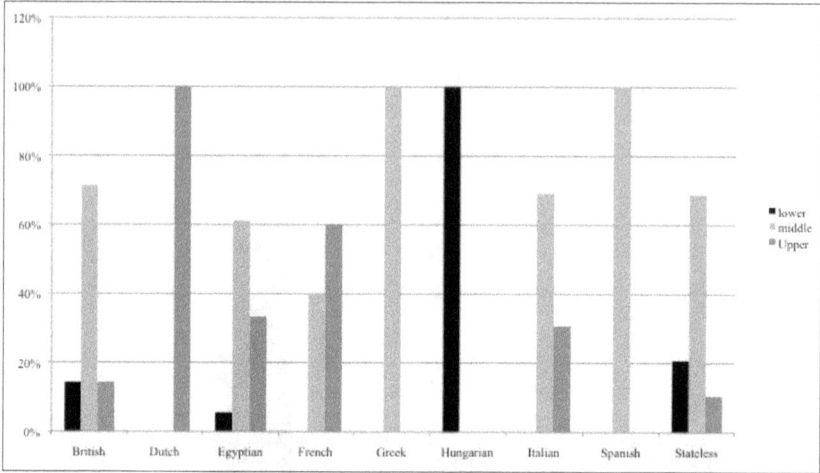

general trend of a rising bourgeoisie within Egyptian Jewry from the second half of the nineteenth century. Beinin attributed the success of that bourgeoisie as follows:

> Kinship connections throughout the Mediterranean basin, a long tradition of diasporic commercial activities, and participation in the local cultures of the Levant and overseas French culture, enabled Jewish businessmen to function as commercial intermediaries between Europe and the Ottoman realms.[392]

Indeed, with the expansion of the economy coupled with the political stability caused by the British presence, members of the local non-Muslim minorities, including a large number of Jews, found themselves in great demand for their language skills and Western-style education. However, as noted by Krämer, "statistical data on occupation and social stratification are, even for the twentieth century, rare and not very reliable".[393] Therefore, it is difficult to state with authority that the statistics established for the Australian sample group give a true reflection of Egyptian Jewry in general. As previously noted, Laskier's research on the emigration of the Jews from Egypt to Israel from 1948 on indicated that, apart from youths aged sixteen and under, the largest group of migrants were non-professionals and of low socioeconomic status. The Jewish Agency paid their fare and transit expenses.[394] No mention was made of their nationality in the official records, which probably meant that they were stateless. It seems that, unless they were driven by a strong Zionistic motivation, the Jews of Egypt who had better education, some professional training, more financial resources, and a European passport had more options than just going to Israel when they were forced out of Egypt. Those at the lower end of the socioeconomic scale would not have had those options.[395] As such, the profile of the Australian interviewees appears fairly representative of the Egyptian Jews who migrated to other diaspora communities.

SCHOOLING/OCCUPATION/CLASS

It has already been established that Jews, like other minorities, attended in droves the elitist foreign schools, mainly English and French, which disseminated a highly desirable Western culture.[396] The group under study provided the perfect illustration of those conditions. The whole gamut of schools was represented in the various testimonies I gathered in the course of my research.

In modern democratic societies, education is usually the key to upward mobility, and the case of Egyptian Jewry clearly illustrates this principle. According to the census of 1907—comparing the literacy of Muslims, Copts, Jews, and other ethnic groups—"the proportion of literacy was higher among Jews than among the rest of the population" on a pro-rata basis.[397] According to Landau, the reasons for that high benchmark were both the Jewish tradition of study and the standard of education available. As mentioned previously, the Jews of Egypt could choose from a number of educational institutions. In the great majority of cases they went through either their own communal school system or through the foreign private school system, but seldom through Egyptian government schools. Evidently, their socioeconomic status, their ethnicity, and their world view determined their preference. The choices fluctuated between a religious or secular education administered in French, English, or Italian schools. The communal schools were the only ones teaching Jewish religion, whereas the private schools were either secular—such as the French lycées and some British institutions like the prestigious Victoria College—or Christian missionary schools of various denominations.[398]

The data I gathered indicated a comparatively high level of respondents with secular education. Seventy-six percent of the sample group, male and female, completed varying levels of secondary education by the time they left Egypt, whereas 18 percent had a tertiary education, leaving 6 percent with just primary education. The culmination of secondary studies consisted of either a diploma in business studies or accountancy, the French baccalauréat from the lycées, or an Oxford and Cambridge matriculation from the British schools. Tertiary education in Egypt was more problematic, although some of my respondents attended Egyptian Universities or foreign institutions, such as the British Institute, the French Law School, or the American University. The level of education of the whole group was, therefore, unusually high for that period, especially compared to the Muslim and Christian groups.

Research undertaken by Ethel Carasso on the Jewish community between 1947 and 1957 suggested a number of fundamental reasons for the privileged cultural position held by the Jews: their concentration in the two main cities of Egypt, which gave them a more immediate access to education; and the combined roles of the AIU schools and the Lycées de la Mission Laïque Française in spreading French culture, notwithstanding the role played by missionary French and English schools in the education of minorities in general. Extrapolating from the statistics provided in the *Statistical Handbook of Middle Eastern Countries* for 1937, showing that only 22.9 percent of the total Egyptian population was literate, the comparative percentage of literacy for the Jewish minority was 83.3 percent for men and 67.7 percent for women, an average of 75.4 percent for the total Jewish population. The Muslim population's literacy rate was 24.9 percent for men and 7.9 percent for women, which represented an average of 16.5 percent; for the Christian population, it was 48.6 percent for men and 29.8 percent for women, on average 39.3 percent.[399] This profile of high Jewish literacy, combined with a stress on education, is a feature of most diaspora communities, including Australian Jewry.[400]

Chart 6 illustrates the individuality and variety of the respondents' choices of schooling. However, the resulting statistics were sometimes misleading because a given respondent could have changed schools not only within the same strand—which was not unusual—but also changed systems from communal to private, or from religious to secular, or again from French to English. Therefore, the figures—55 percent in Christian schools contrasted against 22 percent in Jewish schools and 44 percent in secular schools—do not paint an altogether true picture. Similarly, the statistical results of 78 percent with French education compared to 36 percent with an English education and a mere 4.5 percent with Italian education—only at the primary level—were not mutually exclusive because the same student could have started in a French or Italian secular school and ended up in an English missionary institution.

A perfect example of that scenario was the case of one interviewee (#44) who switched from a secular communal Italian school, Scuole della Regina Elena, to the Presbyterian Scottish School for girls and subsequently to Alvernia, an English convent school.[401] Another notable case was Interviewee #84 who started in a Jewish school, Abraham B'tesh, then attended a French Catholic school, Saint Vincent de Paul, up to the equivalent of the School Certificate (Brevet Elémentaire), and was finally moved to the French secular lycée for her baccalauréat. In 1946 she was offered a scholarship for a Paris university but decided to sit for the matriculation examination at the British Institute in Cairo.[402] Although this case was indeed exceptional, it still illustrates the remarkable diversity of educational opportunities available in a country such as Egypt in the 1940s.

A separate analysis of the middle-class section of the sample group confirmed that 73 percent had a secondary education, predominantly French, 23 percent had a tertiary education, and 3 percent had a primary education only.[403] An analysis of the upper-middle-class standard

CHART 6. Types of schooling.

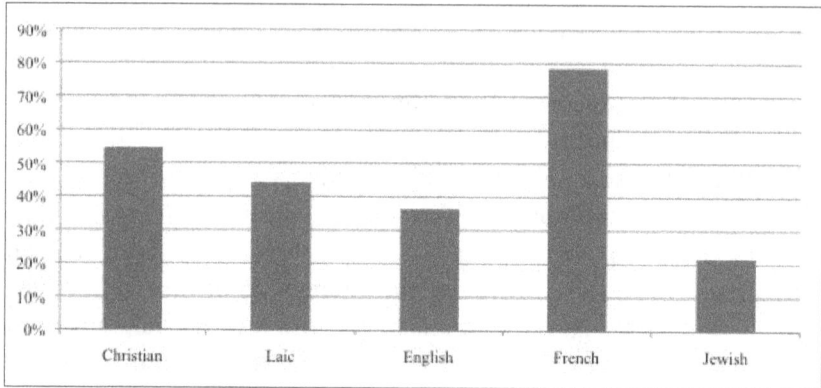

of education within the sample showed a similar trend: 78 percent with secondary education, 17 percent with higher education, and 6 percent with primary education only. Data on religious and secular education showed a preference for secular schools, which were attended by 56 percent of the sample, whereas 44 percent went to Christian schools, and only 17 percent went to Jewish schools. Furthermore, only 22 percent of my respondents attended English schools, compared to 72 percent educated in French schools. A separate examination of the female respondents' level of education revealed the highest percentage of secondary education, 85 percent, but only 9 percent with higher education—not surprising for those days—and 6 percent with only primary education. There were no other significant variations between men and women in the overall analysis of the field of education.

Although the data clearly demonstrated that the majority of the sample group had French education, there were many instances of parents switching their children from one system of education to another, as previously noted. Apart from the common desire of most parents to give their children the best education possible, the reasons ranged from peer pressure to issues of prestige, cultural preferences, or individual perceptions of better opportunities in one system than another. Interviewee #70 related that her mother removed her from an excellent Catholic school, Ecole des Soeurs de la Miséricorde, under pressure from a close relative who was president of the Jewish community school.[404] However, a Christian missionary school was sometimes the only private school offering a Western-style education if the respondent lived in a village or a small country town where there was no Alliance school.[405] The education offered in Christian schools was usually of an excellent standard. The only problem it presented for Jewish students was the missionary zeal of some of the teachers. In one particularly salient case, the interviewee (#73) recalled that the English Mission College would convert anyone who was slightly interested. In his case, the missionaries converted both his brother and him because they were orphans. At age 26, when he wanted to marry a Jewish girl, he had to convert back to Judaism. Interviewee #38, who attended the English Mission College for Girls, also remembered the pressure that was brought to bear upon Jewish pupils to convert. However, she added, "although our class was more than 50 percent Jewish, only one student converted in the ten years I was there".

The issue of conversion gradually became less problematic with the establishment of the secular Lycées de la Mission Laïque Française in Cairo and Alexandria and the UJE in Alexandria, as corroborated by Ziza Lester (#20):

> My brothers went to the Jesuits at Khoronfish. They had the best schools at the time. They tried to convert my brother David. My parents found out when my brother David tried to sneak a book of catechism under his bed. My parents took both of them out [of that school], and put the three of us in the Lycée. A lot of our friends followed suit.

In fact, all my respondents were the products of an English or French education, whether religious or secular, except for the two respondents who attended Egyptian state schools because they had no other choice.[406] This finding alone was indicative of the overall Westernisation of the sample group, a Westernisation that was considered the key to modernity, civilisation, and success by the majority of the Jews of

Egypt, as well as by other minorities. It is obvious that, together with their multilingualism, their relatively high level of Western education compared to other migrants of the same period proved to be an important asset in their acculturation process in Australia.

The data also showed that the questions of occupation, class, and level of education were closely related. A gender-based examination of the occupations of the sample group revealed that most of the men of working age were white-collar workers, either as owners/professionals (59 percent) or as employees (41 percent) engaged in small and large trading or retail businesses, ranging from bookkeepers, to office administrators, to salespersons.[407] In contrast, 75 percent of the women were occupied with home duties, with only 8 percent working in the family business and 17 percent employed as secretaries or receptionists. An overall analysis showed that 7 percent of the whole sample group were still students or had just finished high school at the time they left Egypt; 14 percent were in the liberal professions as engineers, pharmacists, lawyers, and teachers (both male and female); and a mere 3.4 percent—only four out of eighty-eight—had a trade. In the last category, two were women working respectively as a dressmaker and a manicurist.[408] Of the two men, one was a printer (#24) and the second an apprentice dental mechanic (#77). Two out of those four cases placed themselves in the lower-middle-class bracket.

Among the 14 percent of professionals who arrived in Australia with a tertiary education, not all were able to continue in their chosen profession. Two were fully-fledged lawyers who had studied law in Egyptian and French universities. Both were highly educated and cultured gentlemen. One had practised in Egypt, working at the Mixed Courts until they were abolished. He did not practise law in Australia because laws were different and he would have had to go back to university.[409] The other lawyer (#43) decided to branch out into business. The wife of the only doctor in the group stated that her husband's qualifications from an Egyptian university were not recognised in Australia, and he went back to England in order to requalify. There was one pharmacist (#5) who graduated from Kasr-Al-Aini University in Cairo, but he also had to requalify in Australia.[410] He ended up owning a very successful pharmacy where his clientele was mostly of migrant origin, and with whom he could communicate, thanks to his multilingual skills. The other professionals were mostly engaged in business administration, property development, and teaching at primary, secondary, and tertiary levels. Most of the interviewees who were students when they left Egypt proceeded to higher education once they arrived in Australia.

Analysis of the data on schooling, occupation, and class shows a definite correlation between those three elements. Furthermore, the statistics reveal that every one of the male participants within the sample group was educated, participated fully in the work force, and pursued different and respectable careers. As for the women, the fact that twenty-eight of them held jobs in one capacity or another was remarkable considering where they lived and the patriarchal society that sustained them.

MULTILINGUALISM

A predominant characteristic of the sample group was its language skills. First, all the participants spoke French at different levels of proficiency because French was the lingua franca of minorities in Egypt. They also spoke a variety of other languages more or less fluently. On average, they were proficient in 4.3 languages, mainly Arabic, French, English, Italian, and Greek. According to their respective ethnic backgrounds, they might also speak one or more languages, such as Ladino,[411] Spanish, Yiddish, Turkish, Corfiote[412], Hebrew, German, or even Russian.[413] A statistical analysis across the variables of language skills, birthplace, ethnic origin, and nationality only confirmed those figures, showing for instance that within the sample group the Egyptians spoke 4.3 languages, the foreigners 4.7, and the stateless 4.5 languages as demonstrated in charts 7, 8 and 9.

These results were not surprising, in view of the cosmopolitan nature of Egyptian society until the 1960s because most of the Jews and other minorities were exposed to a variety of languages and cultures. At home, they heard or spoke at least three languages, depending on the ethnic ori-gin of the family. For instance, one interviewee stated that her parents, originally from Smyrna, spoke either Ladino or French to the children, but they also knew Turkish, Greek, and Arabic. Another classic exam-ple was Interviewee #71 whose parents, ethnically Russian and Ruma-nian, spoke Yiddish and German at home but were also fluent in Italian, French, and English. Furthermore, in the various types of schools the Jews attended—whether they were private or communal, French or English, religious or secular—at least three languages were taught at all times, from a very young age. Beinin very aptly noted:

> Many Jews were multicultural and multilingual, but some social status was attached to speaking Arabic, Judeo-Spanish, Italian, Yiddish, or French at home. The cosmopolitan character of the Jewish community, especially its commercial middle and upper classes, is captured by the casual remark of a son of an upper middle-class Sephardi family holding Italian citizenship that emi-grated from Anatolia to Alexandria in the nineteenth century in

CHART 7. Number of languages spoken according to nationality.

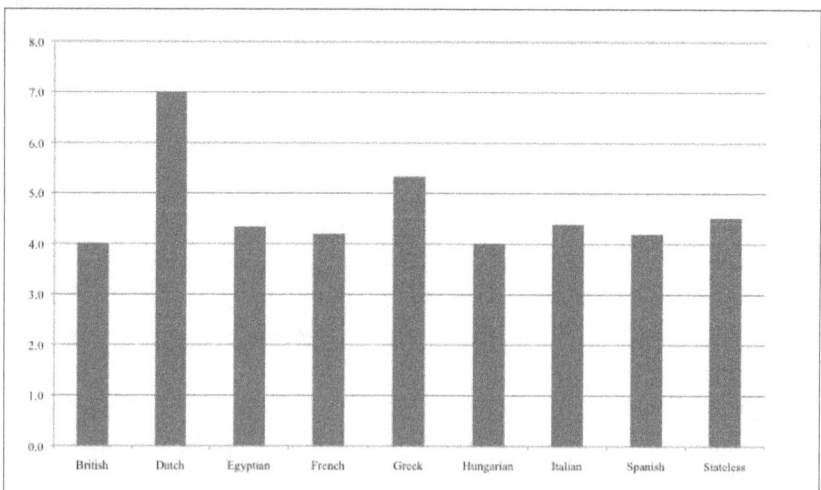

CHART 8. Number of languages spoken according to birthplace.

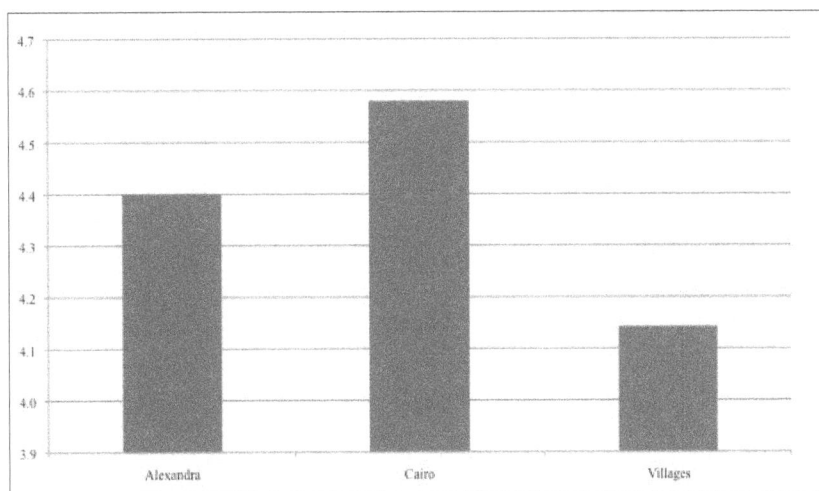

describing the ambience of his family: "We spoke French and English at school, Italian at home, Arabic in the street, and cursed in Turkish". Alexandrines were typically more cosmopolitan than Cairenes. However there were also thousands of indigenous, poor, Arabic-speaking Jews in Alexandria whose existence has generally been ignored because the cosmopolitanism and commercial elements of the community were so prominent. Even in Cairo...it was rare to find monolingual Jews.[414]

These linguistic skills proved to be an invaluable asset wherever Egyptian Jews eventually settled. A number of interviewees stressed the advantage it gave them in their job searches and in their contacts with other migrant groups. Thanks to their thorough knowledge of the French culture and language, some found jobs with local French institutions or created their own import-export companies in partnership with overseas French firms.[415] Others, mostly women, went into the teaching profession, specialising in French or Italian after gaining a Diploma of Education in Australia.[416] In the case of Interviewee #76, it was her sound

CHART 9. Number of languages spoken according to class.

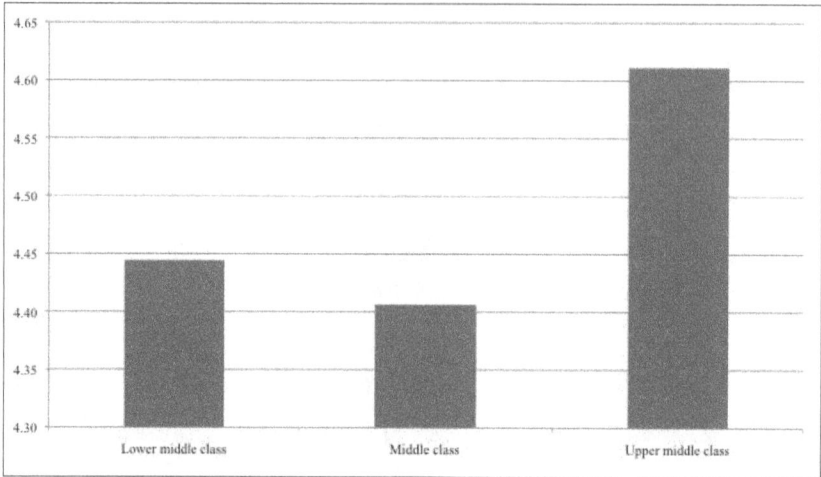

knowledge of Arabic, as well as French and English, that first propelled her into the field of education. She taught in a Sydney public school in the suburb of Lakemba, where there is a high Arabic-speaking student population. Another participant insisted that his elderly mother's knowledge of Italian and Greek helped her cope with the initial culture shock she experienced upon her arrival in Australia. She could at least communicate with the large number of postwar Greek and Italian migrants who settled in Australia in the 1950s and 1960s.

It is evident that a good command of the English language facilitates the smooth integration of any migrant group, and the Egyptian Jews were no exception. When they first landed in Australia, their panoply of languages did not always include English, except for a rudimentary acquired knowledge from their school years or from American movies. When questioned, the interviewees assessed their own English skills on their arrival in Australia as: poor (18 percent), fair (30 percent), or advanced (48 percent); a minuscule 3 percent had no skills at all. Data confirmed that the 38 percent of the sample group who had attended

English schools in Egypt accounted for the lion's share—85 percent—of the advanced speakers. Moreover, of the 62 percent who did not attend English schools, 27 percent described their initial English skills as poor, 42 percent as fair, 25 percent as advanced, and 5 percent as having no skills at all. However, these differences did not affect their professional lives as dramatically as one might have expected. The figures showed that 50 percent of the fluent English speakers immediately went into white-collar jobs compared to 41 percent of those self-rated with fair to low English skills, not a significant difference.

It is still fair to say that good English skills facilitated employment. None of the respondents with an English education had difficulty finding work immediately, whereas 9 percent of the second group did. The advanced English speakers dominated in both the professional and the business/white-collar fields, albeit by a small margin. Nevertheless, thanks to their innate gift for languages, the non-English speakers caught up relatively quickly. One can deduce that, for the Jews of Egypt, an English education was not the only key to successful integration. The French educational system had laid enough groundwork to enable them to apply their skills without major problems.

The fact that Egyptian Jews maintained the use of French in the Australian context raised a number of important questions. Who continued to use the mother tongue and why? Was it transmitted to the children as part of their cultural heritage, and what were their reactions? How did the dominant Anglo-Celtic population react to their use of a foreign language? In 1984, Suzanne Rutland interviewed some of the Egyptian and German Jews in Adelaide. On the issue of language, she quoted the words of Rabbi Jeffrey A. Kahn, then minister of the Temple Shalom, in Hackney, South Australia:

> [The Egyptian Jews]…continued to speak French among family and friends in Australia and at communal functions. Their love of the French language had not been diminished by events in Egypt. For most of the German Jews, on the other hand, the German language had unpleasant associations and so they chose to use

English rather than their mother tongue. Their children who grew up in Australia usually could not communicate in German. The fact that the Egyptian Jews continued to speak French disturbed many European Jews who had sacrificed the use of their native language.[417]

In fact, at the time I conducted my interviews thirteen respondents—14.6 percent—elected to proceed in French because they considered it their mother tongue, but not necessarily because of a low level of fluency in English. Only two cases out of those thirteen admitted they were not proficient enough in English.[418] The majority had no problem expressing themselves in English. They all held responsible white-collar jobs or successfully ran their own businesses. A case in point was Interviewee #54 who spoke Arabic, French, Italian, Ladino, and English fluently. However, her bond with the French language was so strong that she seized every opportunity to speak it. As argued by the French researcher Alain Lévy, who based his doctoral thesis on the history of a Jewish Egyptian family from 1899 to 1980, choosing to speak French in that context was the expression of a deliberate choice of civilisation:

> De fait, aujourd'hui, quarante ou quarante-cinq ans après avoir vu leurs itinéraires diverger et les conduire à des situations, modes de vie et lieux notablement différents les uns des autres, ils [les Juifs d'Égypte] communiquent spontanément et systématiquement en français lorsqu'ils se retrouvent. Ce n'est pas une simple commodité, puisque l'anglais, l'italien ou l'arabe conviendraient tout autant. C'est l'expression d'un choix de civilisation.[419]

I also found that wherever Egyptian Jews settled, and whenever they met other Egyptian Jews, they would automatically and spontaneously communicate in French. They seemed to make a conscious, or possibly even unconscious, effort not to lose their connection with the French language and culture, although not necessarily with France as a national entity. The result was often a constant switching from one language to the other, with some borrowing from Italian and Arabic in the process. In Australia, depending on their age on arrival, older participants would speak French to their children and grandchildren, who would answer them in a more-or-less hesitant French or, more often than not, in English. In the case of the younger respondents, the use of French with their children depended on whether their partner also came from Egypt. The attitude of the children towards the use of French by their parents has changed over the years. In the 1950s and 1960s they resented it because it made them feel different from their schoolmates. The advent of multiculturalism, and the promotion of foreign cultures and languages in the broader community—through the introduction of ethnic radio in 1975, with its foreign language broadcasting, and the creation of SBS, a multiethnic television station—rendered the knowledge and use of a foreign language not only more acceptable but even desirable.[420] In the course of my research, I found that when parents were French-speaking, their children not only spoke French but also demonstrated a propensity for at least one other foreign language acquisition. With even one French-speaking parent, most of those children still claimed a certain level of communication in that language, particularly with grandparents whose fluency in English was below average.

The information gathered throughout my interviews makes clear that the multicultural environment of 1950s Egypt—where a plethora of ethnic and religious traditions, languages, customs, and mentalities cohabited more or less in harmony—bred a cosmopolitan, multilingual, and multinational group of Jews. Their ability to connect with different cultures simultaneously, their linguistic abilities, and their standard of education stood out as fundamental traits of their identity, and were common across the boundaries of class, education, and ethnic origin. It served them well in their migration experience in Australia and elsewhere.

CHAPTER 5

JEWISH ETHNICITY, RELIGIOSITY, AND POLITICS

Egyptian Jewry, and by extension, the sample group under study, embodied a very diverse community, divided into subgroups along the lines of ethnicity, culture, education, and socioeconomic status. This diversity was also reflected in the religious domain where significant and jealously guarded differences in rituals, language, and customs existed among the Sephardim, the Ashkenazim, and the Karaites.

SEPHARDIM, ASHKENAZIM, AND KARAITES

The wide umbrella of *Sephardim*—literally meaning from Spain—used to include all the Jews from the Old Ottoman Empire, North Africa, Greece, and the Middle East. Obviously, they did not all share the same traditions and rituals, and their origin could not always be traced back to Spain. Some were indigenous to Egypt and other Arab countries—such as Iraq, Iran, Syria, Lebanon, and Yemen—for many generations.

These Jews are now catalogued as *Mizrahim* or Oriental Jews and are differentiated from the Sephardim. In Egypt, they were more likely to live in separate Jewish quarters called *haret-el-Yahud* or *hara*, and—as far as lifestyle, language, mode of dressing, and cuisine—were unrecognisable from their Muslim or Coptic neighbours. Then again, they were more religious than their Westernised and cosmopolitan brethren of the middle and upper classes. By the mid-twentieth century, the majority of Oriental Jews had gradually moved out of the *hara*, leaving behind their poorer co-religionists. The fact that none of the participants in the present research admitted to having ever lived in the *hara*—whether in Cairo or Alexandria, or even in a provincial town—was a clear indication of their standing in the socioeconomic ladder.

Italian Jews are also categorised as Sephardim seeing as a sizeable number of Spanish Jews settled in the various principalities of Italy after their expulsion from Spain in 1492. However, their Spanish origin is not always clear-cut. The ancient Jewish community of Rome, for instance, claims a presence in the city from the time Judea was a province of the Roman Empire. Jews first came to Rome as free settlers and, after the destruction of the Temple in Jerusalem in 70 CE, they were brought in as slaves and prisoners.[421] Interviewee #8, who claimed an old Italian origin, resented being "lumped in with the Sephardim", insisting that, given that there was no trace of a Judeo-Spanish tradition in his background, neither through language, food, or rites, his family could not be of true Sephardic origin. The ongoing use of Ladino (*judesmo*) at any level of competence by the descendants of the expelled Spanish Jews, five hundred years after the fact, is clearly seen as an identity marker in the debate about who is and who is not a true Sephardic Jew.[422]

As indicated earlier, the first Sephardic migration to Egypt dated back to the fifteenth century, at the time of the Christian *Reconquista* of Muslim Spain and after the Expulsion in 1492. However, the majority of Sephardim came to Egypt in the late nineteenth and early twentieth centuries, via different provinces of the Old Ottoman Empire, in search of a better and more secure future, as testified by several of my interviewees. The official records clearly showed that they were at the helm of the

Egyptian Jewish community. Ziza Lester (Interviewee #20) proudly recalled the origin of her family:

> My father's family came from Spanish Morocco in the late 1870s by ship, landed in Alexandria, and settled in Mehalla-el-Kobra, which is a township halfway between Cairo and Alexandria. I remember my father telling me that our family history went back to the times of the Inquisition. They spoke Ladino. My grandfather was president of the Jewish Community and my father was vice president.

By the twentieth century, the leaders of Egyptian Jewry were all Sephardim. The whole community was headed by the Sephardi chief rabbi of Egypt, regardless of origin or affiliation, and, except for the Ashkenazim and the Karaites, everybody followed the Sephardi rite with some local variations.[423] Jacques Hassoun, in *Histoire des Juifs du Nil*, poetically evoked the ancient Egyptian ritual as "des bribes du très vieux rituel égyptien".[424]

Sephardim constituted the majority of the Australian sample group, thus reflecting the overall Sephardic predominance within Egyptian Jewry. Nevertheless, the group included 22 percent Ashkenazim and 9 percent of mixed affiliation, plus one Karaite. The percentage of Ashkenazim was uncommonly high, given that they had never represented more than 8 percent of the total Jewish population of Egypt, even after the wave of immigration of eleven thousand Polish and Russian Jews expelled from Palestine by the Ottomans in December 1914.[425] According to Fargeon, there were only five thousand Ashkenazim living in Cairo in 1939.[426] Krämer added that they remained a minority of five or six thousand individuals in the interwar period, and most of them were based in Cairo, in the Ashkenazi quarter of Darb-el-Barabra.[427] The predominance of Cairo as a place of residence for Ashkenazim could be the reason why, out of a total number of twenty-six Ashkenazim in the Australian group, twenty were from Cairo and only six from Alexandria. It is also possible that a higher number of Ashkenazim were attracted to Australia because of its predominantly Ashkenazi Jewish community.

According to the comments from the majority of interviewees, the relations between the two communities seem to have been mostly harmonious, notwithstanding a certain feeling of superiority from the Sephardim, who considered themselves the aristocracy of Egyptian Jewry. A mixed marriage between an Ashkenazi and Sephardi couple was sometimes considered *une mésalliance* (marrying below one's status). As related by Interviewee #43, he was jokingly chastised when he announced his engagement to an Ashkenazi girl: "Why do you marry a *schlecht*?[428] Don't we have enough girls in our community?" However, he claimed he did not take these remarks to heart. For him they were the expression of a superficial sibling rivalry and were not rooted in deeply founded prejudice. My data confirmed that intermarriage between the two groups was not systematically discouraged, as noted by this Sephardi interviewee (#66):

> Two of my uncles married Ashkenazi girls and jokingly, probably not knowingly, we used to call them "*schlecht*". It is much later that I found out what it meant and I felt awful about it.

As for the interviewees of mixed affiliation, they also did not recollect any bad feelings between the two communities. Interviewee #22 expressed it pragmatically: "I am Ashkenazi and Sephardi. Was I aware of any tension between the two groups? No, but I was aware I was different; I spoke Yiddish at home". She recalled that she regularly attended the Ashkenazi synagogue of Cairo with her father and other Cairene respondents, whereas the Ashkenazim of Alexandria usually attended the same synagogues as the Sephardim.[429] As stated earlier, the fact that the Alexandrian Jewish community gathered the three ethnic groups under one single umbrella fostered a climate of greater unity. Supporting evidence of this aspect of communal interrelations came from a representative of the Zionist Executive in 1925:

> In Alexandria, conditions are different from Cairo…There too, you have the separation between Sephardi and Ashkenazi Jews… but relations are much better there and the differences have been significantly reduced under the influence of the seaport…Social

intercourse, too, is more highly developed; even intermarriage is
more frequent and does not have the diffamatory [sic] character
attached to it in Cairo.[430]

The third constituent of Egyptian Jewry was the Karaite population,
whose estimated size varied from thirty-five hundred to nine thousand,
depending on the source.[431] According to the Karaite Jews I have interviewed formally and informally, both in Australia and overseas, it seems
that most of them left Egypt between 1952 and 1957, the same as the
bulk of Egyptian Jewry. Beinin, whose research of that group was more
extensive, claimed that few Karaite Jews departed before the Suez War
because of their close identification with Arab-Egyptian culture and
stronger attachment to the land:

> A significant proportion of the Karaites remained in Egypt until
> the 1960s. Because most Karaites were thoroughly Arabized
> and defined themselves in terms rooted in their experience as
> an Ottoman millet, they tended to remain in Egypt longer than
> Rabbanites.[432]

Whereas Beinin found a well-established Karaite community of about
four hundred people in the San Francisco Bay area, Karaite Jews were
hard to trace in Australia.[433] Through the network of Egyptian and Turkish Jews in Sydney, I located only one Karaite couple and obtained a
very informative interview from the husband. He was married to his second cousin and knew of only another five or six Karaite families also
in Sydney, all related either directly or by marriage.[434] Although this
respondent articulated most of the issues relating to Karaite Jews, it is
obvious that I could not draw significant conclusions based on only one
interview. Therefore, I decided to group his testimony with the testimonies of the other two Karaites I formally interviewed in Paris and San
Francisco. These interviews, complemented by Beinin's findings, helped
to construct a more informed picture of the way Egyptian Karaites maintained their sense of identity while acculturating to Western societies,
whether in the United States, France, or Australia. They also provided

some degree of comparison with the findings related to the experience of Sephardim and Ashkenazim. Furthermore, I decided to use the
singularity of the Australian case study to evaluate what happens when
the reference group of a minority already has a minority status within the
broader reference group. Thus, similar to Russian dolls, Karaite Jews are
enclosed within four concentric social circles: the Rabbanite Jews from
Egypt, the Sephardic community, the Ashkenazi Australian community,
and finally the broader Australian society.

The first concern raised by my Karaite interviewee related specifically to
the minority aspect, obviously a very sensitive issue. As was the case with
the other Karaites I met overseas, he saw himself first as a Jew of the Karaite tradition. He resented a categorisation because it suggested separation
and alienation between the Karaite minority and the Rabbanite majority.
He claimed that in Israel the ancient conflict between the two groups has
been put aside and that the Jewishness of the Karaites was not questioned
anymore. Actually, in spite of some reluctance expressed by the Orthodox
rabbinate of Israel, the official stand of the State of Israel is to include and
accept the Karaite Jews as part of the broader Jewish family.[435]

However, this interviewee emphasised the fundamental difference
between the Karaites of the Middle East and the Karaites of Crimea and
Lithuania.[436] From the early nineteenth century, the latter claimed they
were not ethnically Jews, and their claim was accepted by Tsarist Russia.
They made the same claim to the Nazi authorities in January 1939 and,
after confirmation from the rabbinic authorities that they did not consider
Karaites to be Jews, the Nazis ruled accordingly:

> The Karaite sect should not be considered part of the Jewish reli-
> gious community...and the racial classification of the Karaites
> should be decided not according to their attachment to a specific
> people, but according to their personal genealogy.[437]

Although over two hundred Karaites were "mistakenly" massacred in
September 1941 at Babi Yar (Ukraine) by the *Einsatzgruppen*, this ruling saved most of them from death.[438]

As for the relationship between Karaites and Rabbanites in Egypt, the Australian Karaite interviewee claimed that it was mostly harmonious,[439] in spite of their differences on matters of rite and practice, such as the calendar, some aspects of dietary law, and the exclusion of certain festivals like Hanukkah.[440] It is also not customary for Karaites to have a *bar mitzvah* ceremony, and even less a *bat mitzvah*.[441] The American Karaite interviewee had a vague recollection of having some kind of coming-of-age celebration at the Karaite synagogue of Cairo, together with other boys of the same age, at the time of the festival of *Simhat Torah*.[442]

The Parisian Karaite interviewee, who had maintained a very strong sense of her Karaite identity, did not always agree with the assessment of her Sydney counterpart. Although she left Egypt at the age of sixteen after the Suez War, and later married an Ashkenazi Jew, she was very much aware of tension and even antagonism between the two communities. Even when I interviewed her in 1998, she still felt rejected by Rabbanite Jews: "Vous me demandez mon sentiment d'identité, d'appartenance. Je serai toujours la petite fille de mon grand père, juive karaïte en premier lieu, sauf pour les Juifs qui nous rejettent, les rabbanites".

Conversely, the Sydney interviewee did not feel estranged or excluded from the Rabbanite community, whether in Egypt or Australia, although he admitted to not being observant enough in his religious practice to be significantly affected one way or the other. In his view, Egyptian Karaites felt more alienated from the last Karaite Rabbi of Egypt, Tobia Bobovitch (1879–1956), who came from Crimea and hardly spoke Arabic, whereas the whole Karaite community was very fluent in that language.[443] In the Egyptian Jewish context of religious communalism of the 1940s and 1950s, the Karaite Jews were recognised as "a Jewish minority and lived as other minorities in the Middle East, endogamously and self-governing".[444] In spite of this *modus vivendi*, marrying Rabbanite Jews was often discouraged and even frowned upon. It was customary for Karaite Jews to marry within their community and often within the extended family, in order to maintain continuity of their particular traditions and cohesion in their midst.[445] Thus, most of the Karaite Jews I came into contact with, whether in Australia or overseas, were related in some way.

One point on which all three Karaite interviewees agreed was their close ties to the land of Egypt. "We were the oldest existing indigenous group in the Middle East…and long pre-date the Arab conquest of the region in the seventh century", proudly stated the American Karaite, whose relative, Mourad Farag Bey, helped draft the Egyptian constitution in the 1930s.[446] It is well known that Karaite Jews in Egypt were totally acculturated to the Arab-Egyptian culture, unlike the majority of Rabbanite Jews.[447] Although they remained fully Jewish on their own terms, their religious practices were strongly influenced by the Muslim tradition. For instance, Karaite Jews removed their shoes before entering a synagogue, like Muslims before entering a mosque. Instead of a *kippah* (traditional skullcap) as a head covering, Karaites wore the fez or *tarboush*, a traditional Turkish headdress adopted by Arabs. In addition, although the synagogue service was conducted in Hebrew, any additional blessing or special announcement was expressed in Arabic, the mother tongue of the Karaites. In the Sephardi or even Ashkenazi synagogues, a European language—in most cases French—was used to address the congregation.

In contrast to the Sephardic Rabbanites, Karaite Jews, like other Mizrahi Jews, often adopted Arabic patronymics. For instance, the Australian Karaite respondent explained that, back in 1840, his ancestors had "arabised" the family name—which used to be typically Jewish—in order to blend in better with Egyptian society. When asked the date of his family's arrival in the country, he hesitated, "maybe around 1,000, from Iraq or Persia", but he was adamant that they had been in Egypt for several generations. Both his grandparents used to wear the traditional Arab garb, whereas his father, who was a teacher in a government school, had adopted European attire, but still had to wear the fez, which was compulsory in government schools. Contrary to the growing trend among Jews in Egypt to educate their children in private French or British schools and to distance themselves from Arabic culture, he was sent to a *madrassa*, or Koranic school, for two years and then to an Egyptian public school in order to acquire a perfect knowledge of Arabic, given that Karaites considered it to be their national language.[448] It was also the language used within the family, as was the case for most Mizrahi Jews, although few would admit it today.[449] Consequently, and again contrary to the majority of respondents (65 percent), the Australian Karaite was and still is fluent in both the colloquial and literary strands of Arabic.[450]

The Karaite respondents all expressed a strong attachment and feelings of belonging to Egypt. Unlike half of their Sephardi and Ashkenazi compatriots within the sample group, they regarded themselves as Egyptians. The Australian Karaite evoked his university days at Cairo Fuad University:

> There were demonstrations all the time against the King and the British. I felt very nationalistic, very anti-British. I felt Egypt should be independent. I was politically active. I used to join the demonstrators, shouting the slogan "Down with the British", until the day they started to shout "No Jews after today", while passing near the Jewish *hara*. So I slipped out, disgusted.[451]

In fact, despite their strong allegiance to Egypt and Arab culture, Karaites still experienced problems being accepted as legitimate Egyptians. As explained by Beinin, they had not quite assimilated the "notions of citizenship and nationality recently introduced to Egypt".[452] When asked by the Egyptian state to prove their citizenship, they tried to comply but met with a lot of bureaucratic resistance, nearly as much as the Rabbanite Jews. As a perfect illustration of this covert discrimination, the Australian Karaite interviewee said that his family had to take the Egyptian government to court on that issue. In order to prove their eligibility, they produced a record found in the Cairo Citadel's archives relating to the arabisation of their name back in 1840, which attested to their presence in the country. The court ruling went in their favour and the state was ordered to grant citizenship to all the family members. This ruling paradoxically pointed to the independence of the judiciary within a system where the arbitrary often ruled.[453]

With the establishment of the State of Israel in May 1948 a rude awakening was in store for the Karaites, despite their closeness to Egypt and its culture. In June 1948, a bomb was exploded in the Karaite section of the Jewish quarter of Cairo, "killing twenty-two Jews and wounding forty-one".[454] The younger generation of Karaite Jews gradually came to realise that there was no future for them in Egypt. The Australian Karaite pointedly said: "I felt I would never be accepted as a 'real Egyptian', although in my heart I felt Egyptian". This realisation pushed him into joining the underground socialist Zionist youth movement, *Shomer ha'Tsa'ir*, with the intention of eventually migrating to Israel. In fact, when he decided to leave Egypt after the Suez War, he was stripped of his citizenship and issued a *laissez-passer*—a travelling permit, stamped with the dreaded Arabic words *rihla bi-dun raj'a,* literally meaning "one journey without return"—just like most of Egyptian Jewry.[455]

RELIGIOUS OBSERVANCE

When asked about their degree of religious observance, the majority of interviewees—68 percent—considered themselves traditional, which usually meant that their families attended synagogue services intermittently and kept the traditional rites of passage. They did not necessarily keep a *kosher* (Jewish dietary laws) home except during the festivals, as stated by Interviewee #66: "My mother was traditional. We kept kosher only at festivals but very strictly. A lot of Jews from Egypt only kept kosher at festivals". Interviewee #81 confirmed this practice: "My father was not a religious man but my mother was traditional. When came the High Holy Days, she would do what she had to do and got the kosher meat".

Then again, one-quarter of the interviewees stated that they practised minimal religious observance by celebrating only the three main Jewish festivals, Pessah, Rosh Hashana, and Yom Kippur. Only two out of the ninety-two people interviewed stated that their family was strictly Orthodox; that is, they kept a kosher home, observed the Sabbath, and attended synagogue every week. In view of the minute size of that subgroup, the only significant conclusion that could be drawn from these findings was that the Orthodox Egyptian Jews did not immigrate to Australia. This could be attributed to any number of reasons: their socioeconomic status, the geographical distance from *Eretz Israel* —the land of Israel— their lack of English skills, the absence of a family contact, or simply the unknown Jewish character of the place. Furthermore, given that the majority of those who came to Australia belonged to the more affluent and more cosmopolitan middle and upper-middle classes, it was to be expected that they would be less religiously observant than their counterparts in the lower strata because religious laxity in Egypt often went hand-in-hand with Westernisation.

My interviewees were also asked about their bar or bat mitzvah. All the male respondents answered in the affirmative to the question of bar mitzvah, which again was not surprising in the context of a traditional Jewish community.[456] What was unexpected was that seven of the female interviewees remembered having a bat mitzvah ceremony, although the majority insisted that it was never practised in Egypt, even unheard of. Actually, one can find in the memorial book *Juifs d'Égypte: Images et Textes*, a picture of such a ceremony, dating back to 1927, labelling it a religious initiation.[457] Interviewee #52 confirmed that not only did she have a bat mitzvah but so did her mother, who used to attend the Jewish communal school where this practice was apparently encouraged from the early 1920s. It seems to have been an Italian-influenced innovation introduced by the Chief Rabbi of Alexandria at the time, Rabbi Raphael della Pergola (1910–1923).[458] It was a collective ceremony held at Alexandria's main synagogue, when the girls recited the Ten Commandments, the Thirteen Articles of Faith, and the *Shema*.[459] Interviewee #66 recalled having her bat mitzvah in the early 1950s:

> We were eighteen girls. We sang all together and it was the most magnificent experience. We were all dressed in a long white gown in piqué, with a short veil, walking into the synagogue Eliahu Hanavi. After the ceremony, a lunch was served at the back of the synagogue for the poorer members of the community, which we shared with them.[460]

The ceremony did not have the pageantry and glamour of today's *bat mitzvah* ceremonies. The focus was more on sharing that special day with others girls less fortunate. All the girls had to wear exactly the same style of dress, modest and simple, in order not to embarrass those who could not afford a more expensive outfit.

The percentage of women who did have a bat mitzvah ceremony stood at 14.5 percent out of a total of forty-eight, which is not negligible for those days. In addition, the fact that this relatively new custom was practised as early as 1927, so soon after the first American *bat mitzvah,* is a further indication that the Egyptian Jewish community, although fundamentally traditional and patriarchal, was not closed to progressive trends within Judaism.

In order to further assess the level of Jewish affiliation of the Egyptian community, it was essential to examine the crucial issue of intermarriage. One-third of my interviewees stated that there was intermarriage in their immediate or extended family, but only six respondents were actually married to non-Jewish partners, which represents a mere 6.5 percent of the total sample. They were all women, whose family religious observance ranged from orthodox to minimal. Only three remained in a Jewish framework in Australia, due to the proximity of parents and siblings. All except one had intermarried a number of years before emigration, but the span of the marriage did not fit into any obvious pattern, given that the ages varied greatly from case to case. Therefore, no significant conclusion could be drawn on the issue of intermarriage being more prevalent in one particular age group within my sample. In only one case was there strong opposition and subsequent ostracism by the father, who was strictly Orthodox.[461] In the remainder of cases, no major family conflict was reported over the choice of a non-Jewish spouse, apart from the initial outcry. On the contrary, three of those cases declared that their respective spouses were greatly respected by the rest of the family.[462]

Based on those findings, it seems that before immigration, marriage within the faith was usually the norm; intermarriage remained a rare occurrence and was, in principle, considered unacceptable. In most cases, if it happened families eventually accepted it, albeit reluctantly. According to Egyptian censuses, mixed marriages constituted only 5 to 6 percent of all marriages contracted by Jews annually, which shows that the marital status of my sample group was a true representation of the general trend.[463]

This somewhat lenient attitude towards intermarriage was consistent with the rather low level of ultra-orthodox religious observance within the sample group. As one would expect, most respondents indicated that their parents or grandparents had been more observant than they were. Interviewee #5, who spent his childhood in the 1920s in a remote village of Upper Egypt, remembered that his father, in spite of the distance and logistic difficulties, made sure that all the Jews of the area celebrated the Jewish festivals according to tradition:

> At *Rosh Hashana* and *Yom Kippur*, my father used to go to Cairo to get all the kosher products. He used to hire a rabbi and convert one of his properties into a synagogue. The rabbi would bring a *Sefer Torah* and we would have services. The Jewish families would come from all around, from Minieh [a neighbouring village] so that we would have a *minyan*.

Another determining element in the level of religiosity of the respondents was the age factor. Out of the 68 percent who declared themselves traditional Jews, 74 percent were born before 1923, whereas 62 percent of those with minimal to nil observance were born after 1923. The older they were, the more likely they were to be more observant, and vice versa. Clearly, modernity, Westernisation through education, and upper class mobility brought a growing laxity in religious practices.

The picture that emerged from those statistics was one of a community very much aware of its Jewish identity, still close to its traditions—although not adhering to them as strictly as its elders—and surprisingly open to the outside world, in both the Jewish and non-Jewish domains. Although these findings cannot be assumed to reflect the religious character of Egyptian Jewry as a whole, especially in view of its innate diversity, they still reflected the trend demonstrated by broader studies. Krämer commented on the lack of deep religiosity of Jews in Egypt, although "they were traditional enough to reject the secular".[464] Jacques Hassoun confirmed that ultra-orthodoxy was mostly found in the Jewish *hara,* among the economically disadvantaged members of the community, whereas he described the privileged group paradoxically as *dévots, vibrants et frivoles* (pious, vibrant, and frivolous).[465]

ZIONISM, COMMUNISM, AND EGYPTIAN NATIONALISM

How did the participants of this study respond to the three modern "isms" that were so fiercely debated at the time: Zionism, Communism, and nationalism? Did their response reflect the traditional detachment of Egyptian Jews from politics, or did it reveal a definite level of involvement in one of those ideologies?[466]

As previously discussed, involvement in Zionism was always a sensitive issue for the Jews in Egypt. The questionnaire presented to my respondents listed three categories of participation:

- "high" for people who played a significant role in Zionist youth movements before and after 1948;
- "marginal" for those who were sympathetic to the Zionist cause but whose activism was limited to attending a few meetings and fundraising; and
- "nil" for those who had no involvement whatsoever.

Historical sources show that the Egyptian Jewish establishment's response to Zionism was not altogether positive. Apart from the B'nai B'rith leaders, who ardently supported it, most of the influential leadership of Egyptian Jewry remained opposed to any open manifestation of Zionist aspirations by the community in order not to stir up anti-Jewish feelings or be accused of dual loyalty. Egypt's delegate to the nineteenth Zionist congress in Lucerne in 1935 had already articulated this particular concern:

> The Sephardim of the Mediterranean basin and elsewhere did not dare to advertise their attachment to the Yishuv openly. They had to conceal their enthusiasm in order not to create an atmosphere of doubt and suspicion before the Muslims about their loyalties and patriotic sentiments.[467]

The leader of Sephardi Jewry in Palestine, Avraham Elmaleh, who visited Cairo frequently on fact-finding missions, reported in 1939 that "even when the affluent Jews made contributions to these funds [JNF and Palestine Foundation Fund], they refused to accept receipts so that no record of donations to Zionist causes would be entered into their accounting books".[468]

This ambivalent attitude towards political Zionism was discernible in the testimonies of most Australian interviewees, such as the following comment by Interviewee #55:

> You're asking about my feelings towards Israel back in Egypt around the time of the creation of the state in 1948. We were not very involved although we were very happy about it. We could not show our true feelings because of our environment.

In some cases the response was totally negative. Interviewee #8 recalled that his father believed so strongly in the future of Egyptian Jewry that he strictly forbade his son to be associated with any Zionist entity.[469] Nevertheless, as previously discussed, Zionist youth movements established by emissaries from Palestine attracted middle-class Jewish youth, particularly from the Jewish schools in Alexandria where, according to Beinin, "socialist Zionism was hegemonic":

> The largest and most active of these movements was ha-'Ivri ha-Tza'ir (The young Hebrew), the Egyptian branch of ha-Shomer ha-Tza'ir (The young guard) that sought, usually unsuccessfully, to blend Zionism and internationalism...A second Marxist Zionist youth movement formed in 1949–50: Dror—he-Halutz ha-Tza'ir (Freedom—the young pioneer)...established a strong base at the Lycée de l'Union Juive pour l'Enseignement of Alexandria, where, according to one graduate, the dominant ideology was Marxism-Leninism. Students learned dialectical and historical materialism in geography class from Alexandre Roche.[470]

These observations were confirmed by a number of respondents, both in Australia and in France, who attended the same Jewish school. One Sydney-based interviewee (#8) remembered quite vividly that particular young and charismatic teacher "who constantly digressed from his geography lesson to preach the merits of Communism".[471] Although the collected data revealed that indeed half of the Zionist activists were a product of Jewish schools, that data also showed that of the 38 percent of interviewees who attended English schools at some stage, 58 percent called themselves Zionists. For instance, Interviewee #62, who went to a prestigious British school in Alexandria, joined a Zionist youth movement as early as 1945. The Zionist emissaries were preparing the group for life on a kibbutz. Eventually, he was smuggled into British-mandated Palestine in 1946, at the age of nineteen, with another fifty-six youngsters:[472]

> It was a few days before Pesach. We were given the uniforms of Jewish soldiers who were stationed in Alexandria. They were British soldiers. We took their paybooks, we had to memorise their numbers, and once we arrived in Israel [Palestine] we already had identity cards waiting for us and the uniforms and papers were sent back to Egypt. We crossed the desert by train…We arrived at the kibbutz Deganya Bet the first night of the Seder. There were 350 people around the table. I will never forget that night.

In actual fact, his story was part of a well-documented operation in April 1946, called Operation Passover, which was organised by the Hagana with the help of local Zionist emissaries as a series of initiatives to smuggle youth out of Egypt wearing British army uniforms.

The Australian sample included the whole gamut of Zionist involvement. Out of ninety-two participants, only 15 percent acknowledged being Zionists and having an active involvement in the Zionist movement; less than one-third (31 percent) registered a limited involvement; more than one-half (55 percent) never participated in any Zionist activities; and one interviewee claimed to be anti-Zionist. In view of the official stand of the Egyptian/Jewish establishment towards Zionism, it is not surprising that interviewees between eighteen and twenty-eight years of age were the most represented in the active Zionist category, as opposed to those over the age of twenty-eight, who were the least represented in that category.

As for Egyptian nationalism, it has already been demonstrated that the vast majority of Jews in Egypt showed little interest in the local political scene. Under King Fuad I (1917–1936)[473], a small number of prominent Egyptian Jews who had direct entry into the Royal court were active participants in the nation-building process, either as members of government, such as Senator Cattaoui (1861–1942)[474], or as strong advocates of Egyptian nationalism, such as the man known as Abu-Naddara (1839–1912).[475] By the late 1940s, this was no longer the case; there was no Jewish representation in government circles. Jewish political activism on behalf of an independent Egyptian state was rare in the context of a rising Islamic and pan-Arab nationalism. Actually, this trend was one of the dominant features of the Australian participants, who all claimed they had no involvement in Egyptian political life, with two interesting exceptions.

The first case was the Australian Karaite interviewee. He stated that during his days at university in Cairo he had identified strongly with a left-oriented Egyptian nationalism. Together with fellow students, he participated in several anti-British and anti-government demonstrations, where patriotic slogans such as "Egypt for the Egyptians" were shouted. As mentioned earlier, he only withdrew when these demonstrations turned anti-Jewish.

The second exception was a woman who was involved with the Egyptian Communist movement from a young age. According to Beinin, the ideology that attracted Egyptian Jewish youth more than Zionism was Communism:

> One thousand or more Jews participated in the Egyptian Communist movement from the 1930s to the 1950s. Thousands more were sympathetic to Marxist ideas in one form or another... Excluded by definition from both Islamic currents like the Muslim Brothers or the quasi-Fascist Young Egypt, Jewish youth searching for political expression in the 1930s and 1940s (a minority of the community, to be sure), turned towards Marxism or Zionism or, as in the case of ha-Shomer ha-Tza'ir, a combination of the two.[476]

The political activism of that particular interviewee (#54) went totally against the trend of the Australian sample. She perceived her activism as part of her Jewish existential condition: *"j'étais activiste de par ma condition d'être juive d'abord"*. At the age of fifteen, following in her brother's footsteps, she joined the underground Egyptian Communist Party. She rejected political Zionism as a solution for all Jews.[477] She professed the popular notion circulated among a section of Egyptian Jewry that the State of Israel was a much-needed and deserved safe haven for the Jews of Europe who had endured unspeakable racist persecution throughout the centuries. It did not apply to the Jews living in the safe and tolerant Egyptian environment, where she personally never felt threatened until the establishment of the State of Israel in 1948. Egypt was her home; she did not feel a foreigner and said it pointedly: *"je ne me sentais pas étrangère"*. She felt a deep attachment to the people and empathised with the plight of the ordinary downtrodden Egyptians, especially the women. Particularly gifted in languages, in addition to French and English, she spoke Ladino with her parents, who were originally from Smyrna (Izmir), and Portuguese. She was also fluent in Arabic, both written and oral, which was rare for a woman of her generation. In the French lycée where she was enrolled, Arabic was taught as a third language for a few meagre hours a week. Her political activism was not confined to the Egyptian scene. She relentlessly continued her fight against social inequality when she migrated to Australia, always on the left of the political spectrum, organising migrant women support groups, informing them of their rights, and working with the Ethnic Communities Council. She died of cancer in 2001.

Notwithstanding these two exceptional cases, the bulk of the Australian respondents declared they were apolitical in Egypt, in terms of Zionism, Egyptian nationalism, and Communism. The same applied to their new country, at least on the federal level of politics. In Egypt, their focus was directed more towards their jobs, financial needs, and Jewish communal and family life. In Australia, they also seem to have been more concerned with rebuilding their lives economically, professionally, and socially, as well as quietly consolidating their integration and acculturation within both the Jewish and broader communities, without disturbing the status quo.

FEELINGS OF BELONGING

Before assessing the level of Egyptian Jews' integration into Australian society, it was important to analyse the depth of their feelings of belonging in the Old Country. In view of the fact that the issue was more about perception than about objective evidence, I raised the following questions with the participants: Did they feel Egypt was their home? Did they feel included in the national project? How did they react when confronted with the adverse political reality of Egypt in the late 1940s? A statistical analysis of their responses showed that over half the sample (53 percent) voiced strong feelings of belonging in Egypt, at least until the seminal events of 1948. Egypt was their home and, for most of them, as one interviewee so aptly put it, it was the only one they knew. The rest of the group was equally divided between those who qualified their sense of belonging as moderate (23 percent) and those denying it outright (24 percent). The question was: Why did the last two subgroups feel such an alienation from a land where they had been living for at least two generations in apparent comfort and freedom?

On one hand, the controversial issues of foreign citizenship and Zionist activism did not impact significantly on those feelings one way or the other. In fact, 57 percent of the respondents across the board expressed a strong attachment to their country of birth before 1948, regardless of whether they were foreign nationals, Egyptians, or stateless.[478] These findings seem to validate the claim that, for the Jews of Egypt, the adoption of a foreign nationality was more often one of convenience than of conviction. As for the Zionist activists or sympathisers, my research surprisingly revealed that they were just as likely to have strong feelings of belonging in Egypt as those with a minimal Zionist involvement (59 percent compared to 51 percent). These results also tend to validate Krämer's contention that "at least until the late 1930s, even local Zionists supported the national aspirations of the Egyptian people. It was by no means rare to find Egyptian Jews who, like Léon Castro, sympathised and collaborated with both the Egyptian and the Jewish nationalist movements".[479]

Because the criterion of citizenship or political activism did not appear to determine the degree of closeness to Egypt, I looked at the issue of age to check if there was a direct correlation between those two factors. For that purpose, the group was divided into three age categories: over twenty-eight, under eighteen, and those in between the two. The resulting statistics confirmed that a majority (63 percent) of the older constituents admitted to a strong sense of belonging when they lived in Egypt, whereas the younger ones were equally divided between those who declared themselves to be moderately attached and those totally unconnected to their birthplace. It was to be expected that the respondents who left the country before the age of twenty-eight would be more estranged from their Egyptian roots than their parents and older compatriots. One of those interviewees (#8) admitted that, whereas he grew up considering himself part of a tolerated minority, his father, an Italian national whose family had settled in Egypt three generations earlier, believed until 1955 that Egypt, not Italy, was his home. These contrasting attitudes were the result of a growing perception among younger Egyptian Jews that there was no place for them in the emerging political conjuncture. They were also the manifestation of a new world vision implanted in the minds of young Jews by Western schools. The appropriation of a Western cultural identity was often at the expense of an Egyptian cultural identity.

COMPETENCE IN THE NATIONAL LANGUAGE

This trend was again apparent when I compared the respondents' level of fluency in the Arabic language with the respondents' respective age groups. The figures showed that out of the ninety-two interviewees, the majority (65 percent) rated their fluency as poor to fair, compared to only one-third (34 percent) rating it as good to excellent. With the exception of two cases, the speakers with excellent Arabic skills were all over the age of twenty-eight at the time of their departure from Egypt, whereas three-quarters of the speakers with poor skills were under that age. Conversely, those with a higher level of fluency in the Arabic language were more likely to feel a strong attachment to Egypt than those at the lower end of the scale (67 percent compared to 33 percent).

Generally speaking, the older members of most migrant groups start their new lives with a poor command of the national language of the adopted country, whereas the younger generation acquires a better linguistic fluency with ease and speed, gradually becoming unidentifiable from the dominant national group. In the case of Egyptian Jewry, particularly the Mizrahi Jews, the opposite was the norm. The parents were better Arabic speakers than their children, who were again better speakers than their own children.[480] When they finally abandoned the use of Arabic as their home language for the more prestigious foreign languages, they also tried to shed their Oriental/Middle Eastern identity and mentality, often equated with a lack of sophistication. Except for the Australian Karaite who was under the age of twenty-eight when he left Egypt, only one interviewee—who died in 2009 at the age of one hundred—admitted to speaking exclusively Arabic at home with her parents.[481] Another fourteen respondents (15.5 percent) said that an adequate level of Arabic was spoken at home as well as one or two European languages. The rest of the group stated that they only spoke a "kitchen" Arabic with servants and shopkeepers.

Interestingly, the statistical study showed that of the 35 percent of respondents who admitted possessing good to excellent Arabic skills, 55 percent were of lower-middle class. On the other hand, of the 32 percent with fair skills, only 11 percent situated themselves in the lower social echelon. It seems that, at least for the younger generation of respondents, the declining status of Arabic was directly linked to flagging competence in the language, which was in turn related to age and position on the social ladder. Conversely, competence in European languages was identified with high culture and social standing and was a determining factor in the perception of self. Krämer confirmed that this phenomenon was already in motion during the interwar period:

> Arabic, by contrast [to French], was increasingly losing ground, and…was relegated to a low rank as the language spoken by the poor inhabitants of the Cairo *hara,* the provincial towns and the Karaites…Most local Jews knew just enough colloquial Egyptian Arabic to be able to deal with shopkeepers, waiters, domestic servants and the man in the street; a minority had a sufficient command of Modern Standard Arabic to be able to read and write it.[482]

Did the Jews of Egypt gradually exclude themselves, or were they excluded from the national process? Were they actors, victims, or maybe both? Could the Egyptian leaders of the time have done more to embrace their non-Muslim minorities through education, as Turkey's Atatürk did for his minorities?

During the lifetime of the Ottoman Empire, the language issue was very similar in both Egypt and Turkey. The same multicultural ambiance prevailed; minorities, such as Greeks, Italians, Armenians, and Sephardi Jews, continued to use their own languages in the public and private domains. As was the case for Arabic in Egypt, "knowledge of Turkish was not considered to be a necessary condition for interaction in everyday life…In the case of the Jews, the educated elite spoke French as well as Judeo-Spanish because of the French influence the Alliance [*AIU*] had on the community", stated Mary Altabev, who extensively researched the status of Judeo-Spanish in the Turkish social context.[483] It was the mirror image of the situation in Egypt, where French was "the lingua franca of the local foreign minorities and the Turko-Egyptian elite".[484] Only after the collapse of the Ottoman Empire—and the establishment of the new Turkish Republic in 1923 by Mustafa Kemal Atatürk (1881–1938)—did extensive socio-political reforms overturn the status quo regarding education and language policies. The historians Esther Benbassa and Aron Rodrigue, who have written comprehensively on the Sephardi diaspora in the Levant, studied the process of Turkicisation of Turkish Jewry.[485] With the view of constructing a new secular national identity,

Atatürk embarked on a modernisation and secularisation program of the education system. In November 1928, he mandated that Turkish be written using the Roman script instead of the traditional Arabic script and, at the same time, he instituted compulsory Turkish primary education for all Turkish citizens, regardless of religion or ethnicity. Benbassa and Rodrigue confirmed that "the use of Judeo-Spanish was also viewed unfavorably and a number of organizations were founded to encourage Jews to speak Turkish".[486] The proclaimed message of these sweeping reforms was one of inclusiveness for all ethnic groups in building the new nation, through the medium of a unifying national language. From what I have observed in my informal meetings with Turkish Jews now living in Australia, the process of Turkicisation was a success as far as fluency in the national language and sense of self are concerned, although some reservations were expressed by Altabev:

> I argue that the Turkish Jewish identity is marginal because they [Turkish Jews] feel that they are not considered as part of the national majority mainly because of their different religion (cf. Lewis, 1961; Akçam, 1995; Bora, 1995).[487]

In Egypt, a similar program of Egyptianisation was started after the Montreux Convention of 1937, with the abolition of the Mixed Courts and the phasing out of special privileges for foreign nationals. In an effort to raise the status of Arabic fluency, while at the same time alleviating the growing problem of unemployment, the Egyptian government targeted the workplace by making "Arabic obligatory in all business dealings", thus forcing "shop owners and businessmen unable to read and write Arabic...to take on additional Egyptian personnel".[488] The government also targeted education, although not as ambitiously as the Turkish example, by introducing compulsory Arabic tuition in the curriculum of prestigious private schools, which were patronised by the Egyptian elite and the middle and upper classes of non-Muslim minorities.[489] Implementation of these reforms was not felt in earnest in those schools before the early 1950s, when government regulations demanded that students who failed their Arabic examinations not be allowed to proceed to the next class, regardless of their achievements in other subjects. For the majority of my younger respondents—who rightly or wrongly considered themselves European—these changes were not met with great enthusiasm, although Arabic tuition was still limited to a few hours a week and was effectively relegated to second or third rank behind French and English studies. However, the Egyptian education system was under the scrutiny of leading Egyptian intellectuals and scholars, such as Taha Husain (1889–1973), who was very critical of the didactic method used to teach Arabic, which "exaggerates its difficulties even further, making it into an esoteric language that repels the students".[490] Therefore, it is not surprising that only a small percentage of my sample group possessed excellent Arabic skills. Had the teaching methods undergone fundamental reform, could they have reversed the trend as far as non-Muslim minorities were concerned? The answer to that question remains in the domain of the hypothetical.

At the end of the day, the reasons for the failure of the Arabisation or re-Arabisation of the Jewish community of Egypt—as compared to the Turkish Jewish community—were deeply rooted in cultural, social, and political conditions. The combination of: (1) Egyptian Jewry's adoption of Western culture and world view; (2) its growing uncertainty of ever being accepted as "real Egyptians"; and (3) the looming Palestinian conflict made it a "mission impossible." The government's efforts towards Egyptianisation were not truly embraced by all ethnic and religious groups. The Jews, for one, do not appear to have embraced it, in spite of the initial support of Egyptianisation by prominent leaders of the Jewish community, such as the Chief Rabbi Haim Nahum and Joseph Aslan Cattaoui.[491] According to Krämer—and I tend to agree with her—Egyptianisation of all non-Muslim minorities, except for the Copts to some degree[492], was already doomed in the 1940s:

> Even if the Jews had all become Egyptian patriots, learned Arabic, and applied for Egyptian nationality, it would still not have changed the basic fact that they overwhelmingly were not of Egyptian origin, not "real Egyptians", and not Muslim.[493]

After 1948, any question about inclusion or exclusion, nationalism or Zionism, activism or apathy proved irrelevant. All the participants in this study—whether they felt they belonged in Egypt or felt unwelcome, whether they remained close to the Egyptian culture or distanced themselves from it—agreed that everything changed for the worse after the outbreak of hostilities with Israel in 1948, and particularly after the Suez War in 1956, when they were all implicated as fifth columnists. Interviewee #20, one of the earliest ones to have acquired Egyptian nationality, expressed her growing feelings of alienation:

> After 1948, the climate started to change in Egypt...We found ourselves stateless from one day to the next. I started to feel I did not belong and we were not welcome. Around 1949, the government sequestrated everything we owned, and that is when we discovered we were blacklisted because my father had properties and money. We were kicked out of our apartment. We then became determined to get out of Egypt.

Even though over half of the respondents initially considered themselves an integral part of Egypt, this study demonstrated the fragility of that bond when confronted with adverse political and economical conditions. The demise of the liberal and inclusive style of Egyptian nationalism and the rise of an exclusive, pan-Arab, anti-foreigner nationalism, further fuelled by the creation of the new State of Israel and the plight of the Palestinians, shattered what proved to be an illusion of inclusiveness. It caused the Jews to flee or be forced out of their country of birth, which, since the early nineteenth century, had been remarkably welcoming and tolerant towards its minorities.

CHAPTER 6

FORCED EMIGRATION

THE THREE "TRIGGER EVENTS"

As a general rule, the Jews left Egypt in three successive waves, after each of the first three Arab-Israeli Wars. I have labelled these wars the "trigger events". The 1948 Arab-Israeli War triggered the first wave, forced or otherwise. In fact, the Jewish Agency records showed that twenty thousand Jews, a sizeable 25 percent of the total Jewish population of about seventy-five to eighty-five thousand[494], left between 1948 and 1950, of which 14,299 settled in Israel.[495] The second and major wave left in the wake of the second trigger event, the 1956 Suez War, when, in the space of just four months between November 1956 and March 1957, another 14,102—23 percent—Jews departed. The emigration of another seventeen to nineteen thousand continued steadily until the outbreak of the 1967 Six-Day War, leaving only between twenty-five hundred and seven thousand Jews in Egypt.[496] The third Arab-Israeli War brought about the nearly total demise of Egyptian Jewry.

The measures taken by the Egyptian government against its Jewish minority after each of those three seminal events included arbitrary detention, expulsion, denaturalisation, and economic strangulation through sequestration of assets or workplace discrimination. Given that all the respondents of my sample stated they were affected by at least one of these measures, I tried to determine who was forced to leave, who left "voluntarily", and under what circumstances they left. Although one-third (34 percent) stated they were given no choice but to leave the country, an equal percentage declared they feared the hostile environment, and about one-quarter (28 percent) stated they could see no future for Jews in Egypt. From these findings, one could deduce that, although the last two subgroups did not experience the same degree of persecution suffered by the first group, they still left Egypt under some form of duress that permeated from the prevailing climate of anti-Jewishness, fear, and uncertainty.[497]

THE 1948 ARAB-ISRAELI WAR

The relation between the trigger events and their time of departure was clearly reflected in the testimonies of my interviewees. In fact, the overall data collected through the interviews indicated that out of ninety-two respondents in Australia, twenty-four left between 1946 and 1951, eleven between 1952 and 1956, and fifty-seven after 1956, whereas only one left after 1967. These numbers roughly reflected the trend for the overall Jewish population and undoubtedly demonstrated that the Suez War was the catalyst for the departure of the bulk of my respondents. Nonetheless, those who left earlier—both after the 1948 Arab-Israeli War and the Cairo fire of 1952—represented a far from negligible segment (38 percent), further proof that the Jews of Egypt were already experiencing destabilisation and discrimination before the events of 1956.[498]

There were some variations in the emigration patterns of the Sephardim and the Ashkenazim within that timeframe. My findings seem to echo those of Beinin about Sephardim emigrating later than Ashkenazim.[499] The reason suggested by Beinin was that Ashkenazim had shallower roots than the Sephardim because of a more recent migration to Egypt and difference in culture and mentality. The analysis of my data did show a vast gap between the two ethnic groups in relation to their attachment to their country of birth and also revealed that a larger proportion of Ashkenazi participants emigrated before 1952, whereas the opposite was true for the Sephardi participants.[500]

In the wake of the first Arab-Israeli War, the authorities officially targeted all Zionist activists and sympathisers, even though Zionist youth groups had been tolerated up to 1948 and operated semi-legally in Egypt. They also targeted anybody suspected of being a Communist or being associated with a Communist. Seeing as the authorities had imposed martial law throughout the country, the criteria for these arrests were broad. Anyone deemed "prejudicial to the safety and security of the state" was a potential target.[501] There were three such cases among my sample group. The experience related by Interviewee #46 was particularly significant because it demonstrated the arbitrary nature of those arrests. He was a student at the Faruk University, in his last year of engineering, and was never involved in Zionist or Communist activities. In April 1948, members of the Muslim Brothers Society tried to stop him from entering the grounds of the university on the pretext that "they did not want Egypt to help the enemies of Islam". When he tried to force his way in, they physically assaulted him. The dean of the faculty, who did not want any problem with the powerful Muslim Brotherhood, worked out a compromise where the Jewish student collected his lecture notes from friends without attending classes personally. This arrangement was short-lived. On 15 May 1948, the day Egypt and the other Arab states declared war on Israel, the authorities formally arrested him. He related the precise circumstances:

> The guy from the secret police was there and he said: "The Egyptians on one side and the foreigners on the other side". I went towards the Egyptian side because that is what I thought I was. He said: "You are not an Egyptian, you are a foreigner, you are a Jew". Until then, I had never been impressed by the arguments of the Zionists. This is when I realised that it was not going to help to try and integrate in Egypt because they were never going to accept us. That was the turning point for me. I started to study Zionism and Hebrew while I was in prison.[502]

He was subsequently interned for fifteen months with other Jewish students in the Abukir camp, twenty kilometres from Alexandria.[503] Although their treatment at the hands of Egyptian authorities was fair, it was still a traumatic experience for these young people, who were never officially accused of any wrongdoings or put on trial.[504] The only way to be released was to agree to leave Egypt immediately and forever.[505] Paradoxically, during his time in prison this particular respondent, together with other students in the same predicament, appealed to the Prime Minister of Egypt, al-Nuqrashi Pasha—the same one who had declared repeatedly to the British Ambassador in Egypt that "all Jews were potential Zionists but that anyhow all Zionists were Communists"—to allow them to sit for their final examinations. Strangely enough, they were granted permission to do so, albeit separately from the rest of the student body. The respondent recalled that his diploma was delivered to him in the internment camp, together with a signed picture from the King, in recognition of his outstanding performance in the examination. He pointed out: "This was Egypt, it couldn't have happened anywhere else". Eventually, the covert efforts of the Jewish Agency and Mossad Le'Aliya helped secure his release from prison, together with other detainees, and immediate travel arrangements were organised to Israel through Naples.[506]

To further illustrate the random nature of these arrests, the next example was a case of mistaken identity. Interviewee #35 was put under house arrest and given one month to leave the country because he was mistaken for a Zionist activist bearing the same name. As previously mentioned, there was also the case of the Rabbi of the Port Said community, arrested as a suspected Zionist sympathiser, held in solitary confinement for forty-four days, then shipped out with his family.[507] One could be arrested just for a perceived empathy for the enemy.

Other interviewees reported they felt threatened by the anti-British street demonstrations because, as #43 said, "Invariably, at the end, they turned anti-Jewish".[508] Often it was the sudden and unjustified arrest of a brother or an uncle that galvanised them into leaving, as testified by the following interviewee:

> We could see our stay in Egypt was coming to an end. My cousin
> M. [who used to do land valuations] had been arrested because
> the police found maps of the farms he was supposed to value and
> thought they had a Zionist spy on their hands.[509]

Apart from the fear of being arrested, the Jews also had to contend with
daily harassment in the street. One respondent claimed he was beaten
up twice by a group of young Egyptians and treated to a variety of
insults both as a Jew and as a foreigner. In 1951, he decided, "enough
is enough". He obtained some information about Australia from the
Australian Ambassador at the time, Sir Roden Cutler, bought his ticket,
and landed in Sydney in September 1951.[510]

The growing climate of distrust towards the Jewish population was
another disquieting feature. Jewish families, who lived too close to so-
called sensitive areas, were "advised" to move. Needless to say, they
could not disregard that advice. Such was the case of Interviewee #83
who reported that after 1948, the family were forced out of their apartment because it was considered too close to the royal palace of Abdin in
Cairo, where King Faruk resided.

Another debilitating measure imposed on a number of Jews after the
1948 Arab-Israeli War was the government sequestration of their assets,
as explained by Laskier:

> On 30 May [1948] Proclamation N26 subjected to sequestration
> the property of any person who was interned in Egypt and of any-
> one residing outside Egypt whose activities were deemed "preju-
> dicial to the safety and security of the state as well as of those
> who had merely been placed under surveillance". Since there was
> no legal barrier to placing people "under surveillance", the proc-
> lamation could be, and was, applied indiscriminately.[511]

Considering the fact that the government targeted the business assets and
properties of "the most celebrated figures of Egyptian society and of Jewish communal life", it is difficult to believe that the motivation for this
proclamation was purely a question of security.[512] In fact, the previously
mentioned Ziza Lester (#20), whose father, an Egyptian national, was

"one of the pillars of the textile industry in Egypt" and vice president of the Cairo Jewish community, attested that around 1949 the government unilaterally sequestered everything the family owned, and their apartment was seized. At the same time, her brother, who had a key position with a foreign company, found himself barred from his office. There was no other avenue left for them than to leave the country. Another interviewee, whose family owned a very successful bullion business, said that in 1952, while his parents were travelling overseas for business, their work premises, properties, and bank accounts were seized without prior warning. A warrant was issued for his father's arrest, charging him with tax evasion, while other members of the family were imprisoned.[513] His father never returned to Egypt and lost everything he owned.

Another seminal event in the history of modern Egypt, the Cairo fire on January 26, 1952—known as Black Saturday—deeply affected the psyche of non-Muslim minorities.[514] Contrary to the other three trigger events, this was an internal matter, a so-called spontaneous uprising against the hated British and their indiscriminate killing of forty policemen, as well as the corruption and mendacity of King Faruk's rule. Although it was not directly aimed at the Jews, the excesses and the violence displayed on that day shook the community to its core. According to the testimonies of my Cairene respondents, it played a significant role in their decision to leave the country more or less urgently. This is how Interviewee #22 remembered it:

> I witnessed many demonstrations and riots because we lived in the centre of Cairo. The one that is the most vivid in my mind is when they burned Cairo down in 1952. They were burning people alive. We could see the Shell building from the back of our flat, and we could see the people being torched alive as they were trying to get out of the building. I was terrified.

A second respondent (#47) was so traumatised to see the frenzied mob, totally out of control, burning and looting systematically every symbol of Western presence—particularly British and Jewish symbols—that he decided there and then to leave Egypt immediately. One week later, he

was in Italy with his son. Interviewee #63, who worked for the British
Institute in Cairo, luckily was away from his office on that day because
the whole building was torched and many people were hurt. Although he
was already considering leaving Egypt since 1947, these riots caused him
to hasten his preparations, and he left the country within a few months.

Even for respondents who did not witness those nightmarish scenes
of January 1952, their significance was compounded when they were
followed in July of the same year by the Free Officers' coup that over-
threw the ailing monarchy of King Faruk. A climate of uncertainty and
fear, generated first by the violence in Cairo and then by the change of
regime, permeated the Jewish community. The rise of Colonel Gamal
Abdel Nasser as the new leader in 1954 consolidated those fears, which,
according to Beinin, was understandable:

> There were good reasons for Jews to be alarmed when a group
> of unknown army officers overthrew the monarchy and seized
> power on July 23, 1952. The army had no social or political links
> to the Jewish community.[515]

THE SUEZ WAR OF 1956

As already stated, it was the tripartite attack by Britain, France, and
Israel on October 29, 1956, that sealed the fate of the Jews in Egypt.
Harsh measures taken by the military government in retaliation for this
attack "directly and radically affected the rights, status, and very existence of many Jews in Egypt".[516] They were subjected to arbitrary police
detention, sequestration of their businesses and assets, expulsion from
the country, and denaturalisation. The oral testimonies of my interviewees reflected very closely the reality on the ground. Fifty-seven of my
respondents (63 percent) left the country in 1956 or later. I estimated
that twenty three (42 percent) were forced out, among which twelve
were actually expelled after being interned or kept under house arrest.[517]
The rest emigrated "voluntarily", although the distinction between the
two categories was often blurred. Their motivation was either the fear

of repercussions from the political situation or the realisation that Jews had no place in the new Egypt. One can safely assume that in fact all the Jews of Egypt faced forced emigration sooner or later.

As enemies of the state, the British and French were immediately expelled. Among the Jews, those who were French or British nationals were doubly targeted for expulsion and sequestration by the authorities. They accounted for 14 percent of the sample group. The story as related by British Interviewee #4 expressed her fear and disarray:

> The expulsion of the French and the British started. As a British subject, my mother was expelled, her shop seized, and she had to leave within three days with only E£10. I was also expelled and was supposed to leave without my family but was saved by the Dutch Consulate, who gave me a false passport declaring I was Dutch since my marriage. It was a very difficult time. We were living in fear of our servants who were brainwashed every day, during their prayers at the mosque or by loudspeakers in the streets. They were coming back to work with hate in their eyes. I remember walking along the streets and hearing some Arabs yelling, "We will cut your throat".

The authorities used to detain one member of each British or French family and then issue an order of immediate expulsion for the entire family. The prisoner would be released on the condition he would leave the country immediately, and he was brought directly to the ship to join his family. Such was the case of the fiancé of Interviewee #51, who was arrested for being British and Jewish and imprisoned for a month before being deported to Britain. At the same time, the family business was sequestered, and the rest of his family left with nothing but their clothing and the allowed sum of E£20 per person.[518]

The six French nationals in the group reported that they were immediately served with expulsion orders after being kept under house arrest. House arrest also meant no communication with the outside; therefore, they were not allowed to have a radio or use the telephone.[519] Deliberate intimidation and bullying was used to further demoralise them. "The doors had to remain wide open. We had no right to close them, and anyone could come in and take anything they wanted", recalled Interviewee #69 who, together with her parents, husband, and one-week-old child, was given notice to leave the country within three days. However, it seems that strict enforcement of the expulsion orders varied from case to case. Interviewee #9, who had been under house arrest for over two weeks, was given twenty-four hours to leave the country after being woken up at midnight and taken to the police station with her husband and baby. Her husband pleaded and managed to obtain an extension for health reasons, but the rest of the family was not granted any such reprieve.[520] As with the British nationals, the business and personal assets of all the expelled French nationals were sequestered under Military Proclamation No. 5, and they left the country with little else than their clothes.[521]

It is important to note that these measures particularly affected the British and French Jews because they were not really expatriates with a permanent home and assets in their mother country. Their home was Egypt and, in most cases, those Jews had never set foot on French or British soil, except maybe on holiday. Everything they owned or built, whether on a large or modest scale, was physically and metaphorically rooted in that country. When they were forced out of their familiar surroundings, they experienced not only the material loss of their possessions but also the emotional loss of the only home they knew.

It is evident that, in the context of the Suez crisis, Zionists—real or imagined—would bear the brunt of the emergency laws. Although the percentage of active Zionists within the Australian group was low (13 percent)—which reflected more or less the situation in Egypt—one of them (#24), a Greek national, was arrested by the *mukhabarat* (the Egyptian secret police) on charges of espionage for Israel because of his past activities in Zionist youth organisations. His brother was also arrested, although he was not a Zionist activist, and they were both kept at the infamous Tura prison in Cairo, together with common criminals.[522] Upon intervention from the Greek Consulate and given that the authorities did not have enough evidence to convict them, the two brothers were taken from prison straight onto a ship bound for Greece, remaining handcuffed until the ship was out of Egyptian territorial waters. Any connection with known Zionist activists, however tenuous, was considered suspect. Such was the case of a Jewish doctor who was arrested and interned for months at the Huckstep prison near Cairo, just because he used to work in the same hospital as Moshe (Mussa) Marzuk, the Karaite who was hung in 1954 for his part in a conspiracy to commit acts of sabotage on behalf of Israel.[523] Again, there were no charges, but the doctor, his wife, and their child were issued an immediate expulsion order.

The Suez War was also a wake-up call for the Karaites of Egypt. Beinin claimed that 40 percent of them departed between October 1956 and March 1957, although there were still one thousand Karaites in October 1966, out of an overall Jewish population of about seven thousand on the eve of the Six-Day War.[524]

The French, British, and Zionists were not the only besieged groups. Egyptian and stateless Jews, as well as Jews of other nationalities, were also targeted and saw their properties and businesses seized under Military Proclamation No. 4.[525] It was clear that the largest and most important Jewish-owned ventures were the prime objectives of the sequestration policy. I have identified seven such cases out of the fifty-seven respondents who left after 1956. For example, Interviewee #8, whose well-respected and prominent Italian family owned a large cotton ginning and export company, reported that in November 1956 their offices were occupied by a military-appointed sequester, the ginning mills seized, and their bank accounts frozen unilaterally. The owners were barred access to their business premises and expelled from the country within a few days, with nothing except a few suitcases of clothing. The husband of Interviewee #10, an Egyptian national, owned a factory that manufactured and supplied uniforms for the Egyptian army. He was under the misapprehension that his privileged connections with people in government would always protect him from any adverse reaction. In 1963 he was arrested, his business sequestered and subsequently nationalised. The couple was forced to leave the country with only a few of their personal belongings, having lost everything:

> La fabrique a été nationalisée, la maison séquestrée. Tous les
> meubles ont été notés. Nous n'avons rien pu vendre. Nous avons
> quitté la maison avec juste quelques valises avec nos habits.[526]

Interviewee #19, who was of Spanish nationality, worked in the family
business, an important enterprise manufacturing concrete pipes. After the
Suez War it was nationalised, and two of the co-directors were arrested
on trumped-up charges of espionage. He consequently lost his job and
had to leave the country, due to the fact that by that time nobody would
employ a Jew.

It is clear from these examples that neither foreign nor Egyptian
nationality guaranteed Jews immunity from harassment, sequestration,
or expulsion. The situation was even more precarious for stateless Jews,
as noted by Laskier:

> It is estimated that as early as the end of November 1956, at
> least five hundred Egyptian and stateless Jews had been expelled
> from Egypt…Because in most cases the individual served with a
> deportation order was responsible for supporting his family, all
> members of the family had to leave the country.[527]

The stateless refugees represented about a third of my sample group.
They equally attributed their departure to expulsion, loss of livelihood,
and a hostile environment. They also experienced the erratic enforcement
of the emergency laws. For instance, my brother, whose application to
the University of Montpellier in France had been intercepted by the government censor, was expelled within a week for corresponding with an
enemy of the state. Interviewee #7, whose brother had gone to Israel a
few months before, was suddenly ordered to leave the country. On the
contrary, his father, whose extensive property and assets were seized, was
not officially expelled. It is obvious that, in this case like in many others,
to be expelled or to leave "voluntarily" was a question of semantics, seeing as the family of the expelled individual was often left destitute and
had no choice but to leave. According to Laskier, this was the result of
a deliberate policy of "ethnic cleansing" by the Egyptian authorities to
get rid of its Jewish population, using "more subtle, potent techniques of

intimidation and psychological warfare against the Jewish population as a whole", together with "simultaneous economic harassment of Jews".[528]

It stands to reason that the closure of major Jewish-, French-, and British-owned businesses meant the loss of jobs for a large segment of the Jewish community, even when they did not suffer directly from expropriation or expulsion. For instance, Interviewee #1 recalled that her husband, as the accountant of a large French company whose Jewish managing director had been arrested and subsequently expelled, was ordered to stay at his post until he had shown all the financial records to the military administrator. As soon as his work was completed, his employment was terminated. With six mouths to feed, no job, and no possibility of finding another one, he had to look elsewhere. Sponsored by his sister, who had immigrated to Canada immediately following World War II, he applied for a landing permit and eventually settled in Montreal. Other respondents remember that they were just asked not to come to work anymore, without any explanation, although they guessed the true reason: "We were stateless. We had to leave Egypt because my husband was fired from his job like all the Jews".[529]

Furthermore, many Jews in private enterprise were prevented from conducting their business efficiently because of continual obstructions created by arbitrary government regulations. As a result, they had to close down or relinquish their share of the business to Muslim Egyptians at a minimal price. This state of affairs was again corroborated by the testimonies I have gathered. For instance, the father of Interviewee #90, who had run a prosperous customs agency for years without any restrictions, suddenly found himself barred from entering the Egyptian customs area, which had suddenly been declared out of bounds for Jews. Because he could not continue working under those conditions, he had to close his agency and found himself deprived of his livelihood. Until that time he had never considered leaving Egypt.

Although it is true that not all Jews were expelled or stripped of their property or even made jobless, all my respondents testified to the atmosphere of panic that overtook Egyptian Jewry in the days and months following the Suez War, as illustrated by the following interviewee (#7):

> The people in Cairo were in such a panic. Every time I went to my shop, I noticed that all my [Jewish] neighbours who had shops were leaving one by one, going all over the world. We used to meet in my house with friends; we would look at the map and one would say, "I am going to the Belgian Congo", another one, "I am going to Argentina". They all had different destinations. I decided to come to Australia.

The scenes at the offices of both the Cairo and Alexandria Jewish communities, as well as at various consulates, embassies, and travel agencies, were to some extent reminiscent of the pictures of the Jews of Germany trying desperately to flee after the events of Kristallnacht in November 1938. Clearly there was no comparison with the extent of violence experienced by the German Jewish community during the Nazi pogrom.

The fact that the government was engaged more or less overtly in a policy of encouraging Jewish emigration did not indicate that the Jews were free to pack their bags and go. They first had to obtain exit visas, which were equally compulsory for foreign, Egyptian, and stateless Jews. Those who were Egyptian nationals were stripped of their nationality once they applied for an exit visa.[530] They had to leave the country as stateless, with a *laissez-passer* valid for only one one-way trip (*valable pour un seul voyage sans retour*).[531] The acquisition of those visas was often capricious, time-consuming, and onerous, as public servants were notorious for their venality.[532] The experience of Interviewee #40 encapsulated the general feelings of exasperation, frustration, and panic:

> I was stateless. I had to go to the authorities to obtain an exit visa. They gave me a visa but said that my son, a newly born baby, had to stay behind because he was born in Egypt. therefore he was Egyptian. I took my son and went to the offices of the Red Cross and told them I wouldn't move until they got me an exit visa. There were thousands of other women in the same predicament. The Red Cross eventually obtained permission for us to leave. It was the worst time in my life. I left in a great hurry, and I didn't take anything with me.

As a matter of fact, most of the respondents who left at that time said that, according to regulation, they were allowed to take only their personal belongings, such as clothes and household linens, plus the sum of E£10 or E£20, and E£50 worth of gold per person. They had to dispose of all their larger and precious possessions—furniture, cars, jewellery, and household goods—at prices well below their true value, given that profiteering was rife. Often, the Jews just closed their doors and departed, leaving everything behind.[533] One respondent (#37) declared: "I didn't get one penny for my house. I had to give everything away. I left without telling anybody". When he tried to sell his car, he had to reveal his religion to the prospective buyer, who then proceeded to pay him one-quarter of the asking price.

At the point of departure, which was usually the port of Alexandria or the airport in Cairo, the customs inspectors were ruthless in their searches and confiscated arbitrarily any items considered to be too valuable. Most of my respondents recalled the humiliating body searches they had to endure, particularly in the period immediately following the outbreak of the Suez War.[534] Here is what Interviewee #65 remembered:

> We had to pack in six days. We were putting boxes after boxes in the basement for my uncle to take care of. The porter saw what was happening and, although we had given him money to appease him, he denounced my mother to the authorities, saying that she was putting diamonds in the suitcases. The day that we left, we just closed the house as if we were coming back. Our ship was delayed because we were all bodily searched. They didn't find anything and finally they let us aboard.[535]

A handful of respondents reluctantly revealed they were so desperate at the idea of leaving the country empty-handed that they took the huge risk of smuggling out some money, either personally or through the black market, by conceding a hefty percentage.[536] "I converted all my money in gold ingots", said one. "My brother made some wooden boxes with a double cavity big enough to fit the gold. I bribed a guy £50 to look after our luggage". If caught, they would have faced years in prison. In some cases, they entrusted small amounts to Egyptian friends who arranged somehow for the money to reach them once they were on board, without exacting a share of that money.

Interviewee #8 recalled a particularly colourful and touching episode. His father, who, together with his brothers, was at the head of a large cotton trading company, had been expropriated and ordered to leave the country with his whole family, although they were Italian nationals. Because his bank account was frozen he could not access any of his money, but managed to gather about E£800 from the sale of personal items. He entrusted that amount to one of his most loyal Egyptian employees, who promised to pass it on to him on board the ship. He waited in vain on deck for a sign of that money, but the ship was ready to leave and he thought all was lost. Suddenly, as the ship's gangway was being removed, he saw his employee running up to the ship, sobbing and screaming, begging to hug his boss one last time. In the ensuing confusion, the man managed to slip into his pocket the money that had been entrusted to him. Another interviewee (#81) reported that all his mother's jewels were passed through customs clandestinely by an Egyptian friend and mysteriously delivered directly to his cabin on the ship.

Nevertheless, these cases were more the exception than the rule and, taking into account all the testimonies I gathered, it is fair to say that most of my respondents were more or less forced "Out of Egypt"—the title of André Aciman's colourful memoir—with little more than their clothes.[537]

THE 1967 WAR

In the years between 1956 and 1967, Jews were increasingly pushed out of the workforce, and the private sector was eliminated through a campaign of widespread nationalisations. The Jewish community gradually lost all of its prominent members who had previously held positions of leadership in the various Jewish institutions. The few respondents who stayed on after 1956 until the early 1960s did so mainly for economic reasons. They claimed they were still making a living from their ongoing businesses and were reluctant to leave the country empty-handed.

For instance, the family of Interviewee #14 owned an upmarket lingerie shop that used to supply Queen Narriman, King Faruk's second wife. Their business somehow escaped the various waves of sequestrations and nationalisations. Nevertheless, my respondent feared for his children:

> I wanted to leave since 1948. One had to think of the children and their future, but my brothers were very comfortable, they had the shop, they owned buildings, and they didn't want to budge. So we left without them in 1962.

The consequences of the 1967 Six-Day War proved catastrophic for the remaining Jews of Egypt. As mentioned earlier, at least 425 Jewish males between the ages of eighteen and fifty-three were rounded up as soon as the war started. The seventy-five who were foreign nationals were taken directly from prison to a ship to be deported. The Egyptian and stateless Jews remained in prison, some for over three years, and were released only after intervention from foreign governments and international agencies. As already mentioned, it was mainly thanks to HIAS secret diplomacy, the unpublicised cooperation of the Spanish government, and the vital role played by Angel Sagaz, Spain's ambassador in Cairo, that all the Jewish prisoners were eventually freed and allowed to leave Egypt.[538]

With one exception, my Australian interviewees did not experience the dramatic events of 1967 personally seeing as they had already left Egypt by 1963. Interviewee #57, who was married to a Syrian Christian, remained in Egypt until 1970. Although she was not particularly targeted during the Six-Day War, she confirmed that the living conditions for all non-Muslim Egyptians gravely deteriorated after 1967. She reported being threatened with dismissal from her workplace because of her Jewish maiden name, which by law had to appear on all her identity papers.

I obtained only one first-hand testimony, from an Italian Jew—now living in London—who was still in Egypt when the Six-Day War broke out. He was arrested in June 1967 and spent six traumatic months in prison before being expelled. He witnessed some horrific incidents, although he claimed they were caused by the sadistic and brutal initiatives of the prison guards rather than by official directives from the Egyptian government in relation to its Jewish prisoners.

The scarcity of testimonies post-1967 is proof enough of the fact that the Jewish presence in Egypt had declined dramatically by 1967 and continued its downward trend until today, when it has been reduced to less than a hundred individuals at best, mostly older women.[539] After twenty-five centuries of continuous history, Jewish life in Egypt has shrunk to such an extent that the few remaining Jews cannot even form a *minyan* (quorum) of ten male Jews—the minimum number required to conduct the traditional service—in the two main synagogues of Cairo and Alexandria.

From analysis of the gathered data, it appears that the sample group I studied is a close representation of Egyptian Jewry before its forced emigration and dispersion. Like the bulk of the community, my respondents had led tranquil and privileged lives under the protection of the foreign powers. Until 1948, Egypt was considered home by most of them, although some had already felt a mounting tension since 1937 due to the abolition of the privileged status of foreign nationals, the rise of a new brand of exclusive pan-Arab and Islamic nationalism, and the escalating conflict in Palestine. In the space of less than twenty years—triggered repeatedly by the three wars between Israel and Egypt—Egypt was emptied of its Jews, a mostly middle-class population whose dominant characteristics were its ethnic, religious, cultural, and national diversity, its Western-style education, and its multiple language skills. How did they fare "Out of Egypt"? How prepared were they for their new lives? Apart from Israel, who took them in and why? Why Australia? The next section of this book examines the transit period when my interviewees suddenly became refugees looking for a new home, and the many challenges they had to face before they settled down at the Edge of the Diaspora.

CHAPTER 7

A JOURNEY TO THE
"EDGE OF THE DIASPORA"

The three successive wars between Egypt and Israel and the dramatic repercussions upon Egyptian Jewry—including imprisonment, sequestration, and expulsion, as well as various other intimidation measures— triggered an authentic, panic-stricken, second exodus-type emigration, which permeated the whole community and brought about its self-liquidation. From a population of about eighty thousand Jews before 1948, nearly one-half—47.5 percent—migrated to Israel.[540] The rest chose other destinations, such as Brazil, France, the United States, Argentina, England, Canada, and even Australia.[541]

Egyptian Jews migrated to Australia mainly in the wake of the first two trigger events, the 1948 Arab-Israeli War and the 1956 Suez War. The small number of those immigrants can be attributed to a number of basic elements about Australia: fear of the unknown, geographical distance, the higher cost of transportation compared to other more accessible destinations, the culture, and, most importantly, the restrictions inherent in Australian immigration policy. Contrary to the United States, Canada, and Australia, immigration to Brazil, for instance, was not restricted by a quota system, particularly under the Presidency of Juscelino Kubitschek (1956–1961).[542] According to the research of Ruth Leftel on the Egyptian/Sephardi community of Sao Paulo, the Brazilian Embassy in Cairo received instructions not to limit the number of visas issued to Egyptian Jews.[543] Because Brazil was not involved in the confrontation between Egypt and her enemies, the immigration formalities were conducted in Egypt. Its embassy was instructed to process visa applications gradually, at a rate that would allow the establishment of the necessary infrastructure to accommodate the refugees.[544] The approval rate for migrants' applications was increased for cases in which the head of the family had a profession and for applicants with family already settled in Brazil.[545] In cases of hardship, HIAS or the Brazilian Jewish community compiled lists of people who wished to immigrate and forwarded those lists, already bearing a permanent visa authorisation, to the Brazilian officials in Egypt. This *modus operandi* was particularly helpful for stateless applicants. A local doctor, recommended by the Brazilian Embassy, conducted the medical screening in Egypt. The only exclusions concerned applicants suffering from certain conditions, such as trachoma, an eye disease endemic to Egypt.[546] As one would expect, a clean police record was also mandatory, and applicants had to prove they were never engaged in unlawful—meaning Communist—political activities.

In contrast, Australia's immigration policy in the late 1940s and 1950s was not particularly welcoming of migrants from the Middle East. In fact, as a general rule, during the first one hundred and fifty years of Australian colonisation, the only immigration that was encouraged was from English-speaking countries, such as the United Kingdom, New Zealand, Canada, and the United States. Migrants of Nordic and Germanic origin were exceptions because they were considered part of the Anglo-Celtic race. James Jupp, a renowned scholar on Australian migration, clearly stated: "The ideal type of an Australian was of English culture and Nordic racial origin".[547] My research in government archives of the late 1940s revealed, through the exchange of correspondence between immigration officers in Europe and ministers in Canberra, the unabashedly ugly face of the White Australia Policy.

The White Australia Policy was the backbone of the Immigration Restriction Act of 1901, the first year of Australia's federation. It was central to the government's aim of building a white British Australia from which all other racial groups would be excluded, although this aim was never spelled out in so many words. In *Old Worlds and New Australia,* Janis Wilton and Richard Bosworth wrote, "any sense of special identity that Australians possessed had largely sprung from a belief—and fear—that they were the 'white guard' keeping the pass against a hostile world".[548]

With the use of practices, such as the infamous "dictation test", this policy was "almost completely effective between the 1890s and the 1960s as a form of immigrant exclusion".[549] It granted immigration officers all the necessary powers to admit or to exclude anybody based on their racial characteristics or for any other reason.

It was a post-Second World War Labour government that first introduced a radical program of non-British immigration based on the principle that, in order to resist invasion from Asia, Australia must "populate or perish". The landing permit system, interrupted during the war, was resumed, and immigration officers went looking for suitable migrants in the DP camps of Europe. For Jewish survivors in those camps, there was an initial period of optimism.[550] However, due to Australian isolationist attitudes, fear of economic competition, shortage of housing, and the surfacing of anti-Semitic feelings, a negative reaction to Jewish refugees manifested itself in the media and among some elements of the general population. As a consequence, in 1946 Arthur A. Calwell, the first Minister for Immigration, imposed a quota system, "which limited the number of Jews permitted to travel on any boat to 25 per cent".[551] Calwell also introduced other policies to limit the number of European Jews travelling to Australia in the postwar era, and immigration records of the postwar period continued to show evidence of an exclusionist policy on the basis of race.[552]

To ensure that no undesirables would slip through the net, the official instructions were to refuse permanent residency to British subjects as well as aliens who were not of "pure European descent", an obvious euphemism for "white."[553] This ruling targeted specifically the applications of British subjects whose ethnic origin was India or Singapore. Following a 1948 report that large numbers of Indian Jews who wished to immigrate were non-European in appearance,[554] the Calwell ministry decided to prohibit entry to Australia to all Jews of Middle Eastern origin except under special circumstances.[555] Applicants had to declare on their immigration application (Form 40) whether or not they were Jewish.[556] No other religion was indicated on that form. Although the question was deleted in 1954 after the leaders of Australian Jewry registered their protest, the immigration officers were still under instructions to try to determine during the interview if the applicant was of the Jewish faith. Calwell's immigration policies continued to be implemented by Robert Menzies' Liberal government, with Harold Holt as Minister for Immigration from 1949 to 1956. The late Aaron Aaron, one of the founding members of the NSW Association of Sephardim, who migrated to Sydney from Calcutta in 1950, related to me during an interview how he had fought the Australian government for two years to get his wife and children to join him from Calcutta.[557] Another respondent (#25), who landed in Australia in 1958, reported that his family had been trying to obtain a landing permit since 1951. He presumed that the reason their application was rejected consistently until 1957 was because they were Egyptian nationals and therefore considered non-Europeans, despite their ethnic origin being Italian and Spanish.

How did such an immigration policy affect the Jewish refugees from Egypt wishing to immigrate, seeing as in principle they were labelled undesirable? Why did they choose faraway Australia of all places as their new home, and where in Australia did they choose to settle?

Australia was no stranger to Egypt, despite the great geographical distance. Australia had been involved with the Middle East since 1914. Australian soldiers—particularly those of the 4th Light Horse Brigade—played a key role in the Battle of Beer Sheva in 1917 and ultimately in the British conquest of Palestine. They were also heavily involved in the defence of Egypt during World War II.[558] The Australian politician and diplomat, Richard G. Casey, was in Cairo in 1942 as Minister Resident in the Middle East, appointed by Sir Winston Churchill.[559] Again, in 1956, the Australian Prime Minister, Sir Robert Menzies, was personally drawn into the Suez Canal crisis. Chanan Reich, an Australian academic and political writer who studied the relationship between Australia and Israel, noted Australia's reaction to Nasser's unilateral nationalisation of the Suez Canal in July 1956:

> The Australian government felt strongly that Nasser had acted contrary to international law, and that the Canal, being vital to the security of countries including Australia, should be returned to international control with guaranteed freedom of navigation.[560]

In fact, in September 1956, Menzies headed the committee of eighteen countries sent to Egypt to negotiate with Nasser the regaining of international control of the canal.[561] However, Menzies was not exactly an objective observer. On the contrary, he was a staunch supporter of the United Kingdom and "had publicly and trenchantly damned Nasser and defended the United Kingdom's militant response to nationalization".[562] Furthermore, Australia, "as a power dependent on maritime communications", had important interests in the region, which included "the Suez Canal as a 'life line' of the Empire and of trade with Britain and Western Europe; oil; the creation and maintenance of Israel".[563] Thus, an untempered use of the canal seemed vital to Australia because 60 percent of all Australian trade went through the canal and any diversion from that route to the nineteen hundred kilometres longer Cape of Good Hope route would have increased annual freight charges significantly.[564] The meeting between Menzies and Nasser was a total failure in diplomatic terms. According to Menzies' own reports to London and Canberra, he was angered with Nasser's reaction to the proposal handed to him and had "entered into a personal argument with Nasser, and...Nasser had taken great offence".[565] On November 7, 1956, as a consequence of the tripartite attack by Britain, France and Israel, Egypt severed diplomatic and all other relations with Australia, in retaliation for its support of Britain. The Australian Legation in Cairo was closed and the Canadian Embassy agreed to act as protecting power for Australian interests.[566]

The Australian government was kept well informed of the situation in Egypt, post-Suez, through the various reports tabled at the UN on this very issue. From early November, immediately after the outbreak of hostilities, reports on the alarming situation of Jewish residents in Egypt started appearing regularly in the Australian Jewish press.[567] Under pressure from the leaders of Australian Jewry, the government voiced a strong protest at the UN General Assembly about the ill treatment that Jews, as well as British and French residents, were reported to endure at the hands of Egyptian authorities.[568]

Was there a direct correlation between Menzies' personal interaction with Nasser and the granting of visas to Jewish refugees from Egypt, as claimed by some of my interviewees? I found no hard evidence supporting such a claim. However, I found clear evidence in archival records that, by March 1957, a special immigration policy was promulgated in favour of Jewish and non-Jewish refugees from Egypt, in recognition of the hardship they had endured as a result of the Suez War.[569] Was this policy a spontaneous and humanitarian gesture by the Australian government to the victims of the Suez crisis, or was it more a response to the strong representation and numerous appeals made by the leaders of Australian Jewry in this respect, particularly in Sydney and Adelaide?

Based on the evidence I have uncovered in both government and community archives, I suggest that it is fair to say that—as far as Egyptian Jews are concerned and notwithstanding the goodwill of the Australian government—the implementation of that particular immigration policy was mostly due to the tireless efforts of the AJWS of NSW and its president, Sydney D. Einfeld.[570] Not to be forgotten was also considerable political lobbying from the South Australia Jewish Board of Deputies with the help of Patrick Galvin, the Labor Federal Member for Kingston, South Australia.[571]

Einfeld, who was also president of the Executive Council of Australia Jewry, reacted immediately to the outbreak of hostilities on October 29,

1956, by sending a telegram to the Prime Minister, R. G. Menzies in Canberra, urgently requesting Australia's "intervention against ill treatment of Jews in Egypt", and pointing out the establishment of concentration camps for Jews, together with the "seizing of one so-called hostage from every Jewish family seeking escape".[572] Subsequent letters were sent by Einfeld to the Prime Minister and to the Minister for External Affairs, R. G. Casey—dated December 11 and 12, 1956, respectively—urging the government to instruct the Australian Delegation at the UN "to support protests made against this harsh and brutal treatment of the people of [his] faith who are still in Egypt".[573] In fact, the AJWS records showed that from November 1956 and as late as September 1962, Einfeld was in constant contact with the Department of Immigration at the highest echelons, pleading the case of Egyptian Jews because of the fundamental reluctance at official government level to allow Oriental Jews into Australia on the assumption they were not white.[574]

Einfeld became aware of this attitude in the course of his negotiations with Canberra and asked to be accompanied by the leader of Sydney Sephardi Jewry, Aaron Aaron, so that the Secretary of the Department of Immigration, T. H. E. (later Sir Tasman) Heyes, could see for himself that Sephardi Jews were not black.[575] Heyes' initial response pointed to the difficulties caused by the closure of the Legation and the fact that it could no longer secure checks on health and character of applicants in Egypt. Therefore, although the government sympathised with the predicament of the Jews of Egypt, the answer was that "there is nothing more that can be done by the Department at this juncture". Only the applications that were received and sent back to Cairo before the closure of the Australian Legation in Cairo could be considered at that stage, provided they met the following criteria:

- Holders of recently expired visas may be given renewals.
- When screening was completed by the Australian Legation and visas were about to be issued, visas may be issued.
- When screening had not been completed but the applicants are the dependent relatives of residents of Australia, [the Immigration

Department] will be prepared to consider waiving normal screening on compassionate grounds.

- In regard to persons whose admission has been applied for since the Legation was closed, the Department will consider the grant of visas, without screening, to the wives and minor children of residents of Australia.[576]

Interviewee #9 testified to the crucial role played by Einfeld in the admission of Egyptian Jews into Australia. As a French national, she had been expelled from Egypt in 1956 and was subsequently lodged in a refugees' hostel in Paris while waiting for a landing permit for Australia:

> At first, we were refused permission to come to Australia…Life in France had not been very easy. I felt a foreigner, I felt a refugee… It is only when Syd Einfeld got special permission for refugees from Egypt that we were accepted under that category.

Rutland's research revealed that there was considerable political lobbying by Egyptian members of the Adelaide Jewish community between December 1956 and March 1957, to facilitate the admission of relatives from Egypt into Australia. The South Australia Jewish Board of Deputies called a public meeting on December 20, 1956, to discuss the problem of the Jews in Egypt and invited Patrick Galvin, the Labor MHR for Kingston, as the guest speaker. A subcommittee was formed and "it was decided that a list of names of families seeking permits to enter Australia should be drawn up and that this list be submitted to both Canberra and the Australian Jewish Welfare Society".[577] Further recommendations were made, such as sending cables to U.S. president Dwight D. Eisenhower, to Secretary of State John Foster Dulles, and to UN Secretary-General Dag Hammarskjold, with copies to Prime Minister Robert G. Menzies. Furthermore, every effort was to be made to meet Menzies during his visit to Adelaide in January 1957, although this request was subsequently denied. Nevertheless, following the public meeting Galvin sent a telegram to the Prime Minister that read as follows:

> Urge you to give special consideration to allow into Australia persons in Egypt and those expelled from Egypt who have relatives in Australia prepared to give guarantee of accommodation and maintenance. In addition as it seems impossible in Egypt at present for screening and medical checks to be completed for people who have already been given permission from Australia is it possible for visas to be issued subject to such checks being completed at Australian legations in Paris or elsewhere…Suggest on humanitarian basis these people receive same consideration as Hungarians as they are suffering because of their sympathy with Britain and their Jewish faith.[578]

In spite of Einfeld and Galvin's combined representations, the initial response from the new Minister of Immigration, Athol G. Townley, to Galvin in January 1957 once again disappointed the Jewish community, reiterating that only the Egyptian Jews "who had been nominated already and had their applications accepted and sent to the Australian Legation in Cairo before its closure could have their screening and medical checks in another country if they could manage to leave Egypt".[579] Townley further elaborated that it had become necessary since April 1956 "to reduce the number of applications being accepted for nationals of the South European and Mediterranean countries in order to avoid the number of migrants exceeding the program approved by the government". Entry permits were granted to nationals of Southern European and Mediterranean countries only if the applicants "had dependent relatives of residents of Australia or were single women under 35 years of age".[580] Interviewee #90 reported that her father's application for the admission of his sister with her husband and child into Australia was rejected on the basis of that particular policy, as shown by the letter he received from the Department of Immigration:

> The very considerable increase in the number of applications for the admission to Australia of nominated Southern European

and Middle Eastern migrants paying their own fares has made it necessary to place some temporary limitation upon the number which can be approved.[581]

It is clear from this statement that the federal government had decided there would be no mass migration from Egypt and refused to broaden the categories of Egyptian refugees, pointing out, not unreasonably, that these were not people without a country, in view of the fact that "Italians and Greeks could return to their homelands and Israel was prepared to accept all Jews expelled from Egypt".[582]

Nevertheless, Galvin[583] and Einfeld persisted in their representations, and by March 1957 Townley agreed to broaden somewhat the categories of such persons eligible to come to Australia:

> On humanitarian grounds I have now decided that up to 30th June next applications may be accepted from residents of Australia for the admission of any relatives, dependent or not, other than cousins provided that the nominees:
>
> • Are residents in Egypt, or were residents there on 1 November 1956.
> • Can reach a country outside Egypt where they can be seen by an Australian overseas post.
> • Are found to comply with normal immigration standards as to health, character, etc.
>
> In cases where such applications are accepted before 30th June, but the nominees are found to be still living in Egypt as at 30 September next, it will be necessary to consider then whether the application should be regarded as having lapsed.[584]

This development was welcomed by Australian Jewry and led to the second most important wave of Egyptian Jewish migration. Although the relative relaxation of immigration requirements explains why a few thousand Jews of Egypt ended up in Australia, it still meant that only those with close relatives in Australia who could act as sponsors were considered suitable. It is not surprising therefore that the majority of my respondents—68 percent—invoked the presence of family in Australia as the main reason for their immigration, clearly reflecting the impact of that particular aspect of government immigration policy.

Even for those who were considered eligible, the procedure was not straightforward because the Australian Legation in Cairo had been closed from the early days of the Suez War. Therefore, the first hurdle for would-be applicants was to leave Egypt and present themselves personally at the office of the Australian Embassy in Rome, Paris, or Athens for their initial interview and medical screening. The circumstances under which the Jews were departing, especially in the wake of the Suez War, have already been discussed at length. The harsh political and socioeconomic measures implemented by Egyptian authorities vis-à-vis their Jewish population were obviously aimed at provoking their hasty departure. As previously indicated, the travel documents given to stateless and Egyptian Jews were valid for a one-way trip only, even when they were leaving Egypt "voluntarily" and forced to relinquish any claim for compensation from the Egyptian government.[585] It was inevitable that, in this context, a great number of people would have required considerable help for their relocation, as far as tickets, visas, transit accommodation, and other essential needs were concerned. The Jewish Community of Alexandria and Cairo and the ICRC worked hand-in-hand to provide that help, with secret funds supplied by international Jewish organisations, such as the JDC, the Jewish Agency, and United HIAS Service. ICRC records showed that:

> [Its delegates in Egypt] actively concerned themselves with stateless Jews and those stripped of their Egyptian nationality who wished to emigrate, and the ICRC organised a shipping schedule from Alexandria to Greece and Italy…Upon arrival, they were assisted by the Greek and Italian Red Cross Societies and by the local branches of international Jewish organizations, which sought to find a country of permanent asylum for them.[586]

Around the same time, from about early 1957 and at least until 1959, the UN High Commissioner for Refugees (UNHCR) "declared that many of the escapees from Egypt came under the mandate of his Office" and, as refugees, were entitled to UN assistance and funding. Once the Egyptian refugees landed in European ports, the Jewish Agency directed the emigration to Israel and HIAS took care of emigration to other areas, such as Latin America, the United States, Canada, and Australia. The refugees, particularly those who were stateless and without means of support, were met upon arrival and were offered assistance for food, accommodation, or any other basic need during that interim period.[587] The immigration process to Australia generally took between two and twelve months and sometimes even longer, depending on each case. About 26 percent of my respondents reported they were assisted by Jewish relief organisations at some stage of their exodus, particularly while waiting for their visa applications to be approved. The refugees were accommodated in HIAS-nominated hotels in Paris or *pensione* in Rome or Genoa. If needed, they were given meal tickets or medical help. Joseph Claude Bentata (#18) kept a diary of that period and was kind enough to share some of his notes. He was twenty years old at the time and had left Alexandria with his brother in December 1956 for Genoa, on an Egyptian ship, the *ss Nefertiti*. As they were approaching the coast of Italy, he recorded the following observations in his diary:

> All day long passengers reorganise, lock up suitcases and make themselves ready for disembarkation. We are close to Corsica. At 7 p.m. we arrive at the port of Genoa. It is no great fun to arrive at night in winter in a foreign land not knowing where we will spend the night with "umpteen" suitcases. The consuls of France and UK are on the dock, greeting their nationals. Jews on board huddle around representatives of a Jewish organization. At 10 p.m., we are driven to *l'Albergho Torinese*. Completely lost!

At a later stage, he added this explanatory note for his children:

> Our accommodation and board was provided by the HIAS and I seem to remember that the hotel used to billet Jews from Egypt

and from Hungary who had escaped the USSR invasion. They considered us as the rich refugees as we had full suitcases and £10. Many of them had nothing!

Only 12 percent of my respondents acknowledged having their passage to Australia paid for by HIAS. The majority declared they paid their own fare, which was consistent with their middle- to upper-middle-class background. They circumvented the prohibition to take any funds out of Egypt, except for £20 or even £10, by purchasing open-dated tickets to Australia before leaving Egypt, often without knowing if their applications would be successful. Some even spent all the money they possessed on first-class cabin tickets because they had received adverse reports on the living conditions in the tourist-class cabins, as heard in the following testimony (#55):

> At the time, we could take some of our furniture and household possessions (but no money or jewellery) because we already had our migration papers. We were allowed only £20 each. As we couldn't take any money out, we bought ourselves first-class tickets for our trip. We tried to smuggle some money out through a customs agent in Alexandria who was supposed to bring the money on the ship for a 10 percent commission. We got to Alexandria—we could not leave via the Suez Canal as it was blocked due to the war—and gave him the package, but on that night he came on the boat and said that the customs had found the money. We were so scared at the time because they were putting lots of Jews in prison. We had lost everything. We went to Genoa where we stayed thirty days waiting for the boat to Australia. HIAS accommodated us into a pensione.[588]

Even the foreign nationals, particularly those who had been expelled, needed assistance with accommodation and living expenses while waiting for their visas in Paris, Rome, or Athens, and government or local Jewish organisations provided that assistance. One such case (#71), a French national, landed in Paris after being expelled from Egypt as an enemy alien, with her husband, a week-old baby, and her parents. She described that period as "the best and worst year of my life":

> We ended up living all together in one room in the attic of a hotel
> for one year. We had help from the French government. Every
> Thursday, we had to queue up at the Palais Chaillot and we would
> get tickets for milk, restaurant, and rent.

Another French national (#9), who was also expelled in November 1956
with her baby and parents, had a similar experience:

> We had already bought our first-class tickets to Australia back
> in Egypt. We stayed in France for nine months [waiting for our
> landing permit] and were helped by the French government as
> refugees. We were staying at l'Hotel Brebant, which was requi-
> sitioned by the government for the accommodation of Egyptian,
> Algerian, and Hungarian refugees. These refugees received assis-
> tance from the HIAS.

Interviewee #51, a British national who had been imprisoned then
expelled in November 1956, immediately after the Suez War, was accommodated in a Jewish refugee hostel in London with his fiancée. Their
wedding ceremony at the Spanish Portuguese synagogue was apparently
organised and paid for by the local Jewish community.[589]

In accordance with JDC data, 591 Jewish refugees from Egypt were
assisted by HIAS in their emigration to Australia from 1956 to 1963,
although the extent of that assistance was not specified.[590] In fact, it
was the combined efforts of relief organisations—such as the ICRC,
the Intergovernmental Committee for European Migration (ICEM), the
UNHCR in cooperation with HIAS, the JDC, the French Comité Juif
d'Action Sociale et de Reconstruction (COJASOR), and the Italian,
Greek, and British Jewish communities—that facilitated the transfer of
the Jewish population from Egypt, through Europe, and to their final
destinations.[591]

Because, as a general rule, the Jews of Egypt who were leaving the
country "of their own accord" were not allowed to take anything more
than their personal clothing and the sum of E£10 or E£20 per person,
they packed enough clothes to last them for the first two to three years of
emigration, in anticipation of difficult times ahead.[592] The end result was

CHART **10.** Reasons for migration.

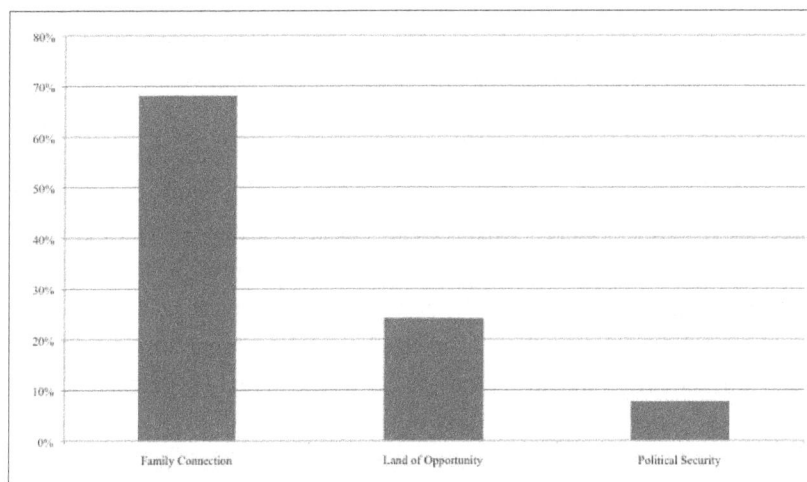

an "umpteen number of suitcases", as noted by Joseph Claude Bentata (#18) in his diary.[593] It is not surprising therefore that the majority of respondents preferred to travel to Australia by ship, in order to have all these suitcases carried at no extra cost. The Lloyd Triestino or Flotta Lauro shipping lines seem to have been the most popular choices.[594] The voyage usually took about thirty-two days from Genoa to Sydney, with stopovers in Naples, Messina, Port Said, Aden, Colombo, Fremantle, and Melbourne.[595]

Even as the refugees from Egypt were moving from one hemisphere to the other, Hungarian refugees escaping Soviet reprisals after the 1956 Hungarian revolution were also heading for the same destinations, using the same travel routes. Furthermore, those ships were carrying large numbers of assisted Italian migrants from Sicily and Calabria, in search of a better life in Australia. The ships were therefore fully booked and the conditions were poor, particularly in tourist-class cabins. Those among my respondents who were privileged to travel in first-class cabins retained beautiful memories of a leisurely month at sea and reminisced about the excellent food, accommodation, and entertainment. In contrast, those who travelled below deck or in more modest cabins complained of crowded conditions, poor choice of food, and even at times segregated quarters, which meant that married couples were separated for the duration of the month-long voyage.[596]

The reasons invoked by the interviewees for choosing to migrate to Australia were characteristic of all displaced individuals looking for sanctuary. Family reunion was the predominant attraction (68 percent); the perception that Australia was a land of opportunity was second (23 percent), followed by the search for political security (8 percent).

The picture was slightly different when a comparison was made between the migrants pre- and post-1956. About 42 percent of the "pioneers"— those who migrated to Australia pre-1956— were searching for a better future in a safe country far from the Middle East. In fact, political security and better economic opportunities rated about the same. Moreover, cultural affinities and proficiency in English contributed significantly to the final decision of where to settle; nearly one-half of the group possessed an advanced level of English, whereas one-third had an adequate knowledge. Nevertheless, the dominant reason for migrating to Australia remained the presence of a family member or friend who could act as a sponsor. Family reunion led to a chain migration phenomenon, accounting for two-thirds of the sample. One of the first Egyptian Jews to arrive in Australia in 1948, at the age of twenty-six, stated that he alone was responsible for the migration of over forty Egyptian Jews who settled in Adelaide because he was there.[597] Chart 11 clearly shows that family reunion was the dominant feature of the post-1956 migration from Egypt:

The son of the late Elie Ovadia, an Egyptian Jew who landed in Sydney on Australia Day 1957, delivered the eulogy at his father's funeral and praised him for sponsoring forty-four members of his extended family:

> My father went on to sponsor the immigration of the entire extended family, both on his side and my mother's. Three generations and

CHART 11. Reasons for migration according to date of arrival.

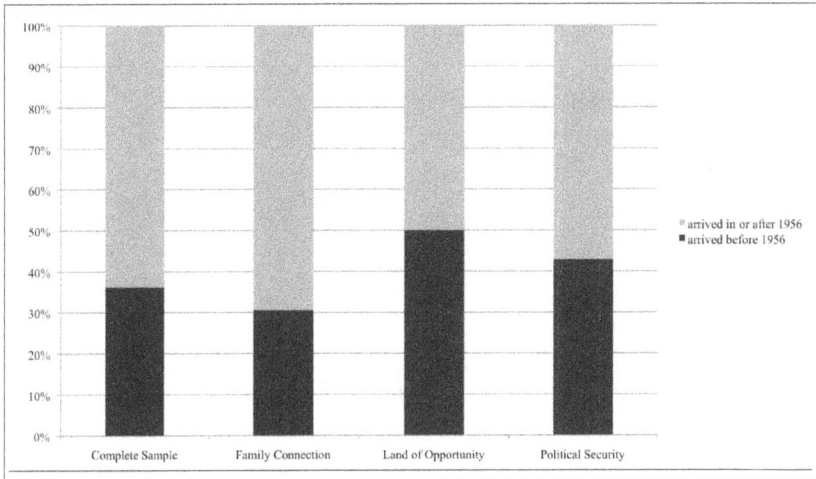

several families followed in the next eighteen to twenty-four months, all of these using our home as a halfway house until they themselves were established.[598]

According to one of the beneficiaries of Ovadia's hospitality, there were as many as thirteen people living under the same roof at any given time.

There were several other cases of chain migration and extended families pooling their resources until they could cope on their own, as illustrated by Interviewee #55:

[My first wife's cousin] bought a house in Homebush and we moved in with them, renting one of their rooms. As soon as we arrived, I started the formalities for my sister and her family and for my younger brother. They had to leave Egypt and go to Italy for these formalities as the Australian Embassy in Egypt had closed down. They were there for six months. They sent us a little bit of money, which we used as a deposit for a house at Bondi Beach, where the Swiss Grand Hotel is now, a big semi with four rooms. They arrived nine months after us and moved in with us. Then my first wife's uncle and family of four arrived and also moved in with us. We were three families plus my younger brother. At one stage we were thirteen living together in the house.

Having a British passport in those days virtually ensured entry into any Commonwealth country. Therefore, the British members of the sample group were privileged applicants, provided they complied with the usual conditions applicable to all British subjects.[599] Interviewee #41, who had been drafted into the British navy between 1942 and 1945, "wanted to see the world" and his dream was to come to Australia. He seized the opportunity to emigrate as soon as possible after the end of the war. Nevertheless, he had to wait eighteen months for passage on a boat to Australia because troop repatriation had priority over any other kind of travel.[600]

Mayer Harari also served in the British Army for the duration of the war. He could foresee that life in Egypt as he knew it was coming to an end, particularly after witnessing numerous anti-British riots post-1945 and the voting on the partition of Palestine.[601] When two of his relatives were arbitrarily arrested in May 1948 on charges of Zionist espionage and imprisoned in the infamous Huckstep camp[602], he decided it was time to get as far as possible from the Middle East.[603] Although his British passport gave him the choice of any Commonwealth country, he dismissed Canada because of the climate and South Africa because "it was another country with problems". He decided, therefore, "to go as far South as possible", originally planning to settle in New Zealand, where an ex-colleague and his wife had emigrated. However, as experienced by the previous respondent, there was a two-year waiting list on ships going in that direction.[604] The hardship of travelling such a long way in the immediate postwar years has been documented by social historians and writers who studied that crucial period of migration to the southern hemisphere, and the conditions on the so-called hell ships.[605] Mayer Harari remembered the old fifteen-hundred-ton Greek ship *ss Rena* on which he travelled to Australia from Port Said. He called it "a ferry", seeing that it was apparently used originally for a shuttle service between Cyprus and Haifa. My respondent claimed they were four hundred passengers instead of eighty, travelling under "terrible conditions", with stringent water restrictions, and some passengers sleeping on deck. The voyage took forty-seven days and my respondent, who was travelling with his spouse and a fourteen-month-old baby, thought they would never make it to their destination. He even claimed that after disembarking its last passengers, the ship eventually sank outside Sydney Harbour.

What most of the respondents knew about their faraway destination was often very schematic and idealised and did not match the reality of life in Australia, particularly in the late 1940s. This was particularly true of the desperate postwar European refugees who relied on the promotional material provided by Australian Consular officials, as noted by Catherine Panich, daughter of migrants who came from Europe at the end of World War II:

> The active advertising in Europe to recruit migrants included posters depicting a beautiful girl plucking oranges from a tree. People in white shoes were walking through Sydney with the bridge in the background. These, apparently, were the conditions in Australia.[606]

Equally, my respondents had read about Australia in library books, and often based their decision to emigrate on that scant information.[607] Those who did not wish to migrate to Israel and could not stay in Europe, either because they were stateless or because of limited economic opportunities, had to select a country where they had the best chance of being accepted and making a decent living. It was often a process of elimination, as explained by Interviewee #67:

> We realised that the situation in Egypt was not good. We took the world map and looked at Canada, too cold; South Africa, looming problems with the majority black population; Rhodesia, bound to be trouble; so Australia was the best place with the best climate, a country for the future.

For others it was a waiting game, just a matter of accepting the first visa that came through, after applying to three or four countries, such as the

Chart 12. Date of arrival according to Jewish ethnicity.

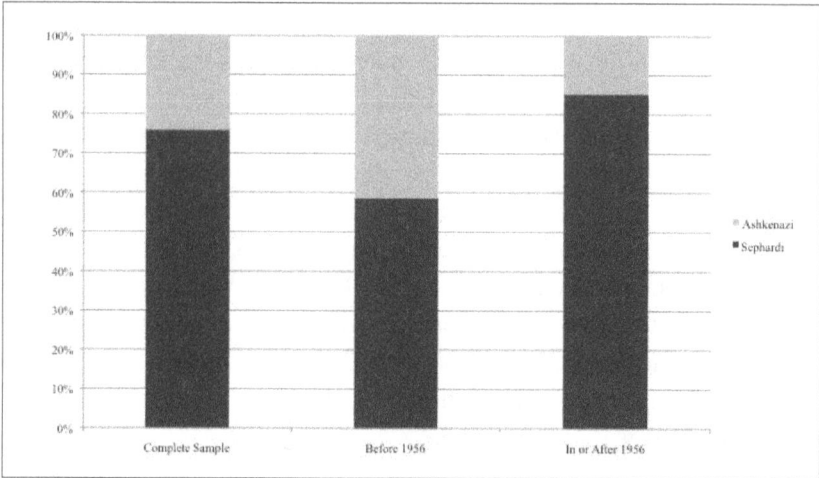

United States, Brazil, Canada, and as a last resort Australia. Interviewee #91 admitted that after, witnessing some of the rioting in the streets of Cairo after World War II, he just wanted to leave the place. "L'Égypte, ce n'est pas pour moi", he told his wife. Waiting for his American landing permit to be approved would have taken at least six to eight months. He had been told that Australia was a fantastic country, *un pays formidable*, and in 1947 he decided to come on a tourist visa to see for himself. He liked what he saw and settled in Adelaide. Why Adelaide? At first, it was just a fortuitous decision because of an acquaintance made on the ship on his way to Australia. He was searching for investment opportunities and found Adelaide friendlier and the authorities more accessible and helpful than in Sydney or Melbourne.[608]

My research also noted two interesting trends concerning the immigration pattern of the Ashkenazim compared to the Sephardim. First, as shown in the next chart, Ashkenazim represented nearly one-quarter of the sample group, whereas in Egypt they had constituted only 8 percent of the total Jewish population. Secondly, contrary to the migration trend of Sephardim, relatively more Ashkenazim migrated to Australia before the Suez crisis (39 percent) than after (15 percent).

Why did such a relatively high percentage of Ashkenazim choose to settle to Australia? The search for political security seems to have been the highest motivating factor for the Ashkenazim, given that the motive applied to over half of them, as demonstrated in chart 13. For instance, Interviewee #22, who arrived in Australia as a teenager, said her grandparents escaped from Russia to shield their children from being drafted into the Russian army. She recalled what her father told her:

> The reason we came to Australia was because my father said he did not want to live again in a country that could be involved in another war. So he did it by process of elimination. France was rejected because of the Algeria issue; Israel was rejected because of the war with the Arabs…whereas Australia was far enough for him to know that he was going to lead a peaceful existence.

The second motivating factor for the Ashkenazim within my sample was the belief that Australia offered more opportunities, and the third element was probably the fact that more Ashkenazim than Sephardim had attended English schools in Egypt and proportionately more of them possessed advanced English skills. In fact, 55 percent of the competent English speakers were Ashkenazi, compared to 43 percent Sephardim. Nevertheless, the fact that 46 percent of the whole group fitted in the top category, with only 3 percent having no previous knowledge of English, amply demonstrates the overall level of proficiency of my sample.

I suggest three other reasons for the earlier emigration of the Ashkenazi participants, as shown in chart 13. On the one hand, because of their shallower roots in Egypt, the Ashkenazim were more likely to have family already overseas—in this case, Australia—who would encourage an earlier migration and provide vital support. On the other hand, an instinctive understanding and experience of persecution might have made them more sensitive to the ominous signs of danger looming ahead. Or again, maybe they just realised sooner than their Sephardim compatriots that "the good old days" in Egypt were coming to an end, given that their

CHART 13. Reasons for migration according to ethnicity.

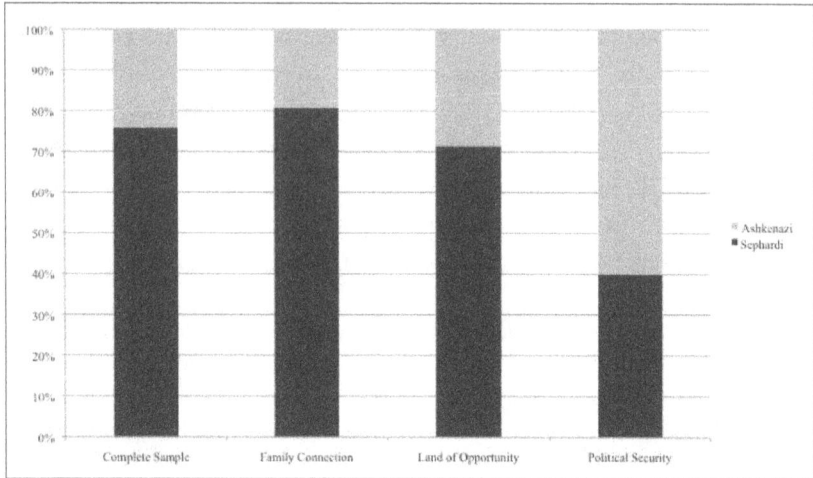

predominant reason for leaving Egypt pre-1956 was the lack of opportunities for the future.

The majority of the sample group of Egyptian Jews chose Australia as their destination in order to be reunited with family or close friends, trying to alleviate the trauma of dispersion and displacement that they had all experienced at different levels of intensity. However, it is clear that the road to Australia was not without its problems, due to the political situation in Egypt, the restrictions imposed by the Australian immigration policy, and the complicated logistics of obtaining a landing permit. It is also clear that Australia often represented the second or third choice, and that its distance from Egypt and from Europe was daunting for some and attractive for others.

My research did not attempt to determine the exact number of Egyptian Jews who migrated to Australia because of inconsistencies in the numbers recorded in official government censuses, estimates by various researchers, the educated or uneducated guesses of members of the group, and my own assessment based on the number of people with whom

I came into contact about forty years later, taking into consideration the inevitable depletion of the original group due to natural attrition.[609] Equally, demographers and Jewish historians have also debated the size of the somewhat larger group of Hungarian Jews who found refuge in Australia at about the same time, in the wake of the 1956 Hungarian revolution.[610] Whatever the total number of Egyptian Jews in Australia, it is undeniably much smaller than the broad postwar Jewish migration from Eastern Europe. This could be one of the reasons why they have not attracted much attention and why so little official data on the specifics of the group is available.

The Australian census of 1971 listed as 944 the number of Jews born in Egypt who had migrated to Australia, out of an overall Jewish population of 62,208.[611] This figure related only to people who chose to register their religion as well as their place of birth, which was not always the case.[612] Furthermore, it did not take into account those who were not Egyptian-born. The issue of under-numeration of Jews is an ongoing problem for demographers of Australian Jewry; most argue that the level of under-numeration is at least 20 percent. Because of these uncertainties about the size of the group, I elected rather to study the profile of who came to Australia, when, why, and where. Although it was difficult to draw a definitive picture because of the diversity and pluralism inherent to all Egyptian Jews, a certain number of characteristics emerged from the analysis of my data.

The majority of my respondents (about 60 percent) arrived in Australia after the 1956 Suez crisis, which was consistent with the general pattern of emigration of Egyptian Jews. The rest had emigrated just prior to or after the first war between Egypt and the fledgling State of Israel in 1948.[613] As has already been established, the reasons for leaving Egypt were closely linked to the political situation on the ground. In fact, nearly two-thirds of the sample group were either expelled for political reasons or forced to leave because of loss of livelihood, and one-third saw no future for Jews in Egypt.

Looking at the Australian landing permit criteria, it was obvious that, after race, the emphasis was on youth, which generally presumes good

Chart **14.** Age according to date of arrival.

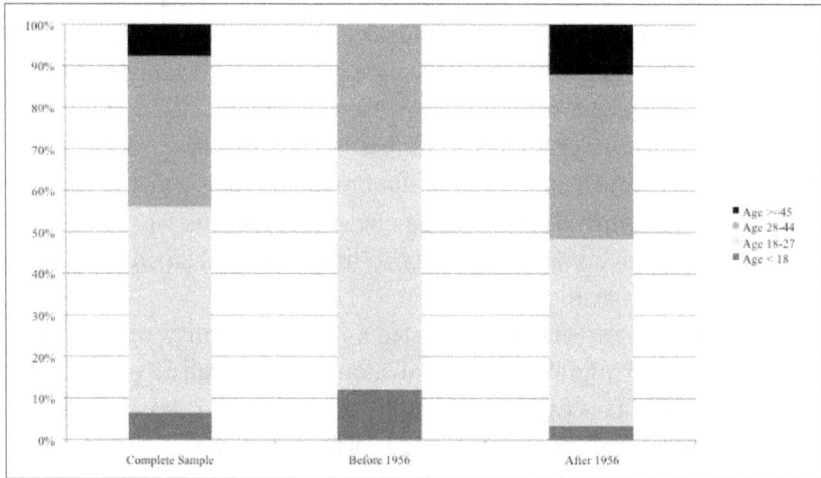

health. Australian immigration officials strictly monitored the health requirements for would-be migrants. The applicants had to submit to a thorough medical examination by an Australian doctor at various screening centres in Europe. Preference was clearly given to young, healthy single men and women and young families, whereas older—over fifty—and/or ailing applicants were discouraged and often rejected outright.[614] Interviewee #65 recalled that his family's application was consistently rejected because of the advanced age and declining health of his eighty-year-old grandmother and her seventy-five-year-old sister. It was only when those ladies passed away after three years of waiting in Rome that the rest of the family was allowed into Australia.[615] Furthermore, the fact that about 90 percent of my sample group were under the age of forty-five upon arrival on Australian soil is a clear indication that the age factor played an essential role in the migrant selection process, as shown by the following chart:

Overall, 49 percent were aged between eighteen and twenty-seven, 37 percent between twenty-eight and forty-four, and only 8 percent forty-five and over. Actually even more—about 57 percent—of the respondents who had immigrated before 1956 were in the eighteen to twenty-seven age range.[616] This particular phenomenon was not surprising because, apart from occasional contact with Australian soldiers stationed in Egypt during World War II, the image of Australia in the minds of would-be migrants was comparable to that of the Far West in nineteenth-century America. As already indicated, very little of substance was known about the actual living conditions, and the overall impression left by the Australian soldiers on leave in the streets of Cairo and Alexandria during the war years was that the country was not for the faint-hearted. It was, therefore, natural that anyone who dared to venture so far from a comfortable and familiar environment to the other side of the world would be young and adventurous, looking for new horizons in what was perceived to be an uncharted and distant land. In fact, nearly one-third of the pre-1956 subgroup—twelve out of thirty-seven—considered Australia to be a land of opportunity, in addition to being far from the troubles of the Middle East. They saw themselves as pioneers, and their youth was an asset that facilitated the immigration formalities.

The post-1955 respondents were mostly young adults, although slightly older than the first group.[617] However, the most significant difference was found in the over forty-four group, where my chart shows a leap from 0 percent pre-1956 to 12 percent post-1955. This phenomenon was obviously linked to the further degradation of the status of the Jews in the context of the Egyptian political climate from 1956 onwards, when most of the Jewish population had no option but to leave the country. As indicated previously, their choice of destination was often determined by the presence of family or friends. Most of my interviewees were sponsored by a family member. It was also not unexpected that the majority of my respondents had been young on arrival, seeing as it was a physical impossibility for me to access most of the older cases. The odds were that migrants over fifty years old arriving in Australia in the 1950s were not likely to be alive or well enough mentally in the late 1990s and early 2000s to be able to contribute to this study.

Where did the Egyptian Jews settle once they landed in Australia? In view of their predominantly urban background, it was not surprising they chose the three capital cities—Sydney, Melbourne, and Adelaide. Big cities usually offer better work opportunities, as well as a stronger community network. Strangely enough, the city that attracted them most, at least initially, was the smallest of the three, Adelaide, which was the preferred place of settlement for nearly half of the pre-1955 arrivals. It was certainly the place where they became the most visible and where they formed the largest single ethnic group within the broader Jewish community. Out of a population of 985 Jews in Adelaide recorded by the 1961 census, Jews from Egypt numbered about four hundred, although the people I interviewed quoted much higher numbers.[618] Whatever the case may be, they had a much more significant impact on the Adelaide community than their compatriots in Melbourne and Sydney.

A number of factors could have contributed to that phenomenon. Three key individuals were responsible for facilitating the immigration and settlement in Adelaide of Egyptian Jews. The role played by the Labor MP, Patrick Galvin, in securing a relaxation of the quotas for Egyptian Jews after the 1956 Suez War, has already been outlined. Another key individual was the late Reverend Abraham Berman (1891–1982), who served the Adelaide Jewish congregation for many years, from the late 1940s to 1977. His role has not been recorded in official archives but was revealed by his wife in the course of a series of interviews conducted by Rutland in 1984 as part of her research on oral history.[619] Franziska Berman related that the Chief Rabbi of Egypt, Haim Nahum Effendi (1872–1960), wrote to Reverend Berman, appealing for his help in obtaining a landing permit for a congregant and his family, who had been rejected twice by Australian immigration because of the advanced age (fifty) of the parents-in-law.[620] Apparently, thanks to Berman's intervention they were finally accepted in principle in 1955 and arrived in Adelaide in September 1956, just before the outbreak of the Suez War. Franziska Berman also claimed that her husband facilitated the entry of another hundred people from Egypt into Australia because of his close contacts at the Immigration Department in Adelaide.[621] Some of these individuals became the most prominent members of the Adelaide Jewish/Egyptian community.

The third individual who spearheaded the establishment of Egyptian Jews in Adelaide was Max Liberman, who came to Australia from Egypt in late 1947 with his young wife—on a tourist visa while waiting for his immigration papers for the United States to come through—and subsequently decided to settle in Adelaide. Having brought with him some capital, he very quickly made contact with the South Australia Department of Industrial Development and the Premier of South Australia to discuss investment possibilities in that state. Against all odds, he succeeded in obtaining the necessary permits to start a textile factory in Adelaide, in partnership with a friend who was a textile manufacturer in Egypt. He remained in constant touch with his friends in Egypt and some of them, now living in Adelaide, concurred in saying that it was his enthusiastic letters about conditions in Australia that undoubtedly induced a number of them to join him. The friend who was in textiles had apparently already received a landing permit for Brazil when he read Liberman's glowing reports on the South Australia government's policy of encouraging establishment of new industries, which caused him to change his previous plans. His brother also remembered those circumstances:

> Nous avons lu la lettre de Max qui disait que tout manquait à Adé-laide et qu'on pouvait s'installer très facilement. Le gouvernement de Playford en Australie du Sud encourageait les grandes industries à s'établir à Adélaide. Nous avions déjà le permis pour aller au Brésil mais mon frère a voulu d'abord passer par l'Australie. Quand il est arrivé ici, naturellement il a voulu rester et il n'était plus question d'aller au Brésil.[622]

Through his contacts in local government, Liberman was able to secure landing permits for over forty of his relatives and friends within the first three years of his own arrival. He commented on how easy the whole procedure was in those early days:

> C'était tellement facile d'avoir des visas à ce moment-là. J'allais à l'Immigration Dept et je disais que j'avais une famille de douze

personnes en Égypte qui voulait venir ici. Le type me disait, je suis très "busy". Il me faisait remplir les formulaires, mettre la photo dessus, mettre le "stamp" et ensuite il signait et j'envoyais les "landing permits".[623]

From thereon, through chain migration, more Egyptian Jews landed in Adelaide, where they found a growing network of their compatriots, as well as a welcoming Jewish community.[624]

Was the presence of family and friends the only reason why so many Egyptian Jews chose to settle in Adelaide? Some respondents spoke of a special bond between members of the same Masonic lodge in Cairo as the root of their decision. Although my research did reveal that a higher proportion of Adelaide respondents or their parents were Freemasons in Egypt, this claim was not otherwise substantiated. Others stated that Adelaide's climate was an important factor. For instance, Interviewee #35 and her husband chose Adelaide because she was asthmatic and wanted a place where the climatic conditions were similar to Egypt's. They believed that Adelaide, with its Mediterranean climate of winter rainfall and sunny summers, and the desert never far away, fitted their requirements perfectly.

Adelaide's compact size—the "twenty-minute city"—was possibly another attraction, compared to the sprawling character of Sydney and Melbourne, which could be quite alienating for a newcomer, even one familiar with urban living.[625] In a smaller environment, human contacts are generally easier to establish, and most of my Adelaide interviewees spoke with gratitude about the warmth of the welcome and support provided by people like Reverend and Mrs. Berman. Their home became a haven for the newcomers who had nowhere to go. The Bermans helped the new migrants adjust to Australian conditions by holding an open house every Sunday evening, bringing together thirty or forty Egyptian refugees who met and interacted around a Lazy Susan filled with nuts and snacks. Many of my Adelaide interviewees personally experienced their hospitality, including Max Liberman (#91): "nous allions chez lui chaque dimanche jouer aux cartes et il nous donnait à manger. Il était formidable. N'importe qui venait et tapait à la porte, il lui ouvrait la maison". Indeed, the role played by the Bermans was an important factor both in the process of chain migration from Egypt to Adelaide and in smoothing out the newcomers' initial feelings of alienation. They provided a focal point, a point of social contact for people who otherwise might have felt totally isolated. In addition, the small Adelaide Jewish community, only too happy to boost its membership with the newcomers, welcomed them with open arms.

Another possibility is that Egyptian Jews did not really choose Adelaide but Adelaide chose them. Since the arrival of displaced persons after World War II, the Australian government has tried to influence immigrants to settle in regional areas. Today, a growing number of initiatives—such as the State Specific and Regional Migration Schemes—have been developed to direct migrants away from the bigger centres of Sydney and Melbourne, with the aim of encouraging the development and industrialisation of the smaller capital cities.[626] Actually, Max Liberman, who was responsible for attracting so many of his friends and relatives to Adelaide, claimed that it was easier to obtain landing permits for people willing to go to smaller centres, such as Adelaide. Based on his personal experience, he also felt that setting up new businesses and industries in Adelaide was greatly facilitated by local government bodies. His contacts there served him well over the years and, at the time of the interview in 2005, he was still vigorously involved in various development projects in South Australia, although he was well past the age of retirement: "I am more active in my work than I was when I was younger. I just finished eight buildings twelve months ago and I am looking for another big development in the centre [of Adelaide]".[627]

As verified by other testimonies from the Adelaide group, settling in a more contained environment and sharing their experiences with their compatriots proved to be—at least for some—more congenial to a successful socioeconomic integration, while they were still able to maintain a sense of personal identity.

I suggest another underlying reason for Egyptian Jews' preference for Adelaide, the smallest of the capital cities—a reason probably rooted in the trauma of the migration experience as a whole. It is possible that they were trying to recapture and recreate what they had lost in their particular exodus, such as a united, close-knit community where every-body is familiar. The Maccabi Club—an institution they built themselves and patronised assiduously for at least the first ten to fifteen years—was not only a congenial meeting place, similar to the sporting clubs of Egypt, it was also an attempt to replicate that familiar ambiance and strengthen their bond and identity as Jews from Egypt living in Austra-lia. In fact, this was exactly how Rabbi Jeffrey Kahn, who served as the first Rabbi of the Beith Shalom Progressive Synagogue in Adelaide from 1981 to 1986, described the group of Egyptian Jews in the course of an interview with Rutland in 1984: "a very tight-knit group, with very close relationships between them".

Nevertheless, despite the sample group's earlier settlers' preference for Adelaide, Sydney was a popular destination, particularly for those who arrived post-1956. My study demonstrated that immigrants to Syd-ney were latecomers—even when compared to those from Melbourne and other locations—considering the initial attraction exerted by Ade-laide and its familiar social network, as shown in the next chart.[628]

The majority of the Sydney-bound migrants (68 percent) settled there for the same reason as the Adelaide group, namely the presence of fam-ily and friends. Furthermore, the attraction of a big city like Sydney, the hope of better socioeconomic opportunities, and the geography of the place, with its pristine beaches and temperate climate, were undoubtedly important components of the equation.

While recognising that all these factors played a part when it came to choosing a place to settle within Australia, it is also important to remem-ber that often the newcomers had no choice but to stay, at least initially, at the place of residence of their sponsor (relative or friend)—whether it was Adelaide, Sydney, or Melbourne—and this was found to be true across the board. The class privileges they enjoyed in the Old Country were long gone—although not forgotten—when they landed in Austra-lia, unknown and disoriented, with very little money or no money at all. Social services for migrants were minimal in that period, the distances were daunting, and the topography of the place was totally unfamiliar.

CHART 15. Date of arrival according to city of settlement.

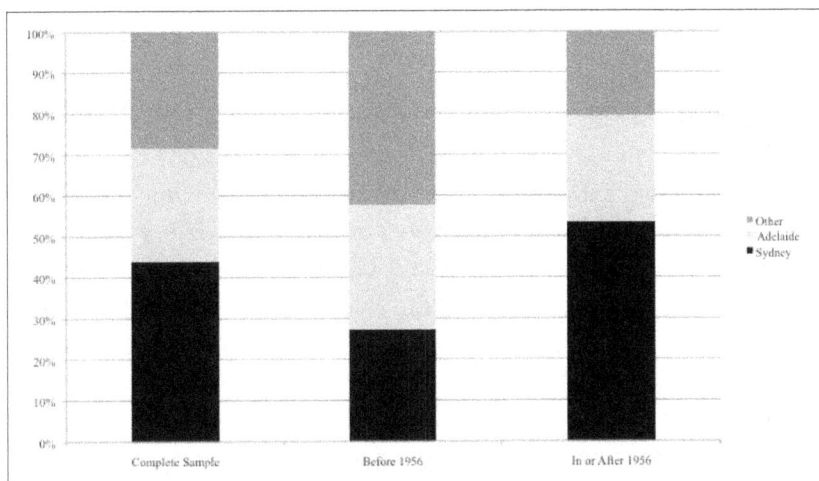

Consequently, the newcomers tried to settle in close proximity to each other in an attempt to create their own network. Egyptian Jews did not always settle in traditional Jewish areas, such as the eastern suburbs of Sydney or Elwood and St. Kilda in Melbourne, nor did they seek accommodation in government or Jewish migrants' hostels.[629] As pointed out by Rutland, most of the postwar Jewish refugees were already not being accommodated in government migrant camps (such as Bonegilla in northern Victoria or Bathurst in New South Wales):

> The Australian government, both Labor and Liberal, insisted that the reception and integration of the refugees was the responsibility of the Jewish community. No government funds were to be expended on Jews because of the fear of political repercussions. The task of accommodating the newcomers and helping those in need to find their feet in a new land was assumed by the sponsors of the refugees. Australian Jewish Welfare Societies (AJWS in Sydney and AJS&RS in Melbourne) directly sponsored some of

the refugees and acted as a backup service for those who were sponsored privately but required assistance.[630]

Among my sample group, there was only one Egyptian Jew who went through the Bonegilla Migrant Centre when he first arrived in 1968 via Israel.[631] As for the Jewish hostels, I also encountered only one case of a couple with two children who needed a place to stay while their house was being built and lived in one room at the Greenwich Jewish hostel in Sydney for eleven months in 1961. This did not mean that Egyptian Jews had no trouble finding places to live. Coming from Egypt, where most people lived in rented apartments, they were confronted with a totally different situation in Australia, where people usually bought their own home and where rental accommodation was scarce. All the pre- and post-1956 arrivals without family connection in Australia complained about the scarcity of housing in Australia after the war. Children were not welcome in rented accommodation and guesthouses. Conditions in Adelaide were particularly difficult in the early days of Egyptian migration, and most respondents confirmed that life was hard in this respect. They also remembered that food coupons were still being distributed and building material for new houses was in short supply. One interviewee (#91) related that, in the late 1940s, because returned soldiers were given priority as far as housing was concerned, "migrants had to obtain a building permit and wait two years before they could build their own home and new houses could not exceed ten squares in size".

Migrants with babies experienced the greatest difficulties. One of my Adelaide respondents (#67) reported that, when she finally found a room to rent, she was not allowed "to stay in the house during the day with the baby because the lady of the house did not want to be disturbed". Interviewee #35 recalled that she had to move when her baby was born because babies were not allowed in that particular guesthouse. Another couple lived in a rented caravan for over eighteen months before moving into their house. A Melbourne respondent said he lived two years with his wife and child in a rented room at £12 per week until he had saved £500 for a deposit on a house worth £3000.

Apart from a few privileged cases among those who arrived before 1956, accommodation was the main source of anguish for most respondents in the early days of their immigration. Despite those initial difficulties, my survey showed that within two years of arrival 68 percent of the sample had bought their own homes and the rest achieved that goal within an average of four years. This was largely due to the buoyancy of the work market. Looking at the whole group—both men and women— all of the respondents who were of working age stated that they joined the workforce almost immediately upon arrival without major difficulty. Those were the days of full employment in Australia. The level of occupation of the newcomers usually matched their qualifications, but not necessarily their former status. In fact, 42 percent were in white-collar jobs, whereas 19 percent started their own professional or business enterprises. A very small proportion, 9 percent, worked as technicians, 7 percent were still students, and only 11 percent—mostly those with low English skills—were initially engaged in factory or menial work.

When I compared the differences in the level of occupation between men and women in the group, it became apparent that displacement and hardship due to migration disrupted the structure of the traditional family in Egypt—the man at the helm, sole provider for his wife and children. Suddenly the man was not the only breadwinner; the woman had to assume a collaborative role in meeting the financial needs of the family. Her status changed significantly from what it had been in Egypt, where middle-class married women seldom worked for a living. Once in Australia, Egyptian/Jewish women were often—willingly or unwillingly— "liberated" from the ancient structures prevalent in their country of birth and their specific role as homemakers. Although homemaking remained exclusively the domain of women within the study sample, the change was particularly noteworthy in the white-collar category. Whereas in the Old Country only 9 percent of wives or mothers were employed outside the home in any capacity, in Australia they constituted nearly half of the white-collar workers from the sample group. One respondent claimed that she developed as a person in Australia because she was able to do what she wanted. She opened her own women's wear factory; she designed and cut the patterns, and her husband organised the machinists and the distribution of orders.[632] Among the women who arrived in their early teens and finished school in Australia, the majority went on to become primary and high school teachers.[633] The adult women took office jobs as clerks or secretaries, depending on their training.

As expected, my data also showed that women at home with low or no English skills fared worse emotionally than working women, particularly the older ones. Some expressed feelings of isolation and alienation as they faced a social structure and cultural traditions that were totally foreign to them. Although on a much less tragic scale, they were confronted with the same predicaments experienced by Holocaust survivors who, as noted by the sociologist Naomi Rosh White, "having left behind all that was familiar to them, deprived of family, former friends, social networks, and material goods, had to try and find a place in a new community, to start their lives again".[634] They found solace only within their own ethnic and linguistic microgroup. For example, the mother of Interviewee #8 was left in charge of the household while her husband, two sons, and daughter-in-law went out to work to pay three mortgages on the home they had just bought. They were living away from the traditional Jewish areas. After leading a life of luxury in Egypt, surrounded by servants, the mother found herself not only trying to make ends meet on a very tight budget, but also alone all day, having to clean, shop, and cook for five adults and an eleven-year-old child. Her English skills were poor, and communicating with her Australian neighbours was made even harder by the unfamiliar Australian accent. Her only support came from extended family members, who were themselves experiencing similar difficulties. In such cases, integration was a longer and more arduous process.

Overall, my study consistently showed that working women within the sample group engaged in lower-status occupations than the men. They represented only 15 percent of the owner/professional section, in which tertiary-educated men dominated.[635] This trend was a reflection of the patriarchal nature of Jewish society in Egypt, where higher education was considered more essential for men than for women because the latter were destined for marriage and home. This mentality sometimes persisted even after immigration to Australia, and it was not unusual for Egyptian Jewish families to make all the necessary sacrifices for the sons to pursue university studies while pushing their daughters into secretarial jobs with little prospect.

It is also true that the women—particularly the older ones—did not remain in the workforce in the same proportion after the initial period of settlement. As the socioeconomic situation of the family improved, the financial contribution of the women became less essential. It is important to note that Australian working conditions in the 1950s were not particularly friendly to mothers—especially those from migrant communities—due to a severe shortage or even lack of public childcare facilities, combined with inflexible working hours. One respondent remembered that at her place of work, Prudential Insurance Company, the policy still prevalent in the late 1960s was to avoid employing young married women because they were more likely to quit their jobs prematurely to have children.

Taking into consideration all the information referenced to this point, a clearer profile of the Egyptian Jewish migrant to Australia can be outlined. It has been demonstrated that the selective nature of the Australian immigration policy ensured that migrants were young, healthy individuals and families, as demonstrated by the majority of my respondents. It has also been established that, although they came mostly from a privileged middle and upper-middle class, those privileges had been stripped away when they landed in Australia, with few resources, particularly after 1956. In spite of the initial and inevitable culture shock, their integration and acculturation were reasonably smooth thanks to a Western education, multiple language skills, a cosmopolitan culture, and sound business training. Although most Egyptian Jews have generally maintained their use of the French language within the family circle and with their compatriots in social situations, the majority of the sample was proficient enough in English to function relatively well in the workplace. As previously mentioned, all the respondents who were of age joined the workforce almost immediately after their arrival without major difficulty. Those were days of full employment in Australia, and the type of occupation usually matched their qualifications. The fact that only a small percentage engaged in factory or menial work is a further sign of the overall education and skill levels of the sample.

As previously demonstrated, the sample group also reflected a traditional community with robust family structures, a strong sense of Jewish identity, a traditional but somewhat low level of religious observance, and no significant involvement in politics.

By retracing every step of my respondents' long journeys to the Edge of the Diaspora, I have tried to create a comprehensive picture of the conditions under which they immigrated to Australia, during the time of the White Australia Policy, when Jews from the Middle East were considered undesirable migrant material. I examined the historical and political connections between Egypt and Australia, focusing on the period of the nationalisation of the Suez Canal and the role of the Australian Prime Minister, Sir Robert Menzies, in negotiations with the president of Egypt, Gamal Abdel Nasser. I looked into the reasons why my respondents elected to migrate to Australia, a country they knew nothing about, and I examined the long and tedious process my participants had to go through to obtain their precious landing permits. I assessed the support provided by Jewish and international organisations during their transit period in Europe and the extent of the lobbying by communal bodies in Australia, as well as a few exceptional individuals, who fought for their admittance into the country. I tried to evaluate the profile of each respondent: who was allowed in, who was refused, and why. I found that those who were accepted represented an excellent prototype of the "model" migrant, seeing as they fitted the strict criteria set by the Australian immigration policy of those days.[636] Their assets were not necessarily money, but youth, health, education, and a network of family and friends, which made them self-sufficient although their beginnings were difficult. As a general rule, they did not go through the government-sponsored migrant centres or the Jewish migrants' hostels. However, I found that the traditional family structure of the respondents was significantly eroded by the hardship of forced emigration. As the women were forced to take on new roles, men were displaced from their privileged position as sole breadwinner. I looked into the ethnic distribution of the group between Sephardim and Ashkenazim and tried to find a migration pattern related to that distribution. I examined the reasons why such a relatively high proportion of the sample group chose to settle in Adelaide and the role played by a few key individuals in that trend. My research shows that, in spite of differing cultures and traditions, the Jews of Egypt quickly entered the work force and blended into Australian society, thanks to multicultural skills and cross-cultural strategies acquired and practised in Egypt. Because of their small number and their diversity, they were able to integrate without much fanfare and, as a result, did not raise their profile as a distinct group within the broader Jewish community—especially in the larger cities of Sydney and Melbourne, whereas the Jewish community of Adelaide was small enough for Egyptian Jews to make a difference. Today, the ranks of the original community of Egyptian Jews of Adelaide are much depleted through the processes of natural attrition and movement to the bigger cities of Sydney and Melbourne, mainly to follow their young. Will that group of young people retain some traces of the distinctive identity of the Jews from Egypt, or have they totally acculturated to the host society? Will they at least know the chequered history of their parents and grandparents? These are some of the questions raised in the next chapter.

CHAPTER 8

A MULTILAYERED IDENTITY

For any group of migrants, the questions of identity and identification are fraught with problems and contradictions. In a multicultural society such as Australia's, identity and identification are determined by a composite of national, ethnic, social, and religious elements that often coexist in a state of lesser or greater tension. They are inevitably shaped by the strength of the migrants' connection to their former homeland, its traditions, culture, and language; by their acceptance of the value system and mentality of the adoptive country; and by the ability to balance the merits of both, aided by government initiatives towards a smooth social integration. The level of identification with their new home can depend greatly on the context of their migration—political or economic, voluntary or forced—and on the strength of the respective parochial institutions, whether ethnic or religious. Their age, education, and proficiency in the national language; the level of support granted to them by public or private welfare bodies; the success of their social and professional integration; and their own strategies of acculturation can all influence how well they identify with their new home.

In view of those considerations, I chose to raise the question of identity with my respondents towards the end of the interview, on the assumption that—after recounting their lives in Egypt, the reasons for their departure, and their migration experience in Australia—my respondents would be more attuned to the nuances of the issue of identity and their answers would reflect these nuances. I asked them to reflect on the way they saw themselves, to consider their level of self-identification with Australian society in general and the local Jewish community in particular, to assess their religious observance, and to evaluate the place Egypt and/or Israel occupied in their hearts and minds. The aim was for them to sort out the various layers of their identity, then try to define their core identity. It became obvious very quickly that they could not identify themselves with a single definition. Their answers were as multifaceted as my questions, and I realised that trying to define the specific identity of Egyptian Jews through their perception of self, as well as through the way they were perceived by others, was not going to be straightforward. From the onset, that identity was full of contradictions. For instance, they came from a Middle Eastern country, without being necessarily ethnically Oriental. Only a small proportion had Egyptian nationality, although most were Egyptian-born. Although they were all multilingual, French was their primary language, but very few were technically French. They saw themselves fundamentally as Jews, regardless of the fact that for the most part they were not strictly observant. Furthermore, as Sephardim within a predominantly Ashkenazi Australian community, they were a minority within a minority. All these paradoxes rendered the task of labelling them concisely even more intricate. Therefore, I had to consider their perceptions of self while bearing in mind the other features of their profile that either reinforced or contradicted those perceptions. The ultimate aim was to uncover whether the tensions among the various layers of their identity helped or hindered their integration into Australian society.

The issue of identity in general, and Jewish identity in particular, has been studied by eminent contemporary sociologists, such as Steven M. Cohen, Samuel C. Heilman, Zvi Gitelman, Stephen J. Whitfield, and numerous others who have defined what constitutes the essential components and characteristics of modern Jewish identity or identities. Most of them agree that Jewish identity in Western societies today is more a matter of choice than a matter of fate.[637] Stuart Z. Charme, for instance, argued:

> In modern culture, where identity is open, affirmations of the given and traditional are as much dependent on choice as more dramatic creations of new identifications and commitments... Identity, formerly objective and imposed, has become constructed and chosen—Jewish identity, like all others.[638]

It is undeniable that Jews, by essence, have multifaceted identities, as a consequence of their history of peregrinations. This characteristic is a major feature of Egyptian Jews' distinctiveness, which has remained constant wherever they have settled. The "sociological ambivalence" discussed by Samuel Heilman in his study of Orthodox Jews in the United States—generated by a possible contradiction and therefore conflict between an inner and an outer Jewish identity—is a significant feature of the sample group under study here.[639] This was already true for the Jews in Egypt where, on both the national and cultural levels, they were torn between their Western outer identity and their Egyptian roots, their inner identity. Then again, living in a country where they were defined by their religion, they were perceived as "others" by the Muslim majority and therefore perceived themselves as "others". Even when they felt a strong sense of belonging in Egypt, even when they were Egyptian citizens, they knew that they would never be considered "true Egyptians", and consequently they did not really consider themselves Egyptian. Technically speaking, one can argue that the Jews in Egypt were still *"Galuth"* Jews[640], although they lived in privilege and comfort under the protection of the colonial powers. They remained the perennial outsiders, and eventually the time came when they were not wanted anymore and they had to leave. It seems that their forced departure unequivocally resolved the conflict between their inner and outer identities.

What happened once my respondents landed on Australian shores? How did they resolve the new conflict between their own Egyptian/

French culture and the contextual Anglo culture? What model of acculturation did they choose to resolve that conflict: assimilation or integration? Which strategies did they use to fit into Australian society? To answer these questions, I compared their perceptions of self-identification, both in Egypt and in Australia, and checked for any variation resulting from their displacement. I evaluated the content of their Australian identity because a fair number of respondents claimed it had now become not only part of the way they saw themselves, but also part of the way they wanted to be seen. As stated by Chanan Reich in his comparative research on the ethnic identity of the Jewish and Greek communities in Melbourne, "the formation of identity is an ongoing process of interaction between external identification and self-identification".[641]

It is important to remember that most of the Jews of Egypt migrated to Australia as impoverished refugees. As previously demonstrated, they came mostly from a middle- or upper-middle-class background. They left their homeland under duress, officially banned from ever coming back. Before 1977, when Egyptian president Anwar el-Sadat started peace negotiations with Israel, they were not even allowed to visit Egypt. Catherine Panich, who studied the Australian postwar immigration experience, explained that such a migration process could be compared to:

> a metaphoric…"death" of the former self, the permanent loss of close relationships, the recognition that a chapter of one's life is closing with great finality. The action of emigrating thrust one irrevocably into a new frontier…Slowly and subtly the newcomer would be absorbed and moulded by this new environment.[642]

Furthermore, Egyptian Jews arrived in Australia before the term "multiculturalism" was coined, at a time when the country still "dealt with cultural diversity fundamentally through exclusion" via the White Australia Policy, and migrant groups were defined in racial rather than ethnic terms, as pointed out by Geoffrey Levey in his discussion of the challenges to Jewish identity presented by Australian multiculturalism.[643] Assimilation was the currency of the day, and it demanded "all previous allegiances be relinquished, along with traditions and languages".[644]

How did the Jews of Egypt fit into that single mould, bearing in mind the multiple nature of their identity?

The answer to that question is that, like other migrants, they did not fit neatly into any single category. The majority of my respondents, like most Australian Jews, identified themselves as being primarily Jewish, in spite of a below-average level of religious observance.[645] Their Jewishness was more a sense of belonging to the Jewish people by sharing a number of rituals and traditions. Therefore, it was not "the sole emblem of their being" as it usually is for ultra-Orthodox Jews.[646] One must not forget that this was how they were identified and how they identified themselves during their time in Egypt, regardless of their religious laxity or orthodoxy. They continued to perceive their Jewishness as the essential component of their identity, although it was more of an ethnic marker rather than a strictly religious one. For instance, one of my respondents insisted that being Jewish was very important to her even though she had just stated she was totally secular: "It is something that I cannot reject or deny. I am the product of a traditional Jewish family".[647] Another respondent, who considered his Jewish identity an issue of culture, not of religion, admitted nevertheless that he was affiliated to a synagogue and attended services on the High Holy Days.[648]

Moreover, all my respondents listed a range of other identities, which might not be as fundamental as their ethno-religious identity, but nevertheless remained an important part of who they were. Interviewee #89, an Italian national—who had declared at first: "My heart is Jewish. Now I am Australian" —must have realised that the issue was not as simple as his statement implied, and quickly corrected himself:

> I see myself as a person with more than one identity, Italian to some extent but more Egyptian. I think like them [the Egyptians]. I was brought up with them…I lived with them all my life; we spoke the same language.[679]

It is obvious that in his case all his different inner and outer identities were cohabiting quite happily and there was no question of relinquishing any one of them in order to adopt a single national identity, however desirable.

Having lived in a country like Egypt where the outer identity was often negotiable, Egyptian Jews had acquired the necessary strategies to juggle national and ethnic identities according to time and place. I encountered many such examples in the course of my research. The case of one of the Karaite respondents was particularly relevant. As stated previously, most of the Karaites in Egypt were not as Westernised as their Sephardi compatriots. Until the early part of the twentieth century, they were very acculturated to the local population as far as language, clothing, and food were concerned, however not their religious practices. This respondent's first language was Arabic, both at home and at school. Unlike his Jewish middle name, his first name and surname were typically Egyptian. Through the omission of one of his names, he used to switch from one identity to the other according to context. On university campus, he emphasised his Arabic persona in order to be accepted by his Egyptian/Muslim fellow-students while in the workplace. When he dealt with Jewish, British, or French businessmen regarding employment, he emphasized his Jewish persona by revealing only his Jewish name. His Egyptian acculturation became an added asset because it allowed him to enter a domain that was not always accessible to his Westernised bosses. He was thus able to operate in both worlds and move with ease from one to the other because of this duality.[650] His inner and outer identities were interchangeable. As argued by Erving Goffman in *The Presentation of Self in Everyday Life*, "when the individual presents himself before others, his performance will tend to incorporate and exemplify the officially accredited values of the society, more so, in fact, than does his behaviour as a whole".[651] When he left Egypt, this respondent spent thirteen years in Israel before immigrating to Australia in 1969, which added another layer to his identity. Today, depending on the circumstances, he sees himself either as an Australian Jew or as an Israeli Jew, but he is also a Karaite Jew from Egypt. There is no simple answer to the question of which aspect of his identity is predominant. Levey commented upon the complexity of Australian Jewish identity:

> The twin worlds that Jews occupy are reflected in how they choose to call themselves...Jewish institutions and individuals in this country typically refer to themselves as "Australian Jews"... The noun "Jews" signifies the presumed primary identity; the adjective "Australian" is the qualifier.[652]

That particular issue is still hotly debated within the various diasporas of Egyptian Jews. Are they to refer to themselves as Egyptian Jews, as Jews *of* Egypt, or as Jews *from* Egypt?[653]

My respondents used different strategies to deal with their Egyptian identity. Some claimed they had no identity conflict, denying the Egyptian content altogether. Such was the case of Interviewee #63 who, having always mixed in British circles in Egypt, both at school and at work, stated that he never felt part of the country and saw it purely as an accident of birth. Since arriving in his adopted country, he has defined himself first and foremost as an Australian, and this was his presentation of self to others. As for his religion, it belonged in the private domain of his inner identity, and he revealed it only when it was appropriate.[654] This was exactly the way Jews traditionally negotiated life in liberal democracies before the advent of multiculturalism, "by downplaying their Jewish distinctiveness" and stressing their national loyalty, noted Levey.[655] The next interviewee (#31) also considered herself much more Australian than anything else. Although she acknowledged that Egypt had given her precious multicultural skills, she never felt she belonged there. As for her Jewish identity, it constituted a part of her ethnic background but did not play a significant role in her present life, given that she was not a practising Jew—she was married to a non-Jewish person—and she did not socialise with Jews, even those from Egypt.[656]

Exposure to a multiplicity of cultures of the type experienced in Egypt made it difficult for the Jews of Egypt to identify with a single and dominant national or cultural distinctiveness. An example is the case of Interviewee #10, born of an Austrian father and a Russian mother who migrated to Egypt towards the latter part of the nineteenth century. She spoke Yiddish at home with her parents and had a French education dispensed by Catholic nuns, while her brother went to a Jesuit school. She did not identify with either her Russian or Austrian origins but felt she belonged in Egypt, although she did not speak Arabic. That sense of belonging probably had more to do with the comfort of her privileged lifestyle. Typically, she never called herself Egyptian, although she had acquired Egyptian nationality through marriage. On the contrary, she maintained that she had no distinct sense of identity and therefore could adapt herself to any environment: "Je ne sens pas que j'ai une identité distincte. Je m'adapte à tout le monde. Je me décris comme quelqu'un qui vient d'Égypte, de culture française". Another respondent stated: "I am a citizen of the world…I am comfortable anywhere".[657]

In fact, the collected data indicates that, in spite of having been rejected by what was after all their mother country, the majority of the Jews of Egypt have kept a positive memory of their birthplace and preserved certain elements of the culture they left behind, such as the languages, the food, even the sense of humour. For instance, within my sample group the majority (68 percent) still reminisced with pleasure about their lives in Egypt and did not harbour any resentment towards Egypt. Some of them even spoke Arabic—albeit brokenly—whenever they had the opportunity. As noted, the use of the French language within the circle of family and friends was maintained, particularly in households where both spouses were from Egypt, and close to half the sample group—44 percent—expressed a deep and continuous affinity with the French culture.[658] The same proportion declared that they socialised mostly with ex-Egyptian Jews, mainly in the "over twenty-eight" category, sharing some of the traditional Egyptian dishes; 40 percent stated that at least some of their friends were originally from Egypt. The older they were, the more they identified with the past, which is usually the case, particularly for migrants for whom the past represents a familiar anchor to which they remain attached while they try and chart their way in unfamiliar waters.

Nevertheless, for most of the respondents, Egypt symbolized the past and, as specified by Interviewee #19: "Egypt has very little relevance except in memories". Nearly half of the Sephardim within the sample

CHART **16.** Feelings of belonging in Egypt versus identity in Australia.

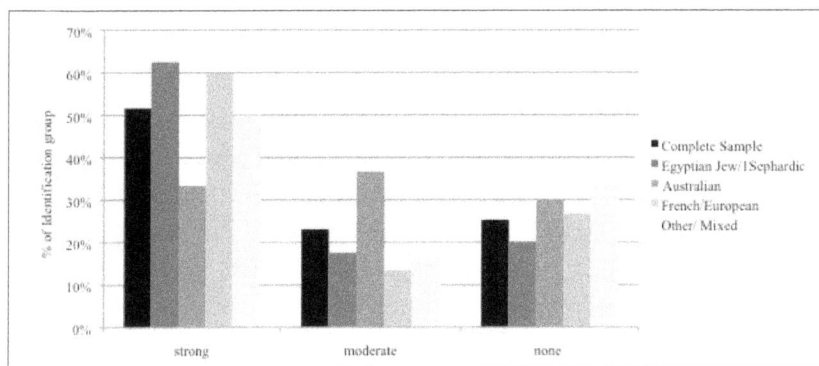

refined their definition of self as primarily Sephardi Jews from Egypt, a definition that consciously or unconsciously excluded the national connotation of the label Egyptian Jews, while still retaining the ethnic and religious aspects. One-third of the sample—33 percent—claimed they now saw themselves as Australians, as succinctly articulated by the next respondent: "I feel Jewish because I was born Jewish, and then I feel Australian, as if I was born here. I feel nothing for Egypt".[659] Interviewee #55, who was stateless when he arrived, declared that because his first citizenship was Australian, that was his only national identity.[660] As a general rule, my data showed that those who had a strong sense of belonging in Egypt were more likely to define themselves as Jewish/ Egyptian, whereas those who did not tended to prioritise their Australian identity, as seen in Chart 16:

The complexity and ambivalence of Egyptian Jews' multiple and conflicting identities were not really understood in any of their countries of immigration, and the old dilemma lingered. Whereas in Egypt they were never considered Egyptians, in their new country they were labelled as Egyptians or even Arabs, both by the general population and by the Jewish community. The confusion on the part of the general population was somewhat tolerated and humoured, but it was resented coming from the Jewish community who, in the eyes of my respondents, should have known better. This attitude was part and parcel of the bigger issue of the internal cultural divide between the Ashkenazi and Sephardi Jews that is discussed further in this chapter.

On the other hand, in the late 1950s when the main wave of Jewish Egyptian migrants arrived in Australia, the general population, staunchly monolingual and still quite insular, was just starting to get accustomed to the ways of the New Australians—their broken English, their funny accents, their strange food, and their peculiar customs. On the whole, my respondents did not complain about the way they were greeted by Australians. They considered them mostly helpful and pleasant despite their innate Anglo reserve. There was at times some venting of anti-immigrant feelings, especially when migrants communicated in their own language in front of the locals. One respondent (#77) stated, "they [the locals] felt that somebody talking in a different language was strange…you have to speak English, they said".[661] Interviewee #8 remembered an unpleasant episode in 1959, when he was having a private conversation in French with his wife on the train on their way to work, and an older commuter intervened loudly by poking her umbrella at his wife, saying: "Speak English, you wogs!"[662] This was obviously a reflection of the mindset of assimilation, whereby migrants were encouraged to shed their old culture and adopt unilaterally the Anglo culture. A number of parents within the sample group remembered that the issue of language deeply affected their children, who begged them not to speak French in front of their school friends.[663] Even in the late 1960s, when the Department of Immigration had already dropped from official usage the term "assimilation" and replaced it with "integration", I personally remember being admonished by a primary school headmistress for speaking French to my children. Nevertheless, nobody in the sample group could recall a significant anti-Semitic incident originating from non-Jewish Australians.

The multiple identities of the Jews of Egypt seemed to baffle Australians, and it was not uncommon for the former to be submitted to a lengthy interrogation by the latter trying to work out who these newcomers were. They would be asked why French was their mother tongue when they were not French citizens, why they did not consider themselves Egyptian when they were born in Egypt, what it meant to be Jewish in Egypt, and a string of other related questions. According to numerous testimonies of Egyptian Jews who had settled all over the map, they were subjected to the same type of questioning and repeatedly had to explain themselves to others.[664] Even in France where they shared the same culture, they were often asked: "Mais d'où venez-vous?" because their accent was not recognised as an authentic French accent and therefore they could not be "true French". It is obvious that their multilayered identity was confusing for the various host societies.

If one were to assess which types of migrants were expected to acculturate better than others in Australia during that time, it would be the young, European-looking, educated, English-speaking, and middle class. It is undeniable that these factors played a major role in the degree of identification and communal involvement of my sample group. Within the sample, those who were under the age of twenty-eight upon arrival in the country felt much more connected to Australia than those over that age. One can assume that this would be true across the board for all migrants. Early integration difficulties are usually more easily overcome by the younger members of any migrant group, and the structure of my sample group confirmed that the majority—about 60 percent—of those between the ages of eighteen and forty-five had an easier integration experience than those over forty-five. More specifically, the respondents in the upper-middle-class category, aged between eighteen and twenty-eight, with a tertiary education and advanced English skills were more likely to be involved in communal affairs than the older respondents. Furthermore, respondents under the age of eighteen upon arrival would have attended primary and/or high school in Australia, which would significantly improve not only the identification process but also the degree of professional achievement. The younger migrants were more likely to become professionals or self-employed than those who arrived over the age of forty-five, as demonstrated by the next chart.

By the time the present research was initiated—about forty years after my participants' arrival in Australia—the overall proportion of

CHART **17.** Age distribution according to level of occupation achieved in Australia

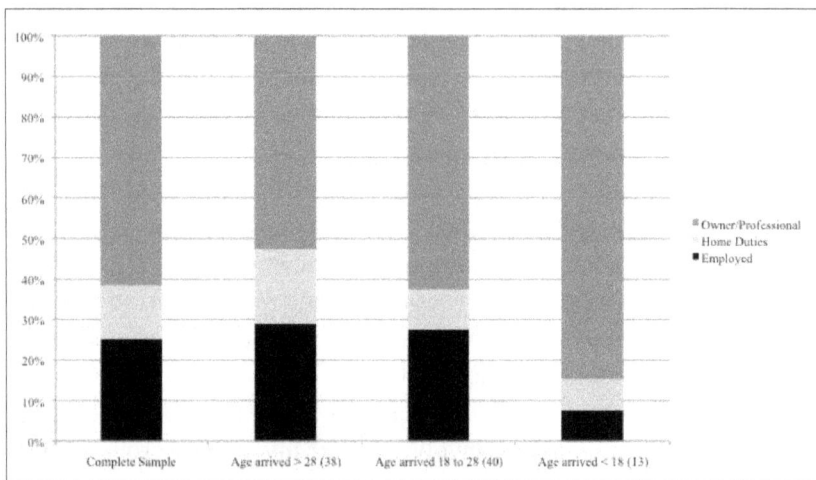

those who achieved the highest status professionally was a remarkable 62 percent, which means they had reclaimed a place in the middle or upper-middle class. Moreover, virtually all the participants had become more or less fluent in English, through either formal education or auto-didactism. Their English remained accented and identified them immediately as non-Australian-born; however, due to the multicultural nature of modern Australian society, they were not alone in this respect. Some even declared that, through the years, their accent was often considered "interesting", particularly when they revealed that they came from Egypt. If they did not look too "ethnic", the response would often be: "You don't look Egyptian", as if in consolation.

My next task was to address the issue of the dynamics between the sample group and the broader Jewish Australian community. Both the size of the existing Jewish community and the support system organised by the local Jewish institutions were crucial to the newcomers' identification with that community. As noted, the profile of Egyptian Jews was higher in the smaller Adelaide context, where they were accepted "on face value" by the established community. As claimed by Interviewee #35, "they were more interested in us than we in them". Their profile was definitely lower among the much larger Sydney and Melbourne Jewish communities, where some of my respondents complained they were made to feel like outsiders by their fellow Jews. One notable example was the case of Interviewee #63, who was a highly educated graduate of the elite Victoria College in Alexandria and the British Institute and was fluent in four languages. He remembered that some of his Ashkenazi colleagues used to call him an Arab because he did not speak Yiddish.

The feeling of being patronised by the Jewish establishment was often shared by my Sephardi and Ashkenazi interviewees. Interviewee #26 confided that, to this day, the only people who accepted her as an equal and with whom she felt most comfortable were the more recently arrived South African Jews. They were also considered outsiders at times by some of the local Jews. According to that respondent, her complex identity as Ashkenazi, francophone, Egyptian-born, Jewish, and now Australian was often considered exotic and distinctive.[665] This phenomenon was probably due to the fact that the Egyptians' migration preceded that of the South Africans, and therefore the former were perceived as more-seasoned New Australians. How did South African Jews weather their own immigration experience, and was there any parallel between the two migrations? It is true that their migration to Australia was greatly facilitated by the fact that they were not refugees when they first arrived. Moreover, they found in Australia a familiar culture, education system, lifestyle, and communal structure. Because of the size of the Jewish South African population in Australia—estimated at around fifteen thousand—they were able to rely on their own support group, and most of them very quickly re-established themselves within the ranks of the Jewish and wider communities.[666] Nevertheless, no uprooting is easy, and they must have experienced difficulties adjusting to life in their new country. A comparative study of their exodus would be an interesting topic for future academic research.

Gitelman has argued that "identification with Jews is generally expressed in the diaspora…in two ways: affiliation and philanthropy".[667] To what extent were Egyptian Jews affiliated to Jewish institutions, such as synagogues, communal bodies, and welfare organisations? How did they generally interact with the local Jews, and particularly with the Iraqi/Indian Sephardim? Was there a sustained effort on their behalf to build separate institutions in order to preserve the specificity of their Sephardic religious traditions and cultural identity or identities? In other words, how strong and distinctive was their Sephardi identity, and how did it fit in with the dominant Ashkenazi identity and with that of the other Sephardim in Australia?

First, it is important to state that in Egypt synagogue affiliation was quasi-axiomatic for the Jewish population. As noted by Krämer, "all Jews residing in town for a certain period of time, usually one year, were regarded as members of the community, regardless of rite and personal observance".[668] However, the system of synagogue member-ship where congregants must "pay to pray" was quite foreign to Sep-hardim given that it was customary in Egypt for the rich families of the community to maintain and subsidise the various religious institutions. Everybody attended the synagogue of their choice "without having to pay any fee". Consequently, in Australia many resisted the notion of membership payment that was common practice in all the diasporas of the Western world.[669] My research also revealed that, as a consequence of uprooting and dispersal, a fair number of Egyptian Jews in Australia seemed to neglect the practice of regular synagogue attendance, except on the High Holy Days. Nevertheless, the fact that the majority of the sample group—close to 80 percent—remained affiliated to Sephardi, Ashkenazi, or Reform synagogues, however loosely, proved a persist-ing self-identification as Jews despite the laxity in religious observance. The distribution among the three types of institutions was not necessar-ily based on ethnicity and has fluctuated over the years. For example, about 20 percent of Sydney and Melbourne Sephardi respondents who had the choice between the two rites chose to affiliate with Ashkenazi synagogues, whereas the opposite was almost never true.[670]

As for Sephardi identification, the early records of the Sydney Sephardi synagogue showed that a significant number of Egyptian Jews joined the predominant Iraqi and Indian Jews as founding members of this synagogue, and some of them served on the Executive Board and/or in the ladies auxiliary for many years.[671] Scholars, such as Myer Samra and Naomi Gale, have both compared and contrasted the issue of identity between the Iraqi and the Egyptian groups, studying their inter-action, as well as their relations with the wider Jewish community.[672] According to Samra, the Iraqi and Indian Jews came to adopt the label of Sephardim by the mid-1950s, partly out of a need to differentiate themselves from the predominant Ashkenazim and partly because they considered the Sephardi/Spanish/European background to be more pres-tigious. Apparently, they were not aware of the Egyptian Sephardim:

> For many of my informants, "Sephardi" had become synonymous with Iraqi culture, so to learn about Sephardi Jews from Egypt with different customs has been quite a surprise.[673]

The encounter between the two different Sephardi traditions encouraged a degree of acceptance of certain aspects of these traditions, such as "the liturgy and culinary endeavours". Samra noted that the "tunes identi-fied with the Yerushalmi tradition [practised by Egyptian Jews], occa-sionally used in the Sephardi Synagogue" were favourably accepted by Iraqi Jews, who used the Babylonian Talmud. Furthermore, the dishes prepared by the Egyptian women, although different from Iraqi cuisine, were more appreciated than Ashkenazi cuisine. This was an example of a sharing of cultures. However, added Samra, notwithstanding the positive aspects of their identification with each other, the dissimilarities between the two communities led to episodes of friction and even estrangement, arising "from differences in cultural taste and education", as well as dif-ferences in self-identification.[674]

According to some of my respondents, the Iraqi establishment con-sidered the Egyptians not knowledgeable enough of their own religious traditions[675], whereas the Egyptians found the Iraqis too rigid in their approach to ritual differences and often unwilling to compromise.[676]

Here again, the Egyptians' continued use of French as their lingua franca became an issue. According to Samra, the fact that they spoke French between themselves and had "developed friendship networks which included other Jews from around the Mediterranean who had also adopted the French language", further alienated the Iraqi/Indian group. Conversely, although the Egyptian Jews accepted the general principle of a common Sephardiness, they still claimed they were the "real" Sephardis, with a true Spanish origin, unlike the so-called Sephardi Jews from Asia.[677] According to Gale, "members of the Egyptian group invariably regarded themselves as superior to the Iraqi and Indian-born members…more modern and more advanced".[678]

Gradually, due to natural attrition as well as disaffection and/or general apathy, the original Egyptian membership of the Sephardi synagogue dwindled considerably. Some joined other Egyptian families who were already affiliated to Ashkenazi synagogues, as a result of their children attending Jewish day schools and therefore becoming acculturated to the Ashkenazi tradition. Others were already settled in more isolated neighbourhoods with a small Jewish community, as was the case for the Egyptian Jews who lived in Sydney's St. George district. The travelling distance to the Sephardi synagogue in Bondi Junction constituted a significant obstacle, particularly for the older members who often could not drive. It was much more convenient for them to join the only local synagogue, based in Allawah, which followed the Ashkenazi tradition.[679] Furthermore, some of the disaffected members of the original Sephardi synagogue, who considered themselves "true Orthodox Sephardim", pooled their efforts with other Sephardim from Israel, North Africa, and Iraq, and formed their own Sephardi *minyan,* now based at Beit Yosef (the Caro synagogue) in Bondi.[680]

In the case of Melbourne, it was a group of dedicated Egyptian Jews, wishing to emulate the example of the NSW Sephardim and also seeking to define themselves vis-à-vis the dominant Ashkenazi community, who enlisted the help of the Melbourne Baghdadi Jewish community to establish the Sephardi Association of Victoria in November 1965. The first president was Maurice Tueta, an Egyptian Jew.[681] A Sephardi synagogue was subsequently built, inaugurated in March 1977 by Malcolm Fraser, then Prime Minister of Australia, which was a momentous occasion. Unfortunately, Gad Ben-Meir, who also served as president of the association, claimed that the new leadership who took office in 1987 had sown "seeds of division and dissension", which "brought about the alienation of almost the entirety of the Iraqi constituency and of the intelligentsia".[682] It is noteworthy that some of my respondents, who were part of the original committee and were still very involved in running the synagogue, did not mention any significant internal conflict, either because they considered it irrelevant by the time of the interview or because they had simply occluded the memory of that conflict, which is often the case in oral history. On the contrary, they showed great pride in the self-sufficiency and strength of their small congregation. Only when specifically asked about any friction between themselves and the Baghdadi members did they acknowledge that it existed, but that they still managed to maintain a reasonably harmonious working climate between the two ethnic subgroups. One of the founding members, the late Maurice Gamil, proudly showed me the Commonwealth Award presented to him in February 2002, in recognition of his unique dedication to the Sephardi synagogue and to the Sephardi tradition.[683]

Overall, the identification of the Egyptian Sephardim with the Sephardim of Asia encountered a number of difficulties, particularly in Sydney, due to differences of culture, religious practice, and mentality. The larger problem of the children and grandchildren of Egyptian Jews in Adelaide, Sydney, and Melbourne identifying with the Sephardi tradition is really the issue here and should be more closely monitored. How can they be motivated to retain a distinctive Sephardi identity when their parents' congregations are ageing and shrinking? The allure of the bigger and better-organised Ashkenazi synagogues, the influence of the Jewish day school system—where Ashkenazi history and traditions are predominantly taught, with at best a token Sephardi content—and the prestige of the upwardly mobile young Ashkenazi adults often prove too much of an attraction, preventing the young from developing a strong Sephardi identity. Unless a systematic educational program is established, this does not augur well for the growth of the Sephardi community of Australia, at least as far as the Sephardim from Egypt are concerned.

How did Egyptian Jews interact with the broader Jewish community, a community that was, as already stated, predominantly Ashkenazi? Although the Sephardim and Ashkenazim within the sample group were very much aware of their own history and traditions, they did not see themselves as fundamentally different, and they dealt with one another as equals. Together in Egypt, they had already undergone the process of Westernisation through education and socialisation, and in Australia they experienced the same trauma of displacement and alienation. However, according to the testimonies of various respondents, the attitude of the dominant Ashkenazi community in Australia towards the small Sephardi community was often unsympathetic. Interviewee #56, who was herself Ashkenazi, stated: "there was no warmth from the Anglo-Jewish community. They looked down upon us. They did not like us to speak French".[684] Others recalled the patronising behaviour of the dominant group and the subtle discrimination they experienced in the early days of their arrival. This negative perception was confirmed by Gale's research on the Sephardi Jews of Sydney. It seems that when Sephardim started to arrive, "neither AJWS nor the ECAJ displayed much enthusiasm in helping them", whereas the 1956 Hungarian refugees, who arrived at the same time as the Egyptian refugees, were welcomed with open arms.[685] Apparently, many Jews from Egypt were particularly bitter at the way they were treated. According to Gale, the attitude of the Ashkenazi establishment stemmed partly from ignorance of the existence of Sephardi Jews and partly out of fear of a new wave of anti-Semitism sparked by the arrival of presumably undesirable "black" Jews who would undermine their status as White Australians.[686] Maybe it was no coincidence that the only three instances I noted where Egyptian Jews complained of discrimination by local Jews in positions of authority concerned respondents who were visibly ethnic or, in other words, of Middle Eastern appearance. The three cases, two in Sydney and one in Melbourne, approached the Jewish Welfare offices upon arrival in Australia, asking for help, and in all three cases they were told to address themselves to "their own people", which they interpreted as being the Sephardi community.[687] The impact caused by such an expression of exclusion at a particularly vulnerable time in their life, when they had already suffered dispossession and dislocation, seems to have had a deep and lasting effect, seeing that they still remember those incidents over forty years after the fact. Gale aptly recalled Max Weber's differentiation between self-identification and identification by others:

> While self-identification refers to common descent and cultural traditions, identification by others is based mostly on physical and behavioural characteristics which are different from those of the identifier.[688]

It is understandable that the Egyptian Sephardim, who were considered the aristocracy of their community in Egypt, did not appreciate being snubbed by the dominant Ashkenazim. Nevertheless, except for those few cases, and unlike the Baghdadi and Indian Jews, the majority of my interviewees said they were not systematically discriminated against by the dominant Ashkenazim, maybe because of their ethnic heterogeneity, Western acculturation, and generally more European appearance.

The experience of Egyptian Jews in Adelaide constitutes a case in point. Contrary to the situation in Sydney, the Adelaide respondents reported that their relationship with the established Ashkenazi community was mostly harmonious, borne out of respect and genuine interest for the cultural and religious differences between the two traditions. Adelaide Jewry was so small that all newcomers to the community were welcomed, regardless of their ethnic background. Some locals reproached the Egyptian newcomers for their low level of involvement in communal activities. They also reproached them for their continued use of the French language, when the local Jewish population had abandoned their native German for English.[689] Nevertheless, the consensus was that they contributed significantly to the community by more than doubling its size and thereby reinvigorating it. Despite various promptings from the Sydney and Melbourne Sephardi associations, Egyptian Jews in Adelaide never wanted to establish a separate Sephardi synagogue.

In view of the overall small size of the community, they did not wish to isolate themselves and thus divide the community. They preferred the strategy of acculturation, integrating the existing structure while retaining certain features of their identity.

Again it was in Adelaide that the communal involvement of the Jews of Egypt was most prominent. After the initial struggle to settle and earn a living in a foreign land, a number of Egyptian Jews came to hold leadership positions in the established Adelaide communal institutions. Aaron Aaron, leader of the NSW Association of Sephardim (NAS), praised them in his book:

> They helped to regenerate Jewish life into what was becoming a fast-fading assimilated Jewish community. Their presence has been felt in the synagogue where they introduced parts of their Sephardic *Minhag*, blending this with the Ashkenazi *Minhag* so that the result reflected aspects of the background of every Jew.[690]

This was reiterated to me by one of my Adelaide respondents, the late Albert Ninio, who served many terms on the board of the synagogue, eventually becoming president. He was responsible for the introduction of some of those Sephardi *minhagim* (traditional liturgical rites") and melodies in the predominantly Ashkenazi ritual. Furthermore, he headed the Jewish Welfare Society of Adelaide and ran it single-handedly for many years.[691] He was also past and acting president of the B'nai B'rith lodge (1969–1970). A number of other prominent Adelaide Egyptian Jews were mentioned by Aaron Aaron, such as the late Victor Ades, who was president of the South Australia Jewish Board of Deputies from 1963 to 1970. The Jewish kindergarten of Adelaide still bears his name. Dr. Albert Hassan was Treasurer and president of the AHC, the only synagogue in Adelaide at the time. The late Joseph Bolaffi was Treasurer of the South Australia Zionist Federation from 1962 and then became president in 1974 for six years.[692] Victor Baroukh was president of the Nat Solomon's House for the Aged. The lord mayor of Adelaide between 1993 and 1997 was Henri Ninio, Albert Ninio's younger brother. He was also president of the Beit Shalom Progressive Synagogue, established in

1963. Today, his daughter is a rabbi at Temple Emanuel in Woollahra, Sydney. As stated earlier, Egyptian Jews were also very active in the establishment of the Maccabi Sports Club in 1960, supporting it for many years, probably because of their familiarity with the social club scene in Egypt. The high level of communal activism of the Adelaide respondents is undeniable. Only in South Australia were Egyptian Jews visible in state and local politics, however modestly. Max Liberman, the pioneer among Egyptian Jews in Adelaide, was chairman of the Housing Commission from 1975 to 1980. Others, such as the Hassan family and the Barouch family, achieved great success in the business realm.

From these observations, it seems that the strategies of identification and acculturation of Egyptian Jews with the wider Jewish community worked relatively well in spite of some early difficulties, again due to cultural differences and the racist attitudes of a few individuals within the ranks of the predominantly Ashkenazi institutions. Once they were more established and more financially secure, they often joined Ashkenazi synagogues, sent their children to Sunday schools and, when they could afford it, to Jewish day schools, Jewish sports clubs, and Zionist youth groups. Through their children, they gradually entered Jewish society, and because of their innate ability to adapt and fit in, they were accepted and integrated within the fold relatively quickly. However, in the case of the Sydney respondents, for financial reasons some did not always conform to the traditional Jewish pattern of settling in the more affluent and cosmopolitan eastern suburbs and moved to more "Australian" suburbs, where they relied on their own network for support and socialisation. In the case of the Adelaide respondents, the acculturation was more a two-way process, as has just been discussed.

Another important component of the overall Jewish identity is the level of identification with the State of Israel. As noted by Samra, "Israel is central to the identity of all Jews, even if the elements from which that identity is built may not necessarily be identical".[693] Attachment to and identification with Israel function at several levels: ideological, religious, national, and personal. How close did my respondents feel to the

Jewish State, and what did it represent for them in Australia compared to what it represented in Egypt?

Virtually all in the sample group stated they had family, close or extended, living in Israel and hence were connected on a personal and emotional level. They felt implicated on a national level with the Jewish State, with varying degrees of intensity, although few would elect to settle there at this stage of their lives. Nearly 10 percent of my respondents had lived in Israel for a number of years after leaving Egypt. They migrated to Australia to be reunited with family and for economic reasons. Close to 17 percent of the interviewees have never visited Israel. Nevertheless, the majority openly expressed feelings of pride and solidarity with the Jewish State, and 44 percent claimed they actively supported Zionist organisations by promoting or attending functions and contributing financially to Zionist causes. Interviewee #56, for instance, always encouraged her sons to attend Zionist youth movements. As for many other Jews, the Six-Day War was a watershed event that strengthened her identification with the Jewish State. Rutland noted:

> Unlike the 1956 Suez crisis, the 1967 war had a significant impact on Australian Jewry because it brought together all members of the community, including the unaffiliated. More importantly, the community expressed this sense of unity and solidarity in a public manner, either through attending rallies or donating to the emergency appeal.[694]

Interviewee #56 revealed to her granddaughter that "it was through this war that she developed a sense of identity with Israel and Judaism and has never felt so proud of being Jewish".[695] One must remember that in Egypt, except for the idealistic young men and women who joined the Zionist youth movements overtly or covertly, most Jews had only covertly sympathised with Israel. Not only were Zionist activities banned after the establishment of the Jewish State, but also any outward sign of support for Israel by members of the Jewish community was construed as an act of treason and could be severely punished. "We could not show our true feelings [towards Israel] because of our environment. You had to be very careful and very restrained", remembered Interviewee #55.[696] Those who did not toe the official line paid the heavy price of imprisonment and expulsion, which was the case of a number of my respondents, both in Australia and overseas.[697] The establishment of the State of Israel formally constituted the final link in the chain of events that gradually forced the Jews of Egypt to undertake their second exodus.

In Australia, as in Western democracies, Jews feel free to express their solidarity with Israel or to criticise its policies, and they often exercise that freedom. Some of my respondents stated that the existence of Israel was essential to their security and to their status as diaspora Jews: "Les juifs du monde sont en sécurité de par l'existence de l'Etat d'Israël".[698] Interviewee #55 went even further, saying that for him and his wife, "the existence of Israel made the area and the world in general a safer place"[699], but Interviewee #9 disagreed, stating that for her, Israel could not be considered a safe haven in the current political context. A respondent who had lived in Israel for eight years prior to coming to Australia declared he could not separate his identity as a Jew from his identification with Israel: "outside Israel, you have to identify yourself as Jewish, whereas in Israel you just are".[700] Interviewee #61 admitted to a lingering sense of culpability for not settling in the "Promised Land" and opting instead for the relative comfort of life in Australia.[701] Even for those who were not always in agreement with the Israeli government's policies, being loyal to the State of Israel remained a constant.[702] Some chose to qualify their feelings of solidarity by insisting that, as Australian citizens, their first loyalty was to Australia and then to Israel, except in the unlikely event of Australia turning against its Jewish population.[703] In contrast, Interviewee #54 was totally against the idea of Israel's centrality to the identity of all Jews. She identified more with Egypt and the Egyptians: "je me considérais très égyptienne. J'étais très fière de l'être". She also violently disagreed with the policy of occupation of the Israeli government vis-à-vis the Palestinian population. Again, I have outlined the varying extent of identification with Israel as expressed by my respondents, demonstrating once more the diversity of the group, which included staunch Zionists, Zionist sympathisers, and even anti-Zionists.

Up to this point, it has been established that my interviewees strongly related to their Jewishness as a combination of ethnic and religious identity distinct to the Jews of Egypt. Some tried to assert their collective identity through the establishment of and affiliation to Sephardi institutions, but without resounding success, due to their small numbers and internal division. Others, drawing on their multicultural skills, successfully blended into the ranks of the broader Australian/Jewish community, even though they rarely held leadership positions, with the exception of Adelaide Jewry, where Egyptian Jews were more numerous and therefore more prominent. There were, however, individual cases of communal achievements in Sydney and Melbourne, such as the past president of the Great Synagogue of Sydney, Herman Eisenberg[704]; the past president of the NSW Council of Jewish Women (JCWA), Dinah Danon; the late Jacques Balloul, who was president of the Sassoon Yehudah Sephardi Synagogue of Melbourne and sat on the Executive Board of the Zionist Federation of Australia; and others who worked for communal organisations in different capacities. The majority have maintained some fundamental aspects of their previous or "inner" identity and affinity with the French culture, as well as their Egyptian and Mediterranean roots, which, to quote Levey, constitute a "salad bowl" of multiculturalism.[705] Most of my respondents seemed well integrated and have accommodated both their Jewish identity and their newly forged national identity as Australians.

It is important to point out that, apart from a feeling of nostalgia for their past life in Egypt, as well as a lingering sadness and some resentment about the way that period of their lives was abruptly terminated, none of my respondents expressed any regrets about choosing to live in Australia. On the contrary, many of them declared: "being kicked out of Egypt was the best thing that could have happened to us". What Chanan Reich wrote about the broader Jewish community of Melbourne seems particularly relevant to the sample group:

> The 1967 survey of the Melbourne Jewish community revealed a
> marked satisfaction with life in Australia and positive emotional

feelings about being Australians…This pattern of positive feelings towards Australia prevailed side by side with a high degree of Jewish identification…[These feelings] stem from economic success, or upward social mobility and a relatively high degree of tolerance which they enjoy in Australia.[706]

Nevertheless, their memories of the past were part of a precious cultural heritage held close to their hearts. When asked whether their children were interested in their history in Egypt, the majority of my respondents (76 percent) answered in the affirmative. How can that heritage be transmitted to the next generation? Oral history is certainly one tool, and it has been used by a number of Australian-born grandchildren of Egyptian Jews for the Hans Kimmel Memorial Essay Competition in Contemporary Jewish History at Sydney and Melbourne Jewish day schools. The requirements of that competition are to research the life story of one member of the family. This exercise proved to be an enriching experience at every level because it gave the students the opportunity to learn directly about their parents' or grandparents' origins and early beginnings in Australia and, at the same time, motivated them to delve into the contextual history of the twentieth century. One such student was faced with the dilemma of a family with roots in a number of countries—Austria, Russia, Greece, Italy, Algeria, and France—before even getting to Egypt:

> This "dilemma" however, soon translated itself into an opportunity as I decided to focus my research on the different Jewish communities and lifestyles that my family had been part of over the last 120 years.[707]

Another student realised the importance of her grandmother's testimony and the rich legacy she has entrusted to her:

> My grandmother lived through a period of great changes in the world, which had a significant influence on her life…The languages, customs and traditions that she has kept and brought from her youth enrich my life as well as my family's life in Australia.[708]

Oral history as a direct transmission method of one's cultural heritage to the younger generation, particularly when it reflects the life of a community that is no more, deepens and enhances one's understanding of a specific period of history and its people.

It is clear that from the two possible models of acculturation to the Australian way of life, assimilation or integration, my respondents did not choose the former, at least at the level of the first generation. As defined in the introductory part of this book, assimilation meant foregoing one's cultural and religious traditions and fusing into the host society by either changing name, intermarrying, converting, or just leaving one's ethnic community. Apart from a few exceptions, my respondents maintained ties with their cultural background and religious community while interacting with Australians. What strategies did they use in their efforts to "become Australians and remain Jewish"? They tried as much as possible to reside close to centres of Jewish life.[709] They provided Jewish education for their children, either through Sunday schools or Jewish day schools. They contributed to the general welfare of the Australian Jewish community by being active in Jewish organisations, such as B'nai Brith, the National Council of Jewish Women (NCJW), the Women's International Zionist Organisation (WIZO), United Israel Appeal (UIA), Jewish Communal Appeal (JCA), and the various Jewish museums.[710] They also made a contribution to the wider Australian community by donating their time to organisations, such as Meals on Wheels, Rotary International, the Wesley Mission, and both major political parties.[711]

In addition, most of the interviewees did not abandon their language and culture in spite of some adverse reactions from both the Jewish and the wider Australian community. They did not reject their religious tradition, even if their level of observance had generally waned compared to what it was in Egypt.[712] They did not turn their backs on their own community, whether they stayed within the inner circle of Egyptian Jews or the wider context of Australian Jewry.[713] Socialisation with non-Jewish Australians was described as cordial but often superficial. In fact, among the ninety-two respondents, there were only four cases of name Anglicisation. For instance, Interviewee #23 removed the "a" at the end of his name, which made it sound more "Anglo", but he did not show any other sign of shedding his identity as a Jew from Egypt. In the case of Interviewee #31, it was her father who had started the process of assimilation in Egypt, by changing the obviously Jewish family sur- name to a British one after World War II, and the daughter followed suit. The other two cases had intermarried. The husbands were Maltese and Greek, also from Egypt.[714] Generally speaking, the practice of Anglicis- ing surnames in order to better identify with Australia's Anglo society seems more prevalent in the Maltese community.

Intermarriage was rare at the level of my respondents' generation. However, it was definitely on the rise with the Australian-born gen- eration and constituted a growing source of concern for many of my respondents. Their concerns in that respect were no different from those of the broader Jewish community, in view of the fact that "recent demo- graphic studies indicate a significant increase in intermarriage amongst the younger generation", as well as a declining birth rate.[715]

It is undeniable that the Egyptian Jewish heritage of my sample group has remained a significant ethnic marker. It identifies them as a group, sharing common characteristics, such as collective memories, both bitter and sweet; a language or two, or even three, apart from English, mainly French, Arabic, and Italian; a religious tradition, primarily but not exclu- sively Sephardi; a diverse cuisine, Sephardi, Egyptian, and Western; and a European education and culture. Because of what Beinin called their "Levantine cosmopolitanism", the respondents internalised strategies for accommodating the different layers of their identity and for living in symbiosis with people from other ethnic backgrounds without assimi- lating.[716] In their new diaspora, they have tried to integrate success- fully in Australian society, finding a comfortable place in the middle or upper-middle class while preserving some aspects of their identity by re- acculturating the characteristics of their original diaspora to the Austra- lian diaspora, thus adding another layer to their identity. They represent the last generation of authentic Jews from Egypt, but that specificity is bound to be diluted and gradually disappear as their children acculturate more and more into Australian society. Clearly, the dwindling Jewish community that remains in Egypt is not likely to reproduce itself. One would have to study the first generation born outside Egypt in order to assess what—if anything—is left of those distinguishing features.[717]

I have attempted to identify the interviewees' perception of self to determine their level of integration in the Australian social landscape and their contribution to the broader Jewish community. Earlier I investigated the depth of their feelings of belonging in Egypt and discovered how these feelings gradually evaporated after 1948 and were totally shattered by their forced departure. They arrived in Australia with a multilayered identity because of their diverse ethnic and cultural backgrounds. Into the monolingual and monocultural Australia of the 1950s they brought multilingual and multicultural skills, a deep sense of family, a different Jewish tradition, and a strong connection with Israel. They distanced themselves from political involvement, and few were visible within the ranks of Australian Jewry leadership, apart from the Adelaide group. Although they were mainly of Sephardi stock, in Australia they mixed freely with the Ashkenazi majority in the synagogues, the day schools, and the various communal functions. Today, they claim that their predominant feeling of identity is Jewish Australian, but they still carry the signs of their previous identities, through their accent when they speak English, the language they use in their close family circles, the food they eat when they get together, and the way they think and see the world.

CHAPTER 9

THE FRENCH
MIGRATION EXPERIENCE

A CASE STUDY

The analysis of the various aspects of the migration of Jews from Egypt to Australia, at a time when Australia was still overwhelmingly Anglo-Celtic in its culture and world view, led me to compare the immigration experience of the same ethno-religious group to a different cultural and social context, again using oral history as a methodological tool. I chose France because, after Brazil, it is supposed to be the country that received the largest number of Egyptian Jewish émigrés. Whereas fewer than two thousand Egyptian Jews migrated to Australia, at least ten thousand migrated to France. Both the secondary sources and the oral history responses of the French interviewees indicated significant differences in their integration experience. However, despite their contrasting contexts, there were also interesting similarities between the interviewees' stories within the two groups.

The French sample consisted of an elite and, for the most part, highly educated group of former Jews from Egypt, all living in Paris, who arrived in France from the early 1950s to the late 1960s. Through their testimonies I was able to probe the interconnected themes of culture, integration, and identity, as well as preservation and transmission of memory. Because the majority of Egyptian Jews were more or less steeped in French culture, it was important to assess how significant this element was to the overall success of their integration in French society, compared to the situation in Australia where most Egyptian Jews had to adjust to a new language and a foreign culture. Did the fact they were already familiar with the national language and culture render them more acceptable to French society, and at what level? I evaluated the link between the size and the socioeconomic configuration of the French migration and the migrants' ability to organise themselves as a distinct ethnic entity, to gain recognition from the broader French Jewish community, and to develop their own sense of identity, taking into account their inherent diversity. Finally, I looked at the extent of their commitment to the preservation and transmission of the Jewish Egyptian cultural heritage to the next generation.

FRANCE IN THE 1950s

The Jews of Egypt who migrated to Australia in the late 1940s and 1950s landed there at a time when Australia was experiencing a dramatic increase in its population base. It was trying to absorb hundreds of thousands of non-British migrants while still reintegrating its returned soldiers into civilian life. To cope with this mass influx of people, housing and jobs had to be provided; new infrastructure needed to be built and new industries had to be developed. Equally, when the Jews of Egypt arrived in France in the early 1950s, that country was going through a period of dynamic social and economic change while it was being reconstructed after the physical and psychological ravages of wartime occupation. The country was in the middle of what popularly became known as *les Trente Glorieuses,* the thirty glorious years between liberation in 1945 and the first oil crisis of 1973, a period of consistent economic growth, unbroken prosperity, and abrupt social change.[718] As reported by Interviewee #15F, there was a crucial need of workers to rebuild France's economic base:

> A ce moment-là en France, on demandait des gens qui savaient travailler. Non seulement il n'y avait pas de problème de chômage mais on manquait de main d'oeuvre. Le pays était à reconstruire. En 1956, on a très facilement absorbé les dizaines de milliers de Juifs qui sont venus, pour lesquels on avait commencé à préparer des cités-dortoir, comme Villiers-le-Bel, dans lesquelles on les a installés.

In fact, the economic recovery of France was largely due to the active role of the state in revitalising its industries and its program of nationalisation of public utilities such as electricity, gas, coal, banks, airlines, and many private companies.[719] Another critical factor of that recovery was the implementation of the Marshall Aid Plan, an American initiative, which gave grants, loans, and subsidies to struggling postwar nations, including France.[720] All these initiatives contributed to the increasing modernisation of both industry and agriculture. It was a period of full employment, rising wages, and new patterns of consumption and leisure.

In order to repopulate and respond to labour demands, the French State was offering attractive incentives to encourage couples to have more children. Consequently the birth rate rose sharply. Families with more than three children were entitled to generous *allocations familiales,* housing allowances, tax relief, and cheaper transport.[721] Furthermore, the rapid process of urbanisation that characterised the 1950s, 1960s, and 1970s, popularly known as *les années de béton* (the years of concrete), led to an extensive program of massive reconstruction of France's housing infrastructure to alleviate the acute shortage of accommodation in the big cities. At the end of the war, what was available was old and lacked modern amenities like bathrooms and running hot and cold water. The situation was predominantly critical in Paris and remained so in the late 1950s, as experienced by most of my respondents, who were there either in transit or permanent residence. They reported that it was common for the hotels where the various welfare agencies had placed them to have only one toilet per floor, no bathroom or hot water, which meant they had to use public baths for their daily ablutions. Cooking in the rooms was strictly forbidden, but out of sheer necessity, especially with young children, this rule was surreptitiously and regularly broken. The housing shortage was gradually eased by the large-scale construction of council estates in the periphery of nearly every French city.[722] As indicated by Interviewee #15F, the newly built council estate called Villiers-le-Bel accommodated a large number of Jewish refugees from Egypt.

FRENCH JEWRY AND THE EGYPTIAN REFUGEES

During that period, French Jewry was also in the process of reconstruction and renewal. The Holocaust devastated a community that had stood at approximately 330,000 at the end of 1940. The Nazis murdered approximately eighty thousand French Jews.[723] Between 1945 and 1948 there was a large influx of Ashkenazi refugees from Eastern Europe, who swelled the ranks of the depleted French Jewish population. In his study of contemporary French Jewry, Laskier pointed out:

> Already in 1944 and 1945 the French Jewish communities, consisting of over 200,000 Jews, were the only ones outside Israel to be inundated by consecutive waves of immigrants. The French government's liberal policy of keeping the gates open to refugees meant that the Jewish communities in France became havens for those who had fled their homelands for Western Europe. Hundreds of thousands of refugees were granted temporary asylum, pending permanent resettlement elsewhere. However, tens of thousands preferred to make France their permanent home.[724]

Laskier added that the task of assisting these refugees to settle in France was undertaken largely by the JDC beginning in 1944, with the help of Jewish communal leaders and local welfare institutions, such as the COJASOR, established in 1945. To streamline the various local Jewish agencies, JDC encouraged the creation in 1949 of an umbrella organisation, the FSJU, with the major objectives of organising relief, raising funds, and distributing them where they were needed most.[725] Nevertheless, it is obvious that a task of this magnitude could not have been undertaken without the cooperation and contribution of the French government.

At this juncture, French Jewry was still predominantly Ashkenazi—Germanic and Eastern European—including a small number of veteran Sephardi families, well integrated into the broader French society. By the early 1950s, the Muslim nationalist struggle against French colonial rule in North Africa gained momentum, even as the rise of the Arab-Israeli conflict compounded the existing tension. The Jews of Algeria, Morocco, and Tunisia came to the realisation that their status in their native lands was becoming increasingly precarious. Following decolonisation, between 1955 and 1965, a massive exodus of North African Jews occurred in the direction of Israel and France. The eminent Orientalist, Michel Abitbol, whose specialty is the history of the Jews of Morocco, noted that the wave of migration to France radically altered the face of French Jewry, not only demographically but also geographically and ethnically.[726] In just one decade, confirmed Laskier, "the Maghribi Jewish segment emerged as the majority of the Jewish population" and French Jewry, now predominantly Sephardi, became the "second largest Jewish community in the Western World, with over 550,000 people".[727]

The huge task of resettlement and absorption of such a large group required a great deal of assistance from both government and Jewish institutions. Algerian Jews were French citizens since 1870 by virtue of the Crémieux Decree, and 120,000 chose to relocate in France after Algeria gained independence, whereas only ten thousand went to Israel. The option to settle in France was not automatically available to the Jews of Tunisia, who had been naturalised as French on "a selective and individual basis", nor to the Jews of Morocco, who were never granted French citizenship under the French protectorate regime.[728] This fundamental difference in status between the three groups of North African Jews often determined their final destination. The majority of Moroccan Jews—more than two-thirds—immigrated to Israel, together with half of Tunisia's Jewry, with the help of the Jewish Agency. Nevertheless, a significant number of Tunisian and Moroccan Jews preferred to settle in France because of their affinity with the French language and culture. Although they were granted right of asylum and were allowed to work, they were not eligible for the substantial assistance the French government bestowed on its repatriated citizens. Therefore, they had to rely heavily on the various Jewish welfare agencies, subsidised by the JDC and FSJU.[729]

The North African Jewish communities were not the only Jewish communities of the region being uprooted in the 1950s. As has been sufficiently demonstrated, the Jews of Egypt were also being forced out of their native country, escaping discrimination and persecution in the wake of the Suez War. In addition to considering Israel as a destination, a relatively large number of those refugees looked towards France because of its geographical proximity and its reputation as the traditional haven for political refugees, as well as their own cultural and linguistic affinity with France. The group that landed in France was generally made up of repatriated French nationals and stateless refugees. The latter included those who were forced to renounce their Egyptian nationality before leaving the country and the *sujets locaux* who had not been naturalised for the reasons previously outlined. How did they face the challenges posed by their forced emigration, such as finding accommodation, food, work, and schooling for the children, while trying to acculturate to a society with whom they shared the language but not much more? As pointed out by Laskier, the plight of the French national repatriates was somewhat alleviated because the French government had "organised complete reception services that included emergency housing, financial aid, and employment assistance", the same as for the repatriates from Algeria.[730] They were also eligible to receive social security benefits and medical assistance. The situation of the stateless refugees was more complicated. Some were in need of a temporary sanctuary while waiting for visas to other countries, such as Australia or the United States. Others were allowed into the country because, as already mentioned, France traditionally supported stateless refugees, through the Office Français de Protection des Réfugiés et Apatrides (OFPRA). Their knowledge of French facilitated the formalities. According to Interviewee #15F, France probably felt responsible for their plight, in view of her role in the 1956 Suez War, although other respondents commented that Great Britain, which was just as responsible as France, did not extend the same degree of assistance to the stateless refugees who landed on her shores.

Notwithstanding the subsidies of both the French government and UNHCR, most of the funds needed to settle and integrate the refugees from Egypt into the local economy, or to assist their emigration to other countries, were provided by JDC. France was its main theatre of operation, particularly between 1957 and 1960. A large number of stateless Egyptian Jews wished to settle in France and they needed urgent assistance. A Special Programs Assistance Fund was established by JDC specifically to cope with the needs of Jewish refugees from Egypt and Eastern Europe.[731] This fund subsidised local Jewish agencies, such as COJASOR and the Service Social des Jeunes (SSJ), who were in charge of "Care and Maintenance" and provided the refugees with cash relief, as well as assistance with rent, food, child care, and housing for a year or until the head of the family found suitable employment.[732] Two of my respondents were immediately recruited by COJASOR to assist in dealing with the needs of the Egyptian refugees.[733] The financial help and moral support provided by this relief agency were acknowledged by all the respondents. They testified to its invaluable contribution towards their initial integration into French society, as illustrated by the following statement from Interviewee #14F, whose parents were lodged and fed by COJASOR for an entire year:

> Quand mes parents sont arrivés, les premiers cinq jours, ils ont été logés et nourris par la Croix Rouge...Ensuite le COJASOR les a pris en charge. Ils ont été mis dans un hotel, rue Cadet. Ils recevaient une prime de logement et une prime de bouffe. C'était un hotel où toutes les chambres étaient prises par des immigrés juifs, essentiellement des Égyptiens mais il y avait aussi des Marocains et des Algériens. Ils ont vécu un an là-bas.[734]

However, the French authorities' welcoming attitude towards the stateless refugees was not open-ended. To be able to reside in France on a permanent basis, the refugees still had to obtain a work permit (*carte de travail*), which in turn would give them a resident permit (*permis de séjour*). Often they found themselves in a vicious circle because prospective employers would not offer them work until they held a resident permit. Egyptian-born Frédéric Galimidi noted in his memoirs, *Alexandrie-sur-Seine,* that the JDC saved him *in extremis* from deportation, by offering him a position in their personnel office.[735] Another respondent decided to go back to university, which gave him a student status and allowed him to extend his stay in the country until such time as he could secure a job:

> N'ayant pas de permis de séjour, on tournait en rond. On ne pouvait avoir ce permis que si on avait un contrat de travail et on ne pouvait pas avoir un contrat de travail sans permis de séjour. Finalement, j'ai repris mes études à l'université. J'ai eu un contrat de travail et donc le permis de séjour mais il a fallu que ce soit grace à des gens de chez nous, des Juifs d'Égypte qui étaient de nationalité française.[736]

There were obviously cases of hardship, particularly among the economically vulnerable and the older members of the group, which was not very different from the situation in Australia, but the 1956 wave of young and old refugees seems to have been better taken care of. After a few years, most of them had adjusted reasonably well to their new conditions. Interviewee #14F remembered that some of his compatriots were even blessing the circumstances that had brought them forcibly to such a wonderful country as France, an attitude also prevalent within the Australian sample:

> La plupart d'entre eux s'étaient refaits et finissaient par dire: nous allons élever une statue en or à Nasser, pour nous avoir chassés, parce qu'ici nous avons des voitures, des autobus qui marchent, une vie culturelle, des écoles, des cinémas.

From this overall picture of France in the mid-1950s, it appears that the social welfare infrastructure was more developed than in Australia where social services were still in their infancy. Moreover, French Jewry was significantly larger, more established, and possibly better funded to deal with a large influx of refugees. The subsidies granted by the JDC to local Jewish welfare agencies for the purpose of assisting refugees from Egypt were comparatively generous, and that assistance covered many of their essential needs. Furthermore, the presence of a relatively large Egyptian network in France around 1956 constituted a safety net for the incoming refugees from Egypt, just as it did in Australia, particularly in Adelaide, albeit on a smaller level. Solidarity was found to be the key to facilitate their integration. Interviewee #15F, who lived in France since 1952, recalled that by joining forces with other émigrés from Egypt they were able to establish their own enterprises, thus creating employment opportunities for themselves and their compatriots:

> Quand nous sommes venus ici, nous nous sommes retrouvés à essayer de gagner notre vie. On s'est aperçu qu'en définitive…il n'y avait qu'un seul moyen, c'était de nous rapprocher les uns des autres, de nous entr'aider et de créer nos propres affaires.

The Egyptian refugees seem to have successfully confronted the many challenges posed by their forced emigration and acculturation to French society through personal and group solidarity, with the support of international and local Jewish agencies and government-funded assistance programs.

There was nevertheless a fundamental difference in the status of Egyptian Jews landing in France and those landing in Australia. Whereas in France the majority arrived stateless, on a temporary visa, and seeking asylum, those who came to Australia arrived as legal migrants after a rigorous screening procedure. As such, they were automatically entitled to permanent residency in Australia whether they found employment or not, as long as they remained in the country for two consecutive years. They were also entitled to the relevant social services—however modest—enjoyed by the general population soon after their arrival. In addition, although the conditions for entry of refugees into France were not as stringent *a priori* as for Australia, permanent resident status

272   EGYPTIAN-JEWISH EMIGRÉS IN AUSTRALIA

was far from assured, as confirmed by the personal experiences of the majority of the French respondents. They had to find work and accommodation within a certain time frame and present themselves regularly at the *Préfecture* to apply for residency extensions. The French bureaucratic process reportedly caused undue hardship and humiliation to the already traumatised refugees. The obvious question is: Why did so many Egyptian Jews choose to settle in France in spite of this uncertainty? I have attempted to answer this question by identifying the ethnic, socioeconomic, cultural, and ideological characteristics of the participants in the French study, and by evaluating the extent of their similarities to and differences from the Australian participants.

ETHNIC AND SOCIOECONOMIC CONFIGURATION OF THE FRENCH SAMPLE GROUP

The Egyptian background of the Australian and French sample groups did not differ significantly as far as ethnicity, nationality, class, level of education, and language skills were concerned. There were, in some instances, slight variations, but due to the disproportionate size of the two groups, these variations could not be considered truly representative of distinct characteristics pertaining to one group or the other. As was the case for Australia, the French group typified the ethnic diversity and linguistic pluralism that constituted the intrinsic components of modern Egyptian Jewry. For instance, the wide Sephardi category, which characterised the majority of the French respondents, included several ethnic subgroups: Ladino-speaking Sephardim from, for instance, Istanbul, Izmir, Salonika, Algeria, and Morocco; Arabic-speaking Oriental or Mizrahi Jews from Egypt, Syria, Iraq, and Palestine; *Romaniot* or Greek Jews from mainland Greece and Corfu; and Italian Jews from Leghorn.[737] On the other hand, the Yiddish-speaking Ashkenazim were greatly underrepresented when compared to their proportion within the Australian group. There were only two cases of mixed Sephardi and Ashkenazi origins, and they were mostly acculturated to the Sephardi tradition.[738] There were also two cases of Karaite Jews. The three categories of passports that Jews from Egypt could possess—Egyptian, European, and stateless—were represented in about the same proportions for both the French and the Australian respondents, except for the fact that there were no British subjects within the French sample, as was to be expected.

The Egyptian socioeconomic configuration of the French group broadly replicated the Australian findings of an educated and multilingual group, consisting of a predominant middle class, a small upper-middle class, and an even smaller lower-middle class.[739] As was the case for the Australian group, few within the French sample were strictly observant, although the majority strongly identified with their Jewish roots and with Israel. On the issue of intermarriage in Egypt, although the French data showed a slightly higher percentage of intermarriage—9 percent compared to 3 percent for the Australian group—the difference was not important enough to indicate a definite trend.[740] However, according to my data the percentage rate of intermarriage in the generation born in France was significantly higher and could signal a deeper assimilation in France than in Australia. One would need to consult demographic studies, such as those undertaken by Sergio Della Pergola in which intermarriage within French Jewry is seen as growing steadily.[741]

The circumstances surrounding their exodus from Egypt followed a similar pattern for both samples. Comparable to the Australian participants, over half of the French group left Egypt in the aftermath of the 1956 Suez War, which confirmed the general trend of Jewish migration from Egypt between 1947 and 1967, and the reasons for leaving were more or less the same in both cases. A slightly higher proportion of French respondents—about 40 percent compared to 35 percent for the Australian group—had been expelled for their political convictions, either as Communists or Zionists after the 1948 Arab-Israeli War or as French nationals after the 1956 Arab-Israeli War, and others were forced out by the government sequestration of their assets or by the sudden loss of their livelihood. About the same proportion of French and Australian respondents stated they left Egypt because they believed there was no future for them as Jews. As previously stated, the interviewees who were looking for a better and safer future, as far as possible from the troubles of the Middle East, chose Australia because of its distant location. Paradoxically, for some of the French respondents it was in fact Australia's isolation and remoteness that were perceived as negatives. To be so far removed from Europe, the hub of Western civilisation, was considered a long-term sentence. The saying on the street was that Australia was a place where one went "for work and forever".

A Question of Culture

The most salient difference between the immigration experiences of the two sample groups arose from the all-important issue of culture. Beyond the incentives of family reunion, economic opportunities, and search for political security, which, in that order of preference, motivated immigration to Australia, the fundamental reason that France was chosen as a refuge by such a relatively large number of Egyptian Jews was their deep affinity with the French language and culture.[742] According to the sweeping statement of one of the original founders of ASPCJE, those who settled in France were obviously not the true Zionists, nor the uneducated, but the middle classes who came out of the French schools of Egypt and who had appropriated the French culture as their own. "They were the true intellectuals", he said.[743] My research confirmed that not only had the majority of the French sample group attended those schools, which was to be expected, but also a significantly greater percentage of that group—61 percent—had attended Jewish day schools at the primary or secondary level, compared with 22 percent of the Australian contingent, which might explain their greater commitment to the preservation of their cultural heritage as Jews of Egypt. Nevertheless, seeing that both the Jewish day schools and the secular French lycées had been following the French education curriculum, these findings mainly corroborated the solid foundation of French culture inculcated into the Jews of Egypt and embraced by them.

Another reason motivated young Egyptian Jews to turn to France, even before the outbreak of the Suez crisis—their wish to pursue their university education in France, a dream that was facilitated by both the geographical proximity and the somewhat cultural continuity between Egypt and France.[744] In fact, seven French respondents—33 percent— were in that category. Initially, these students had every intention of eventually going back home at the end of their studies. Clearly, these plans were never carried out as a consequence of the political events that unfolded. Then again, although these students were not necessarily French citizens, university education in France was an attractive proposition given that it was nearly free of charge at the time, except for books, library fees, and a small contribution to social security.[745] At first, their living expenses were mostly subsidised by their parents or, in cases of hardship, by philanthropists from within the Jewish community in Egypt.[746] Their personal situation and official status changed dramatically as a result of the outbreak of the Suez War and France's involvement. Because no Egyptian-sourced allowance could reach them due to the breakdown of relations between Egypt and France, they found themselves financially stranded. Their foreign-student status changed. They became political refugees and therefore were entitled to assistance from the French government. Such was the case of Interviewee #2F who, after two preparatory years at the selective high school, Lycée Louis-le-Grand, had just been accepted at the prestigious Ecole Supérieure de Physique et Chimie Industrielle (ESPCI) when the Suez War erupted.[747] As his personal funds were exhausted, he appealed to the French government and succeeded in obtaining a scholarship, as a dissident of Nasser's regime:

> J'étais venu ici faire des études et franchement je n'avais aucune idée de quitter l'Égypte. Mais, en 1956, j'étais dans l'incapacité de continuer mes études parce que la situation des Juifs en Égypte s'était définitivement détériorée. Il n'y avait plus aucune possibilité de me faire envoyer même un centime quand finalement j'ai été admis à l'Ecole…Il me restait 100 Francs à la banque, de quoi vivre pour une semaine. Je suis donc allé chercher cet argent avec mon passeport égyptien et là j'ai appris que les passeports égyptiens étaient bloqués…Un copain musulman m'a suggéré d'aller

au Quai d'Orsay, pleurer et dire que le gouvernement égyptien m'enverrait faire mes études en Russie (!), et que moi j'aime la France…C'est comme cela que j'ai pu avoir une grosse bourse de quatre ans du gouvernement français comme Égyptien résistant à Nasser.

Another respondent (#14F) also reported that because he had been arrested and then expelled from Egypt in 1956, he arrived in France as a political refugee. As such, he was subsidised during his first four years of university studies by the French government and Jewish institutions. In general, all these students, popularly called *les Juifs de Nasser*, were eventually allowed to remain in France, and their parents joined them when they in turn were forced out of Egypt. A comparative analysis of the research data revealed that the number of university graduates amongst the respondents in France was significantly higher than in Australia, whereas the number of white-collar workers and businessmen was higher for Australia. I suggest that this disparity was not surprising if one considers that migrants with French university degrees were more likely to be gainfully employed in France, but those with business experience and no diplomas would have had better opportunities to use their skills in a promising new country like Australia, either by working for somebody or starting their own enterprise. It is also probable that, judging by the restricted size and elite character of the French case study compared to the total number of Egyptian Jews who settled in France, I did not have access to the whole variety of categories within the group of Egyptian Jewish émigrés in France.

Another characteristic of the French sample was a higher ideological involvement both in Egypt and later in France.[748] Confirming what Beinin wrote about "the political inflection of a French education" in Egypt as being generally tilted to the left, a relatively greater proportion of my French respondents, particularly those who went through the Jewish schools, confirmed that they had been introduced to Marxism and socialist Zionism through their French teachers or the Zionist youth movement emissaries from Palestine.[749] Often their Zionist and/or Communist activism was mainly restricted to attending a few meetings.

It still caused their arrest in 1948 and subsequently their expulsion from Egypt.[750] Once in France, they joined the French Communist Party for a number of years but were eventually forced out or opted out due to the anti-Israel stance adopted by the party.[751] However, they still favoured the left side of politics, as opposed to the Australian respondents who, with one single exception, were mainly conservative in their world view.[752] Interviewee #4F, for instance, stated that he felt very close to the ideals of the 1968 student revolution and its efforts to change the rigidity of French bourgeois society:

> Pendant la révolution des étudiants en 68, nous étions pour. C'était une révolution de bourgeois. On avait commencé à bien gagner notre vie, mais on avait gardé l'esprit étudiant. Il y avait beaucoup de Juifs activistes dans cette révolution. Cette révolution m'a marqué pendant très longtemps.

Notwithstanding those few differences, the majority of French interviewees agreed that their deep acculturation to the French language and culture was indeed the determining factor that made them choose France over other countries and was also the prime facilitator of their migration experience. Egyptian-born Jewish author Eglal Errera pointed out that in Egypt, French was perceived as the language of cultural sophistication. In the new reality of the forced exile of the Jews of Egypt, it suddenly acquired the attributes of a refuge, of an existential tool in the idealised space of France:

> Ils [les Juifs d'Égypte] ont, au début de ces années1960, le sentiment de l'imminence et de l'irréversibilité de leur exode. La langue française qui jusqu'ici avait été la langue du raffinement et du luxe culturel devient refuge et arme existentielle. Riche de son bilinguisme, le "Juif d'Égypte", débarque en France...[753]

For Interviewee #2F, it was more the impact of French thought on impressionable young minds that made the move out of Egypt inevitable, rather than the rise of Egyptian-Arab nationalism and the creation of the State of Israel:

> Je pense donc que, plus que la montée du nationalisme arabe, plus que la création de l'état d'Israël, le fait que nous avions déjà l'esprit à la française nous a amenés, un jour ou l'autre, à quitter l'Égypte, malgré nous.

This special affinity with France and French culture was intense at several levels. Year after year, teachers of various persuasions had rigorously and persistently taught their students in the French schools of Egypt about French history, geography, literature, and ideals. A typical example was the writer Frédéric Galimidi, whose love of France was so deeply ingrained that, when the time came to leave Egypt, he would not even consider migrating to any other country:

> La police [égyptienne] avait fait se former plusieurs files selon les pays de destination les plus "demandés"...Je pris place, avec ma mère, dans la file d'attente "France". Pourquoi celle-ci et non une autre? Je ne m'étais même pas posé la question, tant cela allait de soi. Non seulement parce que j'étais titulaire de trois diplômes de droit français, ce qui était déjà en soi une bonne raison, mais surtout parce que Monsieur Dumont, ce cher et vieux professeur de français avait su, tout au long de notre scolarité, trouver la voie du coeur en nous distillant jour après jour l'amour de la France et de la langue de Descartes.[754]

Based on the perceptions of the sample group—bearing in mind its elite characteristics and the restricted numbers of French testimonies—it can be said that the cultural integration of Egyptian Jews in France was understandably smoother than that in Australia.

ECONOMIC INTEGRATION

A proficiency in the national language facilitated the employment prospects of even older Egyptian refugees in France, particularly in the economic climate of those "glorious" years. They were able to secure respectable positions, sometimes within their field of expertise. This was not always the case for their Australian counterparts, who were considered too old at the age of fifty and had to content themselves with menial work if their English was not adequate. Interviewee #2F believed the success of his father's immigration experience was due to his French cultural background. Long before his exodus from Egypt in 1957, he was already prepared for his eventual uprooting. As a result, although he was already fifty-two years of age, once in France he immediately found work in his profession as an engraver. He even boasted that for the first time in his life he was entitled to holiday pay, weekends, medical cover, and social security:

> Mon père était très bien en France…bien qu'il soit arrivé ici à 52 ans, parce que pour la première fois, il avait un mois de vacances; pour la première fois, le samedi et dimanche, il ne travaillait pas; il avait la sécurité sociale. Quand il tombait malade, il était couvert. Il est rentré tout de suite dans une usine où il a travaillé comme graveur.

Obviously there were exceptions, even within this elite sample group, particularly among the respondents' parents. In one instance, Interviewee #56, who lived in France for two years before migrating to Australia, reported that her fifty-year-old mother could not find work in her profession as a teacher and had to content herself with being a nanny. Others were never able to re-enter the workplace in France, due to age, ill health, or because they were psychologically overwhelmed by the traumatic economic and social upheaval in their lives after their forced emigration. However, even those extreme cases drew some sense of comfort and continuity from being in a free country where they knew the language and could at least communicate. One respondent (#8F) related that his father was too sick to work, but still felt more at home in France than anywhere else because of the culture. Interviewee #14F recalled that after being forced out of Egypt, his sixty-year-old father never regained enough self-confidence to find work in France. Still, he never expressed any regrets for leaving Egypt and the police-state atmosphere that was so prevalent towards the last few years: "en France, mon père s'est senti totalement libéré. Il était heureux à ce point de vue". In fact, the majority of the French respondents claimed that their parents had acculturated remarkably well to the French conditions, considering their age and lack of local qualifications or specific expertise. It is important to point out that the success of that integration was not necessarily a question of great financial achievement, as Egyptian Jews in France—like those in Australia—are not generally reputed to have reached the highest pinnacles of economic achievement.[755] Whereas young and old managed to achieve varying degrees of financial comfort and professional success, the majority just felt particularly privileged and lucky to be living in a country such as France:

> Quel que soit l'âge, finalement, tout le monde était content de vivre ici. Pour ceux qui sont venus ici à l'âge de 18 ans, dans une démocratie, à l'époque où l'éducation était gratuite, c'était une chance incroyable.[756]

One particular interviewee (#2F) went as far as stating that even the experience of his Zionist friends, who chose to settle in Israel to follow their ideals, was disappointing, both culturally and economically, compared to the French experience:

> L'expérience de plusieurs de mes amis qui sont partis en Israël avec un idéal a été négative...Par contre, ceux qui se sont installés en France sont très heureux parce qu'ils sont venus dans une culture qu'ils connaissaient. Economiquement, la France a eu des années glorieuses entre 1960 et 1975 où tout le monde a fait de l'argent.

In fact, most respondents gradually reintegrated into the comfortable ranks of the middle class. Once they secured stable employment, they were able to buy their own apartment through loans provided by COJASOR, the same institution that helped them when they first arrived.[757]

SOCIALISATION WITH THE HOST SOCIETY

When asked to what extent their fluency in the national language actually facilitated social interaction within French society, the interviewees'

responses varied, in line with the diversity of the group. The age factor proved to be a determining element in that respect. The majority of
respondents concurred that, as far as their parents' generation was concerned, socialisation was mostly a closed-circuit phenomenon, at least
during the initial years. They interacted mostly with other members of
their own group, as can be the situation for migrant groups anywhere in
the world. At times the older generation experienced a sense of alienation
due to the difference in mentality and acceptable behaviour between
Egypt and France, in spite of the familiar language. Only by socialising
and sharing their experience with people of the same background could
they cope with the inherent difficulties of their new circumstances. This
was one of their strategies of acculturation. Interviewee #4F recalled
the high spirits of his parents and compatriots, living together in a very
basic Paris hotel requisitioned by COJASOR for Egyptian and North
African refugees, where they stayed for nearly a year: "ils étaient là, tous
ensemble. Quand j'allais les voir, ils étaient là à se lamenter et à rigoler
en même temps".[758] Later, when they were in a position to buy their
own apartments, they happily ended up in the same housing complexes
known as Habitation à loyer modéré (HLM), at Villiers-le-Bel and Gen-
evilliers, in the Paris *banlieue* (outer suburbs).

Even for those who settled in the south of France, where the locals
were reputed to be friendlier than the more xenophobic Parisians, they
were still far from the easygoing openness of southern Mediterranean
societies. Interviewee #14F recalled the sense of isolation experienced
by his parents and others like them when they came to settle in Montpellier, to be close to their children attending university there. Again
their strategy for coping with uprooting and dislocation was to form
their own familiar social nucleus. Although this structure was more
common in Australia because of the cultural divide, it also gave the
French migrants the kind of support that no amount of financial aid or
social services could provide.[759] Here again, by forming a united insiders' group and a strong network of their own, they were better equipped
to cope with the angst of exile and the difficulty of adapting to a new
environment.

Adjusting to such a fundamental change as forced immigration and trying to face up to its many challenges proved even more daunting for the older and less resilient refugees, particularly those whose mentality had remained fundamentally Middle Eastern. The clash between the value systems of the two cultures necessarily impacted their identification with and integration into the host society, causing them to feel even more alienated. One interviewee recalled how shocked his seventy-year-old father was whenever he witnessed the amorous behaviour of young people in the streets of Paris.[760] He used to complain to his son—in Arabic—about bringing him to such a wanton place: "mon fils, dans quel pays m'as-tu emmené?"[761] He could never get used to the permissiveness of French society, and his immigration experience was consequently very unhappy. It is clear that in such cases the confrontation between different customs and codes of behaviour puts a strain on any relation with the host society.

As was the situation for the Australian sample, socialisation was significantly easier for the younger members of the group. The majority of those who came in their late teens and went to school or university in France experienced much less difficulty in that respect than their older compatriots. Because of their indoctrination in the French schools of Egypt, they arrived in France, "le plus beau pays du monde", with the usual youthful expectations of being accepted as equals. The fact that their country of origin had rejected them made them even more anxious to acculturate and be accepted in their adoptive country. Their proficiency in French and affinity with Western culture ensured that they did not have any serious problems of communication on the professional or personal level. They all stated that they loved France and had never regretted their decision to settle there.[762]

In spite of these glowing reports, a few more aspects of the integration of the French respondents—such as the level of interaction with and acceptance by the locals—still needed clarification. Again, the stories varied. One common denominator was the clear sign of an enduring connection between the respondents. For instance, Interviewee #2F, who came to France at the age of eighteen, claimed that although he had developed an excellent rapport with his French colleagues during his professional life as a scientist, he still considered his old friends from Egypt as family and socialised with them even more since his retirement: "les copains d'Égypte, c'est comme mes frères; c'est notre enfance". Interviewee #14F also stated that he mixed very comfortably with French people at both the personal and professional levels. However, in his retirement years he has realised the importance of his relationship with his ex-compatriots, a relationship he neglected after his early university years.[763] Other interviewees claimed they very rarely socialised with the French on a personal level due to the fact that they found them generally cold and inhospitable. The same respondent (#10F) who was earlier quoted for praising the French immigration experience as by far the best for the Jews of Egypt, admitted he did not have a single French friend, Jewish or non-Jewish because of that coldness and indifference. Thus, he only socialised with ex-Egyptians:

> Je suis en France depuis 51 ans et je n'ai pas un ami français, juif ou pas juif. Mes amis sont des anciens Égyptiens que je connaissais avant mon arrivée en France ou que j'ai connus depuis... Je n'ai jamais formé des liens d'amitié [avec les Français] parce que j'ai été frappé par [leur] sécheresse et [leur] indifférence...Ce n'est qu'au parti communiste, quand j'étais jeune, que je me suis fait quelques amis.

Another respondent also admitted that after nearly fifty years in the country, although he had achieved a successful career as an engineer and led a very comfortable lifestyle, he still was never able to break down the social barrier put up by "les Français de France". Until the present day, although he had never regretted settling in France, he did not feel truly accepted as a Frenchman, and consequently most of his friends were Jews from Egypt.[764]

There were a few respondents who had completely lost contact with their compatriots over the years, for a variety of reasons—distance, profession, apathy, or just a desire to blend in, to assimilate into mainstream society, without attracting attention to their differences.[765] However, in the last few years, they also experienced the need to reconnect with their roots, joining various associations founded by expatriate Egyptians, either on a regular or occasional basis.[766]

One other obstacle to the acceptance of the French respondents by the host society was their distinctive Egyptian accent when they spoke French—un français égyptien— with its linguistic idiosyncrasies. It identified them immediately in the eyes of the locals as not authentic.[767] This distinction remains a sensitive issue, even after more than fifty years in France, as demonstrated by the annoyance of Interviewee #4F. He still resented being asked every time he made a new acquaintance, either socially or professionally, the question "Where do you come from?":

> Il faut admettre que nous avons un handicap, c'est l'accent… Chaque fois que je rencontre un gars en voyage et que je veux lui montrer une usine qu'on a construite, au bout de dix minutes, il me demande, "d'où vous venez". J'en ai marre![768]

He interpreted the questioning about his origins as clearly implying exclusion, given that it stated that he was not from France. It reminded him that he would always be an outsider, "one who did not belong", and considered it a handicap. It is interesting to note that in Australia that same question, "Where do you come from?", would not have had a negative connotation, seeing as the majority of the Australian population originally came from somewhere else. On the other hand, according to Interviewee #4F, settling in a country such as France, with an old and established culture and a prestigious past, was potentially more alienating than settling in a new country such as Australia, where everybody had a share in making Australia into what it is today and thus developed a greater sense of belonging:

> Parce que j'ai émigré en France, dans une vieille culture qui a existé sans moi, je me sens redevable de quelque chose. Vous en Australie, non, parce que vous avez fait l'Australie en même temps que les autres…Vous étiez des pionniers.

At times, the issue of a foreign accent even affected the employment opportunities of Egyptian Jews. One respondent (#2F) reported that at first, several of his job applications were consistently rejected, although he was a graduate of the prestigious Grande Ecole, ESPCI, because his Egyptian accent was not considered appropriate in leadership positions:

> Celui qui m'employait à 24 ans, savait qu'un jour j'allais diriger d'autres personnes et donc mon accent égyptien les gênait. J'ai été chez beaucoup de boites américaines, comme IBM, et ils m'ont tous dit "non" à cause de mon accent.

Comparatively, in the Australian study, the issue of accent arose only in one instance, when a respondent (#71) who wanted to work as a primary school teacher was advised by the South Australia Education Department that the pupils could be negatively affected by her foreign accent. After much deliberation, she was given a fifth-grade class, where it was believed her "accent would do the least harm". It is nevertheless interesting to note a certain similarity between the attitudes to foreigners prevalent in the 1950s both in France and Australia, even when those foreigners had a perfect command of the dominant language, albeit with a different accent.

ANTI-SEMITISM

If there was a certain level of discrimination against the Jews of Egypt on the grounds of their national identity, few of the French respondents admitted to overt discrimination on the grounds of their religion. It is well known that in the French Republic, secular by definition, religion has traditionally been relegated to the private realm, and it was and still is considered unpatriotic to identify oneself publicly and solely as a member of a religious community.[769] The majority of the French respondents stated unequivocally that the question of one's personal religion is never discussed in mixed French society.[770] However, they were definitely aware of a certain "in-house" anti-Semitism that would manifest itself only when Jews were not around. One respondent stated that he was never at the receiving end of such derogatory remarks because of his very typical Jewish surname, whereas others with less obvious patronymics would often overhear off-the-cuff anti-Semitic comments in their work or social environment. "J'ai toujours eu des pointes ici et là…Il y a de ceux qui savent que je suis Juif et d'autres qui ne veulent pas le savoir", said Interviewee #12F, who just shrugged his shoulders.[771] Others recalled seeing anti-Semitic graffiti, such as "Mort aux Juifs", on the walls of the underground metro, but they did not consider this kind of manifestation as particularly threatening or significant. Very few reported anti-Semitic incidents in which they were specifically targeted. Only one respondent (#10F) remembered that his son was once called "a dirty Jew" at school, but, he proudly added, the son immediately "punched the offender in the face" and it never happened again. This respondent was in fact saying that even if there was anti-Semitism in France, the Jews were not helpless victims anymore. He was not just proud of his son, he was proud of living in a country such as France where Jews could not be racially vilified with impunity, even in the context of a school playground.[772]

In contrast to these testimonies, there were a few respondents who were deeply disturbed by this kind of covert anti-Semitism that still existed in some circles. One of them declared outright:

> I lived in Paris for twenty years but always felt a foreigner. I feel much more comfortable here [in Australia] than in France, more at home. The people are more accessible and hospitable. The French are antisemitic, arrogant and with [sic] a feeling of superiority.[773]

Another respondent (#21F), who lived in France from 1957 to 1961, claimed that in those days she faced discrimination and antagonism, both as a Jew and as a foreigner, and was happy to leave the country when her visa to the United States came through:

> The minute we landed in New York and saw the blatant signs of Judaism, it blew my mind! We didn't have to hide anymore that we were Jews or foreigners, which we did even more in France than in Egypt.

With the increasing reports of anti-Zionist and anti-Semitic incidents in France today, the next quote—from Interviewee #6F, who has been living happily in France since 1958—was found to be clearly symptomatic of that new climate He is a computer engineer with a PhD from the prestigious Ecole Polytechnique de France and had just retired from the workforce. He confessed that the last few years had deeply affected his sense of belonging in France and, for the first time since his arrival, he viewed his future as a Jew in France as grim. He is convinced that he might be forced to pack his bags one of these days: "Je suis convaincu que nous devrons faire nos valises un jour avec l'antisémitisme croissant au niveau de la presse". Equally, in the context of the 2005 underground suicide bombings in Great Britain, I had to reassess an earlier comment made by a London-based respondent (#8F) about being more at home in France because of the culture, but feeling safer in England as a Jew.[774] That was in 2003. This series of events raises the question of whether, once again, Jews are under threat in Europe.

Notwithstanding those dissenting voices, anti-Semitism does not seem ultimately to have hindered the successful integration of the Jews from Egypt into French society and the French economy. The testimonies gathered in the course of this research have clearly shown the immigrants made good use of the opportunities that were available when they first arrived, such as communal and government assistance, cheap housing, and free tertiary education for the young. They gradually regained a comfortable middle-class status, often through their chosen professions. They did not regret settling in France and would never live anywhere else. By the time this research was conducted, the majority was enjoying a secure retirement, and the picture of integration was not substantially different from the Australian case study. Nevertheless, it is still important to point out that, in marked contrast to the French experience, no Australian respondent reported having experienced anti-Semitism first-hand or suffered from religious discrimination from the general population.

IDENTITY AND IDENTIFICATION

When the time came to compare the issue of identity in the two migration experiences, again there was some commonality. Like their compatriots

at the Edge of the Diaspora, the French respondents reported that they
often found it awkward to describe themselves to others because of their
multilayered identity. Thus, their presentation of self varied depending
on the context and on who asked the question. In France, people are usually very private, and thus Egyptian Jews would suppress their pluralistic identity to outsiders and declare themselves simply as French without
any mention of religion or ethnic origin. To insiders, they would qualify
that answer in a variety of ways: a Jew originally from Egypt and now
French, an Egyptian Jew, a Sephardi Jew, or any other label combination. However, they all recognised that their inner perception of self—
the way they saw themselves—remained a constant: a Jew from Egypt
first, French "by cultural choice and not by birth". For some respondents, there was no conflict between their ethno-religious identity and
their adopted national identity. For instance, Interviewee #7F stated that
although she was Jewish first, she felt deeply French because France had
given her everything.[775] Another interviewee (#15F) dealt pragmatically
with the intricacies of a multilayered identity:

> Si c'est un Français qui me pose la question, je suis français,
> point final. Si c'est Madame Barda qui me pose la question, je
> lui dis: je suis comme vous. Je suis un Juif d'Égypte. Quant à
> moi, je me sens Juif d'Égypte; je me sens français; je me sens
> sépharade.[776]

Others were still struggling with their multiple co-existing identities, trying to construct a succinct definition of self. Interviewee #8F, who came
from a mixture of Venetian, Greek, Turkish, and Ladino backgrounds,
had lived consecutively in Italy, France, and England since his exodus
from Egypt. Not only did he speak all the relevant languages, he also
knew some of the regional dialects. He became a British subject but
could not decide which one of those respective cultures he identified
with most. In response to my question about his core identity, he started
by stating that he was first a Jew, although he was hardly observant, and
then added: "I am closer to the French culture, but I want all my other
cultures together; I don't want to give up any of them". In other words,

the cosmopolitanism that used to be the essence of life in Egypt for the elite minorities—and that he had grown up with—was his permanent and preferred condition. In the same vein, Interviewee #2F, who had obviously reflected on the issue of identity long before our interview, stated that he always described himself to others as an Alexandrian Jew, although culturally he saw himself as French:

> Si on est français par la culture, je suis d'abord français. Si on est français par le sang, alors je suis alexandrin. Je n'ai pas de sang bleu…Dans le passé, je n'ai jamais refoulé mon identité. J'ai toujours dit que j'étais alexandrin et juif en même temps.

In his opinion, Alexandria—because of its ancient association with Hellenism and its geographical position, on the edge of the Mediterranean, facing Europe—was different from the rest of Egypt. It was a place that still resonated from the legacy of a culture that influenced the entire Western world. For him, being an Alexandrian signified much more than merely being born in Alexandria. It meant that one always retained the essential characteristic of the culture that once flourished there, which was an open and tolerant view of the world. This notion that Alexandria had a defining influence on its minorities' world view and aptitude to function anywhere in the world was also raised by Interviewee #14F, in regard to his tolerance towards people from different religious or ethnic backgrounds, a tolerance inculcated in Egypt:

> J'ai continué à fonctionner en France avec ma mentalité du Lycée de l'Union Juive, ou du Lycée français, ou même simplement d'Alexandrie, ce qui est à mon avis notre fonds culturel; c'est-à-dire que pour nous, Juifs ou non-Juifs, c'était la même chose.

It was clear from the complexity of those few comments on identity that this was an issue my respondents, as part of the Jewish/Egyptian/French intelligentsia, had struggled with at a personal level and tried to resolve at an intellectual level. The result was that they still identified with their compatriots, given that they admitted that they socialised primarily with other Jews from Egypt, particularly in their later years. Then again, by the time this research was conducted, they were sufficiently settled and secure in their identity within their ethno-religious boundaries for them not to mention any significant real or perceived discrimination from Jews of different ethnic backgrounds, unlike the situation in Australia between the Iraqi and Ashkenazi Jews. Not only did they create new institutions, but they also rebuilt older ones. As stated in the testimony of Interviewee #15F, very soon after their arrival in Paris, the Egyptian émigrés were able to negotiate with the *Consistoire*[777] the loan of a separate hall, on the same premises as the Grande Synagogue de la Victoire:

> Tout de suite, les Juifs d'Égypte ont voulu avoir leur synagogue, avec son organisation propre, son rite etc., et ils l'ont obtenue très facilement.

It is known as L'Oratoire Égyptien: Eliahou Hannabi, in remembrance of the Great Synagogue of Alexandria, and this is where Egyptian Jews have been conducting their religious services according to the Egyptian/ Sephardi liturgy for over fifty years.[778]

Furthermore, as Sephardim they belonged to the dominant group within French Jewry, the North Africans, with whom they shared an ethnic and religious tradition, a past history in an Arab land, a multiplicity of cultures, and a relatively recent migration experience.

The fundamental differences between the French and the Australian groups related to their numbers and to their visibility and impact as a distinctive ethnic group within the local Jewish community. The French participants represented a community at least five times larger than the Egyptian community in Australia. Given that important numerical difference, the French group was significantly better equipped to retain its distinctive characteristics and assert itself independently.

Preservation and Transmission of Cultural Heritage

Another distinctive feature of the Egyptian French group was a particularly strong awareness of its history, culture, and ethnic identity, and an equally strong and dynamic commitment to the preservation and transmission of its cultural heritage. This awareness was dormant during the early years of settlement in France, while the émigrés were working hard at establishing themselves in their new homes, starting their families, and raising their children. After some twenty years, once their socioeconomic base was more solidly anchored, the realisation of having lived through a unique chapter of Jewish history surfaced, and they joined forces with other ex-Egyptian/Jewish intellectuals who shared the same perspective. They were among the first, if not the first, of all the other groups of Jews from Egypt dispersed throughout the world— outside of Israel—to lobby for a remembrance of things past, as well as to raise the awareness of the larger community to their existence as a minority group.[779] They formed the Association pour la Sauvegarde du Patrimoine Culturel des Juifs d'Égypte (ASPCJE) in 1979, with the specific aim of safeguarding the rich and diverse history of their community. The association requested that all the Jews of Egypt be oral historians and participate in the task of sharing their memories and recording their testimonies for the benefit of present and future generations.

According to one of my respondents, a founding member of ASPCJE, two vastly different but highly significant events triggered that awakening. The first one was Egyptian president Anwar el-Sadat's dramatic visit to Israel in 1977, which led to the signing of a peace treaty between the two countries in March 1979.[780] Beside the political—both national and international—importance of this very public event, it had very personal and emotional significance for the expelled or self-exiled Egyptian Jews. To understand why this represented a watershed event for them, one must remember that when the Jews left Egypt after 1956 their laissez-passer bore the stamp: Valable pour un seul voyage sans retour. Consequently, not only were they forced to leave empty-handed a country where most of them had lived for at least two or three generations, but they were also barred from ever returning.[781] To be suddenly free to revisit their birthplace was like the miraculous re-opening of a door that had long been sealed. It brought back memories of the exceptional lifestyle and carefree days of their youth. Somehow, this event does not seem to have had the same resonance for the émigrés from Egypt living in Australia, probably because the physical isolation and remoteness of their new home had somewhat dulled their sensitivities in this respect. The second event, much smaller in scope but also definitive in its outcome, was the funeral of the Communist militant, Egyptian-born Henri Curiel, shot in the lift of his Paris apartment in 1978 by unknown assassins believed to be from the Far Right.[782] The fact that none of the various eulogies delivered during the official ceremony ever mentioned that Curiel was a Jew from Egypt greatly disturbed the small group of his Egyptian/Jewish friends, also affiliated to the left side of politics, including a number of my respondents who were present at the funeral.[783] Together they decided to act by initiating a series of measures to inform the general public as to the identity of the Jews of Egypt. They started by producing and distributing a small booklet called, "A la Rencontre des Juifs d'Égypte".[784] In 1979 they organised a major reunion, held at the Jewish community centre of Paris, *Espace Rachi*, which attracted over three hundred people originally from Egypt. Following the success of that reunion, the ASPCJE was created and its committee, which included a number of my respondents, decided on a series of initiatives. They organised a four-day colloquium on Jewish, Mediterranean, and Oriental cultures, at the Centre Georges Pompidou.[785] They also planned a series of lectures by academics on various topics of Jewish/Egyptian history and helped with the publication of a number of books written by Egyptian Jews in France. The association's bulletin, *Nahar Misraim*, which appeared from December 1980 to May 1989, was the brainchild of Interviewee #2F who worked very closely with the Egyptian-born historian, Jacques Hassoun:

> A la suite des journées de Beaubourg, j'ai dit à Jacques [Hassoun], il faut qu'on fasse une petite publication pour garder le contact avec tout le monde. Il m'a dit, tu veux t'en occuper? J'ai dit oui, j'ai trouvé un imprimeur, une femme qui tapait à la machine et on a commencé. Ça a marché pendant dix ans.[786]

Several respondents were actively involved in the production of the bulletin by contributing articles or attending to administrative duties at the

ASPCJE, until its publication was suspended in 1990.[787] The association resumed its activities in 1999, with the help of old and new members, again including some of my respondents, who continue to show dedication and commitment to the cause of safeguarding and transmitting the heritage of the Jews of Egypt. The publication *Nahar Misraïm* now appears quarterly as a newsletter and discusses a variety of topics, such as personal memories of life in Egypt, the latest books written by Egyptian Jews, or significant events in the Jewish/Egyptian world, such as the World Congress of the Jews of Egypt held in July 2006 in Haifa, marking the fiftieth anniversary of the events that led to the second exodus from Egypt.[788]

Thanks to the efforts of their intellectual elite, the self-awareness of the Jews of Egypt in France seems to have grown in strength. Not only were they more secure in their identity, but they also tried to inform outsiders of their past history. Their physical and emotional connection to Egypt has not been totally severed; all the French respondents, as well as most of my other contacts in France, made the trip back to Egypt at least twice, individually and on organised group tours, unlike the sample group in Australia, where a much smaller proportion (28 percent) re-visited Egypt.[789] One of those tours, conducted by Jacques Hassoun in 1993, accompanied by Egyptian-born journalist and author Paula Jacques, was recorded live for a special radio program called "Nuits magnétiques, six jours et sept nuits, le temps d'un retour au pays natal" and broadcast nationally over four nights.[790] In 1999—in the context of a school program on the themes of exile, displacement, and revisiting the past—a Jewish student whose family came from Egypt, and who was related to one of my respondents, spoke about the land his mother and grandparents had to leave, their lifestyle, the food they ate, and the many languages they spoke, with a "funny accent". His story sparked the interest of the teacher, who organised a trip to Egypt for the whole class, accompanied by a film crew. The film was shown on television nationally, with that student as the main protagonist.[791] Egyptian Jews were also regularly invited to speak about their specific traditions on community radio programs run by the North African Jews.[792]

In the last decade, inspired by the achievements of the pioneering ASPCJE, similar initiatives have sprung up in France, as well as other countries where Jews from Egypt have settled in sufficient numbers. For example, the Association Internationale Nébi Daniel (AIND), supported by the Association of Jews from Egypt (AJE), United Kingdom; the Association des Juifs Originaires d'Égypte (AJOE), France; and the ASPCJE, is lobbying through official channels, both in France and in Egypt, for the preservation *in situ* of the remaining assets of the Jewish community in Alexandria, such as its synagogues, cemeteries, religious artefacts, and archives, as well as ensuring unrestricted access to its civil records. In the United States, the Historical Society of Jews from Egypt (HSJE) was created in 1995 with the aim of "highlighting the necessity of preserving the memory of Egypt's Jewish community", emphasising the need for "members of the community to learn about their past in order to preserve it". This organisation has adopted a different approach from AIND by strongly lobbying for the return of the patrimony Jews left behind when they were forced out Egypt, and for its transfer to an academic institution in the United States.[793] The IAJE, established in 1997 in New York, has tried to establish a link between the Jews from Egypt living in various parts of the world, in order to preserve the memory of "a glorious past". The late Professor Victor D. Sanua, its director, recognised the debt his association owed to people like Jacques Hassoun and the ASPCJE. He even declared, "If any centre of Egyptian Jewry is established, it should be dedicated in his name".[794] Other associations, such as the Amicale Alexandrie, Hier et Aujourd'hui (AAHA)[795], the AJOE, and the AJE, tend to have more of a mix between intellectual and social activities—organising monthly dinners, outings, occasional conferences, and guided trips to Egypt—with the ultimate aim of bringing people together, sharing the same experience, and keeping in touch with others from the same ethnic background, thus demonstrating their strong attachment to their cultural heritage and their determination not to let it be forgotten.[796]

In the past decade there has been an upsurge of books written by Jews from Egypt, in French, English, and even Italian, about their reconstructed memories of their lives in Egypt, before and after what they called *les événements* (the events), and about their experiences in their respective diasporas. Nevertheless, it has been determined that—from the examination of primary and secondary sources, evaluation of the interviews, and many informal discussions with Egyptian Jewish émigrés—outside of Israel, the push and the motivation to put on record, to remember, and to tell others the personal stories, general history, and cultural heritage of the Jews from Egypt, were initiated in France in the late 1970s by an elite microgroup of Jews from Egypt, some of whom were part of this study. A number of basic elements—such as the size of the transplanted community in France, a tradition of cosmopolitanism, an ethnicity shared with the dominant group within French Jewry, and an affinity with the national culture and language, combined with the professionalism of the microgroup and its preoccupation with intellectual pursuit—seem to have provided the right climate for their creativity to flourish. In that respect, there was no similar climate in Australia, maybe because of a different combination of those basic elements: smaller numbers, greater isolation, multilevel alienation, and unfamiliar culture. The small size of the community of Egyptian Jews in Australia made them a nearly invisible minority. The isolation of the Australian continent and the physical distance between their new home and the Old Country cut them off from their past, and the spread of Australia's main cities separated them from each other. The overriding preoccupation common to most migrants, which is the need to adapt to an unfamiliar culture and language, as well as achieve a comfortable lifestyle, was all-consuming, at least initially. Nevertheless, fifty years later, the memories of the anguish and trauma of new beginnings have somewhat faded. The Jews from Egypt are successfully integrated into their respective host societies at every level: culturally, economically, and socially. Both sample groups, in Australia and France, expressed their gratitude towards the country that had taken them in as refugees and given them freedom, security, and opportunities.

CONCLUSION

In this book I have tried to construct a complete profile of a clearly defined Jewish community from Egypt. Built around the conceptual framework of forced emigration, integration, and acculturation, the book looks into the successful migration experience of this particular group of Egyptian Jews within Australian society and, on a smaller scale, within French society, based on the oral history of a number of Egyptian-born interviewees who migrated to Australia and to France.

Like all other Jewish communities of Arab lands, the strong and prosperous Jewish community of Egypt is no more, notwithstanding the handful of individuals left in Cairo and Alexandria. In view of the political climate in the Middle East, there appears no prospect of that community being revived in the near or distant future. A community of over eighty thousand was either overtly expelled or covertly forced into exile in the aftermath of the first three wars waged between Egypt and Israel in 1948, 1956, and 1967. However, the Arab-Israeli conflict was not the only element that contributed to the demise of Egyptian Jewry. From the early 1930s, long before the establishment of the State of Israel in 1948, the rise of an exclusively Arab-Islamic type of nationalism that did not consider the Jews true Egyptians, as well as the growing threat of Islamic fundamentalism, shook the foundations of the Jewish population. The first cracks started to appear. Egypt wanted to gain independence from British rule and foreign influence and, rightly or wrongly, the Jews were perceived to be in the camp of the foreigners. It was only a question of time before they would be considered *persona non grata*. Maybe the fact that they adopted Western culture and educated their children in foreign schools, as insurance for the future, distanced them even further from their Egyptian roots. With the outbreak of war with Israel they were subjected to overt and covert harassment that led to their expulsion or to a panic-stricken exodus. Although a great number of Egyptian Jews immigrated to Israel, the rest dispersed throughout the Western world, mainly in Europe and the Americas. In Australia, a small group of less than two thousand found a new home.

Before the events that led to their dispersion, the Jews of Egypt occupied what they thought was a safe and respected place in Egyptian society. Their contribution to the economic development and modernisation of the country was considerable, "totally out of proportion to their actual numbers"[797], not unlike the situation in Australia.[798] Apart from a small group of indigenous Jews, most of the Jewish population of modern Egypt had emigrated from countries within the Ottoman Empire, North Africa, and Western and Eastern Europe. Searching for better economic conditions and political stability, or fleeing persecution in their country of origin, the Jews migrated to Egypt from the mid-nineteenth century, attracted by the policy of economic liberalism and legal privilege for foreigners, promoted by Egyptian rulers and guaranteed by British occupation. As a consequence of that immigration, they were not a homogeneous community. They were divided along the lines of ethnic origin, rite, nationality, language, and class. In the Ottoman and Islamic tradition, they were defined by their religion and lived side-by-side with several other non-Muslim communities, such as Copts, Greeks, Syrians, and Armenians, as well as colonies of Italian, French, and British expatriates. Their common characteristics were their multiple language skills, born of their exposure to such a diversity of cultures, and a relatively high standard of Western education, acquired through a network of religious and secular French and English private schools. In the process of Westernisation they grew more and more alienated from the local Egyptian population and from the Arab culture. By 1948, except for a small group of indigenous Egyptian Jews of lower socioeconomic status, most of Egyptian Jewry identified with the Western world and its culture. The middle and upper-middle class spoke French at home and with members of the other religious and ethnic minorities. The use of Arabic was often relegated to communication with servants and shopkeepers.

After their exile, apart from those who migrated to Israel, the majority of Jews from Egypt had to go through a waiting period in the capitals of Europe before they were accepted by any of the countries of immigration except for Brazil. That transit period was facilitated by the assistance of international and local Jewish agencies. The majority of interviewees who chose to settle in Australia did so to be reunited with family members. They first had to overcome the racial discrimination of the White Australia Policy towards Jewish immigrants of Middle Eastern origin. This hurdle was surmounted, thanks to the tireless efforts of leaders of the Australian Jewish community, such as Syd Einfeld and the AJWS, combined with the lobbying by the South Australia Jewish community and the help of a few politicians, particularly Patrick Galvin, Labor Federal Member for Kingston, South Australia.

The interviewees' testimonies revealed that, in addition to their ethnic and national diversity and middle-class background, the newcomers were young, healthy, Western educated, and multilingual, with at least a basic if not a good knowledge of English. They had solid business ethics and were too proud to ask for handouts—in other words, they were "good migrant material". Beginnings in Australia were not always smooth, especially for those who arrived in the late 1940s and 1950s as refugees, without means of support, when Australian social services were in their infancy, accommodation was scarce, and non-British migrants were not made to feel particularly welcome. Nevertheless, they were faced with the necessity of integrating into their new environment.

A relatively large number of Egyptian Jews settled in Adelaide from 1948 on, as a result of chain migration, where they made a greater impact than in Sydney and Melbourne because of the small size of the Adelaide Jewish community.

Due to a combination of factors, such as level of education, linguistic skills, and adaptability, as well as a favourable economic climate, Egyptian Jews entered the workforce as white-collar workers without great difficulty. In a relatively short time they were contributing to the economy of the country. Within two to three years of their arrival they had successfully reintegrated into the ranks of the middle class. Most of them were able to buy their own homes, often thanks to low-interest loans from the Jewish Welfare Building Society. Some of them even owned cars. The younger migrants, who were of school age upon arrival, eventually pursued tertiary education in Australian universities, with the support of Commonwealth scholarships. At the time of the interviews, their Australian-born children were, for the most part, university graduates and professionals. It appears that, as a rule, their socioeconomic integration was remarkably swift.

At first, like all non-British migrants, they were expected to shed distinctive signs of their previous culture and allegiances, particularly their language, and totally assimilate into the host society. The Egyptian émigrés responded to that challenge by creating their own familial networks, sharing accommodation and resources, and helping each other to adjust to their new environment. At the level of government, the failure of the policy of assimilation caused it to be abandoned for the preferred policy of integration of migrants into the emerging multicultural society of the 1970s. In that context, the Jews of Egypt were on familiar ground. Because a multilayered identity constituted the core of their being, they skilfully drew on their past experience of living in a multicultural society. They already possessed the tools for dealing with people from different ethnic backgrounds. They knew how to accommodate the various layers of their identities and gradually re-acculturated themselves within both the Australian Jewish community and the broader Australian society, while maintaining their ties to their religious and cultural backgrounds and preserving a Jewish identity. For the most part they retained the use of French among themselves—sometimes mixed with Italian and Arabic—and their traditional Sephardi and Oriental cuisine, which they introduced to their friends in Australia. In Adelaide, where they were more prominent, they included some of the Egyptian rites and tunes as an integral part of synagogue service.

Their relationship with other Sephardim and with the dominant Ashkenazi community was not without problems. As a group, they were often criticised for a low level of communal involvement. A notable exception consisted of a number of individuals in Adelaide, Melbourne, and Sydney, who distinguished themselves in different fields of communal endeavour. By the time this study was conducted, these early frictions seemed to have been forgotten. Egyptian Jews were generally accepted by their peers as different but valuable members of the Jewish community. They retained their multilayered identity with a strong Jewish core and identification with Israel as the home of the Jewish people.

In spite of the trauma they experienced when they were forced out of Egypt, they seem to have shed long ago any significant resentment towards their country of birth. They still remember with nostalgia the atmosphere of tolerance and conviviality prevalent in Egypt before 1948. The Egyptian/Jewish heritage has remained a significant identity marker for the majority of my respondents, even though they feel very patriotic towards Australia.

In an open society such as Australia, assimilation is regarded as the biggest threat to Jewish continuity. Although intermarriage was rare among the Egyptian-born respondents and even, to some extent, among their children—whose non-Jewish partners often converted—intermarriage within the ranks of the grandchildren seems to be on the increase, confirming Rutland's findings that "recent demographic studies indicate a significant increase in intermarriage amongst the younger generation".[799] My study could not draw a definitive conclusion because most of the grandchildren have not yet married. However, it can be assumed that the generally low level of religious observance of Egyptian Jews, as well as the tradition of liberalism and tolerance towards other cultures, will contribute to a higher level of intermarriage than in more orthodox communities.

Within the framework of forced emigration, integration, and acculturation, the migration experience of this distinct group of Jews has proven to be positive. Thanks to their multiple language skills, multilayered identity, and innate ability to adapt and interact with a variety of ethnic groups, they have succeeded in establishing themselves in an unfamiliar country that initially welcomed them reluctantly before embracing their pluralism. As such, they can be said to have successfully acculturated and integrated into Australian society, while retaining their own cultural diversity.

The high concentration of Egyptian Jews in Adelaide brought them to the forefront of the Jewish community, and they had a significant impact on Jewish community life in that city. In Sydney and Melbourne, in contrast, the small group of Egyptian Jews successfully blended into the existing Jewish communities, but they hardly ever attempted to organise themselves independently or to create their own institutions. There never was a formal association of Egyptian Jews in Australia, but they still to this day practise a high level of unstructured socialisation among themselves.

Furthermore, because the Jews from Egypt did not have a "ghetto mentality"—which was more prevalent among Ashkenazi Jews—they did not always automatically settle in Jewish areas upon arrival in the country. They dispersed in the large cities of Sydney and Melbourne particularly, not realising the consequences of the great distances and the inadequate public transport system on their identification as Jews. Once they realised their isolation, the option of moving had often become too expensive. It took some of the Sydney respondents over fifteen years before they could relocate closer to the stronger Jewish community in the East, so that their children could grow up in a Jewish environment. Furthermore, their diversity and tolerant view of the world, which served them well in their interaction with people from different ethnic backgrounds, did not motivate them to assert themselves as a distinctive group. They preferred to blend into the existing community. Thus their identity was somewhat diluted by the combination of their small numbers, dispersion, intrinsic diversity, and ability to adapt and connect to other cultures.

In contrast to what was happening in France, very few of my respondents—with one notable exception—articulated an active commitment to the transmission and safeguarding of their Jewish Egyptian heritage, although telling their stories to a researcher constitutes in itself an act of transmission and safeguard.[800] They all expressed a high level of satisfaction with their lives in Australia and considered themselves lucky to have ended up at the Edge of the Diaspora, in spite of the different culture and geographical isolation; they had simply added an additional layer to their multifaceted identity.

Comparing the Australian sample with the French sample highlighted some of the similarities and differences. First, the majority of French respondents chose to settle in France because of their deep affinity with the language and culture. Furthermore, they represented a community of over ten thousand, whereas the Australian respondents were part of a community that was estimated to be fewer than two thousand. It is clear that such a difference affected their status as a distinctive ethnic group and their visibility in their ethno-religious community and in the host society. Nevertheless, both sample groups were astonishingly typical of Egyptian Jewry's wide diversity, such as ethnic origin, ideology, and nationality, as well as its common features, such as Western culture, strong Jewish identity, love of Israel, and a distinctive Mediterranean *joie de vivre*.

Although I have made allowances for the small size of the French sample compared to the Australian sample in my conclusions, I had to take into consideration the fact that the French sample represented a very elite group. Made up of a majority of highly acculturated intellectuals who not only talked about their past history but were also actively committed to the preservation of their heritage for the next generation, this microgroup could articulate better than any other the preoccupations and aspirations of the macrogroup. They also inspired other Egyptian diasporas dispersed throughout the Western world to walk in their footsteps, and to gather and record the personal testimonies of the Jews from Egypt. In spite of their strong and active commitment to informing others of their distinctive history and identity, their level of religious observance and Jewish affiliation was significantly lower than that of the Australian respondents. It is obvious that they had been influenced by the secularism of French society. Their identity as Jews from Egypt was, more often than not, an ethnic marker, although the majority expressed solidarity with Israel.

Evidently, the more numerous Egyptian Jews living in France were better equipped to assert themselves within the older Jewish/French community and to retain their distinctive features, particularly because, as Sephardim, they belonged to the dominant group within French Jewry, which added to their prestige. There were a number of reasons for their rapid acculturation. They were greatly assisted by international and local Jewish institutions when they first arrived. Their children were educated free of charge in French universities. Moreover, their deep affinity with the French language and culture ensured a smoother and deeper integration into the host society. However, their integration was not as smooth as one might have expected. Particularly in the initial stages, they were not readily accepted into French society, even though they were fluent in the national language, because their accent and their brand of French exposed them as foreigners. In addition, whereas none of the Australian respondents reported any personal experience of anti-Semitism, the French respondents were aware of a latent anti-Semitism still existing in some circles of French society, and at times found themselves at the receiving end of anti-Semitic remarks. Nevertheless, they also stated that they had never regretted settling in France and felt very privileged to be living there. Since 2000, with the rising level of anti-Semitism disguised as anti-Zionism and found in the general press, I detected a few signs of growing uneasiness among the Egyptian Jews I had previously interviewed.

Obviously, with the passage of time, the history of the Jews of Egypt in modern times will be relegated to the past, *un passé révolu*.[801] That history will be integrated in the greater picture of Jews of Arab lands and their subsequent dispersion throughout Israel and the Western world. My interviewees belong to the last generation of authentic Jews from Egypt, but the reality is that, as a distinct group, they are slowly disappearing. Their stories cannot be found in history books. The features that kept them together are waning as they grow older and as their children and grandchildren integrate deeper into Australian or French society. However, there are lessons to be learned from the migration experience of Egyptian Jewish émigrés, lessons about the process of integration and identity reconstruction, the diverse strategies used to ensure a successful acculturation, and particularly the value of a multilayered identity. These lessons would be lost if studies such as the present one were not undertaken. It is, therefore, crucial to record the personal testimonies of all these individuals who, through the vagaries of history, were forced to leave their birthplace and settle in a foreign land. Otherwise, their voices would not be heard beyond the confines of their closed family circle. The successes and vicissitudes of Egyptian Jewish émigrés and the way they responded to the challenges of a second exodus deserve a greater audience.

NOTES

1. Lana Woolf and I are both Egyptian-born of ethnically different Jewish backgrounds. At the beginning of our project, we still had ageing parents with amazing memories of their past history. The urgency and importance of the task of recording their stories, and the stories of other Egyptian Jews with equally fascinating experiences, were compelling factors in our determination to create, through a series of personal interviews, a record of the history of those Jews. We devised a questionnaire and made the initial contacts. Most of the time we were both present during the Sydney interviews, although only one of us would conduct the actual interview. The rest of the work, such as recording, transcribing, and assessing the collated data, was always my responsibility. When I decided to transform our project into a thesis for a PhD and expand my research to include the Egyptian émigrés in Melbourne and Adelaide, as well as a comparative case study of a similar group in France, I took charge of every step of the research. Ms. Woolf was most cooperative and continued to assist me with the interviews whenever her professional commitments as a high school teacher allowed her to do so.
2. The notion of forced emigration would thus be closer to the notion of exile, defined in *Webster's' Third New International Dictionary of the English Language* (Springfield, MA: G. & C. Merriam, 1976) as "a forced removal from one's native country".
3. WorldReference.com English Dictionary, adapted from Worldnet 2.0 Copyright 2003 by Princeton University.
4. According to UNESCO's definition, migrants—as opposed to refugees— "are people who make choices about when to leave and where to go, even though these choices are sometimes extremely constrained".
5. Forced expulsion of a specific ethnic group is sometimes considered a form of ethnic cleansing. See definition of ethnic cleansing in *Wikipedia, the free encyclopedia*: "ethnic cleansing can be understood as the forced expulsion of an 'undesirable' population from a given territory as a result of religious or ethnic discrimination, political, strategic, or ideological considerations, or a combination of these".
6. According to the definition found in *Wikipedia, the free encyclopedia*, "the term *diaspora*…is used (without capitalisation) to refer to any people or ethnic population forced or induced to leave their traditional ethnic

homelands; being dispersed throughout other parts of the world, and the ensuing developments in their dispersal and culture".

7. *Webster's' Third New International Dictionary* definition of assimilation is a "socio-cultural fusion wherein individuals and groups of differing ethnic heritage acquire the basic habits, attitudes, and mode of life of an embracing national culture".

8. Marion A. Kaplan, "Tradition and Transition: The Acculturation, Assimilation and Integration of Jews in Imperial Germany—A Gender Analysis", *Yearbook of the Leo Beck Institute* 27 (1982): 4 and 5.

9. For instance, Moses Mendelssohn (1729–1786), a German Jew, was one of the main proponents of the assimilation of the Jews in the German cultural community.

10. Kaplan, "Tradition and Transition", 3.

11. Janis Wilton and Richard Bosworth, *Old Worlds and New Australia: The Post-War Migrant Experience* (Ringwood, Victoria: Penguin Books Australia, 1984), 17–22.

12. *Oxford English Dictionary*, 1989.

13. Australian government immigration policies as set by the Department of Immigration and Multicultural and Indigenous Affairs.

14. Suzanne D. Rutland, *Edge of the Diaspora: Two Centuries of Jewish Settlement in Australia* (Sydney: Collins, 1988), 370. Rutland quoted Wilton and Bosworth, *Old Worlds and New Australia*, 34, who stated that the Whitlam era "symbolised the acceptance that multiculturalism had replaced assimilationism or even integrationism as the basis of a national immigration policy".

15. *Oxford English Dictionary*, 1989.

16. Kaplan, "Tradition and Transition", 4.

17. Shimon Shamir, "Notes on Researching the Modern History of Egyptian Jewry", *Bulletin of the Israeli Academic Centre in Cairo* 23 (June 1998): 3.

18. Bernard Lewis, *The Jews of Islam* (Princeton, NJ: Princeton University Press, 1984). Lewis, Professor of Near Eastern Studies Emeritus at Princeton University, has published several books on Islam and on the relations between Muslims, Christians, and Jews in the modern period. They include *Semites and Anti-Semites: An Inquiry into Conflict and Prejudice* (New York: Norton, 1986) and *Cultures in Conflict: Christians, Muslims and Jews in the Age of Discovery* (New York: Oxford University Press, 1995).

19. The body of sacred laws derived from the Koran and from the teachings of the Prophet Mohammed that regulate the lives of those who follow Islam.

20. Bat Ye'or has written extensively on the topics of *djihad* and dhimmitude. Her earlier publication, *Les Juifs en Égypte: Aperçu sur 3000 ans d'histoire* (Genève: Editions de l'Avenir, 1971), gave a critical perspective of Jewish-Arab relations throughout the ages. Her latest book *Eurabia: The Euro-Arab Axis* (Madison, NJ: Fairleigh Dickinson University Press, 2005) presents a conspiracy theory about Europe being gradually taken over by Islam.

21. See Mark R. Cohen, "Islam and the Jews: Myth, Counter-Myth, History", *Jerusalem Quarterly* (Spring 1986): 125–137, and "The Neo-Lachrymose Conception of Jewish-Arab History", *Tikkun* 6 (May-June 1991): 55–60. See the rebuttal of Cohen's argument in Norman A. Stillman, "Myth, Countermyth, and Distortion", *Tikkun* 6 (May-June 1991): 60–64.

22. To name just a few of the historians who researched the lives of Jewish communities of Arab countries, pointing to their chequered history: Renzo de Felice, *Jews in an Arab Land: Libya 1835–1970*, trans. Judith Roumani (Austin: University of Texas, 1985); Harvey E. Goldberg, *Jewish Life in Muslim Libya: Rivals and Relatives* (Chicago, IL, and London: University of Chicago Press, 1990); Michel Abitbol, *Le Passé d'une discorde, Juifs et Arabes du VIIè à nos jours* (Paris: Librairie Académique Perrin, 1999); Shlomo Deshen and Walter P. Zenner (eds.), *Jews among Muslims: Communities in the Precolonial Middle East* (London: Macmillan Press, 1996); Michael Laskier, *North African Jewry in the Twentieth Century: The Jews of Morocco, Tunisia, and Algeria* (New York: New York University Press, 1994).

23. See Norman A. Stillman, *The Jews of Arab Lands: A History and Source Book* (Philadelphia, PA: Jewish Publication Society, 1979) and *The Jews of Arab Lands in Modern Times*, (Philadelphia, PA: Jewish Publication Society, 1991).

24. Stillman, *Modern Times*, 4.

25. Ibid., 7.

26. Ibid., 142–143. Stillman reported that on that day the Ashkenazi synagogue of Cairo was also ransacked and burned and that an apologetic government "offered to bear the expenses for rebuilding the ruined synagogue".

27. Ibid., 149–150.

28. Ibid., 164–165. Stillman claimed that in the case of Egyptian Jewry, apart from the Zionist idealists, it was mostly the lower-middle class of Jews, particularly the "stateless individuals...hurt by the 1947 Egyptianization laws" who left at this time.

29. Regarding the notorious "Lavon Affair", Stillman recommended a series of different perspectives of the events, namely: Eliyahu Hasin and Dan

Horowitz, *The Affair* (Tel Aviv: Am ha-Sefer, 1961) [Heb]; Avri El-Ad with James Creech, *Decline of Honour* (Chicago, IL: Henry Regnery, 1976); and Aviezer Golan, *Operation Suzannah: As Told to Aviezer Golan by Marcelle Ninio, Victor Levy, Robert Dassa and Philip Natanson*, trans Peretz Kidron. (New York, NY: Harper and Row, 1978). For more recent studies, see Uri Bar-Joseph, *Intelligence Intervention in the Politics of Democratic States: The United States, Israel, and Britain* (University Park, PA: Pennsylvania State University Press, 1995); Shabtai Teveth, *Ben-Gurion's Spy: The Story of the Political Scandal That Shaped Modern Israel* (New York, NY: Columbia University Press, 1996).

30. In *The Jews of Arab Lands in Modern Times*, 60, Stillman also expanded on the issue of Middle Eastern and North African Jewries and their confrontation with modernity "as a result of the impact of an ascendant Europe upon the economic, political, and cultural life of the Islamic world". See also Harvey E. Goldberg (ed.), *Sephardi and Middle Eastern Jewries: History and Culture in the Modern Era* (Bloomington and Indianapolis: Indiana University Press, 1996), 59–72.

31. Maurice Fargeon, *Les Juifs en Égypte: Depuis les origines jusqu'à ce jour* (Cairo: Paul Barbey, 1938). Fargeon also published a book on the contribution of Jewish doctors and lawyers to Egypt, *Médecins et Avocats juifs au service de l'Égypte* (Cairo: Imprimerie Lencioni, 1939) and edited two editions of the Jews of Egypt yearbooks, *Annuaire des Juifs d'Égypte et du Proche-Orient, 1942* (Cairo: La Société des Editions Historiques Juives d'Égypte, 1943) and *Annuaire des Juifs d'Égypte et du Proche-Orient, 5706/1945–1946* (Cairo: La Société des Editions Historiques Juives d'Égypte, 1945).

32. Jacob M. Landau, in *Jews in Nineteenth-Century Egypt*, 4, stated "Fargeon's estimate that 30,000 Jews lived in Egypt at the time of the Napoleonic expedition is practically baseless".

33. Landau, *Middle Eastern Themes*, 99–141. "Ritual Murder Accusations in Nineteenth Century Egypt" was first published in *Sefunot* (Jerusalem), 1961, 417–460. The fact that the Greeks were believed to be the major inciters and instigators of these accusations against the Jews was one of the issues raised by Landau. The fundamental reason for that phenomenon was probably economic competition between the two minority groups. Bearing in mind the political tension prevailing at the time and the deep resentment of foreign interference, it is likely that the Greeks—and later the Syrian Christians—"wanted the Jews to be their scapegoat for the mob's hatred of foreigners and thus save their own position". The documents also showed

that the Greeks succeeded at times in recruiting local Arabs to their cause. The Jewish reaction was, for the most part, to ask for the protection of foreign powers, such as Britain, France, and Italy. It was only with the establishment of British rule in Egypt in 1882 that the Jews of Egypt experienced a growing feeling of security. However, Landau concluded that most Egyptians still considered the Jews foreigners, "identifying Zionism with the European infiltration of the Middle East". Therefore, the perception of the Jews as an estranged group, along with "the self-willed isolation of the Jews in Egypt...may have contributed to make it difficult for them to settle down as an integral element of the population in the following years".

34. Landau, *Middle Eastern Themes*, 157–171. "The Beginnings of Modernization in Education: The Jewish Community of Egypt as a Case Study" was reprinted, with permission, from William R. Polk and Richard L. Chambers (eds.), *Beginnings of Modernization in the Middle East: The Nineteenth Century* (Chicago, IL, and London: The University of Chicago Press, 1968), 299–312.

35. Landau, *Middle Eastern Themes*, 172–188. "Abu Naddara: An Egyptian Jewish Nationalist" was reprinted with permission from *The Journal of Jewish Studies*, III (1) (1952): 30–44.

36. Shimon Shamir, *The Jews of Egypt: A Mediterranean Society in Modern Times* (Boulder, CO, and London: Westview Press, 1987), xviii. Shamir holds the Kaplan Chair in the History of Egypt and Israel at Tel Aviv University. He was the first Israeli ambassador to Egypt and the founder and first director of the Israeli Academic Centre in Cairo.

37. Shamir, *The Jews of Egypt*, Appendix A, 215–235, deals with two little-known chronicles in Portuguese about some anti-Jewish rioting that occurred in the mid-eighteenth century in Cairo; Appendix B, 237–242 deals with the original text of the Egyptian Nationality Law of 1929 in French; Appendix C, 243–264, refers to Sanua's correspondence in Arabic.

38. Krämer, *The Jews in Modern Egypt, 1914–1952*, 1989. Originally, this study was a doctoral dissertation published in German in 1982 and then translated into English in 1985–1987. Krämer's article "Political Participation of the Jews in Egypt between World War I and the 1952 Revolution" was published in Shamir, *The Jews of Egypt*, 68–82. Her article "'Radical' Nationalists, Fundamentalists, and the Jews in Egypt or, Who is a Real Egyptian?" appeared in Gabriel R. Warburg and Uri M. Kupferschmidt (eds.), *Islam, Nationalism, and Radicalism in Egypt and the Sudan* (New York, NY: Praeger, 1983), 354–371.

39. Krämer, *The Jews in Modern Egypt*, 116.
40. Laskier, *The Jews of Egypt, 1920–1970: In the Midst of Zionism, Anti-Semitism and the Middle East Conflict*, 1992. Laskier also published a number of journal articles that expanded on the issues discussed in his book, for instance: "From War to War: The Jews of Egypt from 1948 to 1970", *Studies in Zionism 7*, no. 1 (1986): 111–147; "Egypt's Jewry in the Post-World War II Period: 1945–1948", *Revue des Etudes Juives 148* (July-December 1989): 337–360; "Egyptian Jewry Under the Nasser Regime, 1956–1970", *Middle Eastern Studies 31*, no. 3 (July 1995): 573–619; and "In the Aftermath of Israel's Sinai Campaign: The Leadership Crisis and Political and Economical Decline of Egypt's Jewish Communities during the Late 1950s and 1960s", *Africana Journal XVII* (1998): 289–306. He has also written extensively on other Jewish communities of the Muslim world: *The Alliance Israélite Universelle and the Jewish Communities of Morocco: 1862–1962* (Albany: State University of New York, 1983); "From Hafsia to Bizerte: Tunisia's Nationalist Struggle and Tunisian Jewry, 1952–61", *Mediterranean Historical Review 2*, no. 2 (December 1987): 188–222; and "North African Jewry in the Twentieth Century: The Jews of Morocco, Tunisia and Algeria", *Middle Eastern Studies 31*, no. 2 (April 1995): 391.
41. Laskier, in *The Jews of Egypt*, 114–116, mentioned the famed "Operation Passover" when, in April 1946, just before the Jewish festival of Passover, a group of about one hundred Egyptian Jewish youths illegally crossed the desert by train, reaching Palestine under the nose of the British, wearing British army uniforms and carrying British identification cards. One of my respondents was in that group and still remembered how elated he felt being there for that very symbolic Jewish festival.
42. Huckstep was an old American military camp left over from World War II, at Heliopolis, a suburb of Cairo. It had been transformed into a detention centre for Zionists and Communists at the time of both the 1948 war and the 1956 war with Israel. A number of my respondents were detained at Huckstep.
43. Laskier, *The Jews of Egypt*, 205–251. See also Laskier, "A Document on Anglo-Jewry's Intervention on Behalf of Egyptian Jews on Trial for Espionage and Sabotage, December 1954", *Michael X*, (1986): 143–152.
44. Laskier, *The Jews of Egypt*, 246. Two of the conspirators, Shmu'el Azhar and Moshe Marzuq, were executed. Me'ir Meyuhas and Me'ir Za'fran were sentenced to seven years. Robert Dassa, Victor Levy, Philip Natanson, and Marcelle Ninio were still serving out their sentences when they were finally released in the prisoner exchange following the Six-Day War in 1967.

45. Laskier, "In the Aftermath of Israel's Sinai Campaign", *Africana Journal*, 290–291.

46. Szulc, *The Secret Alliance: The Extraordinary Story of the Rescue of the Jews since World War II*, 281–283. I also came across an unpublished article, translated from French by Rabbi Y. L. Cohen of the Sephardi synagogue of Melbourne. It seems that the son of Rabbi Isaac (Zaki) Acher Zal (1870–1963)—who had worked with the chief Rabbi of Cairo, Nahoum Effendi—was President of the Jewish Community of Cairo and, at the same time, the lawyer of the Spanish Embassy in Cairo. Apparently, due "to his high position at the Spanish Embassy, Mayer Acher succeeded to assist a great number of Jews who had no Egyptian identity to leave for Israel by getting them Spanish passports".

47. Beinin, *The Dispersion of Egyptian Jewry: Culture, Politics and the Formation of a Modern Diaspora*, 1998. Beinin is Professor of Middle Eastern History at Stanford University. He also authored a number of books on related topics, such as: *Workers on the Nile: Nationalism, Communism, Islam and the Egyptian Working Class, 1882–1954* (Princeton, NJ: Princeton University Press, 1987); *Political Islam: Essays from Middle East Report* (Princeton, NJ: Princeton University Press, 1989); *Was the Red Flag Flying There? Marxist Politics and the Arab-Israeli Conflict in Egypt and Israel, 1948–1965* (Berkeley: University of California Press, 1990); and *Workers and Peasants in the Modern Middle East* (Cambridge, MA: Cambridge University Press, 2001).

48. Beinin, *The Dispersion of Egyptian Jewry*, 142: "1,000 or more Jews participated in the Egyptian communist party from the 1930s to the 1950s", whereas most of the older members of the middle and upper bourgeoisie rejected political Zionism and professed their loyalty to Egypt to protect their comfortable lifestyle.

49. See footnote 2 on Bat-Ye'or.

50. Beinin, The Dispersion of Egyptian Jewry, 14–15. See Stillman, *Modern Times*; Lewis, *Semites and Anti-Semites*; Martin Gilbert, *The Jews of Arab Lands: Their History in Maps* (London: World Organisation of Jews from Arab Countries and Board of Deputies of British Jews, 1976).

51. See Krämer, *The Jews in Egypt*, 234–235, who postulated that Egyptian Jews experienced "neither uninterrupted persecution and terror nor uninterrupted harmony". See Philip Mendes, "Voluntary Departure or Expulsion: The Jewish Exodus from Modern Egypt, 1948–1967", *Australian Journal of Jewish Studies XI*, (2005): 134–146, where he also examined the two perspectives used to explain the modern exodus from Egypt. The pro-Zionist

perspective is based on the assumption that the "vicarious persecution" of the Jews by the Arabs eventually led to their wholesale expulsion, whereas the anti-Zionist perspective "portrays a harmonious historical relation between Jews and Muslims that was destroyed only by modern Zionist intervention".

52. Edward William Lane, *An Account of the Manners and Customs of the Modern Egyptians 1833–1835* (London: Murray, 1860) Vol. II, 344–349.

53. As stated by Stillman in *The Jews of Arab Lands in Modern Times*, 18, "no native group benefited more from Europe's intrusion into the Middle East than did the non-Muslim minorities".

54. Beinin, *The Dispersion of Egyptian Jewry*, 15.

55. Ibid., 12.

56. Ibid., 250. Beinin points out that until "the capitulations were cancelled by the 1937 Montreux Convention, there were few advantages to becoming an Egyptian citizen. This was a new political category that came into existence only in 1922, and those who had a choice were not eager to abandon foreign citizenship for it. However, by the late 1930s, when the advantages of Egyptian citizenship had become clear, the application of the 1929 Citizenship Law made it more difficult for Jews to claim Egyptian citizenship. Poor and middle-class autochthonous Jews found it difficult to prove that their families had resided continuously in Egypt since 1848, as the law required. They constituted the main group of Jews who were entitled to Egyptian citizenship, and they were often refused or subjected to lengthy bureaucratic delays when they officially applied for it".

57. Ibid., 17–18.

58. Their suffering does not negate the suffering of Palestinians in Israel.

59. Ibid., 19.

60. Ibid., 99–101.

61. Ibid., 6.

62. Ibid., 131–141. Beinin's restricted and restrictive selection of material was possibly the result of his own personal experience, which he revealed in the course of his narrative: his beginnings as a leftist American Zionist, his alienation from Zionism after a stay on a Marxist kibbutz, and his scholarly research in Egypt on the Egyptian working class and the left.

63. Malcom J. Turnbull, *Safe Haven*, 5.

64. In that section I often found references to some of my interviewees' case files.

65. Wilton and Bosworth, *Old Worlds and New Australia*.

66. James Jupp, *Immigration* (Sydney: Sydney University Press, in association with Oxford University Press, 1991), 69–81.

67. Ibid., 70.
68. Ibid., 72.
69. Rutland, *The Edge of the Diaspora*, 233. See also Rutland's article "Subtle Exclusions: Post-war Jewish Emigration to Australia and the Impact of the IRO Scheme", *The Journal of Holocaust Education 10*, no. 1 (Summer 2001): 50–66.
70. Jupp, *Immigration*, 72. For a dissenting view of Australia's treatment of the Jewish refugees, see W. D. Rubinstein, "Australia and the Refugee Jews of Europe, 1933–1954: A Dissenting View", *AJHS Journal 10*, Part 6 (1989): 500–523. Rubinstein was of the opinion that the conclusions drawn by Rutland and other historians, such as Michael Blakeney in *Australia and the Jewish Refugees, 1933–1948* (Kent: Croon Helm, 1985), were "seriously and perhaps fundamentally flawed by…a failure to place the small numbers who came in their proper contextual framework, above all (but not exclusively) in its failure…to acknowledge the force of Zionist opposition to refugee migration to Australia".
71. Catherine Panich, *Sanctuary? Remembering Post-War Immigration*, xv. Interestingly, this is the only reference in the book to Jewish postwar migration to Australia.
72. Ibid., 171.
73. Ibid., 162.
74. Ibid., 186.
75. Glenda Sluga, *Bonegilla: "A Place of No Hope"* (Melbourne: University of Melbourne History Department, 1988).
76. Ibid., x.
77. Ibid., ix-xi. The occupational classifications were mostly "labourer" or "domestic". Because those refugees/migrants were under obligation to work for two years in exchange for their assisted or free passage to Australia, they could be placed wherever the economy needed them or be given any jobs "Old Australians" did not want to take.
78. Rutland, *The Edge of the Diaspora*, 227–243.
79. Rutland, "The History of Australian Jewry 1945–1960", PhD Thesis, University of Sydney, 1990, 104–160; see also *The Edge of the Diaspora*, 251–256. Among my respondents, I only had one who went through the transit camp of Bonegilla. However, he migrated to Australia much later, in 1968, via Israel as a government-assisted migrant with the same two-year work contract.
80. Rutland, *The Edge of the Diaspora*, 1997, 233.

81. For a complete list of Jewish hostels, see Rutland, *The Jews in Australia*, 2005, Appendix 3, 171–173.The great majority of my sample group did not go through the Jewish hostels and seem to have relied on family and friends for their initial accommodation needs. Only one of my respondents (#76) reported being accommodated with her family in the Komlos hostel in Greenwich when they landed in Sydney with a refugee status. All the financial support during their transit period in Paris and their travel expenses to Australia had been provided by the Hebrew Immigrant Aid Society (HIAS).

82. Anne Andgel, *Fifty Years of Caring: The History of the Australian Jewish Welfare Society, 1936–1986* (Sydney: Australian Jewish Welfare Society, 1988).

83. Rutland, *The Edge of the Diaspora*, 242–243.

84. Rodney Gouttman, "A Jew, and Coloured Too! Immigration of Jews of 'Middle East' Origin to Australia, 1949–58", *Immigrants and Minorities 12*, no. 1 (1993): 75–91.

85. Question 17 on a 1950 Incoming Passenger Card asked for racial origin of migrants: European, Asiatic, African, Polynesian (National Archives of Australia).

86. See Rutland, "Are You Jewish? Post-war Jewish Immigration to Australia, 1945–1954", *The Australian Journal of Jewish Studies*, 1991, 35–58.

87. Gouttman, "A Jew and Coloured Too!'"', 1.

88. Rutland, "Egyptian Jews in Adelaide: A Case Study in Oral History", *The Oral History Association of Australia Journal 6* (1984): 19–24. This article was also included as an appendix to Rutland's doctoral thesis, "The History of Australian Jewry".

89. Bernard Hyams, *Surviving: A History of the Institutions and Organisations of the Adelaide Jewish Community* (Adelaide: Hyde Park Press, 1998), 102–105.

90. Aaron Aaron, *The Sephardim of Australia & New Zealand* (Sydney: Aaron Aaron, 1979), 279.

91. Naomi Gale, *The Sephardim of Sydney: Coping with Political Processes and Social Pressures* (Sussex: Sussex Academic Press, 2005). See also her journal articles: "Sephardim and Sephardic Identity in Sydney", *AJHS Journal 11*, Part 2, 332–350, 1991; "A Case of Double Rejection: The Immigration of Sephardim to Australia", *New Community 20*, no. 2 (January 1994): 269–286; "Religious Involution: Sacred and Secular Conflict among Sephardi Jews in Australia", *Ethnology 36* (1997); and "Resi-

dence, Social Mobility and Practice Theory: The Case of Sephardic Jews of Sydney", *Journal of Sociology 35* (1999).

92. Gale, "From the Homeland to Sydney: Kinship, Religion, and Ethnicity among Sephardim", PhD Thesis, University of Sydney, 1990, 409–411.

93. Myer Samra, "Yisrael Rhammana: Constructions of Identity among Iraqi Jews in Sydney, Australia", PhD Thesis, University of Sydney, 1988, vii. Samra explained that the dictum *Yisrael Rhammana* (the Jews are a pomegranate) was central to the Iraqi Jews' perception of their own identity. Apart from his work on Sephardi Jews in Australia, Samra has also conducted research on the lost tribes of Israel and the Benei Menashe tribe in India.

94. Samra, "Yisrael Rhammana", 180.

95. Ibid., 127–128. Samra mentioned a particular meeting arranged by Sydney Einfeld, "in his dual capacity as President of the AJWS and Vice President of the ECAJ", where he took Aaron Aaron, President of the NSW Association of Sephardim, and his Secretary, Monte Moss, to meet personally with the Secretary for Immigration, Sir Tasman Heyes, and plead their case.

96. Ibid., 151–153. Samra noted the relative concentration of Egyptian Jews in the St. George area, somewhat removed from the main centres of Jewish population, which might explain their under-representation in the membership list of the NSW Association of Sephardim (NAS),

97. Ibid., 251.

98. Ibid., 283. Samra claimed: "Despite the divisions and the conflicts apparent within the community, we [the Iraqis and Egyptians] find a shared value of Sephardi unity". See also Samra's unpublished essay "The Founding of Bet Yosef: Conflict and Community among Sephardi Jews", in which he related the history of the split of the Sydney Sephardi community into four congregations, the Sephardi synagogue run by the NSW Association of Sephardim, the Eastern Jewish Association, the Bet Yosef Synagogue, and the Rambam Synagogue. He also commented on the future of the Sephardi community, in view of these internal divisions, predicting that there should be "room for the development of a federation of Sephardi organizations in Sydney".

99. W. J. Hudson, *Blind Loyalty: Australia and the Suez Crisis, 1956* (Melbourne: Melbourne University Press, 1989).

100. Ibid., 8.

101. Chanan Reich, *Australia and Israel, An Ambiguous Relationship* (Melbourne: Melbourne University Press, 2002), 1. H. V. Evatt was Minister for External Affairs at the time.

102. Ibid., 58.

103. Ibid., 16. According to Reich, it was only when the new Labor government headed by John Curtin came into power in October 1941 that "the Australian labour movement expressed its solidarity with the Zionist ideal of establishing a Jewish state in Palestine and pledged itself to accommodate as many refugees as possible in Australia after the war."

104. Ibid., 101.

105. Ibid., 58.

106. Jacques Hassoun, born in Egypt in 1936, joined the largest of the clandestine Egyptian Communist organisations—headed by Henri Curiel—in 1953, at age seventeen. Shortly after, he was arrested, together with other members of the group, and spent six months in prison before being expelled. He relocated in Paris in 1954 where he became a well-known psychiatrist. After his first trip back to Egypt in 1975, he became very involved with a group of Jewish émigrés from Egypt and, within the framework of the ASPCJE and its bulletin *Nahar Misraïm*, he remained very committed to the preservation of the Jewish Egyptian cultural heritage. He edited two books on that same topic, *Juifs du Nil* (Paris: Le Sycomore, 1981) and *Histoire des Juifs du Nil* (Paris: Minerve, 1990). Joel Beinin, in his book *The Dispersion of Egyptian Jewry*, added in an appendix an interview he had with Hassoun in November 1995. Hassoun died in Paris in April 1999.

107. *Nahar Misraïm*, No. 1–33, December 1980 to May 1989.

108. Gilbert Cabasso, et al., *Juifs d'Égypte, Images et Textes* (Paris: Editions du Scribe, 1984).

109. In Hassoun, *Histoire des Juifs du Nil*, chapter I, 15–45: "Splendeurs grecques et misères romaines: les Juifs d'Égypte dans l'Antiquité" by Joseph Mélèze-Modrzejewski. Mélèze's book *Les Juifs d'Égypte de Ramsès II à Hadrien* (Paris: Editions Errance, 1991) was translated into English by Robert Cornman and published under the title *Jews of Egypt: From Ramses II to Emperor Hadrian* (Princeton, NJ: Princeton University Press, 1995).

110. Alfred Morabia, born in Cairo in 1931 and Head of Arabic and Islamic Studies at the University of Toulouse-le-Mirail, wrote an extensive study of the history of Islam and the classic notion of djihad, called *Gihad dans*

l'Islam medieval. He died suddenly in 1986 and his book was published posthumously in 1993 by Albin Michel.

111. Maurice Mizrahi was politically active in the so-called "liberal" period of Egyptian nationalism. He was also the founder of the Cairo branch of LICA (Ligue Internationale contre l'Antisémitisme) and the initiator of the anti-German boycott of 1933–1939 (see Krämer, *The Jews in Modern Egypt*, 128–139).

112. Samir W. Raafat, *Maadi 1904–1962: Society and History in a Cairo Suburb* (Cairo: The Palm Press, 1994). Raafat has also published the following articles—all related to the Jews of Egypt—in the Egyptian press: "Dynasty: The House of Yacoub Cattaui", *Egyptian Mail*, April 2, 1994, 3; "The House Suares Built and How It Became the Mohamed Mahmoud Khalil Museum", *Egyptian Mail*, May 6, 1995; "Garden City's Finzi-Continis: A Look at this Neighbourhood's Last Garden", *Egyptian Mail*, June 17, 1995; "The National Bank of Egypt, 1898–1956", *Egyptian Mail*, May 11 and 25, 1996; "The House of Cicurel", *Al Ahram Weekly*, December 15, 1994; "Ignace Tiegerman", *Egyptian Mail*, September 20, 1997; "The Maadi Synagogue: If It Lights Up Then It's Yom Kippur", *Cairo Times*, October 2, 1997; "Robert Nahman: End of His Era", *Cairo Times*, November 10, 1999. Raafat has also managed the Cairo Jewish community website and the community newsletter, *Bassatine News*, since October 1995.

113. Shamir, "Notes on Researching", 3–7. A number of other researchers of Egyptian Jewry's history also contributed articles to that special edition, including Jacques Hassoun "Can Egyptian-Jewish Identity Be Reconstructed in France?", Michael Laskier "The Jewish Press in Egypt", Inbal Perlson "Jewish Musicians in Egypt", and Jacqueline Kahanoff "My First Passover".

114. As previously indicated, Shamir has published a number of books on Egyptian Jewry, namely *Self-Views in Historical Perspective in Egypt and Israel (Tel Aviv: Tel Aviv University, 1981)*; *The Jews of Egypt: A Mediterranean Society*; and *Egypt from Monarchy to Republic: A Reassessment of Revolution and Change* (Boulder, CO: Westview Press, 1995).

115. Arie Schlosberg was a member of the Zionist youth movement, Hehalutz Hatzair, in Egypt prior to 1948, when those movements were still legal. Upon the declaration of the State of Israel on May 15 of that year, he was arrested together with a group of approximately 350 Jews, including Zionists, Communists, community leaders, and wealthy businessmen. He was interned at the camp of Abukir, an old British Airforce military camp

situated twenty kilometres from Alexandria. When released, Schlosberg immigrated to Israel and became Professor of Psychiatry at the Faculty of Medicine of Tel Aviv University. Through the numerous activities of the centre he has founded, he remains totally committed to the preservation and transmission of the Egyptian Jewish heritage.

116. Professor Michael Laskier spoke about the "Inter-Communal Problems and Conflicts within the Jewish Community of Cairo: The Mid-1950s to the Mid-1960s". The historian Dr. Rami Guinat discussed the Communist movement in Egypt from a Jewish perspective, and Dr. Joseph Marzouq presented a paper on Murad Farag Lisha (1867–1956), the most distinguished Karaite personality in Egypt, who contributed to the writing of the first Egyptian Constitution. The issue of migration was covered by a representative of the Egyptian Jewish community in Brazil, and the paper I presented, "Exodus II: From Egypt to Australia", dealt mainly with the Australian immigration policy of the 1950s, its impact on Egyptian Jewish migrants, and the reason why such a great proportion chose to settle in Adelaide.

117. See editorial of *IAJE Newsletter 1*, no. 1 (1999). Dr. Victor D. Sanua, an Egyptian Jew, born in Cairo, left Egypt after 1956 and migrated to the United States. He was a Research Professor in Psychology at St. John's University, Queens, NewYork. As editor of the *IAJE Newsletter*, he was very active in promoting cultural activities related to the past and present history of Egyptian Jews. He has also written extensively on that topic, for example: "A Study of the Adjustment of Sephardi Jews in the New York Metropolitan Area", *The Jewish Journal of Sociology IX*, No. 1 (June 1967); "Immigration of Sephardic Jews from Egypt", *Sephardic History* (May 1997); "'Egypt for the Egyptians': The story of Abu Naddara (James Sanua) 1839–1912—A Jewish Egyptian Patriot", *Los Muestros 32* (September 1998); "Haim Nahum Effendi (1872–1960), Sephardic Chief Rabbi of Egypt", *Los Muestros 46* (March 2002).

118. For instance, in the ASPCJE bulletin, *Nahar Misraïm 20* (September 2004), an article appeared recalling the Lavon Affair and its consequences. The article also announced the death of Philippe Nathanson, one of the members of the spy ring, who spent nearly fourteen years in an Egyptian prison before being released in the wake of the 1967 War. In addition, the ASPCJE promotes the publication of books written by Egyptian-born French Jews as a testimonial and an homage to life in Egypt prior to the Suez crisis of 1956, such as *L'Égypte que j'ai connue* by Albert Pardo,

2003, and *Je viens d'un pays qui n'existe plus*, 2004, and *Une Jeunesse égyptienne* by Albert Oudiz, 2007.

119. Moise Rahmani's book, *L'Exode oublié, Juifs des pays arabes* (Paris: Editions Raphaël, 2003), retraced the modern history of the Jews in Arab countries and looked at the reasons for their mass exodus between 1948 and 1960. One chapter of this book is devoted to Egypt's Jews (79–203). Rahmani was born in Cairo. His family came from Rhodes and immigrated to Egypt at the end of the nineteenth century. Rahmani left in 1956 just before the Suez crisis and now lives in Brussels, after spending his teenage years in the ex-Belgian Congo in a Rhodesli environment. He was awarded the Marcel Marinower Prize 2003 for the publication of a number of books on Sephardi Judaism and Sephardi Jews.

120. In a quarterly magazine of Jewish culture published in the United Kingdom, *Jewish Renaissance 2*, Issue 3 (Spring 2003): 16–30, a feature on the Jews from Egypt was published with the assistance of the AJE. Egyptian-born British Jews contributed articles on various topics, such as "From Exodus to Exodus" by Alec Nacamuli, which was an exploration of what happened to the Jews of Egypt between the biblical exodus and the "second exodus" in the twentieth century. Other topics included "The Cairo Genizah" by Maurice Maleh, "Jewish Alexandria" by Roger Bilboul, and "Egypt in Israel" by Victor Sanua. A more personal contribution about the bitter-sweet memories of "A Leavened Passover" was written by the late Teddy Nahmias, aboard the ship that took him out of Egypt in 1957 as a refugee, with "no matzah, no harosset, no maror", but instead a huge cake made with flour and yeast, graciously provided by the captain and crew to their Jewish passengers.

121. Ethel Carasso, "La Communauté Juive d'Égypte de 1948 à 1957", Master's thesis, Modern History, Université de Paris X Nanterre, 1982.

122. Alain Lévy, "Topologie sociale d'une migration familiale (Égypte, Algérie, France, Grande Bretagne, Brésil)", Doctorat, Université Paris 7, 1994.

123. Ibid., 18.

124. Ibid., 22–23.

125. Laskier, "The Regeneration of French Jewry: The Influx and Integration of North African Jews into France, 1955–1965", *Jewish Political Studies Review 10*, nos. 1–2 (Spring 1998): 37–72; "France: An Unexpected Centre of Jewish Life", *Judaism XXXIV*, no. 2 (Spring 1985): 231–236.

126. According to the *Encyclopedia Judaica*, Jerusalem: Keter Publishing House, 1971, fifteen thousand Egyptian Jews settled in Brazil in the aftermath of the Suez War.

127. Joëlle Rouchou, "Nuits d'été au parfum de jasmin: Souvenirs des Juifs d'Égypte à Rio de Janeiro—1956/57", PhD Thesis, translated from Portuguese. *Communication and Culture*, University of Sao Paulo, 2003. Rouchou mentioned two other theses that were written on the topic of the Egyptian community of Sao Paulo, but these were not translated from Portuguese.

128. Ibid., 21.

129. Paula Jacques was born in Egypt in a Jewish family expelled in 1957 in the aftermath of the Suez crisis. She spent her early childhood in Israel on a kibbutz and now lives in Paris. She is a journalist and a producer at Radio France. In her first two novels, *Lumière de l'oeil*, and *Un baiser froid comme la lune*, published by Mercure de France in 1980 and 1983 respectively, her characters were made to endure the trauma of exile and dislocation, reminiscent of the émigrés of her parents' generation. These books also constituted the basis of my BA Honours thesis (1987). I looked into the privileged connection between the Jewish community of Egypt and the French culture and its representation in literary works by Jewish/Egyptian writers. Jacques has published a number of other novels that also dealt with the themes of emigration and integration, such as *L'héritage de tante Carlotta*, 1987; *Déborah et les anges dissipés*, 1991, Prix Fémina 1991; *La descente au paradis*, 1995; *Les femmes avec leur amour*, 1997; and *Gilda Stambouli souffre et se plaint* (Paris: Mercure de France, 2002).

130. André Aciman, *Out of Egypt* (New York: Farrar, Straus, & Giroux, 1994). Aciman was born and raised in Alexandria and grew up in Egypt, Italy, and France. A Harvard graduate, he is currently a distinguished professor at the Graduate Centre of City University of New York teaching the history of literary theory and the works of Marcel Proust. He previously taught French literature at Bard College. He has also written *False Papers* (New York: Farrar, Straus & Giroux, 2000), a series of essays on the subject of loss based on his own personal experience: a forced departure from Egypt, an early education in Europe, and college years in the United States, where he finally made his home. Aciman also edited *Letters of Transit* (New York: The New Press, 1999), a book that again looked at exile, home, and memory.

131. Given that my study could not include the Jews of Egypt who settled in Israel because this would constitute the subject of a separate study, the numerous novels and poems written by Egyptian-born Israelis based on their past experiences in Egypt and their migration to Israel are not reviewed in this section; however, they are included in the bibliography.

132. Ronit Matalon was born in Israel to Jewish Egyptian parents in a new immigrant town near Tel Aviv. She has worked as a journalist and now teaches literature at Haifa University. She is also a member of the Council for Culture and Art at the Ministry of Education. Her first novel, *The One Facing Us* (New York, NY: Metropolitan Books/Henry Holt, 1998), translated from Hebrew, was highly praised in Israeli literary circles and has also been translated into Dutch and German.

133. Colette Rossant, born in Paris, landed in Cairo at the age of five with her Egyptian-born father and French mother. After her father's death, she was left in the care of her wealthy grandparents until the age of fifteen, when she was brought back to Paris. Her book *Apricots on the Nile* (New York, NY: Washington Square Press, 1999), described as a memoir with recipes, evokes an Egypt that used to be. Rossant has authored several cookbooks and is a James Beard award-nominated journalist.

134. Claudia Roden, *The Book of Jewish Food* (London: Viking, 1997). Roden has won numerous prizes as a food writer. Her seminal book, *A Book of Middle Eastern Food*, was first published by Thomas Nelson in 1968, then by Penguin books in 1970, with a revised edition in 1985. It is a regular fixture in most Jewish/Egyptian households around the world.

135. Victor Teboul, *La Lente Découverte de l'Etrangeté* (Montréal: Editions Les Intouchables, 2002). Teboul was born in Alexandria. After the 1956 Suez War, his father was jailed and subsequently the whole family was expelled. They arrived in France as refugees and six years later migrated to Canada. Teboul, who holds a PhD in French studies from the University of Montreal and is now professor of French Literature at Lionel-Groulx College, has also written about the representation of the Jew in French Canadian literature: *Mythe et Image du juif au Québec* (Montréal: Delagrave, 1977). The main character of *La Lente Découverte*, Maurice, had been introduced in Teboul's first novel, *Que Dieu vous garde de l'homme silencieux quand il se met soudain à parler* (Montréal: Editions Les Intouchables, 2000), which was about the culture shock experienced by a Sephardi Jew from Egypt when he lands in the province of Quebec, a place with its own identity issues.

136. Meyer Harari, *Second Exodus* (Melbourne: Makor Jewish Community Library, 1999). Harari's family, originally from Damascus, was granted British nationality in Egypt in exchange for services rendered to the Crown. Harari served in the British army during World War II. As a British subject, he was able to migrate to Australia very soon after the end of the war. In his memoir, Harari recounted the story of his life as a young man in Egypt, his early immigration to Australia with his wife, and their difficult beginnings in Melbourne.

137. Freddy E. Dayan, "Growing Up in Egypt in the Thirties" and "From the Banks of the Nile to the Shores of the Derwent, 1940–1988", both translated from the French by Ian Kenneth Smith. These two manuscripts were given to me by the author's son, now living in Melbourne.

138. Andrew Strum, "The Livro de Cantares of Baruch Bentata", in *Los Muestros 29* (December 1997).

139. Strum (ed.), "Wheat, Chickens and the Expiation of Sin, or Vegetarian *Kapparot*: The Ancient Origins of an Obscure Egyptian Jewish High Holy Day Custom", in *Eshkolot: Essays in Memory of Rabbi Ronald Lubofsky* (Melbourne: Hybrid Publishers, 2002).

140. Egyptian-born Robert Solé moved to France at age eighteen. He was editor at *Le Monde* and has published both fiction and non-fiction works. *Le Tarbouche* (Paris: Editions du Seuil, 1992) was his first novel, followed by *Le Sémaphore d'Alexandrie* (Paris: Editions du Seuil, 1994) and *La Mamelouka* (Paris: Editions du Seuil, 1996). His reference books, *L'Égypte, Passion française*, 1997; *Les Savants de Bonaparte*, 1998; and *La Pierre de Rosette*, 1999, were also published by Editions du Seuil.

141. Beth M Robertson, *Oral History Handbook*, fourth edition (Adelaide: Oral History Association of Australia, South Australian Branch, 2000), 2.

142. L. Douglas and P. Spearrit, "Talking History: the Use of Oral Sources", in G. Osborne and W. Mandle (eds), *New History: Studying Australia Today* (Sydney, London, and Boston: George Allen and Unwin, 1982), 51–68.

143. William Foddy, Constructing Questions for Interviews and Questionnaires: Theory and Practice in Social Research (Cambridge: Cambridge University Press, 1993), 11.

144. Paul Thompson, *The Voice of the Past* (Oxford: Oxford University Press, 1990).

145. Lois Foster and Ann Seitz, "Applications of Oral History in the Sociology of Ethnic Relations", *Journal of Intercultural Studies 6*, No. 3 (1985): 5–15.

146. Robertson, Oral History Handbook, 6.

147. Robertson, *Oral History Handbook*, Appendix 1, 78.
148. Foddy, Constructing Questions, 90.
149. Charles P. Thompson, *Autobiographical Memory: Remembering What and When* (Mahwah, NJ: Lawrence Erlbaum and Associates, 1996), 59.
150. Jacques Berque, in *Egypt Imperialism and Revolution*, trans. Jean Stewart (London: Faber & Faber, 1972), 670–671, wrote: "On the morning of 26th January…an immense mob poured into the wealthy districts, setting fire, as though by a prearranged plan, to any establishments displaying a certain degree of luxury or suggesting collusion with the foreigner".
151. Samir W. Raafat, in *Maadi 1904–1962* (Cairo: The Palm Press, 1994), 212–214, also noted what the press had to say about the events of that fateful Saturday: "the following day, the media announced that crowds on the rampage in Cairo had set fire to cafés, cinemas, shops, the Shepheards Hotel, and British-owned businesses. Ten Britishers lost their lives in the Turf Club fire on Maghrabi Street (now Adly Street)".
152. Seymour Sudman and Norman M. Bradburn, *Asking Questions* (San Francisco: Jossey-Bass Inc., 1982), 22.
153. Ibid., 36–39: "In its most general sense, an aided-recall procedure is one that provides one or more memory cues to the respondent as part of the question".
154. Foster and Seitz, "Applications of Oral History in the Sociology of Ethnic Relations", 7.
155. A language that is adopted as a medium of communication between speakers whose native languages are different.
156. To understand this phenomenon, one has to go back to the French expedition to Egypt in 1798 led by Napoleon, the building of the Suez Canal in 1869 by the French, the British occupation of Egypt in 1882, and the privileged status held by foreigners until the late 1940s. All these events impacted greatly on the education of minorities. The combined role of the Christian missionaries, the AIU, and other secular and ethnic schools catering to the different communities contributed to the rise of a cosmopolitan society—especially within the middle and upper classes—that spoke predominantly French.
157. The number of Jews from Egypt who eventually settled in France is estimated to be between 10,000 and 12,000.
158. Sudman and Bradburn, *Asking Questions*, 136.
159. This was the case of my interview with possibly the first Egyptian Jew who migrated to Australia and settled in Adelaide. He was responsible for the settlement of the largest group of Jews from Egypt in Adelaide.

160. See Appendix 2.
161. Suzanne Rutland, "Egyptian Jews in Adelaide: A Case Study in Oral History", *Oral History Association of Australia Journal 6* (1984). Rutland's research indicated that in the days of the White Australia Policy there was great reluctance to grant landing permits to Jews from Egypt because "at an official government level it was widely believed that Sephardi (Oriental) Jews were 'black' in appearance".
162. For example, the *Nahar Misraïm 32–33* (May 1989) included a short story from an out-of-print book written by an Egyptian Jew, Robert Blum, *Histoires d'enfants pour grandes personnes* (Cairo: Théolevi G. & Co, 1942); a chapter out of Egyptian-born Elian Finbert's book, *Les plus Belles histoires d'oiseaux* (Paris: Fayard, 1957); a report on the recent opening of a new Jewish library by the Jewish community of Cairo in January 1989; a recounting of the mysterious assassination of a prominent Jew in Cairo in 1926; the 1918 statutes of a Jewish philanthropic institution for the sick in Alexandria; poems by renowned Egyptian-born Israeli writer Ada Aharoni; and finally, a critical review of the latest book on the history of the Jews of Egypt in the Ottoman period, by Jacob Landau (ed.), published in Israel by Misgav Yerushalaim, in 1988. Next to these intellectual and scholarly contributions, other more mundane items, such as traditional cooking recipes from Egypt, were also included as they were deemed to be just as essential to the transmission of the cultural heritage of the Jews of Egypt.
163. To name just a few of those Egyptian-born French Jews who published their memoirs: Frédéric Galimidi in *Alexandrie sur Seine* (Collection l'Echelle de Jacob IV, Tarascon: Cousins de Salonique Editeurs, 1999), related the story of his exile from Egypt and the long process of integration in French society. Albert Pardo wrote his first book, *L'Égypte que j'ai connue* (Paris: Nahar Misraïm, 1999), in which he remembered with nostalgia the Egypt of pre-1956. He intermingled his own story with little vignettes about Egyptian lifestyle, such as the unusual occupations, the customs, and the superstitions. I also found more testimonies in the newly revived *Bulletin de liaison* of the ASPCJE, in the section "les textes de la mémoire", where personal memories of Egypt and the early days in France are evoked.
164. Shamir, "Notes on Researching", 3–7.
165. Afaf Lutfi Al-Sayid Marsot, *Egypt in the Reign of Muhammad Ali* (Cambridge: Cambridge University Press, 1984), 15.
166. Landau, *Jews in Nineteenth-Century Egypt*, 3.

167. Marsot, *Egypt in the Reign*, 18.

168. Ibid., 19.

169. Robert Solé, *L'Égypte, passion française* (Paris: Editions du Seuil, 1997), 28–30.

170. Mort Rosenblum, in *Mission to Civilize: The French Way*, pointed out the historical meaning of *civiliser*, according to *Oxford Historical Dictionary*: "to bring out of a state of barbarism, to instruct in the arts of life and thus elevate in the scale of humanity".

171. Ibid., 32.

172. Marsot, *Egypt in the Reign*, 20.

173. Robert Solé and Dominique Valbelle, *La Pierre de Rosette* (Paris: Editions du Seuil, 1999).

174. The Arabic printing press was part of the treasures Napoleon had plundered from the Vatican during his Italian Campaign. The first printed version of the Quran was produced thanks to this press.

175. Timothy Mitchell, *Colonising Egypt* (Cambridge: Cambridge University Press, 1988), 133.

176. In *L'Égypte, passion française*, 39–43, Solé pointed out that some of the problems raised during the working sessions of the institute concerned improvement of the judiciary and the education system, the purification of the Nile water and, most importantly, the project of joining the Mediterranean to the Red Sea by the digging of a canal.

177. Marsot, *Egypt in the Reign*, 20–21.

178. Henry Dodwell, *The Founder of Modern Egypt* (Cambridge: Cambridge University Press, 1931, and New York: AMS Press, 1977), 9–21. Muhammad Ali, born in Kavala in 1769, was sent to Egypt in 1801 as head of the strong Albanian contingent of the Turkish forces assembled to expel the French with the help of the British. After the surrender of the French and the subsequent withdrawal of the British, Muhammad Ali manoeuvred himself into power and was granted official recognition by the Sultan. By 1811 he dealt the Mamluk beys a final blow when he lured them into the Cairo Citadel and had them all massacred.

179. Landau, *Jews in Nineteenth-Century Egypt*, 135. In the archives of the Alexandria Jewish community, Landau found the original order issued by Bonaparte, dated September 7, 1798, nominating the various members of the *Consistoire*.

180. Ibid., 161–165. See copy of the French translation from the original Arabic document (probably lost), in *Revue Israélite d'Égypte 21* (1916): 193–196.

181. Emile Gabbay wrote in *Juifs d'Égypte*, 138: "Certains écrits rapportent que Napoléon fit bombarder ce temple sous prétexte qu'il constituait un obstacle au tir de ses canons entre le fort de Kom-El-Dick et la mer, mais ce bombardement ferait, en réalité, suite au non-paiement d'une somme de 50 000 talaris imposée à la Communauté qui n'était pas en mesure de la payer". The policy adopted by the French during their short stay in Egypt was to levy taxes on a community basis, and the Jewish community's share had apparently been set at thirty thousand francs, a sizeable amount for those days.

182. Marsot, *Egypt in the Reign*, 75.

183. Ibid., 76.

184. Faivre d'Arcier Amaury, *Les Agents de Napoléon en Egypt (1801–1815)* (Levallois, France: Centres d'Etudes Napoléoniennes, 1990), 169: "Sur le plan politique, les agents de Napoléon ont eu le mérite de reconnaître en Mehemet Ali—ce chef albanais sorti du rang et sans instruction—le seul homme capable de gouverner l'Égypte. Drovetti et Menguin entretiennent avec lui des rapports privilégiés, et celui-ci les reçoit toujours avec bonté".

185. Marsot, *Egypt in the Reign*, 77.

186. Jean-Jacques Luthi, *Introduction à la littérature d'expression française en Égypte* (Paris: Editions de l'Ecole, 1974), 40. Under British rule from 1882, English had displaced French in the public education system.

187. Dodwell, *Founder*, 222–226.

188. Mitchell, *Colonising Egypt*, 71–72.

189. Dodwell, *Founder*, 238–239.

190. Landau, *Jews in Nineteenth-Century Egypt*, 3.

191. Ibid., 150. Landau also pointed out that "Lane, the orientalist who knew Egypt so well, has left us with what seems to be the first detailed account of 19th-century Egyptian Jewry".

192. Ibid., 148 and 150. Landau reported: "the colours of their turbans are the same as those of the Christian subjects. Their women veil themselves, and dress in every respect, in public, like the other women of Egypt...They are generally strict in the performance of their religious ordinances".

193. Ibid.,158.

194. Karaite Jews reject the authority of the Oral Law and accept as their guide the Hebrew Bible and human reason. The written scriptures include the *Torah* (law), the *Nevi'im* (Prophets), and the *Ketuvim* (hagiography or writings). The Oral Law includes the Mishnah, compiled by Judah ha-Nasi at the end of the second century, and the Gemara, which is a commentary

on the Mishnah with both Palestinian and Babylonian versions. Together, the Mishnah and Gemara make up the Talmud (fifth century).

195. Traditionally, the Karaites—meaning readers of the scriptures—were believed to belong to a Jewish sect founded by Anan Ben David in eighth-century Baghdad. According to Nathan Schur, *History of the Karaites* (Frankfurt, Berlin, and New York, NY: Peter Lang Publishing, 1992), 22, "modern research does not accept the traditional Karaite version, which regards Anan unreservedly as the founder of the Karaite sect. Most scholars stipulate now the existence of two separate groups, the Ananites, followers of Anan and sometimes actually members of his family, and the Karaites, who were the outcome of the coalescence of various sectarian groups".

196. Mourad El-Kodsi, *The Karaite Jews of Egypt, 1882–1986* (Lyons, NY: Wilprint, 1987), 2. El-Kodsi was born in Cairo. A history graduate of the University of Cairo, with a Master's degree from the University of Rochester, New York, he immigrated to the United States in 1959. After retiring from the teaching profession, he continued to research the history of the Karaite community.

197. Information provided by Norman A. Stillman.

198. Landau, *Jews in Nineteenth-Century Egypt*, 4.

199. Beinin, *The Dispersion of Egyptian Jewry*, 39–44: "the Karaites had lived in Egypt for 1000 years, mainly in Cairo's *harat el-yahud al-qara'in*. They were integrated into Cairo's ethnic division of labor, typically working as goldsmiths and jewelers…In the twentieth century, wealthier Karaites began to move to the middle-class districts of Abassiya and Heliopolis and to adopt elements of bourgeois, francophone, cosmopolitan culture".

200. Krämer, *The Jews in Modern Egypt*, 23.

201. Laskier, *The Jews of Egypt*, 6–7.

202. Ibid., 7. Laskier noted two further reasons for this rapprochement: the secularisation of Egyptian Jewry, which attenuated the importance of religious differences; and the rise of Arab nationalism, which caused the two communities to "strive for greater internal unity".

203. Krämer, *The Jews in Modern Egypt*, 16.

204. Ibid., 18.

205. Marsot, *Egypt in the Reign*, 256.

206. Krämer, *The Jews in Modern Egypt*, 8. Krämer indicated that this "wave of massive immigration which began in the mid-nineteenth century, continued well into the 1920s, bringing the number of foreigners living in

Egypt up from about 15,000 in the 1850s to 100,000 in the 1880s and over 200,000 in the years after World War I".

207. From the Latin word *capitula*, meaning chapter, the Capitulations were initially an ancient treaty of commerce and protection, composed of a number of chapters, negotiated between King François I of France and the Sultan Suleiman I of Turkey in 1536, giving France extraterritorial jurisdiction over French expatriates in the Levant and later extended to cover all Europeans.

208. Krämer, *The Jews in Modern Egypt*, 29–30.

209. Ibid., 30. Krämer specified that, beginning in 1875, the "Mixed Courts unified the legal codes and procedures by creating special codes based on the French Code Napoleon, and they were soon able to monopolize all court action involving, however remotely, the interests of foreigners and their companies". This unique institution was in charge of civil and commercial cases between Egyptians and foreigners and between foreigners of different nationalities. Three district courts were established in Cairo, Alexandria, and El Mansurah, each headed by one Egyptian and two foreign judges, with a court of appeals composed of six Egyptian and ten foreign judges in Alexandria. Modifications introduced in 1889 and 1911 gave the court of appeals the right to approve legislation intended to be applied to foreigners.

210. Landau, *Jews in Nineteenth-Century Egypt*, 21. Landau pointed out that "the authorities were forbidden to harm them, conscript them, or confiscate their property without the prior permission of their country's local representative. In some cases the foreign state granted them legal aid".

211. Ibid., 21. Landau wrote: "local authorities generally feared to harm foreign nationals or protected persons in any way, knowing that their state's local representative would protest vehemently and might even demand damages for the persons they affected and punishment for those responsible".

212. Ibid., 25.

213. Krämer, *The Jews in Modern Egypt*, 18.

214. The Empress Eugénie of France was the guest of honour at the palace. The Emperor Franz Joseph of Austria-Hungary was also on the guest list.

215. Mary Jane Phillip-Matz, *Verdi: A Biography* (Oxford and New York: Oxford University Press, 1993), 569–589. Originally, the Khedive Ismail had asked Verdi to compose an inaugural hymn for the opening night of the new Opera Theatre, but Verdi refused and Egypt had to settle for a performance of Rigoletto. However, Verdi relented when he saw the libretto

by Camille du Locle (1832–1903), based on a story set in ancient Egypt written by the Egyptologist Auguste Mariette (1821–1881). The work was supposed to be ready in January 1871 but was delayed by the advent of the Franco-Prussian war. All the costumes, designs, and scenery for Aida were being made in France and could not be taken out of the city until the end of hostilities. The first performance took place in December 1871, nearly two years after the opening of the Suez Canal and the Cairo Opera House. The Khedivial Opera House burned down in October 1971.

216. See Solé, *L'Égypte, passion française*, 153–159. Ismail, grandson of Muhammad Ali, was granted the title of Khedive in 1867 by the Sultan of Constantinople. He was a graduate of Saint Cyr, the most prestigious military school in France. He was reputed to have uttered the famous words: "Mon pays n'est plus en Afrique. Nous faisons partie de l'Europe".

217. André Maurois, *Disraeli* (New York, NY: D. Appleton & Co., 1928), 310–311. Maurois pointed out that it was the world's most prominent banker at the time, Baron Lionel de Rothschild, who granted Disraeli a personal loan of four million British pounds to buy the Suez Canal shares for Great Britain. Once Disraeli secured the deal with the Khedive, he proceeded to convince the British government to reimburse Rothschild.

218. Jacques Berque, *Egypt, Imperialism and Revolution,* 112–124.

219. Contemporary reports on the events of 1882 were typical examples of imperialistic discourse. Evelyn Baring Cromer, first British Viceroy of Egypt, wrote in *Modern Egypt by the Earl of Cromer* (London: Macmillan, 1908) that in view of the political situation, a foreign occupation of Egypt was "necessary in order to prevent anarchy in Egypt", 383. See also Appendix Despatch from Sir Evelyn Baring to Lord Granville, 362–365.

220. Laskier, *The Jews of Egypt*, 1.

221. Cotton is measured in staple length, which is the minimum length of one cotton fibre used in a yarn. A long-staple yarn is needed to spin finer yarns, and the longer the staple the better the yarn. The long staple measures 30 to 37 mm. The Egyptian variety of long-staple cotton bears the name of the man who developed it, the Greek agronomist Sakellarides.

222. For the history of the development of the cotton industry in Egypt from 1820 to 1914, see E. R. J. Owen, "Lord Cromer and the Development of Egyptian Industry, 1883–1927", *Middle Eastern Studies 2* (1966), 282–301, and Alan Richards, *Egypt's Agricultural Development, 1800–1980: Technical and Social Change* (Boulder, CO: Westview Press, 1982), 19–53 and 111–141.

223. Krämer, *The Jews in Modern Egypt*, 37.

224. "No other place in the world in the nineteenth century was transformed on a greater scale to serve the production of a single industry", wrote Timothy Mitchell in *Colonising Egypt*, 16.
225. Maurice Mizrahi, *L'Égypte et ses Juifs: Le Temps révolu, XIXe et XXe siècle* (Genève: Presses de l'Imprimerie Avenir S.A., 1977), 74.
226. H. H. Ben Sasson, ed., *A History of the Jewish People* (Cambridge, MA: Harvard University Press, 1976), 813–869. Ben Sasson pointed to the fact that, from about 1825, in countries such as Tsarist Russia, Rumania, and Poland, anti-Jewish measures were intensified. Jews were subjected to forced conversions, expulsions, pogroms, and residence restrictions. Consequently, they fled in the thousands to America, Western Europe, and the region of Palestine. As for Morocco, Stillman wrote in *The Jews of Arab Lands*, 99–107, that "Moroccan Jewry...lived under one of the most oppressive dhimma systems of the later Islamic Middle Ages", a system which "remained in force for most of the nineteenth century", under which Jews suffered persecution and widespread abuse. In 1863, the British philanthropist and Jewish leader Sir Moses Montefiore paid a visit to the Sultan of Morocco and, with the support of the British government, tried in vain to obtain from him some measure of protection for his Jewish constituency. The emancipation of Moroccan Jewry did not happen for another fifty years.
227. Shamir, *The Jews of Egypt*, xiii.
228. Laskier, *The Jews of Egypt*, 7.
229. Hassoun, *Histoire des Juifs du Nil*, 1990, 3. Hassoun argued that the number of seventy thousand cited by the 1947 British census is not uniform in all monographs, and that a figure of around eighty thousand would be more accurate.
230. Laskier, *The Jews of Egypt*, 7.
231. Krämer, *The Jews in Modern Egypt*, 27: "in the late nineteenth century this was mainly Italian, which until 1876 served as the language of administration and until 1905 as the chief language of instruction in the community schools of Alexandria. By that time, French had become the lingua franca of the local foreign minorities and the Turko-Egyptian elite alike".
232. D. Robino, "1870. Blood Libel in Alexandria", in Landau, *Jews in Nineteenth-Century Egypt*, 182, Document XXXI. This document is a report, written in Italian, by the secretary of the Alexandria committee of the AIU, dated May 29, 1870, regarding the accusation by a Maltese against a sixty-year-old Jew of having kidnapped his four-year-old daughter to use her blood for the making of unleavened bread. See also Document

XXXVIII, "1873–1878: Persecution of the Jews in Damanhur", 199–200. It is a letter, written in French, addressed to the AIU, dated September 15, 1879, relating to a charge brought against Rabbi Moise Salomon—the local *shohet*, or slaughterer—for emasculating a little boy. See also Landau, "Ritual Murder Accusations in Nineteenth-Century Egypt", in *Middle Eastern Themes*, (London: Frank Cass, 1973): 99–141.

233. Landau, in *Jews in Nineteenth-Century Egypt*, 26, reported that in 1855 the Jewish community of Alexandria had asked for and was granted the protection of the Austro-Hungarian consulate.

234. Krämer, *The Jews in Modern Egypt*, 31.

235. Abitbol, *Le Passé*, 161–166. The man responsible for the French naturalisation of Algerian Jews was Adolphe Crémieux (1796–1880), a prominent member of the French Consistoire, a deputy under Napoleon III, and Minister for Justice under the government of Gambetta. The Crémieux Decree read as follows: "Les israélites indigènes des départements d'Algérie sont déclarés citoyens français; en conséquence, leur statut réel et leur statut personnel seront, à compter de la promulgation du présent décret, réglés par la loi française; tous droits acquis jusqu'à ce jour restent inviolables. Toutes disposition législative, décret, règlement ou ordonnance contraires sont abolis". While this decree granted French citizenship to the indigenous Jewish population of Algeria of about thirty-seven thousand, it did not grant it to the Muslim population. This seemingly preferential treatment was apparently due to the fact that the Jews had agreed to be ruled by French law, relinquishing their communal religious status. According to the French sociologist, historian, and political commentator Raymond Aron (1905–1983), the legislation known as *Senatus-consulte*, dated July 14, 1865, granted the status of French "subjects" to the indigenous Muslims, with the option of becoming French citizens, if they accepted to be ruled by French civil and political laws instead of Koranic laws, but the majority rejected that offer.

236. Krämer, *The Jews in Modern Egypt*, 32.

237. Cattaoui is also spelt Kattawi or Qattàwì.

238. Landau, *Jews in NineteenthiCentury Egypt*, 21.

239. Mizrahi discussed the credentials of these families in *L'Égypte et ses Juifs*, 62–71. See also Krämer, *The Jews in Modern Egypt*, 38–46.

240. Regarding the nationality issue, see Shamir, "The Evolution of the Egyptian Nationality Laws", 33–67.

241. One of the most prestigious and oldest schools established by the Brothers of the Christian Schools in 1928, the Collège Saint-Marc in Alexandria, is still functioning today.

242. Landau, *Jews in Nineteenth-Century Egypt*, 73.
243. Aron Rodrigue, *French Jews, Turkish Jews*, (Bloomington and Indianapolis: Indiana University Press, 1984), 1. Rodrigue recounted: "The facts of the blood libel are well known. A Capucin friar, Père Thomas, disappeared in early 1840 in Damascus. Sections of the Christian Arab population of the town accused the Jews of having murdered him to use his blood for ritual purposes...The French consul of Damascus, Ratti Menton, took the accusations seriously. The governor of the town...immediately arrested the accused Jews, some of whom happened to be the leaders of the community, and tortured them to extract a confession to the alleged crime. The terrorised Damascus Jews asked for help from the Jewish community of Istanbul, which immediately appealed for the intervention of the Jewish communities of Europe". For the impact of the affair on European Jewry, see Jonathan Frankel, *The Damascus Affair: "Ritual Murder", Politics and the Jews in 1840* (Cambridge: Cambridge University Press, 1997), and Jacques Hassoun, "Accusation de meurtres rituels en Égypte entre 1870 et 1910—Symptômes", in *Nahar Misraïm*, Bulletin 4–5 (Novembre 1981): 7–27.
244. Landau, *Jews in Nineteenth-Century Egypt*, 73–74.
245. Ibid., 76. Landau summarised as follows: "Hebrew was the holy tongue, Arabic, the locally spoken language, French the vehicle of commerce and culture, and Italian the language spoken by many Europeans in Egypt".
246. Ibid., 74–85. Landau wrote: "In 1862, the first [Jewish] girls' school was established. Despite its small size (it had room for only seventy pupils) it symbolized the beginning of a new educational policy of schooling of girls, which was never reversed in Egypt".
247. Stillman, *Modern Times*, 28.
248. Landau, *Jews in Nineteenth-Century Egypt*, 85–91.
249. Stillman, *Modern Times*, 21, 245–249. According to documents from the AIU's archives, most of these boys "were brought back into the fold" through "legal, political and family pressures". This extraordinary event became an international *cause célèbre*.
250. Landau, *Jews in Nineteenth-Century Egypt*, 182–183, 198–200, 215–217.
251. Laskier, *The Jews of Egypt*, 10.
252. Ibid., 159–160. See copy of the journal of a deputation sent to Egypt by the committee of the Malta Protestant College, discussing a visit to Jewish families, with the view of enrolling their children in their school and converting them.

253. The Lycée de la Mission Laique française was first established in Alexandria in 1909 and in Cairo a year later. The Lycée prepared its students for the Baccalauréat 1ère et 2ème partie, which enabled them to be admitted into French universities.

254. Maître Félix Benzakein, "Souvenirs", in *L'Égypte et ses Juifs, le Temps révolu*, edited by Maurice Mizrahi, 239–248.

255. Victoria College, founded in 1902, was modelled on the prestigious English Public Schools to cater to the Egyptian and British elite. The school founders included three leading members of the Jewish community: Joseph Aghion, Clément Bohor, and Baron de Menasche. See Samir Raafat, "Victoria College 1902–1956: Educating the Elite", *Egyptian Mail*, March 30, 1996, and Sahar Hamouda and Colin Clement, eds., *Victoria College: A History Revealed* (Cairo and New York: American University Press, 2002).

256. Jean-Jacques Luthi, *L'Égypte des Rois 1922–1953* (Paris: Harmattan, 1997), 139.

257. Gilles Perrault, *Un Homme à part* (Paris: Bernard Barrault, 1984). This book is a biography of Henri Curiel written after his assassination in May 1978. Curiel was one of the early promoters of the Egyptian Communist Party.

258. Krämer, *The Jews in Modern Egypt*, 118.

259. Ibid., 120. See also Jacques Berque, *Egypt, Imperialism and Revolution*; and Fayza Hassan, "Right above Might", *El Ahram Weekly On-line*, April 1–7, 1999.

260. Krämer, *The Jews in Modern Egypt*, 121. The Anglo-Egyptian Treaty of Alliance, signed in 1936, abolished those four reservations of British control. The 1937 Convention of Montreux signified the end of the Capitulations and the Mixed Courts system, which took effect in 1949.

261. Ibid., 119, 122. Krämer noted that this issue was "to dominate national politics until the new age after the revolution of the Free Officers".

262. Hassoun, in "Histoire des Juifs du Nil", 74, elaborated on the status of Egyptian Jews under British rule: "l'essor économique sous la domination britannique améliora, de façon sensible, la position économique et sociale des Juifs d'Égypte…En raison des besoins croissants de personnel administratif, les Juifs fournirent un grand nombre d'employés dans les affaires de gestion et d'administration, et furent amplement représentés dans les professions libérales, telles que le journalisme, le barreau et la médecine." See also Fargeon, *Médecins et Avocats'*.

263. Shamir, "Notes on Researching", 4–5.

264. Laskier, *The Jews of Egypt*, 10. Laskier stressed that alongside the Chief Rabbinate, a strong communal leadership was emerging "from the developing modernised middle class after World War I, among the activists of the pro-Zionist B'nai B'rith lodges in Cairo and Alexandria, and among the editors of the Jewish (and pro-Zionist) press…"

265. See in *Nahar Misraïm*, Bulletin 32–33, May 1989, 83, a document on the statutes of a Jewish soup kitchen established in 1916, "Oeuvre Israëlite du Bouillon des Malades—Statuts", (Alexandrie: Société de Publication Égyptienne, 1918). See also in Landau, *Jews in Nineteenth Century Egypt*, 62–70, 235–238, details about the various community institutions and an 1891 report on "Jewish Assistance in Alexandria to Russian Refugees".

266. Krämer, "Political Participation of the Jews in Egypt between World War I and the 1952 Revolution", in Shamir, *The Jews of Egypt*, 68–69.

267. As reported by Krämer in *The Jews in Modern Egypt*, 124, "one of the first advocates of the new idea of territorial nationalism was a local Jew, James (Ya'cub) Sanùa (1839–1912), also known by his Arabic pen name, Abù Naddàra".

268. Ibid., 126.

269. Ibid., 127.

270. Laskier, *The Jews of Egypt*, 46.

271. G. Thompson-Seton, *A Woman Tenderfoot in Egypt* (London: John Lane, 1923), 64–67.

272. Krämer, *The Jews in Modern Egypt*, 33–34.

273. Ibid., 33: "All evidence suggests that the majority of those who lost, or gave up their foreign nationality as well as of the indigenous Egyptian and the Oriental Jews (mostly former Ottoman subjects) in fact did not obtain Egyptian passports".

274. Laskier, *The Jews of Egypt*, 9.

275. Beinin, *The Dispersion of Egyptian Jewry*, 36–39.

276. According to Beinin, the situation had been allowed to continue until that time because no Egyptian leader before Gamal Abdel Nasser had had the political courage to challenge the authority of the powerful Muslim courts.

277. Gudrun Krämer et Alfred Morabia, "Face à la modernité: les Juifs d'Égypte aux XIXè et XXè siècles", in Hassoun, *Histoire des Juifs du Nil*, 77–78. Krämer and Morabia argued that those accusations frequently emanated from Christian communities, mainly the Greek one, not only out of religious animosity, but also for economic reasons, as Jews were perceived as competitors in the marketplace.

278. Krämer, *The Jews in Modern Egypt*, 124.
279. Ibid., 126. See also Beinin, *The Dispersion of Egyptian Jewry*, 18.
280. Beinin, *The Dispersion of Egyptian Jewry*, 63.
281. Ibid., 34–35. Beinin specified that Leon Castro "conducted propaganda for the Wafd party in Europe after the 1919 nationalist uprising and founded and edited a pro-Wafd French language newspaper, *La Liberté*, after returning to Egypt. At the same time, he was the head of the Zionist Organization of Cairo. In the 1940s, he served as the representative of the Jewish Agency for Palestine in Egypt". As for Félix Benzakein, he "was a member of the Wafd, a deputy in parliament, a member of the Alexandria rabbinical court, and the president of the Zionist Organization of Alexandria".
282. Krämer, *The Jews in Modern Egypt*, 141–142.
283. Laskier, *The Jews of Egypt*, 68. The Young Egypt movement was founded in 1933 by Ahmad Husayn, propagating "a new and militant brand of Egyptian nationalism".
284. Hebrew name of the Jewish community in Palestine.
285. The Arab rebellion of 1936–1939 against the British mandate in Palestine or the first *intifada*, as some would call it, was organised by the Haj Mohammed Amin al-Husseini, Mufti of Jerusalem, and his Arab Higher Committee. The Arab High Command started by calling a general strike of Arab workers and the boycott of Jewish goods. These actions quickly escalated into terrorist attacks against the Jews and the British. The second stage of the revolt began in September 1937 after the Peel Commission recommended the partition of Palestine. The clashes with British forces intensified, as did the attacks on Jewish settlements.
286. Krämer, *The Jews in Modern Egypt*, 146.
287. Ibid., 147.
288. Ibid., 149.
289. Ibid., 149.
290. Mizrahi, *L'Égypte et ses Juifs*, 105–119.
291. Laskier, "Egyptian Jewry under the Nasser Regime" in *Middle Eastern Studies 31*, no. 3 (July 1995): 573.
292. Beinin, *The Dispersion of Egyptian Jewry*, 32.
293. Laskier, *The Jews of Egypt*, 10.
294. Ibid., 304.
295. Ibid., 110–111.
296. Krämer, *The Jews in Modern Egypt*, 153. Krämer reported that already in the "1920s and 1930s, Colonel Kisch from the Zionist Executive in

Jerusalem had several meetings with Egyptian politicians, which were arranged by his Jewish friends in Egypt...In February 1938, Chaim Weizmann came to Egypt to meet Prince Muhammad Ali, a prominent member of the royal family, and the British ambassador, Sir Miles Lampson... and in April 1939, Chaim Weizmann met the Egyptian prime minister, the foreign minister, and Ali Mahir".

297. Ibid., 154.

298. Ibid., 157.

299. Klaus-Michael Mallmann and Martin Cüppers, "Elimination of the Jewish National Home in Palestine: The Einsatzkommando of the Panzer Army Africa, 1941", *Yad Vashem Studies 35*, Part 1 (2007) 111–142. According to this article, a special SS taskforce was attached to Rommel's army (Africa Korps) and assigned the task of eliminating the Jewish National Home in Palestine. There is also a mention of the deployment of a similar force "Einsatz Ägypten" (Operation Egypt) to deal with the Jews of Egypt.

300. Laskier, *The Jews of Egypt*, 79–83.

301. Beinin, *The Dispersion of Egyptian Jewry*, 64–65. Following those riots, the government promised to indemnify the victims and placed guards at the entrance of the Jewish quarter.

302. Judith Cochran worked at the Ain Shams University in Cairo as a Fulbright senior lecturer in education in 1980. Subsequently, she accepted the directorship of the DPS English language program at the American University in Cairo. Her book, *Education in Egypt* (London: Croom Helm, 1986), outlined the popularity of foreign schools from 1840 onwards, and the attraction they exerted not only for foreigners but also for the Egyptian secular elite.

303. Luthi, *L'Égypte des Rois*, 139.

304. Cochran, in *Education in Egypt*, 45, pointed out that the only schools that were not sequestered and then nationalised were the American schools and those under Vatican administration.

305. Krämer, *The Jews in Modern Egypt*, 206.

306. Ibid., 207. Krämer reported that in November 1947 the Cairo community registered one thousand applications per week.

307. Ibid., 207.

308. A reunion of all the old members of the pioneer youth groups in Egypt was organised in Israel, on the occasion of Israel's Fiftieth Jubilee in 1998. This event coincided with the date of their arrest in 1948, and on

that occasion a booklet was issued providing personal accounts of their individual experiences.

309. Apart from the armistice with Egypt, Israel signed separate armistice agreements with Lebanon on March 23, 1949, Transjordan on April 3, and Syria on July 20 of the same year.

310. Their journey to Israel was arranged via France or Italy because there was no direct connection with Israel from Egypt. Krämer, in *The Jews in Modern Egypt*, 219, pointed out that it was impossible for the Egyptian government not to notice the number of local Jews who could all of a sudden afford the cost of travelling to Europe and "yet it did nothing to prevent their departure". Krämer suggested a number of reasons for this inaction: the fear of appearing intolerant to foreign observers, the realisation that the local Jews could not be integrated into an Arab-Islamic society, and finally the pragmatic decision that "the departure of thousands of clerks, salesmen and managers would make room for that many 'real' Egyptians".

311. Beinin, in *The Dispersion of Egyptian Jewry*, 68, reported: "on June 20, 1948, a bomb exploded in the Karaite quarter of Cairo, killing twenty-two Jews and wounding forty-one. Several buildings were severely damaged…Jewish witnesses on the scene testified that the response of the authorities was sluggish and negligent". Beinin also mentioned the bombing of Jewish department stores, namely Cicurel and Oreco, in July 1948, as well as an explosion in the Rabbanite quarter of Cairo, killing another nineteen Jews and wounding sixty-two.

312. Ibid., 69. According to Beinin, the Muslim Brothers were considered so strong that they were suspected of preparing an armed insurrection, and many were interned in May 1948. In December of the same year, the prime minister al-Nuqrashi dissolved the society and seized their considerable assets. In retaliation, he was assassinated on December 28, 1948.

313. Ibid., 71.

314. Laskier, *The Jews of Egypt*, 143–144.

315. Shamir, "The Evolution of the Egyptian Nationality Laws", 54–55.

316. Ibid., 58.

317. Ibid., 59.

318. Krämer, *The Jews in Modern Egypt*, 216.

319. Beinin, *The Dispersion of Egyptian Jewry*, 85.

320. Laskier, in *The Jews of Egypt*, 205–251, outlined the whole incident, including the subsequent trial and convictions, where two of the accused were hanged and the rest imprisoned for up to fourteen years. They were

released only after the 1967 War, in exchange for five thousand Egyptian prisoners. The book *Operation Susannah* related how they were recruited in the pioneer youth groups and the details of their arrest and life in prison. The "Lavon Affair", as it came to be known, caused a serious political crisis in Israel because it was later claimed that this misguided and ill-planned operation was organised by military intelligence without the knowledge or approval of the Israeli government.

321. Beinin, *The Dispersion of Egyptian Jewry*, 86.
322. Laskier, in *The Jews of Egypt*, 253–267, outlined very precisely the application of those decrees, which provides concrete evidence of the specifically anti-Jewish intent of the legislation. This bias was not surprising in view of the fact that the Nasser regime was always committed "to deprive the foreign, ethnic, and religious minorities, of the economic and social influence they had exercised for so long" in order to achieve national homogeneity. In a way, the Suez War only precipitated the changeover.
323. Beinin, *The Dispersion of Egyptian Jewry*, 87.
324. See Mizrahi, *L'Égypte et ses Juifs*, 126–136, where Mizrahi compared the prison conditions and the treatment of the prisoners after each war, 1948, 1956, and 1967. He wrote: "Les internements de 1948 et de 1956 n'étaient qu'une manifestation 'courtoise', si l'on peut dire, de l'antisémitisme… En 1967, les souffrances des internés furent de loin les plus dures et les plus longues. Les détenus durent subir de nombreuses brutalités de la part de leurs géôliers". One of my own respondents (#13F), arrested after the 1967 war, reported that he was held at the infamous Abu Zaabal prison for only six months, thanks to his Italian passport, whereas his companions who were either Egyptian or stateless were kept in prison for over three years.
325. Laskier, *The Jews of Egypt*, 256–257.
326. Ibid., 257.
327. Ibid., 268. Laskier pointed out that, at least until 1959, the UNHCR recognised the status of most of the escapees from Egypt as refugees, therefore eligible for UN protection.
328. In 1958 and 1959, the French and the British governments negotiated agreements with the Egyptian government, providing compensation to their nationals for loss of property and/or businesses, whereas the stateless and Egyptian Jews, who had been expelled or pressured to leave, had no chance of redress and lost everything.
329. Beinin, in *The Dispersion of Egyptian Jewry*, 88, noted that the chief Rabbi of Alexandria, Aharon Angel, and the president of the Cairo Jewish

community, Salvator Cicurel, left the country in the post-1956 wave of departures. The Karaite rabbi had died a few months before the Suez War and Chief Rabbi Nahum was ill and died in1960.

330. Laskier, *The Jews of Egypt*, 290. In *The Dispersion of Egyptian Jewry*, 87, Beinin quoted a figure of seven thousand, taken from World Jewish Conference (WJC) records.

331. Laskier, *The Jews of Egypt*, 266–267.

332. See Tad Szulc, "Business with Nasser and Sadam", in *The Secret Alliance: The Extraordinary Story of the Rescue of the Jews since World War II* (New York: Farrar, Straus and Giroux, 1991), chapter XXXII, 280–283.

333. Laskier, *The Jews of Egypt*, 293.

334. During my visit to Egypt in 1999, I was given a figure of about two hundred people in Cairo—most of them in nursing homes—and about twenty in Alexandria. On my second visit, eight years later, I was informed that these numbers had shrunk dramatically, which is not surprising.

335. Interviewee #14 was born in Smyrna (modern day Izmir). He came to Egypt with his mother and siblings in 1921, at the age of six.

336. Tantah is an important railroad junction, situated on a major highway connecting Cairo and Alexandria. Mansurah is also situated in the Delta region, east of Alexandria. Based on Fargeon's research, in *Les Juifs en Égypte*, 287–291, at the beginning of the twentieth century it was a relatively important Jewish community of about one hundred and fifty families, which dwindled to about fifty in the late 1930s. A caption describing Mansurah's lively markets, *Al-Khawagat,* in a modern Egyptian travel guide specified that they were "in earlier times run by Greeks, Jews and Lebanese". The term *Al-Khawagat* or "foreigners" used to be derogatory, but now seems to have evolved to suggesting a kind of nostalgia for the past.

337. One interviewee (#5) was born in Assiut, a village halfway between Cairo and Aswan, where his father had established his business.

338. Fargeon, *Les Juifs en Égypte'*, 189–190; Mizrahi, *L'Égypte et ses Juifs*, 31–32; and Laskier, *The Jews of Egypt*, 4–8.

339. Krämer, *The Jews in Modern Egypt*, 11.

340. Ibid., 18–20. According to Krämer, the five to six thousand Ashkenazim were more concentrated in Cairo, where they had their own synagogue and their own rabbi, whereas in Alexandria, they were part of the general community. Krämer found that they constituted, at most, 8 percent of the overall Jewish population in the interwar period. However, within my Australian sample they had a representation of approximately 25 percent.

The reason for this unusually high proportion might be that a larger component of the sample group was from Cairo.

341. The case of the Karaite Jew is discussed later.

342. Interviewee #14: "J'ai quitté la Turquie en 1921 avec ma mère pour l'Égypte. Il y avait la guerre entre les Turcs et les Grecs. Nous avons quitté pour l'avenir des enfants. Mon père étant mort, les garçons avaient grandi et ne voulaient plus rester en Turquie...Ma mère avait une soeur qui était mariée en Égypte et avait une très bonne position...L'éducation européenne, je l'ai eue en Égypte. J'ai commencé par l'école Harouch, et ensuite l'école Menasche...Nous nous sommes installés à Alexandrie... Jacques, mon frère ainé, travaillait chez un Turc. Albert et Marco travaillaient aussi".

343. The island of Corfu or Kerkira was occupied by the Venetians for nearly four hundred years (1401–1797). After a short period under the French, Corfu was invaded by the English in 1814 and incorporated into Greece in 1864. According to the personal chronicle of a Corfiot family, "Jessula Chronique, Corfou", compiled in 1991 by Jean-François Renaud, who is related to the well-known French writer Albert Cohen (*Mangeclous*, Editions Gallimard Folio, 1938), the Jewish community of Corfu of about five to six thousand was ravaged by a blood libel accusation in 1891, resulting in riots by the local Greek population. According to written testimonies and correspondence between the religious authorities of Corfu and Zante, the situation was considered so serious that the only solution envisaged was emigration: "La question de l'émigration s'impose à nous d'une manière absolue". Over half the Jewish community immigrated to Egypt, and the Germans rounded up those who stayed behind on 10 June 1944, their final destination being Auschwitz-Birkenau. The president of the Association of Friends of Greek Jewry reported that out of the 1,795 Jews of Corfu who were deported only 121 survived. During a personal visit to the Corfu synagogue, I saw a plaque listing the names of the Auschwitz deportees, including members of my husband's family.

344. On Cantonists, see Michael Stanislawski. *Tsar Nicholas I and the Jews, 1825–1855* (Philadelphia: Jewish Publication Society, 1983). According to a report published in January 1863 in the American periodical, *The Occident and American Jewish Advocate*, Russian Jews were subjected to a number of repressive laws during the regime of Tsar Nikolai I, over the years 1825–1855. Among the harshest was the "Cantonist" law, which targeted Jewish boys from the age of eight to be taken from their parents

and trained to serve in the Russian army for twenty to twenty-five years, with the further aim of converting them to the Russian Orthodox faith.

345. Interviewee #37 also said that his grandfather left Rumania in 1882 to save his son from being conscripted in the army. He found refuge in Egypt.

346. Interviewee #3 stated: "As far as I have been told, we could go back possibly to 1840 [in Egypt]. That was the time when somebody from the family in Amsterdam had accepted the invitation that the Vice-Roy Muhammad Ali extended to foreigners to come and develop the country, promising all sorts of benefits".

347. Krämer, *The Jews in Modern Egypt*, 39–41; see also article by Samir Raafat, "The National Bank of Egypt (NBE) 1898-1998", in *Egyptian Mail*, May 11 & 25 (1996), section on "The Suares Brothers of Cairo".

348. See article by Dr. Yunan Labib Rizk, "Battle for Helwan", in *Al-Ahram Weekly 492*, 27 July–2 August (2000). Modern Helwan was founded in 1874 by the Khedive Ismail. Situated twenty-four kilometres south of Cairo, it was renowned for its sulphur springs and salubrious climate and was initially only frequented by the cream of Egyptian society as a holiday place. The article mentioned the construction in the 1880s of a new railway line between Cairo and Helwan by the "Sawaris" brothers (Egyptianisation of the name "Suares"). The new rail service transformed Helwan into a residential district.

349. See Landau, *Jews in Nineteenth-Century Egypt*, 8–9, and Krämer, *The Jews in Modern Egypt*, 10. From a total Jewish population of 59,581 in 1917, 49 percent lived in Cairo, 41 percent in Alexandria, and 7 percent in the villages. In 1947, from a total Jewish population of 65,639, 63 percent lived in Cairo, 32 percent in Alexandria, and only 4 percent in the rest of Egypt, showing a growing urbanisation. According to Landau, during World War I some Jews disrupted the trend by settling in the Canal Zone, "where they could find better opportunities for business with the Allied troops stationed in that area".

350. *The Edge of the Diaspora* is a book by Rutland on the history of Jewish settlement in Australia.

351. Interviewee #74 stated: "J'ai l'impression que les gens du Caire menaient une vie différente de ceux d'Alexandrie. Ces derniers gardent toujours une affection particulière pour leur ville". Interviewee #3 concurred: "My family came to Egypt in 1841. They came to Alexandria. It was more European at the time. Cairo became more important later on. Alexandria was where all the activities were, where you had the harbour, the bankers, where all the cotton was gathered to be shipped…"

352. Landau, in *Jews in Nineteenth-Century Egypt*, 32, also noted: "Alexandria was the most cosmopolitan city in Egypt and the cultural gateway to Europe, which accounts for the fact that European influence was stronger in the Alexandria Jewish community than in any other".

353. Robert Ilbert et Ilios Yannakakis, *Alexandrie 1860–1960* (Paris: Editions Autrement, 1992), 16.

354. Krämer, *The Jews of Modern Egypt*, 82.

355. Ibid., 86.

356. Ibid., 108.

357. Landau, in *Jews in Nineteenth-Century Egypt*, 34–37, pointed out that Port Said had grown from an insignificant settlement to an economically viable town after the completion of the Suez Canal in 1869 and, as a consequence, the Jewish community also grew in importance. The new settlers were "attracted to the town, in the hope of earning a living from trade and tourism". Landau quoted a figure of 594 in 1917 out of a total population of approximately fifty-two thousand, "after which the Jewish population dropped significantly".

358. The data provided by Maurice Fargeon about the Jewish population of Upper Egypt, in *Les Juifs en Égypte*, 308–309—137 Jews for Assiut in 1917, dropping to 62 in 1927—was replicated in all of Upper Egypt with 1,225 Jews in 1917 to 984 in 1927. This data clearly shows the trend away from rural areas. Fargeon also noted that those few Jewish families had more or less adopted the other villagers' lifestyle. Nevertheless, they still maintained strict Jewish traditions, although they did not have the support of Jewish institutions in those villages: "En Haute Égypte...les Juifs ne se comptent que par quelques rares unités insignifiantes...Aucune communauté Juive n'existe en Haute-Égypte où les israélites mènent une vie individuelle et totalement assimilée à celle des habitants au milieu desquels ils vivent...Youssef Wahba m'assure...qu'il n'a jamais enfreint aux Lois de la Sainte Ecriture", 302–303.

359. Fargeon, in *Les Juifs en Égypte*, 287–289, documented the communal activities of all the Jewish families who lived in Mansurah.

360. Landau, *Jews in Nineteenth-Century Egypt*, 38–40, and Fargeon, *Les Juifs en Égypte*, 287–289 and 307.

361. The whole family migrated to Australia in 1948 and settled in Hobart, where the father became head of the French Department of Hobart University and the mother continued to work as a French teacher in high schools.

362. Fargeon, in *Les Juifs en Égypte*, 279, described Tantah as having one of the oldest and richest Jewish communities in Egypt, going back at least two centuries to the days of Muhammad Ali, when the Jews of Tantah were goldsmiths, a profession that attested to their social standing.

363. Krämer, *The Jews in Modern Egypt*, 108–111.

364. Landau, in *Jews in Nineteenth-Century Egypt*, 89–90, described the opening of the Alliance school in Tantah in 1905, which, "unlike the AIU schools in Alexandria, which closed in 1919… continued to function until World War II". In *Les Juifs en Égypte*, 281, Fargeon also pointed out that the influence of the AIU school was such that some of its students eventually became leading figures in the intellectual and social sphere of Alexandria and Cairo.

365. AIU, Egypt, XIII.E.192, Alphandary, Tantah, July 14 (1913), in Krämer, *The Jews in Modern Egypt*, 109–110.

366. In *Les Juifs du Nil*, "Chroniques de la vie quotidienne", 130, Jacques Hassoun reported: "A Tantah, trois synagogues se partagent la ville…les temples Louna, Botton, Chamla et Eskanderany. Une quatrième synagogue réservée aux originaires du Maroc—Kenisset-el-Mogharba—était systématiquement boudée par les notables dont l'établissement dans le Delta du Nil remontait à l'époque Byzantine".

367. In *Les Juifs en Égypte*, Fargeon mentioned three synagogues in Tantah, 280; in *Jews of Nineteenth-Century Egypt*, 42, Landau also mentioned three, and Krämer, in *The Jews in Modern Egypt*, 111, only two. It is obvious that, in the memory of the respondent, the Jewish side of Tantah was larger than life.

368. In the vernacular of the Jews of Egypt, *gabbai* specifically meant the beadle or sexton of the synagogue, whereas the term *gabbai* is usually more generic and means a communal official.

369. See Fargeon, *Les Juifs en Égypte*, 282–286, and Landau, *Jews in Nineteenth-Century Egypt*, 44. Both described the pilgrimage that used to take place in al-Mehalla al-Kubra, every year on the first of the month of Iyar, fifteen days after Passover. The pilgrims used "to congregate in the *Ustadh* (Teacher) synagogue, named for Rabbi Hayyim al-Amshati, which, along with its Scroll of the Law, was greatly revered by all Egyptian Jewry". On that occasion there was much drinking and merry-making.

370. Hassoun, *Histoire des Juifs du Nil*, 128–134: "Le dimanche matin, ils sont plusieurs milliers à se précipiter vers les gares centrales du Caire… et d'Alexandrie…les bras chargés de valises pleines d'échantillons…Mais voici que nos Juifs se précipitent vers les petites villes et les villages du

Delta. Courtiers depuis des siècles, ils assurent la circulation des marchandises et des nouvelles fraîches entre les grandes villes et les campagnes".
371. Krämer, *The Jews in Modern Egypt*, 108.
372. Hassoun in *Histoire des Juifs du Nil*, 91–93, compared the 1917 census to the 1927 census, detailing the distribution of the Jewish populations throughout Egypt. The latter census showed a marked decline in the numbers of Jews from the rural districts.
373. Shamir, "The Evolution of the Egyptian Nationality Laws", 33–67.
374. Golliger's grandfather, originally from Rumania, migrated to Egypt in 1882. He then left Egypt and went to Melbourne with his wife to work as an engineer. His daughter was born in Melbourne and he later died in Australia. When the time came to find a husband for the daughter, his wife wrote to Egypt and found a suitable match in a family also from Rumania. She packed her belongings and travelled back to Egypt with her daughter, who became the mother of this interviewee.
375. Krämer, *The Jews in Modern Egypt*, 29.
376. Ibid., 10; Fargeon, *Les Juifs en Égypte*, 308; Hassoun, *Histoire des Juifs du Nil*, 92–93; Beinin, *The Dispersion of Egyptian Jewry*, 38.
377. Laskier, *The Jews of Egypt*, 8.
378. Beinin, *The Dispersion of Egyptian Jewry*, 38.
379. Krämer, *The Jews in Modern Egypt*, 33. See *Population Census of Egypt, 1937, General Tables* (Cairo: Government Press, 1942), Table 32, 264, and *Population Census of Egypt, 1947* (Cairo: Government Press, 1954), Table 15, 433.
380. Krämer, *The Jews in Modern Egypt*, 35.
381. Ibid., 9.
382. Ziza Lester also claimed that the colour of her passport was blue, reserved for the non-Muslim citizens, whereas the passport of Muslim citizens was green.
383. Krämer, *The Jews in Modern Egypt*, 33.
384. #4 and #77.
385. The island of Corfu, although always ethnically Greek, passed from Venetian domination (1386–1797) to French domination (1797–1814), and then again from British protection (1814–1864) to reunification with Greece after the Greek War of Independence.
386. *The Dictionary of the Social Sciences*, edited by Julius Gould and William Kolb (Great Britain: Tavistock Publications, 1964), 426, defines middle class as "that stratum, within a social structure, that is deemed 'intermediate' between the 'upper class' and the 'working class'. The lines of

demarcation, however, are not precise and are dependent upon a number of varying and ambiguous criteria. The most frequently adopted criterion relates to occupation". For instance, while the upper class is often defined by its largely inherited wealth, the working class consists mostly of manual labourers, and semiskilled and unskilled workers. The middle class includes within its ranks middle- and upper-level clerical workers, technicians, professionals, small shopkeepers, businesspeople, and farmers.

387. After leaving Egypt in 1957, my parents migrated to Canada with my two younger siblings. With the same courage and determination, my mother worked as a dressmaker during the day and at night baked Oriental delicacies to help supplement the family budget. Thirteen years later, she went through a second emigration when she joined me in Sydney, displaying the same ability to adapt to her new environment despite her advanced age.

388. That school was still in existence in the late 1950s. Beinin mentioned it in *The Dispersion of Egyptian Jewry*, 123, as the Heliopolis location of the largest and most developed branch of the Zionist youth movement, *ha-Ivri ha-Tza'ir*. He pointed out that "although the curriculum at the Btesh school included Hebrew and other Jewish subjects, the primary language of instruction was French", as was the case in most Jewish community schools. It was also used as a synagogue, as recalled by Moïse Rahmani, editor of *Los Muestros*: "J'ai la nostalgie des synagogues. Nous fréquentions la nommée Abraham Betesh d'Héliopolis. Je me souviens de la cour intérieure durant les fêtes de Roch Hachana. Les discussions allaient bon train…"

389. The story of this extraordinary woman was inserted in a book by Lysbeth Cohen, *Beginning with Esther: —Jewish Women in NSW from 1788* (Sydney: Ayers & James Heritage Books in association with the *Australian Jewish Times*, 1987), 149–151. In the last two years of her life, Ziza lived in a retirement home, Sir Moses Montefiore Jewish Home, in Sydney. Because she was legally blind, she dictated the first volume of her memoirs, "This is my Life", and distributed it to her friends. Unfortunately, she died in February 2010, before starting Volume 2.

390. The middle class consisted of 68.4 percent of the Eastern Europeans, 71.3 percent of the ex-Ottoman subjects, 60 percent of the Western Europeans, and 68.4 percent of those of mixed ethnic backgrounds.

391. In *The Jews of Egypt*, 191, Laskier stated that in "most cases, the majority of the families and individuals were from the lower-middle and middle socio-economic strata and youth who were not working"; Beinin in *The*

Dispersion of Egyptian Jewry, 71, also wrote: "Except for the minority of committed Zionists, poorer families tended to go to Israel and wealthier families tended to go elsewhere". However, not all the Egyptian Jews who migrated to Israel agree with that assumption. Levana Zamir, president of Israel-Egypt Friendship Association, maintains that the *aliyah* of Egyptian Jews also included a substantial number of middle-class, educated individuals who could have migrated anywhere in the world but chose to settle in Israel.

392. Beinin, *The Dispersion of Egyptian Jewry*, 44.
393. Krämer, *The Jews in Modern Egypt*, 52.
394. Laskier, *The Jews of Egypt,* Table 6.3, 188, Table 6.4, 189.
395. Hassoun, "Le deuxième exode d'Égypte" in Ilbert et Yannakakis, *Alexandrie 1860–1960*, 143–147. While evoking the successive waves of immigration from 1948 to 1973, Hassoun claimed that it was first the political activists—Zionists, Communists, and other troublemakers who were incarcerated—as well as the most destitute members of the community, those living in the *haret-el-yahud* (Jewish quarter), who headed for Israel, via Marseille, where they were greeted by the Jewish Agency. The others—intellectuals, Communists, and members of the upper *bourgeoisie*—chose instead to settle in Europe, the Americas, or Australia.
396. The statistical studies on education and literacy by Hayyim J. Cohen, in *The Jews of the Middle East. 1860–1972* (New York: Wiley, 1972), 110, revealed that by 1945–1946, out of 12,107 Jewish pupils, 59.2 percent of them were attending foreign schools as compared to 41 percent attending Jewish schools.
397. Landau, *Jews in Nineteenth Century Egypt*, 71.
398. Hassoun, "Une Mosaïque méditerranénne", in Ilbert et Yannakakis, *Alexandrie 1860–1960,* 64, pointed out that even the *Lycée de l'Union Juive pour l'Enseignement*, in spite of its name, was an essentially secular institution, founded in 1925 by the B'nai B'rith Masonic lodges. It only taught Hebrew grammar and literature.
399. Ethel Carasso, "La Communauté juive d'Égypte de 1948 à 1957", Maîtrise d'Histoire contemporaine, Université de Paris X, Octobre 1982. See also *Statistical Handbook of Middle Eastern Countries (1835–1944),* Agence juive de Palestine, 1945; and Cohen, *Jews of the Middle East.*
400. Rutland, *The Jews in Australia*, 123.
401. The Italian school was a communal institution created by the Italian government for its citizens residing in Egypt to provide them with an Italian education free of charge.

402. This interviewee had three brothers, all high achievers. The eldest studied medicine at the University of Cairo, the second studied engineering, and the third obtained a degree in engineering from the University of Adelaide.

403. Those 3 percent left Egypt while they were still in primary school and pursued their schooling in Australia.

404. Intervewee #70 insisted that the decision to change schools was not as a result of any pressure exercised upon her by the nuns to convert her to Catholicism. She also added that in the Catholic school she was taught only French, whereas in the Jewish school she had to learn French, Arabic, and Hebrew.

405. Interviewee #5, who was born in Assiut, Upper Egypt, was first sent to the American Missionary primary school and then to the Egyptian state high school because there were no other choices in that village. Interviewee #6, who was born in the country town of Mansurah, attended a Catholic missionary school (*Ecole des Soeurs*) before being sent to Cairo to attend the French *Lycée*.

406. Interviewee #46 first attended the French *Lycée* of Alexandria. He moved to Tantah with his mother after his father died, where he attended the *Alliance Israëlite* school. He moved again, this time to Mansurah, during World War II, where the only high school available was the state public school.

407. As typical examples of respondents from a privileged background, Interviewee #8 worked in his family cotton ginning and export business, a large enterprise established by his grandfather who was a self-taught "cotton classer" (a person who can distinguish and classify the various types of the cotton fibre by touch). Similarly, the husband of Interviewee #10 and their son owned a large factory supplying uniforms to the Egyptian army, the police, and the Department of Transport. In contrast, Interviewee #29, born in the village of Tantah and educated in the Jewish communal schools of Tantah and later Alexandria, left school at thirteen to work and help support his family. Before leaving Egypt, he was a salesperson in the biggest department store of Alexandria, *Les Grands Magasins Hannaux*, founded by a French Jew at the beginning of the twentieth century.

408. Interviewee #11 used to make dresses for British women soldiers during the war, and as a consequence, obtained extra rations of butter and sugar from the Navy Army Air Force Institute (NAAFI)–the British armed forces supply stores.

409. This interviewee (#47) was trained in the Napoleonic Code, which was used in the Mixed Courts.
410. Another interviewee (#25) had just started pharmacy at university in Egypt when the 1956 war erupted. He completed his studies at Sydney University.
411. Ladino, known also as *judesmo*, is a Judeo-Spanish dialect spoken by the Sephardim of Mediterranean countries and written in Hebrew script.
412. A form of Venetian dialect spoken by the Jews in Corfu.
413. The Eastern Europeans spoke an average of 4.8 languages, Western Europeans 4.3 languages, the former Ottoman subjects 4.5, and those from a mixed background 3.9, which makes an overall average of 4.3 languages.
414. Beinin, The *Dispersion of Egyptian Jewry*, 5.
415. His knowledge of French gave Interviewee #8 the start he needed to enter the Pacific Islands trade. Eventually, it allowed him to establish his own export company and later expand into shipping with French partners, dealing mainly with New Caledonia and the Loyalty Islands. Interviewee #24, a printer by trade, secured himself a favourable two-year contract with a printing firm in the French Pacific island of New Caledonia, thanks to his perfect command of both French and English.
416. Interviewees #18, #33, and #59.
417. Rutland, "Egyptian Jews in Adelaide", 22.
418. Interviewee #71 had no English skills on arrival, although she was fluent in Italian, Greek, French, and Arabic. She had quite a large family and still communicated with her children in French but managed to speak some English with her grandchildren. As is usually the case with migrants who do not join the workforce, remaining more or less isolated in the context of the family home, her English skills remained poor in spite of her fluency in four other languages.
419. Alain Lévy, "Itinéraire d'une famille juive d'Alexandrie de 1899 à 1980; de la tradition ottomane à la modernité", *l'Ethnographie,* Vol. 116 (1994), 77.
420. See Rutland, *The Edge of the Diaspora,* 369–377, on "the transformation of Australian society since the late 1960s, with its increased emphasis on multiculturalism".
421. Roman Jews follow an ancient and unique Italian rite called *nusach italki*, which is different from both the Ashkenazi and Sephardi rites and is still used in many Italian synagogues.
422. Judeo-Spanish, known also as Ladino or *judesmo*, is an ancient form of Castillian mixed with Hebrew and Turkish words and often written in

Hebrew script, similarly to Yiddish. See Mary Altabev, "The People and the Language", in *Judeo-Spanish in the Turkish Social Context: Language Death, Swan Song, Revival or New Arrival?* (Istanbul: The Isis Press, 2003), 37–66. This book was the result of her PhD dissertation presented at the University of Sussex, September 1996.

423. See Krämer, *The Jews in Modern Egypt*, 17.

424. Jacques Hassoun, in *Histoire des Juifs du Nil*, 124–137, also mentioned the traditional pilgrimage to the ancient synagogue of El-Ustadh (Teacher), founded in 1044 in Mehallah el-Kobra, and dedicated to the holy man Rabbi Hayyim al-Amshāti. The pilgrimage used to attract *en masse* the Oriental Jews from all over Egypt and was even attended by an official representative of the Egyptian government.

425. According to Krämer, *The Jews of Modern Egypt*, 18, the majority of these exiles returned either to Palestine or to Eastern Europe after WW1.

426. Fargeon, *Les Juifs en Égypte*, 231.

427. See Krämer, *The Jews in Modern Egypt*, 20: "[The Ashkenazim] tried to establish a separate community organisation. The Ashkenazi community, founded in 1865, was, however, denied official recognition—partly because the Sephardi community resisted all attempts at institutionalised separatism. But for all practical purposes, the Ashkenazim formed an independent community in Cairo, with their own rabbi, president, and council...In Alexandria and the provincial towns, where the Ashkenazim formed a small minority, they remained within the larger community".

428. Derogatory Yiddish term for an Ashkenazi, meaning bad or evil.

429. The Cairo Ashkenazim had their own rabbi and their own separate *Beth Din* (Rabbinic law court).

430. Krämer, *The Jews in Modern Egypt*, 76.

431. Ibid., 24. Krämer pointed to different sources quoting varying figures: the 1947 Egyptian census quoted 3,486 Karaites; Maurice Fargeon, seven thousand in 1939; unofficial Karaite sources, eight thousand. Krämer in *The Jews in Modern Egypt*, 86, quoted a problematic figure of six to seven thousand Karaites in the interwar period. Beinin, in *The Dispersion of Egyptian Jewry*, 3, quoted the figure of some five thousand Karaites in Egypt in 1948, probably based on the research of Murad al-Qudsi (aka Mourad El-Kodsi), in *The Karaite Jews of Egypt*, 16, where he stated: "we can rightly assume that the number of Karaites in 1952 was somewhat less than 5,000, but not less than 4,000". Hassoun's claim, in *Histoire des Juifs du Nil*, 103, that the Karaite population numbered seven to nine thousand, seems inflated.

432. Beinin, *The Dispersion of Egyptian Jewry*, 44.
433. Ibid., 185.
434. I was discouraged from approaching them because of their advanced age and state of health. Some members of the original families had already passed away. Although I knew of a few Karaite families who were originally from Istanbul and now lived in Sydney, I made a considered judgment not to formally include them in the present study because they were not from Egypt.
435. Beinin, in *The Dispersion of Egyptian Jewry*, has succinctly covered the Israeli experience of the Egyptian Karaites, 181–184.
436. Tapani Harviainen, in "Ethnic Encounter and Culture Change" (paper presented at the third Nordic Conference on Middle Eastern Studies, Joensuu, Finland, June 19–22, 1995, 2), argued that "the question of the Jewishness of Karaites divides the originally Arabic-speaking Karaites in Israel and San Francisco into another camp: these designate themselves as Karaite Jews, while the Karaims in Eastern Europe stress the independent national character of their community…Besides being a national minority, the Karaims represent an independent religion; they prefer to designate their faith as a religion based on Judaism in the same way as Christianity is an independent religion with a Jewish background".
437. See Shmuel Spector, "Karaites", in *Encyclopedia of the Holocaust* (New York: MacMillan, 1990), Vol. 2, 785–787.
438. My interviewee claimed that the Rabbanite rabbis' intention was to save the Karaites from Nazi persecution. The fact that "groups of Jewish scholars in the Vilna, Warsaw and Lvov ghettos…were prepared to claim, contrary to their real convictions, that they [the Karaites] were not Jews, in order to save their lives" was discussed by Nathan Schur in *History of the Karaites*, "The Karaites in Nazi-Occupied Europe during WWII", 123–125.
439. Krämer, in *The Jews in Modern Egypt*, 26, concurred that the Karaites "tried to keep relations with the Rabbanites friendly, but decidedly distant".
440. The Karaites base their calendar on the observance of the new moon and the ripening of the barley crops in Israel. They do not accept the Rabbanite interpretation of the prohibition on mixing meat and milk products based on the commandment: Thou shall not boil a kid in his mother's milk (Deut. 14:21). They do not celebrate the festival of Hanukkah (or Festival of Lights) and the Fast of Esther, both considered to be post-biblical holidays. As explained by the Parisian Karaite interviewee, "Hanukkah is a

celebration of the Second Temple, and for Karaites, only the First Temple counts since the second one is but a reproduction of the first".

441. According to the French interviewee, a *bar mitzvah* ceremony symbolises the authority of the rabbis over the Jewish community. The Karaite Jews do not recognise that authority given that a Karaite boy is Karaite—literally meaning a reader—from the time he starts to learn to read and not at an arbitrary age set by the Rabbis. However, the Sydney Karaite respondent claimed that Karaites in Israel have now adopted the practice of bar mitzvah, probably under pressure to conform to the dominant tradition.

442. *Simhat Torah*, literally meaning "rejoicing in the Torah", is a joyous celebration, which concludes the annual cycle of the reading of the Torah. Towards the end of the service, all the scrolls of the Torah are removed from the Ark for seven processions around the synagogue, followed by singing children with banners and candles. This is probably the celebration this respondent is referring to.

443. Tobia Simha Levi Babovitch served as the last Chief Hakham (Rabbi) of the Karaite community in Cairo from 1934 till he died in 1956. According to the information compiled by Nathan Schur in *The Karaite Encyclopedia*, Frankfurt, 1995, "he [the rabbi] was used to the different customs and Halakha of Russia and Turkey...he often opposed the local customs, but was not very successful therein. It is obvious that the nationalistic ideology of the European Karaites, who claimed not to be Jews at all, could not be applied successfully in Egypt".

444. Beinin, *The Dispersion of Egyptian Jewry*, 183.

445. Ibid., 193. According to Beinin, the Karaite family tree compiled by David Elichaa of Imperial Beach, California, shows that all the Karaite families of Cairo were related.

446. See Hassoun, *Histoire des Juifs du Nil*, 104, where he mentioned Mourad Farag Bey, "poète et juriste, co-rédacteur de la première constitution de l'Égypte indépendante".

447. Beinin, in *The Dispersion of Egyptian Jewry*, 39, also found that "in all respects except religious practice, the daily lives of the Karaites of *harat-al-yahud al-qara'in* [the Karaite quarters] were undistinguishable from their Muslim neighbors".

448. This interviewee later enrolled at Cairo Fuad University, where he graduated as a Bachelor of Commerce.

449. For instance, the French Karaite respondent remembered that her grandfather, a lawyer at the Islamic courts where all the proceedings were conducted in Arabic, possessed a high level of proficiency in the Arabic

language. Apparently, he used to read the Koran fluently. Because their language at home was nearly exclusively Arabic, she considered it an aberration that her parents succumbed to outside pressure and sent her to a French school to learn French, while her brother was sent to a British school to learn English. The Oriental Jews of the diaspora often deny the fact that they used to speak Arabic at home because that would mean the family had not assimilated to Western culture and, therefore, could be perceived as backward and unsophisticated.

450. Because of his perfect knowledge of the Arabic language, this interviewee is often called upon to translate sensitive material concerning the Jewish community that is published in the Arabic media.

451. He was confronted once more at graduation time with the dichotomy of being an Egyptian Jew when he was not awarded the traditional signed photo of the King, together with his diploma, as was customary for all Egyptian graduates.

452. Beinin, *The Dispersion of Egyptian Jewry*, 40.

453. Ironically, while the family was in court trying to prove their national identity, the son (my interviewee) was called for military service, even though he was not considered an Egyptian national at the time. After spending three months in the army, he was permanently dismissed without any official reason, but he suspected it was because he was a Jew.

454. See Krämer, *The Jews of Modern Egypt*, 26, and Beinin, *The Dispersion of Egyptian Jewry*, 68.

455. After twelve years in Israel after having left Egypt, he immigrated to Australia in 1969. He only went back to Egypt once, in 2000, after forty-three years of absence.

456. The term bar mitzvah signifies a boy's coming of age on his thirteenth birthday and the accompanying ritual and ceremony. The custom of celebrating a boy's first public observance of the *mitzvoth*—commandments—goes back to the Middle Ages, whereas the equivalent ceremony for girls, the *bat mitzvah*, only developed in the United States as a ritual alternative in the Conservative and Reform movements from 1922. The historian Paula E. Hyman reported that the first American bat mitzvah was that of Judith Kaplan, the daughter of Rabbi Mordecai M. Kaplan, founder of Reconstructionist Judaism. However, Arthur Ocean Waskow and Phyllis Ocean Berman pointed out in *A Time for Every Purpose under Heaven* (New York: Farrar, Strauss and Giroux, 2002) that there is evidence of earlier bat mitzvah celebrations in Lwow in 1902, as well as in Italy and France. Within Orthodoxy, the custom has now been adopted. Tradition-

ally, the actual ceremony is not held on a Shabbat, contrary to the Reform movement, although this is also changing. For instance, at the Sydney Great Synagogue, at the end of the Friday night service, the bat mitzvah girl is invited to give an address or *drasha* to the congregation, on a topic set by the rabbi.

457. *Juifs d'Égypte: Images*, 65, "Initiation religieuse des Jeunes Filles en 1927 à Alexandrie".

458. Rabbi R. Della Pergola published a fifty-three-page manual, *Recueil pour l'initiation des jeunes filles israélites*, (Alexandrie: Communauté Israélite, 5682/1922) (French and Hebrew). According to the information provided by Norman Stillman in May 2006, there were "similar rites among Grana [Livornese Jews] of Tunisia at the time of first communion for which we have pictures, again with the girls dressed in a pseudo-bridal gown similar to that used for first communion in the Catholic Church". See also the article "Grand Temple Neve-Chalom: Cérémonie de Bar Mitzva de 55 garçons et initiations de 30 jeunes filles" in the Egyptian Jewish newspaper *Israël*, June 6, 1935, 4.

459. Opening word of a central prayer of the Jewish liturgy, meaning "Hear", incorporating a basic statement of faith.

460. I was one of those eighteen girls and have kept a clear memory of that celebration.

461. Interviewee #28 was eventually accepted back into the fold after a few years, but the father never really reconciled himself to the idea of a non-Jewish son-in-law.

462. Interviewee #51, who married an office colleague, related: "my mother used to tell me, he [the husband] is an angel. There is no one like him". Interviewee #60 married her Greek neighbour who, having fought with the Allied Forces in the Greek Brigade during WWII, was able to immigrate to Australia in 1949 and sponsored his wife's entire family.

463. Krämer, *The Jews in Modern Egypt*, 229.

464. Krämer, in *The Jews in Modern Egypt*, 190–191, stated: "What Jewish visitors from Europe and Palestine, most of them Ashkenazim, deplored most was the apparent lack of Jewish life—as they knew it…In the late 1920s, a teacher from the Alliance Israélite school in Tantah reported…it is true that the Egyptian Jew always says his prayers, and observes all the rites, but he lacks the Jewish soul".

465. Hassoun, *Histoire des Juifs du Nil*, 135.

466. See Krämer, "Political Participation of the Jews", chapter V, 68–82, in Shamir, *The Jews of Egypt*.

467. Laskier, *The Jews of Egypt*, 40.
468. Ibid., 44–45, 50. Laskier also pointed to the report of Moshe Ben-Asher, "Egypt's most formidable Zionist", who estimated that the Arab revolt of 1936–1939 was a wake-up call for Egyptian Jews. Their feelings of security and stability were shaken by the growing support of Egyptian politicians for the Arabs of Palestine. As a result, the idea of a Jewish homeland in Palestine began to sound more attractive.
469. Despite his father's prohibition, Interviewee #8 remained a close friend of a number of Zionist activists, who were subsequently arrested and convicted as spies in the Lavon Affair in 1954. For details on the Lavon Affair, see Beinin, *The Dispersion of Egyptian Jewry*, 94–117, Laskier, *The Jews of Egypt*, 205–251, and Aviezer Golan, *Operation Suzannah*.
470. Beinin, *The Dispersion of Egyptian Jewry*, 51.
471. This particular interviewee also remembered that Alexandre Roche, the teacher in question, had organised some secret meetings outside school hours with a number of over-eager students. When discovered, he was severely reprimanded by members of the school board who were also parents. They were horrified at the thought that their children were being indoctrinated in Marxism and Zionism.
472. Laskier, in *The Jews of Egypt*, 113–115, reported that, although the actual number of youth smuggled out during that particular operation is disputed, the consensus seems to be around seventy to a hundred individuals. Despite these relatively small numbers, "Operation Passover" was important because it was "the *'aliya* of a progressive elite of Zionists, among them people who played an integral role during the late 1940s and early 1950s as Mossad Le'Aliya and Jewish Agency emissaries in Egypt and North Africa".
473. It is interesting to note that, like some of the privileged non-Muslim minorities, King Fuad, born in 1868—son of Khedive Isma'il, a fervent francophile—had an entirely European education. At the age of ten, he went to school in Geneva and in 1885 joined the Military Academy of Turin. He later became military attaché in Vienna. Consequently he spoke Italian, French, and German fluently but "practically no English...and hardly any Arabic", as pointed out by Jacques Berque, in *Egypt, Imperialism and Revolution*, 278.
474. See Krämer in *The Jews of Modern Egypt*, 94–96, who described Joseph Aslan de Cattaoui Pasha (1861–1942) as a man "with far reaching connections in Egyptian business and political circles", who was elected to the Legislative Assembly in 1914 and was sent to London as legal adviser

to the Egyptian delegation (the Wafd) in 1920–1921. Krämer added that "Joseph Aslan Cattaoui entered Parliament in 1922 as deputy of Kom Ombo...The same year he was appointed to the constitutional Commission preparing the new constitution of April 1923...in November 1924, he became minister of Finance...In recognition for his service, King Fuad made him a member of the Egyptian Senate in 1927".

475. Landau, in *Middle Eastern Themes*, 172–187, related the life achievements of one of the most ardent Jewish supporters of Egyptian nationalism, James (Ya'qub) Sanua (1839–1912), also known by his nickname Abu Naddara, meaning "the man with glasses". He made major contributions as a journalist, playwright, political cartoonist, and satirist, exposing the excesses of the ruling class and fighting against the British occupation of Egypt. According to Landau, he was in frequent contact with Colonel Orabi Pasha and his group, who led the 1882 rebellion against the British under the slogan "Egypt for the Egyptians". See also his biography by Irene L. Gendzier, *The Practical Visions of Ya'Qub Sanu'* (Cambridge, MA: Harvard University, 1966), M.S. Monograph XV.

476. Beinin, *The Dispersion of Egyptian Jewry*, 142. See also Krämer, *The Jews in Modern Egypt*, 172–182, about the high involvement of Jewish middle-class youth already in the Communist movement in Egypt in the 1920s and 1930s.

477. This interviewee related that her brother, along with a number of Egyptian Jews, was recruited by Henri Curiel (1914–1978), the legendary and charismatic Jewish Egyptian Communist militant, who was responsible for the foundation in 1943 of MELN, Le Mouvement Égyptien pour la Libération Nationale, the precursor of today's Egyptian Communist Party. He was imprisoned for two years after the 1948 War with Israel. Curiel was then expelled and eventually settled in France, where he remained politically active in unpopular and controversial causes. He was labelled by the French media as the patron of terrorism support organisations, "le patron des réseaux d'aide au terrorisme". He was assassinated in Paris in May 1978 by unidentified killers. See Gilles Perrault, *Un Homme à part* (Paris: Bernard Barrault, 1984). This book was translated into English, *A Man Apart: The Life of Henri Curiel* (London: Zed Books, 1987).

478. Interviewee #54, who was a very proud Egyptian national, recalled her anguish when she was stripped of her passport on her departure in 1957 and given instead stateless travelling papers, valid for one journey without return: "Au moment où je devais quitter, on m'avait enlevé le passeport égyptien et on m'a donné une feuille de route 'aller sans retour'. C'est une

chose qui m'a déchiré terriblement le coeur parce que je me considérais très égyptienne. J'étais très fière de l'être". Interviewee #29, stateless, born in the village of Tantah, never questioned his feeling of belonging before 1948. Egypt was his home, and although he led a very Jewish life, he was not a Zionist. Contrary to the majority of the sample group, he spoke and wrote Arabic perfectly. He was forced out of his job of twenty-seven years because of the 1947 Company Law, which required 75 percent of employees to be of Egyptian nationality. He now lives in Melbourne with his wife and sons.

479. Krämer, *The Jews in Modern Egypt*, 169.
480. The family of Interviewee #53, who lived in the village of Tantah and whose roots went back to the beginning of the eighteenth century, spoke nearly exclusively Arabic at home, but he was sent to British schools in Cairo to gain what was considered the most prestigious education. Arabic was gradually relegated to second place. By the time his children were born, Arabic had been totally suppressed and supplanted by English and French.
481. The parents of this particular respondent (#1) came from Aleppo, Syria, and spoke exclusively Arabic. However, as was often the case, French gradually displaced Arabic and the respondent spoke only French to her children.
482. Krämer, *The Jews in Modern Egypt*, 28.
483. Altabev, *Judeo-Spanish in the Turkish Social Context*, 63.
484. Krämer, *The Jews in Modern Egypt*, 27.
485. Esther Benbassa and Aron Rodrigue, *Sephardi Jewry: A History of Judeo-Spanish Community, 14th–20th Centuries* (Berkeley and Los Angeles: University of California Press, 2000), 101–103. Altabev, in *Judeo-Spanish*, 61–63, also argued that these measures constituted the *coup de grâce* for the status of Judeo-Spanish, already downgraded by the Alliance schools' introduction of French. It had become "the language spoken at home and by the uneducated".
486. Benbassa and Rodrigue, *Sephardi Jewry*, 102–103.
487. Altabev, *Judeo-Spanish*, 142.
488. Krämer, *The Jews in Modern Egypt*, 206.
489. Ibid., 105. According to Krämer, in the early 1930s the Jewish community schools, attended by children of lower- and lower-middle-class families, "were placed under the supervision of the Ministry of Education and adopted the Egyptian curriculum. Arabic was henceforth the main language of instruction, particularly in the senior classes". Clearly, this new

measure did not affect the middle- and upper-middle-class students who continued to flock to private European schools.

490. This was the opinion of Taha Husain (1889–1973), the celebrated Egyptian intellectual and scholar, who thought that "the teaching of Arabic should follow the same rules as that of any other language", reported Berque in *Egypt Imperialism and Revolution*, 639.

491. Krämer, in *The Jews in Modern Egypt*, 168–172, also named "Murad Faraj, the eminent Karaite lawyer, poet, and writer, [who] composed poems in classical Arabic style (*qasa'id*), which dealt with the common heritage of Jews and Arabs".

492. B. L. Carter, *The Copts in Egyptian Politics, 1918–1952* (Cairo: American University in Cairo Press, 1985). The Copts constitute the largest Christian minority in the Middle East, the latest estimates being around 10 percent of the Egyptian population of over eighty-two million. Since the Free Officers' coup in 1952 and the advent of Gamal Abdel Nasser, the Copts have suffered from growing discrimination and marginalisation by the state.

493. Krämer, *The Jews in Modern Egypt*, 205.

494. Estimates taken from WJC records, 1971: 25.

495. Laskier, *The Jews of Egypt*, 187.

496. These figures are quoted by Beinin in *The Dispersion of Egyptian Jews*, 87, taken from the records of the WJC. Laskier in *The Jews of Egypt*, 290, quoted only twenty-five hundred.

497. Only two respondents, who left Egypt before the first trigger event of 1948, stated they did it for personal reasons, one out of Zionist idealism (Interviewee #62) and the other (#41) because "he wanted to see the world".

498. Interviewee #57 was able to remain in Egypt because she was married to a Christian Egyptian. However, she admitted having a lot of difficulty finding work in the last years because she had to reveal her maiden, Jewish surname to her prospective employers, who by law were not allowed to employ her.

499. Beinin, *The Dispersion of Egyptian Jewry*, 1.

500. Eleven of the twenty Ashkenazim in the sample group emigrated before 1956, compared to only twenty out of sixty-three Sephardim.

501. Laskier, *The Jews of Egypt*, 126.

502. One of my contacts in Israel was also interned in the Abukir camp at the same period as Interviewee #46. He recalled that while in prison this particular respondent, from a totally anti-Zionist stand, turned into a fervent

Zionist and migrated to Israel when he was released. Six years later, due to family pressure, he left Israel for Australia and settled first in Hobart before moving to Melbourne.

503. It was an old British air force military camp with hangars where the internees were lodged during the summer and then transferred to wooden shacks in winter.

504. My respondent described the Abukir prison more "like a holiday camp". By bribing camp officials, the detainees were allowed to cook their own food and received regular visits from family and friends, as well as food parcels.

505. In *The Jews in Modern Egypt*, 211, Krämer stated that "on the night of 15 May, 'for reasons of public security related to the present situation', hundreds of Zionists and Communists, mainly Jews, were arrested...Between July 1949 and February 1950, the Zionists and most of the Communists who had been interned over the preceding months were released...The foreign nationals and stateless persons among them were expelled from Egypt".

506. The work of these two organisations has been amply documented by Laskier in *The Jews of Egypt*, 164–183.

507. Interviewee #80, who was only ten years old when her father was arrested, has never forgotten how the whole family waited on the boat for his liberation. They proceeded to Singapore, where the Jewish community needed a rabbi.

508. Interviewee #43 said he remembered the anti-Jewish riots of 1929 when he saw his father take a pistol and put it in his pocket. Laskier, in *The Jews of Egypt*, 18–19, wrote about the anti-Zionist riots of April and May 1938, when Muslim youth paraded through Cairo and Alexandria's centres, shouting "Down with the Jews" and "Throw the Jews out of Egypt and Palestine".

509. As a British subject, Interviewee #43 served in the British Army in Cairo during the war. He chose to settle in Australia because he wanted to be as far as possible from the Middle East.

510. Interviewee #79 was British and thus did not need a landing permit for Australia in those days. His brother had been arrested in 1948 as a Zionist, although he was more of a Communist, and because the family had British nationality, he was deported to England. The whole issue of identity in relation to the Jews of Egypt seems to be encapsulated in that one case: Jewish, second-generation Egyptian-born, in possession of a British passport, arrested for being a Zionist when he was really a Communist.

511. Laskier, *The Jews of Egypt*, 126.

512. Ibid., 129.

513. Testimony of a Karaite Jew in San Francisco (#22 USA).

514. Krämer, *The Jews in Modern Egypt*, 219–220; Beinin, *The Dispersion of Egyptian Jewry*, 48.

515. Beinin, *The Dispersion of Egyptian Jewry*, 85.

516. Laskier, *The Jews of Egypt* 253.

517. Only the men in my sample group actually spent time in prison. I have not personally encountered, either in Australia or overseas, a Jewish woman who was imprisoned as a result of the state of emergency during the Suez War. However, according to a report from the American Jewish Committee, picked up by Laskier in *The Jews of Egypt*, 254, out of about nine hundred Jews who were arrested in November 7, 1956, and kept in different locations, "another forty-two Jews were detained, most of them women, many of them aged", at the Abraham B'tesh Jewish school in Heliopolis.

518. The Egyptian pound (E£) was equivalent to one pound sterling (£STG)

519. According to Laskier in *The Jews of Egypt*, 254, Jewish families under house arrest were "under surveillance by building concierges invested with police authority".

520. In spite of that reprieve, the whole episode was very distressing for this interviewee. When the hostilities first erupted, the whole family left their apartment to avoid a repetition of what happened to them during the 1952 Cairo fire, when insurgents torched the building and her parents had to flee from the rooftop. This time, they had taken refuge at the home of relatives when they heard a radio announcement that anybody harbouring French or British citizens would be considered an enemy of the state. Not wishing to endanger their relatives, they decided to go back home, where they were put under house arrest.

521. Laskier, *The Jews of Egypt*, 254.

522. The common procedure was for the secret police to arrest any male member of the family if they could not find the one they were looking for.

523. The so-called Lavon Affair has already been discussed. Dr. Marzuk was one of the thirteen conspirators involved in that covert operation, known also as Operation Susannah. Eleven conspirators were arrested and charged. Marzuk and Shmuel (Sammy) Azar were the only ones condemned to death. See Laskier, *The Jews of Egypt*, 205–248.

524. Beinin, *The Dispersion of Egyptian Jewry*, 181–203. Laskier, in *The Jews of Egypt*, 290, quoted a much smaller number: "Egypt's defeat in 1967

created problems for the remaining twenty-five hundred Egyptian Jews". Szulc, in *The Secret Alliance*, 280–283, also stated: "In 1967, at the start of the Arab-Israeli Six-Day War, the Egyptian government imprisoned approximately 500 Egyptian Jewish males between the ages of eighteen and fifty-three. They belonged to a Jewish enclave of some 2,500 people".

525. Laskier, *The Jews of Egypt*, 255.

526. His surviving wife recalled that they were forced to renounce their Egyptian nationality and left the country as stateless.

527. Laskier, *The Jews of Egypt*, 256.

528. Ibid., 256.

529. Interviewee #40.

530. Interviewee #10 mentioned the loss of her Egyptian nationality: "Nous sommes partis en tant qu'apatrides bien que mon mari était Égyptien. Il a du renoncer à sa nationalité".

531. Interviewee #72 still had in his possession a copy of that document, with the inscription in French and Arabic.

532. Beinin, *The Dispersion of Egyptian Jewry*, 73.

533. Interviewee #21, who was thirteen at the time, came from a very affluent family. The family owned a jewellery shop, and she remembered vividly the day of her departure: "We closed the door of the apartment and left it as is. The shop was also left. I wasn't even told we were going on that day. My mother didn't trust me".

534. There were several such cases within my sample. I also went through the same experience when I left Egypt in March 1957.

535. There were many similar cases of harassment.

536. Interviewee #14 said he transferred his money to Switzerland through the black market, at the rate of 87 piastres per US$, when the official rate was 24.

537. Aciman, *Out of Egypt*.

538. Szulc, *The Secret Alliance*, 280–283.

539. The gender component of the remaining Jewish community contributed to the surprise election of Esther Weinstein, the first woman president of the Jewish Community of Cairo (JCC), at an impromptu meeting of the board of the Adly Street synagogue in 1996, when a unanimous motion was passed "allowing women on the board of directors for the first time in the history of the 1,000-year-old community". This event was reported both in *The Egyptian Gazette* by Samir Raafat, August 23, 1996, and in the JCC Newsletter, *Bassatine News*, Vol. 1, Issue 3, September 1996.

After her death in 2004, her daughter Carmen Weinstein became the new JCC president.

540. Israel Ministry of Immigration, *National Statistics*, 2002, indicated a total figure of 37,597 migrants of Egyptian extraction between 1948 and 2001, which represented 47.5 percent of the total Jewish population of Egypt of eighty thousand. Israel received 16,024 migrants between 1948 and 1951, 20,484 between 1952 and 1971, and the last trickle in 1971 and later.

541. According to the *Encyclopaedia Judaica* (Jerusalem: Keter Publishing House, 1971), the figures relating to the distribution of that emigration were, apart from Israel, fifteen thousand in Brazil, ten thousand in France, nine thousand in the United States, nine thousand in Argentina, and four thousand in Great Britain.

542. The exceptionally open immigration policy of Brazil was noted at a meeting of the Australian Jewish Welfare Society (AJWS) in Sydney on May 5, 1957, where it was said: "Egyptian Jews…were not allowed to enter any country except Brazil, who accepted these Jews without question".

543. Ruth Leftel, "A comunidade sefaradita egipcia de Sào Paulo", PhD Thesis, History, University of Sào Paulo, May 1997.

544. See also Joëlle Rouchou, "Nuits d'été au parfum de jasmin: Souvenirs des Juifs d'Égypte à Rio de Janeiro—1956/7", PhD Thesis, University of Sào Paulo, 2003, 83–86.

545. Oral testimonies from Egyptian Jews who migrated to Brazil in 1957.

546. In Egypt, hyperendemic trachoma is the leading cause of preventable blindness. It is one of the oldest infectious diseases known to mankind and was first documented in Egypt as early as the Pharaonic era.

547. Jupp, *Immigration*, 69.

548. Wilton and Bosworth, *Old Worlds and New Australia*, 2.

549. Jupp, in *Immigration*, 48, explained how the dictation test was used to exclude any undesirable while avoiding the mention of race: "the dictation test, which was incorporated in the Commonwealth Act of 1901, was discretionary and could thus be used for anyone…[It] required any intending immigrant to pass a written test, originally in 'any European language.' However, the language did not need to be one understood by the immigrant. The object of the test was entirely to facilitate exclusion rather than to ascertain whether immigrants were literate". For instance, the dictation test was used in 1934 to prevent the Jewish Czech socialist writer, Egon Kisch, from landing in Australia because of his political views. Because he was fluent in several European languages, he was given a test in Sydney in Scottish Gaelic and failed. He appealed and the High Court ruled

that Scottish Gaelic was not a European language and he was able to tour
Australia. His story was featured at the Centenary of Federation Exhibi-
tion, "Belonging: a Century Celebrated", at the State Library of NSW in
Sydney, January 2001. Kisch came to Australia for an anti-war conference
and because of his agenda was prohibited from landing in Melbourne.
The dictation test continued to be implemented whenever it was deemed
necessary until its abolition by the Migration Act of 1958.

550. Rutland, *The Edge of the Diaspora*, 225–256.

551. Ibid., 233.

552. In 1948, Calwell extended that quota to the Jewish refugees arriving by
plane; he limited the intake of Jews from Shanghai in 1947 and introduced
the Iron Curtain Embargo in December 1949, "which effectively excluded
Jews who originated from countries under Soviet rule". See Rutland,
"Subtle Exclusions: Post-War Jewish Emigration to Australia and the
Impact of the IRO", *The Journal of Holocaust Education 10*, no. 1 (Summer 2001): 53 and "Australian Responses to Jewish Refugees Migration
before and after World War II", *Australian Journal of Jewish Studies 5*,
no. 2 (2003).

553. National Archives of Australia A 446, Item 72/077857/72, letter from
T. H. E. Heyes, head of the Immigration Department, January 29, 1949,
236/19/2.

554. National Archives of Australia A 446, Item 72/077857/72, Minute No.
339, October 15, 1951, and letter from H. T. E. Heyes, 51/243, February 22, 1952. See also Series D4878 and D4881. The Alien Registration
documentation had to indicate the race of the applicant and, even more
precisely, whether the applicant was European or coloured.

555. Rutland, *The Edge of the Diaspora*, 242. See also National Archives of
Australia A446, Item 72/077857/72, Consular Circular No. 51, July 26,
1954: "In regard to Jews of Middle East origin, it has been found that a
proportion of them show distinct traces of non-European origin and their
admission is generally restricted to the wives and minor children of residents of Australia. Applications for the admission of this class of person,
whether of British or alien nationality, should be referred, accompanied
by evidence that they are at least of 75% European origin, as in the case of
Eurasians who are not Jews. Signed F. H. Stuart".

556. Interviewee #56 obtained from the National Archives a copy of the particular document related to the application for admission to Australia of
her husband's family, dated September 1954. The question "Are you Jewish?" was still included.

557. The *Sydney Jewish News* of April 27, 1956, reported on the Department of Immigration's response regarding the rejection of applications from Sephardi Jews for admission to Australia. That response was: "If an applicant for admission is of 'mixed race', it is necessary for him to be 75 percent European by descent, European by education, mode of living...[and] predominantly European in appearance".

558. Some of my respondents formed personal friendships with Australian soldiers during that time.

559. Thomas Bruce Millar (ed.), *Australian Foreign Minister: The Diaries of R. G. Casey, 1951–60* (London: Collins, 1972). While in Cairo, Casey (1890–1976) played a key role in the negotiations between the British and Allied governments, local leaders, and the Allied commanders in the field. He was knighted in 1960 and was appointed by Menzies in 1965 as the second Australian-born Governor-General after Sir Isaac Isaacs.

560. Reich, *Australia and Israel*, 93. See also Hudson, *Blind Loyalty*, 29–30, where Hudson pointed out: "From Menzies to the bloke in the corner pub", Australians' reaction to the nationalisation was deeply rooted in racial prejudice with "a special category of contempt...reserved for the Egyptians" based on their experience in the Middle East during World War I.

561. National Archives of Australia ACT A1209/23 Item 57/5736 PT1: copy of official message from the Right Honourable R. G. Menzies, Prime Minister of Australia, to his Excellency Gamal Abdel Nasser, president of the Republic of Egypt.

562. Hudson, *Blind Loyalty*, 75.

563. Reich, *Australia and Israel*, 86, 60.

564. National Archives of Australia Series A1838/283 Item 780/6/3 PT1, file 780/6, Subject: United Kingdom and Australian Interests in the Suez Canal, 2: "Any weakening of the United Kingdom economy as a result of the closure of the Suez Canal is a matter of serious concern for Australia, for the United Kingdom is by far Australia's best customer for her exports".

565. Hudson, *Blind Loyalty*, 82.

566. National Archives of Australia A1838/396, Item 1500/2/15/5, Memo External Affairs Dept. 7/11/56.

567. Upon arrival of some two hundred Egyptian Jews in Sydney, the *Jewish News*, November 30, 1956, Vol. XVIII, No. 13, 1, displayed on its front page a large title, "Egypt throws out Jews", denouncing vigorously the arrests, sequestrations, and various types of harassment the Jews had been

subjected to after the 1956 Suez War; on December 7, 1956, more head-
lines appeared in the same paper: "Help Needed for Egyptian Jews", 2,
and "Egyptian Jewry: PM Asked to Get UN help", Vol. XVIII, No. 14, 3;
on March 1, 1957, "Egypt's Jew Baiting", No. 26, 9; on March 15, 1957,
"Egypt Destroyed Jewish Community", No. 28, 3; on October 18, 1957,
"Quiet Despoliation of Egyptian Jewry", Vol. XIX, No. 4, 1. The arrival
of Alec Golliger, with his wife and three daughters—one of them was my
friend Lana Woolf, with whom I started this project—was reported in the
Sun-Herald, March 31, 1957: "A broken-hearted family, victims of Colonel Nasser, arrived in Sydney last night by air".

568. National Archives of Australia A1838/278 Item 175/11/20/15 PT2. Cable-
gram from Australian Embassy in Washington to Department of External
Affairs, 7 December, I.17255, expressing the United States' concern that
"intimidation of various kinds may be being exercised against Jews generally to induce them to leave Egypt and leave property behind".

569. National Archives of Australia A1838/2, Item 1531/115 PT1; Foreign Circular No. 118 (local); Foreign Circular No. 57 (overseas). This circular
instructed immigration officers to grant special consideration to applications by residents or former residents of Egypt "who have been or [were]
about to be forced to leave Egypt as a direct or indirect result of the crisis
there which began at the end of October 1956".

570. Sydney David Einfeld, born in Sydney in 1909, was a leading figure in
both the Jewish and non-Jewish communities. He became president of
the AJWS in 1952 and remained in that position for twenty-five years. He
also alternated as president of the ECAJ with Maurice Ashkenasy from
Melbourne from 1952 to 1968. He was a long-time leader of the NSW
Jewish Board of Deputies. In addition, he was very active in the Australian Labor Party (ALP), representing the electorate of Bondi in the NSW
State Parliament (1965–1971). See Rutland, "The Hon. Sydney David
Einfeld, AO: Builder of Australian Jewry", *AJHS Journal*, Vol IX (July
1991): 312–331.

571. Patrick Galvin (1911–1980) represented this seat in Federal Parliament
from 1951 to 1966.

572. National Archives of Australia A1209/23 Item 57/5736 PT1, PM's file
56/1095, A161 Sydney Sub 166 4–37P: copy of a telegram sent by the
president of ECAJ, Sydney D. Einfeld, to the prime minister, Canberra.
See also in same file, A15 Preston Vic 107 9–40A, copy of a telegram sent
at the same time by Joseph Morello, president of the Maltese community

in Australia, to the prime minister, asking for help in saving "the lives of our unfortunate relatives now in Egypt".

573. National Archives of Australia A1209/23 Item 57/5736 PT1, Prime Minister's Department, 56/1095.

574. Minutes of AJWS Council Meetings, November 19, 1956; January 16, 1957; March 3, 1957; May 5, 1957; June 30, 1958; October 10, 1958; December 1, 1958; May 1, 1959; July 30, 1959; November 11, 1960; February 2, 1962; and September 13, 1962.

575. As noted by Rutland in "Egyptian Jews in Adelaide", this type of information—highly confidential at the time, as well as potentially embarrassing—cannot be found in government archives. It is only revealed through "oral history". Aaron confirmed this occurrence when he granted me an interview in 1999. He stated that he even met with Harold Holt, Minister for Immigration from 1949 to 1956—"really a good man"—and he asked him point-blank, "Am I black?"

576. Letter from T. H. E. Heyes, Secretary to Syd Einfeld, Department of Immigration, December 14, 1956, concerning the plight of Egyptian Jews.

577. Minutes, SA Jewish Board of Deputies, December 20, 1956.

578. Letter from Patrick Galvin, MHR, ALP, Kingston, South Australia, to Dr. E. A. Matison, President of the Board, January 16, 1957, in the South Australian Jewish Board of Deputies, correspondence file, with copy of his telegram to Prime Minister R. G. Menzies, December 21, 1956. Between 1963 and 1969, Leonard Bosman, Liberal MP for St. George District, NSW, supported some of his Jewish/Egyptian constituents in their efforts to obtain permission for their relatives still in Egypt or in transit in Europe to be admitted into Australia. Through chain migration and family reunion, some thirty to forty Jewish families from Egypt had settled from the early 1950s in the St. George area of Hurstville, Peakhurst, Beverly Hills, and Penshurst, NSW.

579. Rutland, "Egyptian Jews in Adelaide", 21.

580. Letter from A. Townley to P. Galvin, January 29, 1957. Galvin subsequently forwarded a copy of this letter to Dr. Matison, Head of the SA Jewish Board of Deputies Sub-Committee, constituted to deal with the plight of Egyptian Jews at the public meeting of December 20. 1956.

581. Letter dated April 16, 1958, from the Department of Immigration, Ref. 1158/11844.

582. Letter from Tasman (later Sir) H. E. Heyes, Secretary, Department of Immigration, to S. D. Einfeld, President of the Australian Jewish Welfare

Society, December 14, 1956, SA Jewish Board of Deputies, correspondence file.

583. Letter from P. Galvin to Dr. Matison, SA Jewish Board of Deputies, correspondence file, January 31, 1957: "I am continuing to press for a more liberal intake from Egypt and should I receive further information in this matter it will be forwarded to you".

584. Letter from Athol Townley to P. Galvin, March 27, 1957, SA Jewish Board of Deputies, correspondence file re "plight of persons in Egypt". I have already pointed out that, as a general rule, nationals from Southern Europe and other Mediterranean countries could only come to Australia if they were dependents of relatives, fiancés of residents, or single women aged eighteen to thirty-five.

585. The Australian government was well aware of the ill-treatment of Egyptian and stateless Jews—as well as British and French nationals—by Egyptian authorities as stated in Australian National Archives A1838/278, Item 175/11/20/15 PT 2, Inward Savingram I.17781, from the Australian Embassy in Washington to the Department of External Affairs in Canberra, dated December 12, 1956, A1838/283, Item 854/10/13/4/4, Savingram I. 1188 dated January 17, 1957, and text of Commonwealth Relations Office telegram No. 760, dated December 22, 1956.

586. Françoise Perret, "ICRC Operations in Hungary and the Middle East in 1956", *International Review of the Red Cross* (31/08/1996): 313, 412–437. The Red Cross chartered fourteen vessels from January to September 1957, which transported 7,910 stateless Jews to Piraeus and Naples.

587. Laskier, in "Egyptian Jewry under the Nasser Regime, 1956–70", *Middle Eastern Studies 31*, no. 3 (July 1995): 589, confirmed that "France, more than other countries of transit, supported stateless refugees. Holders of foreign passports, however, received assistance from AJDC-financed French-Jewish agencies which in January 1958 provided cash relief to 1,400 persons".

588. Ibid., 589: "between 23,000 and 25,000 Jews are estimated to have left Egypt from November 1956 to the end of 1957. These included at least 6,000 stateless persons" and while "the Jewish Agency directed the emigration to Israel…the United HIAS Service…took care of immigration to Latin America, the United States, Canada, Australia, and other regions".

589. It was probably the Spanish and Portuguese Sephardi synagogue of Holland Park, although the interviewee could not remember precisely.

590. Source quoted by Laskier in *The Jews of Egypt*, 273: AJDC, Jerusalem, 308B–309A/80; data published February 14, 1964, by UHS Research and Statistics Department.
591. COJASOR was partly funded by AJDC. It was started in 1945 and helped in the settlement of Jewish refugees in France.
592. Some of the French and British nationals who were expelled and given twenty-four hours in which to leave the country claimed that they were only allowed one suitcase per person.
593. Leaving their homes with only what they could carry has been a common pattern in the long history of forced displacement experienced by Jews throughout the ages. In the 1930s, during the early stages of Hitler's persecution of German Jews, when they were still allowed to leave the country, they were restricted to taking only their clothes and very few personal valuables. The 1956 Hungarian refugees escaped with very little of their personal belongings. Even the South African Jewish émigrés of the 1980s and 1990s, who did not leave South Africa under such duress, were faced with restrictions regarding the transfer of their financial assets.
594. The Lloyd Triestino ships were SS *Australia*, SS *Oceania*, and SS *Neptunia*; the Flotta Lauro's ships were SS *Roma* and SS *Sydney*.
595. The French passenger line, Messageries Maritimes, offered more or less the same service from Marseilles.
596. Interviewee #25 related that he travelled with his family on the SS *Oceania* in what he called "the bottom class", in segregated cabins of six or eight, and the ship was full of Italian migrants. Their voyage took six and a half weeks via the Cape, as the Suez Canal was still blocked.
597. Interviewee #91 related that he had been in constant correspondence with his friends who were still in Egypt, trying to convince them to follow him. A number of my Adelaide interviewees confirmed that his enthusiastic letters about Australia and Australians were read aloud by all his friends in Cairo.
598. Copy of Elie Ovadia's eulogy delivered on February 22, 1999, was provided by his son Charles. Ovadia's name has been engraved on the Welcome Wall, a monument built next to the National Maritime Museum at Darling Harbour, Sydney, to honour the achievements of more than six million migrants who have chosen to make Australia their home.
599. Those respondents did not indicate whether they benefited from the UK Assisted Passage Scheme, instituted in 1947, offering passages to Australia for £10 per adult and £5 for children aged fourteen to eighteen. According to Reginald Thomas Appleyard in *The Ten Pound Immigrants*

(London: Boxtree, 1988), 43, this scheme was followed in 1957 by the "Bring Out a Briton" campaign, with the result that between 1961/62 and 1971/72, only 10 percent of British migrants were unassisted.

600. This respondent landed in Perth in 1947. He lived there for four years in 1947 before moving to Melbourne. The Maltese, another group of British subjects residing in Egypt, were allowed to enter Australia with the minimum of formalities provided they complied with the usual conditions applicable to all British subjects. Eight thousand Egyptian-born Maltese arrived in Melbourne in 1956 after being expelled from Egypt in the wake of the Suez War.

601. As indicated previously, this particular respondent, Mayer Harari, published his autobiography, *Second Exodus* in 1999, as part of the "Write Your Story" Jewish communal project.

602. The Huckstep Camp, situated about fourteen kilometres from Cairo, was an old American military camp with buildings and hangars. For living conditions in the various prisons where Jews were incarcerated in the wake of 1948 War, see the testimony of Professor Arie Schlosberg, "The Internment Camps in Egypt" given at the 1998 Conference of Hagana members, Prisoners of Zion, youth movements, and Aliya Activists in Egypt, as part of the celebration of Israel's 50th Jubilee.

603. This respondent related the circumstances in which both an uncle and a cousin were arrested because of the fortuitous nature of their occupations. The uncle, who worked in the Archives Department of a private company, was accused of burning secret documents. The cousin, who was employed by the *Crédit Foncier Égyptien* and was responsible for the valuations of mortgaged properties, was suspected of spying because of the maps found in his possession.

604. In her doctoral thesis, "The History of Australian Jewry 1945–1960", Vol. I, 63–64, Rutland commented on the "severe shipping shortage which existed after the war", as well as the restrictive official policy of reserving space on British ships "for returning Australians; wives, families, and fiancés of ex-servicemen; and for British migrants".

605. See Rutland's comments on the "hell ships" in "Post-War Jewish 'Boat People' and Parallels with the Tampa Incident", *Australian Journal of Jewish Studies XVI* (2002): 159–176; Panich, in *Sanctuary*, 22–32, also evoked the experiences of postwar refugees seeking a new life in Australia; journalist and writer Diane Armstrong, in *The Voyage of their Life* (Sydney: Flamingo), 2001, has researched the individual stories of Jewish and other refugees who travelled to Australia on the SS *Derna* in 1948.

606. Panich, *Sanctuary*,15; Nojna Peters in *Milk and Honey but No Gold: Post-War Migration to Western Australia, 1945–1964* (Nedlands: University of Western Australia, 2001), 5–6, pointed to "the propaganda posters depicting Australia as a bountiful country of booming industry, full employment" and to "the films, pamphlets, and information evenings at Australian immigrations offices around Europe" where "Australia was portrayed as a plentiful land—a land of milk and honey—with trees laden with succulent fruits and gold nuggets on the streets just waiting to be picked up". See also Sluga, *Bonegilla*, 6, referring to a pamphlet titled "Glück in der Neuen Heimat," (Happy in Your New Homeland), published and distributed amongst prospective migrants by the Australian Department of Immigration in 1948, romanticising "much like the newspaper stories of the time…this 'new life' with pictures of lovers wandering through sunset-lit landscapes".

607. Interviewee #35 arrived in Adelaide in 1948 with her husband, a British national who had been wrongly arrested in 1948 and expelled because he bore the same name as a Zionist suspect. Her in-laws had consulted a book on Australia and, based on what they read, picked Adelaide as a suitable place of settlement. The young couple was sent ahead to pave the way for the rest of the family and was very disappointed with the living conditions in that city in the early years. Although my respondent is now happy to be living in Australia, in hindsight she would never have chosen to settle in Adelaide because it was too isolated.

608. He recalled his first meeting with the person in charge of the Industrial Development Department. The latter arranged for him to meet almost immediately with the premier of South Australia, who helped him set up a textile manufacturing industry. At the time, the Liberal premier was Sir Thomas Playford, who was in office for a record twenty-seven years, from 1938 to 1965. He was known for his achievements in developing South Australia's manufacturing industry. In the 2002 Sir Thomas Playford Memorial Lecture, the Liberal politician Tony Abbott—now leader of the Opposition under Julia Gillard's Labor government—recalled that "when he [Playford] assumed office, South Australia's population was barely half a million and its economy was almost exclusively agricultural. By the time he retired, the population had more than doubled and Adelaide rivalled Melbourne, as the great manufacturing city of Australia".

609. Turnbull, in *Safe Haven*, 34, spoke of "several thousand Sephardi Jews, most of them Egyptians expelled in the aftermath of the Arab-Israeli

conflict, [who] managed to migrate to Australia in the 1950s". However I have not been able to verify this number in official censuses.

610. Rubinstein, *The Jews in Australia*, 80, claimed that "the Hungarian Jews accounted for the bulk of the nearly 3800 Jewish migrants known to the Welfare society who came in 1957–58, with 1619 arriving from Hungary in 1957. Most settled in Sydney rather than Melbourne...In 1961, there were 2,055 Hungarian-born Jews in New South Wales, but only 1,029 in Victoria, according to the (optional) religious statistics of the Census. Even in 1981 these state figures were, respectively, 1,638 and 823". However Rutland, in *The Edge of the Diaspora*, 243, quoted Syd Einfeld who had assisted in the selection of Hungarian Jews, estimating that by December 1957, "1,000 of the 5,000 Hungarian escapees admitted to Australia were Jewish".

611. Rabbi Israel Porush, "The 1971 Census: Interesting Data Concerning Jews", *AJHS Journal VIII*, 1975, Part 1, 15.

612. Charles Price, in *Jewish Settlers in Australia*, Canberra: Australian National University, 1964, 6–8, discussed the very issue of why some Jews would choose not to answer the census question on religious affiliation, as posited by Rabbi Dr. Israel Porush in his article "Some Statistical Data on Australian Jewry", *AJHS Journal IV*, 1953. He argued that a number of Jewish refugees from Nazi Europe had been so persecuted because of their origin that, even when safe in Australia, some would be reluctant to write the word "Jew" or "Hebrew" on any official document. The same could be said of Egyptian refugees.

613. See chart 11: Reasons for migration according to date of arrival.

614. From the annual report of the Australian Jewish Welfare Society for the year ended April 30, 1957, 4: "Although quite a number [of Jews from Egypt] have already arrived in Australia there are serious delays in the issuing of Permits to many who are at present residing in Italy or other countries".

615. See letter from AJWS to NSW Association of Sephardim, July 8, 1957.

616. The oldest respondent among those who migrated prior to 1955 was forty-four when he landed in Australia.

617. Forty-six percent were aged between eighteen and twenty-seven, and 39 percent were between twenty-eight and forty-four, compared to 57 percent and 31 percent respectively in the earlier contingent.

618. Rutland also reported the contradiction between official figures and the perceptions of her interviewees in her article "Egyptian Jews in Adelaide", 24. See also Hyams, whose research into the history of Adelaide's Jewish

community confirmed the obvious gaps in the census figures, presented in *Surviving*, 102.

619. In May 1984, Rutland interviewed Mrs. Franziska Berman, wife of Reverend Abram Berman (1891–1982) who served as second minister and *shochet* (ritual slaughterer) of the AHC from 1944 until his retirement in 1977.

620. An Egyptian Jew, resident of Adelaide, confirmed Franziska Berman's claim to Rutland. Unfortunately, he passed away before I could personally interview him.

621. All my Adelaide interviewees remembered the Bermans' hospitality and the warmth towards the refugees from Egypt. However, the claim that Reverend Berman had helped with such a large number of landing permits seems to have been largely unknown. I encountered the brother of one of the individuals named by Mrs. Berman, who denied outright that Reverend Berman had been instrumental in procuring landing permits for his family. This is the nature of oral history, when individual memories are often contradictory. It is possible that Reverend Berman's influence might have been more general than specific, or that the brother might not have been aware of the Reverend's background work in this respect.

622. Apart from this particular testimony, another two respondents, #35 and #36, had the same recollection of all the friends getting together in Cairo when those letters arrived, to find out as much as possible about life in Australia.

623. Liberman eventually became a giant of the building industry in South Australia. He built satellite towns in Adelaide, Perth, and Sydney and was chairman of the South Australia Housing Trust from 1975 to 1980. He was awarded the medal of Officer of the Order of Australia for services to the building industry (AO) in 1986. In 1992, the SA State government convinced him to come out of retirement to head a large inner-city development in Adelaide, called Garden East, which turned out to be very successful.

624. The phenomenon of chain migration was very aptly defined by Price, in *Jewish Settlers in Australia*, 21, as "the process whereby one member of a family, village, or township successfully establishes himself abroad and then writes to one or two friends and relatives at home encouraging them to come and join him, frequently helping with housing, jobs, and passage expenses. The few who join him then write home in their turn, so setting off a 'chain' system of migration that may send hundreds of persons from one small district of origin to one relatively confined area in the country

of settlement". This was indeed the scenario of the migration of Egyptian Jews to Adelaide.

625. The reasons for that reputation are that most trips are not supposed to take more than twenty minutes, regardless of traffic conditions, and one can walk from one side of the city centre to the other in twenty minutes.

626. Graeme Hugo, "Regional Migration: A New Paradigm of International Migration", *Research Paper* no. 10, *Research Note* no. 56, Parliamentary Library (2003–2004), 2.

627. In the late 1970s and 1980s, Liberman stated that his building company worked in partnership with immigration authorities on the basis of regionally sponsored migration schemes, offering a housing package to prospective British migrants to Adelaide. They would commit to selling the prospective migrants' house in England and provide them with a newly built one in Adelaide. This project was also replicated in Melbourne, Sydney, and Perth. My respondent spoke of about twelve thousand families who migrated to Australia thanks to this plan.

628. Only 9.8 percent of the Sydney group came before 1956, whereas 46 percent of the Melbourne group came pre-1956. However, in view of the small proportion of Melburnians in the whole sample—23 percent—it is difficult to draw a definitive conclusion on that issue. Then again, as previously stated, the higher percentage of Sydney settlers—45 percent—can be partly attributed to the fact that, logistically, being based in Sydney I had a more continuous access to the Sydney component of my sample.

629. As previously mentioned, about forty to fifty Jewish families who, through chain migration, migrated from Egypt to Australia from 1952 on, settled within a few kilometres of one another in the southern suburbs of Sydney, such as Beverly Hills, Bexley, Hurstville, Penshurst, and Peakhurst, where Jewish presence was minimal. At the time, the nearest established Jewish community was the Strathfield community. Later, two more synagogues were established in Bankstown and Allawah.

630. Rutland, "The History of Australian Jewry", 104. Regarding government hostels, see Panich, *Sanctuary*, and Sluga, *Bonegilla*. The first migrants arrived at the Bonegilla Migrant Reception Centre in the Wodonga district in 1947. They were mostly war refugees (DPs). They had come to Australia under the Commonwealth's Post-War Migration Scheme. In return for free or assisted passage to Australia, the new migrants were contracted for two years of labour wherever the Australian government chose to send them. Bonegilla was the largest migrant camp in Australia and was closed in December 1971 after 320,000 people had passed through its gates.

631. Interviewee #7 was twenty-one when he was expelled from Egypt in 1958, and he spent ten years in Israel. In Australia, he first worked as a cleaner before going into the wool business, where he succeeded very well.

632. Interviewee #15 had her own factory for many years, until her daughter grew up, joined her, and expanded the business further into maternity wear.

633. Interviewees #22 and #69.

634. Naomi Rosh White, *From Darkness to Light: Surviving the Holocaust* (Melbourne: Collins Dove, 1988), 171. White is an Australian sociologist who has written on migrants and women. She is herself the daughter of Holocaust survivors. *From Darkness to Light* explores the lives of eleven Holocaust survivors, five women and six men, through their own recollections of their experiences interspersed with historical records.

635. The working conditions of women in general, and particularly migrant women of non-English speaking background (NESB) in post-war Australia, have been the subjects of numerous studies. See B. A. Mitsztal, "Migrant Women in Australia", *Journal of Intercultural Studies 12*, no. 2 (1991): 15–34; M. D. Evans, "Immigrant Women in Australia: Resources, Family and Work", *International Migration Review 18* (Winter 1984): 1063–1090.

636. The Egyptian-born Brazilian researcher Joëlle Rouchou stated in her doctoral thesis on the migration of Egyptian Jews to Brazil that, according to the Vice President of the HIAS committee in charge of Egyptian refugees in Brazil, their integration was one of the smoothest: "Pernidji prit une part active dans plusieurs cas d'immigration, et raconta que celle-ci avait été l'assimilation la plus facile et qu'ils trouvèrent du travail très rapidement" (115).

637. Zvi Gitelman, in his article "The Decline of the Diaspora Jewish Nation: Boundaries, Content, and Jewish Identity", *Jewish Social Studies 4*, no. 2 (January 31, 1998): 112–122, noted that "observers of American Jewry are fond of saying that, today, all Jews are Jews by choice"; Stephen J. Whitfield, in "Enigmas of Modern Jewish Identity", *Jewish Social Studies 8*, no. 2/3 (Winter/Spring 2002): 164–171, stated that "in the twentieth century in particular, the history of the Jews can be recounted in terms of the erosion of a stable identity, so that eventually all of them would be described as Jews by choice…"; see also Samuel C. Heilman, *Cosmopolitans and Parochials* (Chicago: Chicago University Press, 1989).

638. Stuart Z. Charme, "Varieties of Authenticity in Contemporary Jewish Identity", *Jewish Social Studies 6*, no. 2, (January 2000): 136.

639. Samuel C. Heilman, "Inner and Outer Identities: Sociological Ambivalence among Orthodox Jews", *Jewish Social Studies 39*, no. 3 (1977): 227–241.

640. *Galuth* is a Hebrew word for exile. A *Galuth* Jew would be a Jew living in the Diaspora.

641. Chanan Reich, "Ethnic Identity and Political Participation: The Jewish and Greek Communities in Melbourne", PhD Thesis, Department of Politics, Monash University, Melbourne, 1983, 88.

642. Panich, *Sanctuary*, 172.

643. Geoffrey Brahm Levey, "Jews and Australian Multiculturalism", in Geoffrey Brahm Levey and Philip Mendes (eds), *Jews and Australian Politics* (Brighton and Portland: Sussex Academic Press, 2004), 182–184. Levey is Senior Lecturer in Politics and International Relations, and Coordinator of the Program of Jewish Studies, at the University of New South Wales, Sydney.

644. Panich, *Sanctuary*, 171.

645. In that respect, Levey, in "Jews and Australian Multiculturalism", 182, pointed out that "even the most secular Jews strongly self-identify as Jews and with Jewish peoplehood".

646. Heilman, "Inner and Outer Identities", *Jewish Social Studies,* 227.

647. Interviewee #54: "le fait d'être juive est très important pour moi. C'est une chose que je ne peux pas jeter, je ne peux pas nier. Je suis ce que je suis, le produit d'une famille juive qui était traditionelle mais pas religieuse".

648. Interviewee #21 stated: "I am a cultural Jew but nationally I am an Australian. I owe Australia everything I have".

649. Interviewee #89 had been considering emigration since 1953 and finally made it to Australia one month before the eruption of the Suez War in 1956.

650. This stratagem did not always work in his favour. He recalled the time of his graduation when all the students received their diplomas accompanied by signed pictures of King Faruk, except for him. When he queried what he thought was an oversight, he was reminded in a very subtle way that he was not really an Egyptian given that his middle name was Jewish.

651. Erving Goffman, *The Presentation of Self in Everyday Life* (Edinburgh: University of Edinburgh, 1956), Monograph No. 2, 23.

652. Levey, "Jews and Australian Multiculturalism", 187–188.

653. A typical example of that debate can be found in the preamble to the HSJE, based in New York, where it is stated that this organisation shall be known as such, "and not of Egypt or of Egyptian Jews, but FROM

EGYPT, for the purpose will be to include all our co-religionists whose lineage have sojourned in the Jewish Communities of Egypt..." In the course of this study, for the sake of simplicity, I designated them as "Egyptian Jews", although strictly speaking, this label only applied to the small proportion of my respondents who had obtained Egyptian nationality.

654. In spite of his definition of himself as Australian, this respondent recognised that multiple identities were part of the makeup of Egyptian Jews, himself included. His father was an Ottoman subject from Salonika. He remembered how baffled the Australian Immigration Officer was, in 1953, when he landed in Australia and presented his stateless *laissez-passer*; then his wife presented her British passport—her family being originally from Gibraltar; then his mother, originally from Syria, presented her French passport. The officer, puzzled, asked how they were all related and, even when the respondent tried to explain these anomalies, he still could not comprehend the whole picture.

655. Levey, "Jews and Australian Multiculturalism", 181.

656. Interviewee #31 described her immediate reaction to Australia as one of "love at first sight". It was interesting to note that—in spite of her declaration of being totally alienated from her Jewishness—she must have felt it still had some relevance to her because she initiated the contact with me, thus participating through her testimony in a project on the Jews of Egypt.

657. Interviewee #87 had an Ashkenazi father who had been raised by an Italian Jewish family and a Greek Orthodox mother who converted to Judaism. At home, they spoke about seven languages.

658. One is unwittingly reminded of the Sephardi Jews who lived in Turkey for five hundred years after their expulsion from Spain and still maintained the daily use of Ladino.

659. Interviewee #91: "Je me sens juif parce que je suis né juif et ensuite je suis australien, comme si j'étais né ici".

660. It is not surprising that this respondent, who was educated in British schools in Egypt and spoke English fluently, felt immediately at home in Australia.

661. This interviewee, as one of the earliest arrivals in 1949, still maintained that in spite of their insularity, "the Australians were very nice, kind and hospitable".

662. This respondent and his family had initially settled in the southern suburbs of Sydney, a traditional Australian area, which included a number of Italian migrants from Sicily and Calabria. Wog is a derogatory racist

term used in Australian slang to designate a migrant of Southern Mediterranean or Middle Eastern extraction. It was commonly used after the
postwar waves of migration. Today it has lost most of its sting as it has
been appropriated by the groups targeted to broadcast their non-Anglo
Australian ethnic identity.

663. The ingrained bias against foreign languages transcended the fact that
French was the most preferred second language taught in high schools at
the time.

664. On October 15, 2004, Maurice Mizrahi, a Cairo-born Jew who migrated
to the United States as a refugee in 1967, gave a talk at his local synagogue titled "Growing up under Pharaoh", where he spoke about the
baffling nature of Egyptian Jews' identities. He described his family as a
"linguistic and cultural zoo": "My native language is French. I was educated in French, then in Italian, then in both French and Arabic. These
switches were all forced on me by the political winds. My brother was
educated in French and then in Arabic. My sisters were educated in English. My father's native language was Ladino—Judeo-Spanish—and he
was educated in Italian. My mother's native language was Arabic, and
she was educated in French. Her family hailed from Syria and Lebanon.
My grandfather was from the island of Rhodes and my grandmother from
Salonika, Greece, where Greek was spoken. My great-grandfather, Rabbi
Yomtob Mizrahi, was from Smyrna, Turkey, where he built a synagogue
and spoke Turkish. And, of course, everybody went to services at the synagogue and prayed in Hebrew!" Although this example of multilingualism
and multiculturalism might sound hyperbolic, Maurice Mizrahi assured
me that it definitely reflected the reality of his background, and I have no
problem believing it, given that multilingual skills were unquestionably a
dominant feature of the case studies that form the core of my research.

665. This respondent arrived in Australia in 1951 as an eight-year-old, born of
Ashkenazi parents. The family first settled in Melbourne then moved to
Sydney where they socialised with a large group of Jews from Egypt. She
married an Egyptian-born Sephardi Jew. Since she first became involved
with the JNF at the age of sixteen, she has been consistently active in the
Jewish community. She is a past president of the NSW National Council
of Jewish Women of Australia (NCJWA).

666. See Rutland, *The Jews in Australia*, 134: "According to the 2001 Census,
10,473 Jews had been born in South Africa but, allowing for under-count-
ing of 20 percent, the number is likely to be closer to 14,000 to 15,000".

667. Gitelman, "The Decline of the Diaspora", 114.

668. Krämer, *The Jews in Modern Egypt*, 69.

669. Gale, "Sephardim and Sephardi Identity", 338.

670. Gale, in "Sephardim and Sephardi Identity", 334, stated that in 1987, out of a Sephardi population of approximately three thousand, 740 were affiliated to the two Sephardi congregations, while the rest were either members of Ashkenazi congregations or did not belong to any synagogue.

671. See Aaron, *The Sephardim of Australia and New Zealand*, list of foundation members, 79; list of Executive Members of the Board, 100–101; profile of Albert Hassid, who joined the NSW Association of Sephardim upon arrival in Australia from Cairo in 1952 and was closely involved in the negotiations related to the building of the Sephardi synagogue. He represented the Association on the NSW Jewish Board of Deputies. He was also invited to serve on the ECAJ in the matter of Jews in Arab countries, 230.

672. See Samra, "Yisrael Rhammana". See also Gale, "From the Homeland to Sydney".. This thesis has since been published under the title: *The Sephardim of Sydney: Coping with Political Processes and Social Pressures* (Sussex: Sussex Academic Press, May 2005).

673. Samra, "Yisrael Rhammana", 87.

674. Ibid.""", 180.

675. Gale, in "Sephardim and Sephardi Identity", 338, also pointed out the more relaxed religious observance of the Egyptians compared to the Iraqis: "In contrast to the Egyptian Jews, Iraqi Jews adhered strictly to their religion".

676. Two Sydney interviewees (#25 and #26), who had worked tirelessly for many years in every capacity for the Sephardi synagogue and served on the Board of Management of the Association, became disillusioned when they encountered opposition from the Rabbi at the time in regard to the bat-mitzvah of their daughter. They also found that the Indian group was becoming more and more "vociferous and wanted everything their way". When the congregation was left without a rabbi for a certain period of time, they decided to join the membership of the Great Synagogue.

677. Samra, "Yisrael Rhammana", 180.

678. Gale, "Sephardim and Sephardi Identity", 338.

679. Due to the declining Jewish population in that area of Sydney, this synagogue is now part of the southern Sydney synagogue, which also incorporates Bankstown synagogue and South Coast Hebrew congregation.

680. This information was relayed to me by an interviewee who was a member of the Sephardi synagogue for twenty years before deciding to leave the congregation.

681. Aaron, *The Sephardim of Australia and New Zealand*, 33–35.

682. Gad, Ben-Meir, "The Sephardim of Australia", *AJHS Journal XI*, Part 1 (1990): 29. See also, Fiona Kaufman, "The Sephardi Voice: The Sephardi Community of Victoria 1800–1984, A Study", Honours Thesis, 1984, University of Melbourne, Department of Middle Eastern Studies.

683. The vice president of the Sephardi Association of Victoria recalled that Maurice Gamil, without formal religious training, "spent many long hours at home, reciting the prayers with the very unique Sephardi tunes that he had grown up with and wanted to pass on to the next generation". This was part of an article "Reward for work" published in the district newspaper, *The Moorabbin Leader*, on February 12, 2002, 25. Maurice Gamil died in 2006, four years after our interview.

684. This interviewee was expelled from Egypt in 1956 as a French national and arrived in Australia in 1958 after spending two years in France, waiting for a landing permit. As one of the few truly observant respondents, she became affiliated to the Great Synagogue of Sydney where she had her first contacts with the Anglo-Jewish community. She worked for twenty-one years in Jewish education and was the headmistress of the Great Synagogue Sunday School.

685. Gale, "From the Homeland to Sydney", 162. Gale acknowledged that two prominent community leaders, A. Landa and S. Einfeld, did help Sephardim referred to them through friends.

686. Gale also mentioned the case of one Egyptian Jew who, upon arrival in Australia, was met by a Jewish representative on board the ship and asked to prove her Jewish identity by speaking Yiddish. This attitude is reminiscent of the Anglo/Jewish establishment's negative reactions to the European refugees who arrived in Australia immediately before World War II. See Rutland, *The Edge of the Diaspora*, 184–188.

687. One of those respondents claimed that, after being treated in that way, she distanced herself completely from the Jewish community.

688. Gale, "Sephardim and Sephardi Identity", 344.

689. Rabbi J. Kahn confirmed that resentment was expressed by the European Jews towards their fellow Jews from Egypt in respect to their use of French.

690. Aaron, *The Sephardim of Australia and New Zealand*, 20.

691. At the time of the interview, Albert Ninio had been living in Melbourne for a number of years. He died a few months after our meeting. A very warm tribute was paid to him by the former chief minister of the AHC, Rabbi Philip Heilbrunn, praising his involvement in all aspects of Jewish life in Adelaide.

692. J. Bolaffi was also a supporter of a number of Jewish organisations such as of JNF, WIZO, B'nai B'rith, and the Maccabi Sports Club.

693. Samra, "Yisrael Rhammana", 247.

694. Rutland, *The Edge of the Diaspora*, 358–359.

695. Talia Clara Seidman, who stated "In every generation, it is one's duty to regard himself as though he personally had gone out of Egypt (Haggadah)", received the Dr. Hans Kimmel Memorial Prize for Jewish History, Moriah College, Sydney, Year 10, September 2003, 52 and 54.

696. This gentleman was orphaned at an early age and raised by a non-Jewish family. In Egypt, he was very aware of the danger that any sign of support for Israel represented.

697. Interviewee #24 was imprisoned and later expelled for being a member of a Zionist youth movement, and the same for Interviewee #46, who was accused of being a communist.

698. Interviewee #7 was never involved in Zionist activities in Egypt but was nevertheless expelled in the wake of the Suez War in 1956. He suspected that it was an excuse for sequestering his father's business. AJDC arranged for his resettlement in Israel, where he remained for ten years before immigrating to Australia. He is now very involved with the Sephardi synagogue in Melbourne.

699. It was only when this respondent left Egypt and migrated to Australia that he felt free to express his support of Israel. Two of his children, who are now married to Jewish partners, were staunch supporters of *Betar*, the right-wing Zionist youth movement.

700. Interviewee #62 lived in Israel for a few years before coming to Australia to join his mother and sister. He had originally made *aliyah* from Egypt as part of Operation Passover—mentioned earlier—immediately after World War II.

701. Interviewee #61 arrived in Adelaide in 1949 to join her future husband who had migrated earlier. Their beginnings were hard due to the difficult post-war conditions.

702. Interviewee #72 conceded that Israel represented an element of security for Diaspora Jews, although personally he would not choose to live there because of cultural differences.

703. Interviewee #9 was also of the opinion that if Jews were threatened in a country like Australia, they would be doubly threatened in a country like Israel because of its strategic and geographical location in a troubled and unstable part of the world.
704. In January 2006, Herman Eisenberg was appointed a Member of the Order of Australia (AM) for his service to the community at the Great Synagogue of Sydney, as well as the Wesley Mission and Rotary International. See *Australian Jewish News*, "From Nothing to Something", January 27, 2006, 6. (Appendix #4).
705. Levey, "Jews and Australian Multiculturalism", 93.
706. Reich, "Ethnic Identity and Political Participation", 277.
707. This student, who did not wish to be named, was awarded first prize at the Hans Kimmel Essay Competition for her entry in 2001.
708. Talia Seidman's essay also won first prize in 2003.
709. Three families of respondents moved to the eastern suburbs of Sydney, a traditional Jewish area, after more than fifteen years in the St. George area of Sydney, in order for their children to socialise with other Jewish children.
710. Alec Golliger (#37), now deceased, entertained the residents of the Montefiore Home for many years, playing their favourite tunes on the piano. Interviewee #72 is the editor of the quarterly magazine of Jewish Care, *Keeping in Touch*. Interviewee #1K acted as Arabic translator for the NSW Jewish Boards of Deputies on numerous occasions.
711. One particular respondent (#6) worked for over ten years as a volunteer for Meals on Wheels, delivering meals to the old and underprivileged. Interviewee #56 was a volunteer at the 2000 Sydney Olympic Games. She worked at the International Broadcast Centre because of her multilingual skills.
712. Egyptian Jews are not so different from the majority of Australian Jews in that respect. As noted by Rutland in *The Jews in Australia*, 97, "most Australian Jews can best be described as non-practising orthodox…[They] define themselves as Jewish but not religious, and observe some rituals".
713. Forty-five percent of the participants admitted that most of their friends were Jews from Egypt, whereas 40 percent declared they mixed with both Egyptian and Australian Jews. It was not surprising to find that the level of socialisation of the older members of the group—over the age of twenty-eight upon arrival—with other Egyptian Jews, was significantly higher than for those under the age of twenty-eight on arrival (68 percent compared to 33 percent).

714. Interviewees #83 and #60.
715. Rutland, *The Jews in Australia*, 105.
716. Beinin wrote in *The Dispersion of Egyptian Jewry*, 32: "Decades after the liquidation of the community, some Egyptian Jews have reclaimed their Levantine cosmopolitanism through nostalgic literary reconstructions of Egypt..."
717. Rouchou's PhD thesis, "Nuits d'été au parfum de jasmin'", investigated the transmission of memory from one generation to the next, through interviewing the children of Jews who left one diaspora for another, such as the Jews of Egypt.
718. This expression was first used by the eminent French economist, Jean Fourastié (1907–1990). It refers to the emblematic "Les Trois Glorieuses", the three heroic days of July 27, 28, and 29, at the time of the 1830 Revolution when Charles X was overthrown and the so-called "Monarchie de juillet" of Louis-Philippe I was established. Fourastié's book, *Les Trente Glorieuses*, published in Paris in 1979 by Editions Fayard, referred to the extraordinary period of economic growth between 1946 and 1975, when the average standard of living in France trebled in thirty years and impacted every aspect of French social reality: demography, work conditions, buying power, and leisure.
719. Like other large French enterprises, the private company of Renault was nationalised and became the Régie Nationale des Usines Renault.
720. National Archives and Records Administration, Harry S. Truman Library and Museum, Marshall Plan B File, "The Marshall Proposal of Assistance to Europe 10 July 1947"; European Recovery Program; Secretary of the Treasury; Alphabetical File; John Snyder Paper.
721. The French social welfare system was greatly admired, and its reputation had travelled as far as Egypt, particularly the generous *allocations familiales* and other privileges for larger families. Interviewee #1, who, with four children to raise, was always struggling, remembered that her husband spoke often of those privileges and dreamt of settling in France, long before the events of 1956.
722. Those new massive suburban dwellings, called HLM, were vigorously criticised for having no soul by French intellectuals, such as Christiane Rochefort. Rochefort's most popular book, *Les Petits Enfants du Siècle* (Paris: Grasset, 1961), was read as a critique of the growing materialism of postwar French society, of France's birth control policy (*politique nataliste*), and of its impact on women. Marc Bernard, in *Sarcellopolis* (Paris: Flammarion, 1964), blamed the quality of life on those huge

council estates, for a new kind of psychological malaise and alienation affecting mainly non-working women, which he called *sarcellitis* after Sarcelles, one such housing complex near Le Bourget airport.

723. Doris Bensimon, "L'Immigration juive en France, 1945–1999", *Yod 6* (1999): 53–66. See also Susan Zuccotti, *The Holocaust, the French, and the Jews* (New York: BasicBooks, 1993), 280. The general population of France at that time was approximately forty million.

724. Laskier, "The Regeneration of French Jewry: The Influx and Integration of North African Jews into France", *Jewish Political Studies Review 10*, No. 1–2 (Spring 1998): 40.

725. In the case of Australia, it was the AJWS that assisted the Jews from Egypt in the areas of cash relief, employment, and housing loans. According to the minutes of the Jewish Welfare Society of May 5, 1957, in order to maximise and streamline the relief effort, Syd Einfeld proposed that all Welfare Societies—New South Wales, Victoria, South Australia, and Queensland—"decide on a policy and thus act uniformly".

726. Michel Abitbol, "The Integration of North African Jews in France", *Yale French Studies*, No. 85 (1994): 248–261.

727. Laskier, "The Regeneration of French Jewry", 39. See also Doris Bensimon and Sergio Della Pergola, *La Population juive de France: Socio-démographie et identité* (Paris: CNRS, 1984). According to their estimate, the total Jewish population in France is 530,000. The WJC 2004–2005 report estimates six hundred thousand out of a general population of 58,333,000. However, the latest 2005 statistics from the Jewish People Policy Planning Institute (JPPPI) in Israel indicates a contested figure of 494,000.

728. Abitbol, in "The Integration of North African Jews", 250, explained that these differences were a function of the colonial status of each of the three countries. Whereas Algeria was a French colony, Tunisia and Morocco were only French protectorates.

729. In "The Regeneration of French Jewry", 40–44, Laskier elaborated further: "one fourth of Tunisia's Jewry obtained French citizenship during the French Protectorate, whereas Moroccan Jews...remained subjects of Morrocco's Sherifian Sultan". See also Doris Bensimon, "L'Immigration juive en France: 1945–1999", *Yod 6* (1999): 53–66.

730. Those among my Australian respondents who were French nationals confirmed that they were accommodated free of charge in hotels especially requisitioned by the French authorities for this very purpose, until such

time as their Australian visa was processed. They were also offered food coupons and medical assistance.

731. Laskier, in "The Regeneration of French Jewry", 47, indicated that, according to JDC's records, "6,000 families, or over 23,000 Jews, had been received by the JDC-sponsored COJASOR agency" since the Sinai/ Suez War of 1956. It is possible that the Hungarian Jewish refugees were included in those figures.

732. Laskier, "Egyptian Jewry under the Nasser Regime", 595–596.

733. Interviewee #7F was seventeen at the time and ended up settling in France. Interviewee #56, who was twenty, worked for a year while waiting for her Australian immigration papers to be processed.

734. Interviewee #14F came to France alone to pursue university studies in 1954. His parents joined him in 1957.

735. Frédéric Galimidi, *Alexandrie-sur-Seine*, Collection L'Echelle de Jacob IV (France: Cousins de Salonique, 1999), 175–181. In this memoir, the Alexandria-born author evoked the personal trauma of his exile from Egypt and settlement in France.

736. In 1948, upon the establishment of the Jewish State, this respondent (#15F) was arrested for his Communist activities, stripped of his Egyptian nationality, and ordered to leave the country. He arrived in Europe as a stateless refugee and tried to settle in Italy because his wife had an Italian passport, but he was not allowed to work there. In 1952 he moved to France where, thanks to the "Jewish Egyptian network", he succeeded in obtaining a work permit and settled there permanently. Together with Jacques Hassoun, he was one of the founding members of ASPCJE.

737. Eighty percent of the French group was Sephardi, compared to 69 percent in Australia. As noted earlier, the Ashkenazim within the Australian group represented 20 percent, and 9 percent were of mixed origin.

738. There was also one respondent with an Ashkenazi father and a Catholic mother.

739. The two Karaite respondents, #18K & #21K, were committed and active members of their community in France and in the United States respectively. Interviewee #18K was at one stage Vice President of ASPCJE. Interviewee #21K was involved with the Jewish Federation of San Francisco. He was President of the San Francisco Karaite synagogue and co-founder of JIMENA, whose declared goal is "to achieve justice for the Middle East's 900,000 forgotten Jewish refugees".

740. Rutland, in *The Jews in Australia*, 151, reported that the 1996 Census figures "give an overall intermarriage rate of 15 percent for Australian Jewry".
741. Sergio Della Pergola, "World Jewish Population, 2002", *American Jewish Year Book*, Vol. 102 (2002): 601–642. According to the Israeli daily, *Ha'aretz*, June 24, 2004, a report prepared by the Jewish Agency Institute for Jewish People Policy Planning and headed by Sergio Della Pergola, on the condition of the Jewish people in the year 2004, estimates an alarming rate of intermarriage in France at 45 percent and in Australia at 22 percent.
742. Carasso confirmed in her Master's thesis, "La Communauté d'Égypte", that all of her twenty respondents identified their cultural and linguistic affinities with France as the main reason for choosing to settle there.
743. Interviewee #15F argued: "Ceux qui sont venus en France, c'était principalement les classes moyennes qui avaient une culture française, donc les anciens élèves des écoles des Frères, du Lycée français, de l'Union juive…Les vrais intellectuels étaient les élèves des lycées et des écoles chrétiennes".
744. Abitbol, in "The Integration of North African Jews", 251, pointed out that the uniqueness and the success of North African Jews' integration in France was due to the fact that they arrived "with a perfect knowledge of the language, history, climate and geography of their new home". This uniqueness also applied to the Egyptian refugees.
745. Even the prestigious Grandes Ecoles, where admission is still strictly regulated by highly competitive *concours* (university entrance examinations), did not charge student fees.
746. Two of those students, who later became leaders in their fields, medicine and engineering, recognised their debt of gratitude towards the same philanthropist in Egypt, who anonymously subsidised their studies right up to the time of the Suez crisis. Years later, they discovered his identity but he had already migrated to Australia, after he was stripped of his fortune by the Nasser regime. He died in 1987 without ever mentioning his good deeds. As it happened, his son (my husband) was a respondent in the Australian pilot study, and one of the students concerned was a respondent in the French pilot study (#2F).
747. ESPCI is reputed to have produced the greatest number of Nobel prize laureates in France. Graduates of the Grandes Ecoles are usually guaranteed the best positions available in their field.

748. My analysis revealed a significantly higher proportion of Communist activists within the French group, 18 percent compared to 1 percent for the Australian group.
749. Beinin, *The Dispersion of Egyptian Jewry*, 50–51.
750. For instance, Interviewee #14F, who attended the Jewish day school, Lycée de l'Union juive pour l'Enseignement, was initially recruited as a member of DROR, the Zionist socialist youth movement. The same geography teacher cited by Beinin in *The Dispersion of Egyptian Jewry*, 51, introduced him to Marxism. When DROR went underground after the creation of the State of Israel, a Jewish friend recruited him into the Egyptian Communist Party. He was arrested in 1953 after attending a few meetings, then released after four months in prison. As soon as he was able to secure an exit visa, he left Egypt for France. Another respondent (#15F), a comrade of the late Henri Curiel—one of the founders of the Egyptian Communist Party—was also arrested in 1948 and expelled. He eventually settled in France and was highly instrumental in the creation of the ASPCJE.
751. Intervieweee #2F joined the Egyptian Communist Party at the age of six-teen. When he went to university in France he joined l'Union des Jeunesses communistes, but left the party in June 1967 because of its bias against Israel. According to Interviewee #10F, in the mid-1970s the central committee of the French Communist Party issued a directive to unilaterally cancel the memberships of card-bearing Jewish Communists from Egypt. That caused him to leave the party in protest, although he remained a Communist at heart.
752. Only one Australian respondent (#54) declared her political activism for the left both in Egypt and Australia.
753. Hassoun, *Histoire des Juifs du Nil*, 101.
754. Galimidi, *Alexandrie-sur-Seine*, 43.
755. According to Interviewee #4F, who arrived in Paris in 1954 to pursue university studies and who, at the time of the interview, lived in a com-fortable apartment in the sixteenth *arrondissement*, the rich and privileged among the Egyptian Jews settled mostly in Switzerland.
756. Interviewee #2F.
757. These loans were called *prêts d'honneur* because the first repayments of the loan were met by COJASOR, without collateral, on the personal undertaking by the borrower that this debt would be reimbursed as soon as the borrower became solvent.
758. This respondent was at university at the time and lived on campus.

759. Interviewee #14F graduated from the University of Montpellier and now holds a PhD in chemical engineering.
760. In traditional Egyptian society this kind of behaviour was totally unacceptable in public.
761. Interviewee #12F was born in the village of Tantah and used to speak Arabic at home with his parents. He learned French at the AIU school in Tantah. He studied Law in Cairo and completed his doctorate in Paris. He practised as a lawyer before becoming a judge.
762. A few respondents left France within the first three years, given that they were already committed to immigrate to the United States or Australia before their arrival in France (Australian Interviewees #9, #56, #69, French Interviewees #20F, #21F, #22F).
763. This respondent spoke of the support group of Egyptian Jews as his personal ghetto, in the sense of a protective and familiar place: "notre ghetto, c'était les Juifs d'Égypte". He has now become a regular contributor to the resurrected *Nahar Misraïm*. See *Bulletin de Liaison 20* (Septembre 2004): 9; *21* (Décembre 2004): 3–4; *22* (Mars 2005): 16.
764. He attributed that reaction from his contacts or interlocutors to the fact that the French are constrained by the rigidity of their social structures: "les Français sont coincés".
765. Interviewee #1F confessed that for over forty years he consciously cut himself off from his past. By the time of the interview he was socialising mainly with Egyptian Jews.
766. Interviewee #7F, who declared herself unambiguously integrated into French society, has of late become very involved with the Paris branch of AAHA, an association of Egyptians expatriates of all religious persuasions from all over the world.
767. According to Interviewee #10F, this attitude emanates from the chauvinism of the French: "j'ai connu un peu de discrimination à cause de mon accent. Les Français sont toujours un peu méprisants à l'égard de ceux qui ne sont pas purement français".
768. This interviewee came to France around 1954, at the age of seventeen, to sit for his baccalauréat examination and then pursue engineering studies.
769. The French Republic is commonly defined as "indivisible, laïque, démocratique et sociale" (emphasis mine).
770. A few even said that they never mentioned the fact they were Jewish outside their Jewish milieu, "as the question never came up".
771. This respondent (#12F) recalled one significant incident: one day, while watching a television program with some friends, he casually pointed out

that the singer on the screen was Jewish, and the reaction was: "mais vous voyez le mal partout", meaning, "you see evil everywhere".

772. This incident had a profound resonance for this particular respondent. In 1948, when he was incarcerated with other Jews and Communists at the Huckstep camp in Egypt, the fundamentalist Muslim Brothers tried to enter the camp and attack them. The camp commandant abandoned them, and they had to organise their own defence without any outside help.

773. Interviewee #67 is a highly educated and enterprising woman, with degrees from the American University in Cairo, the University of Sydney, and the Sorbonne in Paris. She left Egypt after the burning of Cairo in 1952 and migrated to Australia with her British husband. She lived in Adelaide and Sydney for over twenty-five years before moving to Paris, where she worked as a university lecturer and an interpreter at international exhibitions in Europe and the United States for another twenty years. Since the death of her husband in 1999, she has returned "home" to Sydney.

774. Interviewee #8F indicated that he experienced anti-Semitism in the 1960s, when he worked in the principality of Monaco for a Greek shipping firm. His employers apparently had a policy of not employing Jews and made his life unbearable when they found out he was Jewish, until he had had enough and resigned. He found another job in London and decided to move there, where he resided with his family until he died of cancer in 2008.

775. Her dramatic choice of words illustrates how much she identifies with France: "Je suis française à fond, à mort. J'adore la France".

776. See also an essay by Jacques Hassoun about the complexity of the Jewish/Egyptian identity, "Can Egyptian-Jewish Identity Be Reconstructed in France?", *Bulletin of the Israeli Academic Centre in Cairo* 23 (June 1998): 8–10.

777. The *Consistoire* is the offical representative of Jewish congregations in France. It is a French State creation, introduced by Napoleon in 1808. See Paula E. Hyman, *The Jews of Modern France* (Berkeley and Los Angeles: University of California Press, 1998), 44–48, and Esther Benbassa, *The Jews of France: A History from Antiquity to the Present,* trans. M. B. De Bevoise (Princeton, NJ: Princeton University Press, 1999), 86–92.

778. The Vice President of the Oratoire (#12F) reported that initially this arrangement was supposed to be temporary. The Oratoire had on record five or six hundred congregants. As was the custom in Egypt, there are no fixed membership fees, but seats are sold for the High Holy Days. However, the Vice President explained that people who could not afford a seat

were still welcome. They employed a cantor or *hazan* to read the Torah and chant the prayers. They did not have the funds to employ a permanent rabbi because the congregation was not rich and survived thanks to individual donations.

779. Interviewee #12F stated that, apart from the ASPCJE, there was another organisation called L'Union des Juifs d'Égypte en France to which he also belonged, but he did not specify the nature or the extent of his involvement.

780. One respondent claimed that Sadat published an open letter in a leading Egyptian newspaper, *El-Ahram*, addressed to the Jews of Egypt, inviting them to come back to their birth country. This particular claim could be mythical seeing as I have not been able to locate that letter.

781. In fact, that period was so traumatic for the Jews of Egypt that they used a code word whenever they discussed it, calling it simply "les événements".

782. See Perrault, *Un Homme à part*. After his imprisonment and subsequent expulsion from Egypt for his significant involvement in the Egyptian Communist Party, Curiel relocated to Paris, where he continued to pursue his militant activities. He was heavily criticised for his involvement with the Algerian FLN and other violent Third-World liberation movements.

783. Curiel was known to a number of my respondents who, in their younger years, had been involved with the Communist Party both in Egypt and in France. Curiel's funeral was held at the famous cemetery of Père-Lachaise in Paris, attended by several political figures from the left who spoke only of Curiel's achievements as a Communist in France and never mentioned his Egyptian life.

784. An interesting aspect of that booklet was its cover page. It was a reproduction of an old map of the Jewish quarter in Cairo, drawn by the artists who accompanied Napoleon Bonaparte's expedition into Egypt of 1798. According to Interviewee #2F, who helped compile the booklet, there were no street names on that map. Together with other members of the team, my respondent filled in those names. They claim that this map has since been used by the Egyptian Tourist Bureau.

785. The papers delivered during the colloquium were published, with support from the Centre National des Lettres, in a book called *Cultures Juives méditerranéennes et orientales* (Paris: Syros, 1982).

786. Jacques Hassoun's vital contribution to the work of the ASPCJE and his many books on the Jewish Egyptian cultural heritage have already been discussed at length in chapter I.

787. Apart from the regular and numerous articles written by Jacques Hassoun for every issue of the ASPCJE bulletin, there were contributions by Interviewees #2F, #3F, and #4 in Bulletin no. 1, December 1980. In Bulletin nos. 18–19, October 1985, Interviewee #12F contributed an article on "Maimonide, le symbole de l'espoir", 33–46, and Interviewee #15F on "Témoignages des communautés juives d'Égypte—Le Caire', 54–57.

788. See Albert Oudiz, "Mes années aux établissements de la Mission Laïque Française du Caire" in *Nahar Misraïm: Bulletin de Liaison 22* (March 2005): 3–8; Sarina Rohmer, "Témoignage des Juifs d'Égypte installés au Brésil" in *Nahar Misraïm: Bulletin de Liaison 21* (December 2004): 5–8.

789. It is apparent that, for the Australian group, the issue of distance and cost made a trip to Egypt more problematic than for the French group.

790. I obtained the complete tapes of that special program from one of my respondents (#14F). Paula Jacques had already reported on an earlier trip to Egypt undertaken in 1981, on a radio program called "L'Oreille en Coin". The broadcast was transcribed by Yvette Gabbay and published in the Bulletin of the ASPCJE, nos. 4–5, (Novembre 1981): 28–40.

791. I was shown the film by Interviewee #4F, the young student's uncle.

792. Radio communautaire juive, émission du 19/4/90, "Juifs d'Égypte".

793. "Report on the Inaugural Meeting of the Historical Society of Jews from Egypt" by Victor D. Sanua, October 22, 1995.

794. *IAJE Newsletter 2*, no. 2 (1999): 2.

795. Egyptian-born Sandro Manzoni is based in Geneva. In 1993, he founded the AAHA and has set its agenda as "a cultural and recreational society made up mainly of people who have lived or live in Alexandria". Its aim is to increase the knowledge of Alexandria's past and present. By creating bridges among its members, spread over all continents, it encourages the meeting and sharing of diverse cultures and traditions. The motto of the association "Dispersés, mais unis; unis, mais divers" expresses the essence of former Alexandrians. Its bulletin *Alexandrie Info* is published twice a year and keeps the membership informed of upcoming activities, such as organised trips and reunions, relevant publications, and other news that might be of interest.

796. Most of these associations have established interactive websites and "chat rooms", such as <egyjews@yahoogroups.com> or <aroundtheworld-jews@yahoogroups.com>, and they attract a lot of visitors. Aside from the usual banter, the online exchanges cover a variety of serious topics, specifically relevant to the Jews from Egypt. They often reveal aspects of life in Egypt that cannot be found in any books, such as linguistic expres-

sions that have long been forgotten, personal anecdotes, original memories, and traditional recipes.

797. Krämer, *The Jews in Modern Egypt*, 37.

798. See Rutland, *The Jews in Australia*, 121: "Over the last twenty years, Jews have been featured in the *Business Review Weekly*'s 'Rich List', the 200 wealthiest individuals and families in Australia. Between 20 to 25 percent of these 200 names are Jewish business people…This is a remarkable contribution from a community that constitutes less than half a per cent of Australia's population".

799. Rutland, *The Jews in Australia*, 105.

800. Interviewee #8 has established a foundation, "The Jews of Egypt Foundation", to promote and finance in perpetuity the study and research of the recent history of the Jews of Egypt. He is in the final process of raising funds for a chair at Haifa University in Israel.

801. Based on the title of Mizrahi's book, *l'Égypte et ses Juifs: Le Temps révolu*.

IMAGES

IMAGE **1.** Wedding of Jewish Family from Corfu at the Eliyahu Hanavi Synagogue (Alexandria, 1941).

Source. Courtesy of Teddy Nahmias.

IMAGE **2.** Middle-class Jewish family enjoying an outing in the port of Alexandria (c.1937).

Source. Property of the Barda Family.

IMAGE **3.** Nessim Levi, volunteer in British Army during WWII.

Source. Property of Esther Abécassis.

IMAGE 4. Chief Rabbi of Alexandria Aron Angel at a communal function, c.1953.

Source. The Barda Family.

IMAGE 5. Sha'ar Hashamayim Synagogue (Cairo).

Source. J. & R. Barda.

Image 6. Eliyahu Hanavi Synagogue, Alexandria.

Source. J. & R. Barda.

Image 7. Collective Batmitzvah Ceremony in Alexandria.

Source. Courtesy of Association Nebi Daniel (Property of David Lisbona).

IMAGE 8. Batmitzvah Luncheon at the Alexandria Jewish Community Hall, c.1952.

Source. Racheline Barda.

IMAGE 9. Jewish Cemetery of Chatby in Alexandria.

Source. J. & R. Barda.

IMAGE **10.** Cotton classifiers at the Cotton Exchange of Minet-el-Bassal in Alexandria, c.1952.

persons classifying cotton in Alexandria

Source. The Barda Family.

IMAGE **11.** Travelling to Australia.

Source. Courtesy National Library of Australia.

IMAGE 12. Family of Jews from Egypt posing in the backyard of a modest suburban home (1963).

Source. The Barda Family.

IMAGE 13. The iconic paling fence of a home in the suburbs (c.1963).

Source. The Alphandary Family.

APPENDICES

APPENDIX 1. Sample data obtained from original questionnaire followed by interview.

Responses to Questionnaire   [Listing]   [New Entry]

General information

Gender	Male
Age Group (5 year block)	81 or older
Length of time in Australia (5 year block)	41-45
Marital status	Married
Place of birth	Villages

Year of Birth 1920
Year of Arrival in Australia 1957

Family country of origin:
☒ Turkey ☐ France ☐ Holland ☐ Eastern Europe ☐ Other
☐ Old Ottoman Empire ☐ Greece ☐ Middle East ☐ Morocco
☐ Italy ☐ UK ☐ Spain ☐ Algeria

Summary Ethnic Origin	Old Ottoman Empire
Previous nationality	Egyptian
Occupation in Egypt (male & female)	professional
Socio economic Status	middle class
Jewish Affiliation	Sephardi
Religious practice	Traditional
Intermarriage in Egypt	No

Egyptian
self chemist

Number of languages spoken:
☒ Arabic ☒ French ☒ Ladino ☐ Greek
☒ English ☐ Italian ☐ Yiddish ☒ Other

Type of school attended:
☒ Christian ☐ Laic ☒ English ☒ Egyptian State
☐ Jewish ☐ French ☐ Greek ☒ Other

Arabic skills	good
Level of Education attained in Egypt	Tertiary
Feelings of belonging in Egypt	strong
Community involvement in Egypt	marginal
Connection to Freemasonry	Yes

Notes: self chemist   1. Assistant Pharmacist
Father: electrician /own bus.   2. Opened own pharmacy
mother: home duties   now retired

Involvement in Zionist movement	nil
Date of departure from Egypt	after 1956 Suez War
Reason for leaving Egypt	overt or covert discrimination
Reasons for choosing Australia	family connection
Where in Australia	Sydney

Year departed egypt 1957
hostile environment

Source of assistance pre and post arrival:
☐ HIAS ☐ local Jewish institutions ☒ no assistance ☐ Other
☐ government bodies ☐ family & friends ☐ not applicable

English Skills on Arrival	fair
How difficult was is to settle in Australia	with some difficulty
Occupation in Australia (male/female)	professional 1. Assistant Pharmacist
Level of Occupation	Owner/Professional
Community Involvement in Australia	high
Children's reaction to parents' background	indifferent
Children's level of education	Tertiary

How would you describe your identity:
☒ Jew from Egypt ☐ Australian Jew ☒ Other
☒ Sephardic Jew ☐ Australian
☐ Ashkenazi Jew ☐ of French culture

Years in Australia before own home	0.5
Zionist sympathy in Aust	strong

APPENDIX 2. Article by author in *The Australian Jewish News.*

feature

Jewish Egypt revisited

Racheline Barda recently returned to Egypt, the country of her birth, after an absence of 42 years. It was a journey of nostalgia, of retracing Jewish roots, of liberation.

I LEFT my birthplace in the aftermath of the Suez war of 1956 and for a long time did not want to go back. It was not because I had forgotten the sweet years of my childhood there, but because of what I couldn't forget – the traumatic circumstances of my departure.

Nevertheless, my husband Joe persuaded me to undertake this trip together with our daughters, Daniella and Monique, who live in Paris and Tel Aviv respectively. My son David, a Sydney publisher, was unable to join us.

Singapore Airlines took us direct from Sydney to Cairo. As we land, I feel apprehensive, wondering what kind of welcome we will get. The old fears that I remember from the bad old days – the fear of the arbitrary – come rushing back. I whisper to my husband in a panic: don't let on that you speak Arabic; let's first see what the atmosphere is like. He laughs. He has come back to Egypt once before, 14 years ago, and is relaxed. The knot in my stomach unravels gradually as we are warmly greeted by a pleasant young man who introduces himself in perfect English as our tour operator and says 'Welcome to Egypt.'

The travel agent takes charge of passports, luggage, customs formalities, and we head towards our hotel, mesmerised by the traffic, noise, huge buildings, trying in vain to recognise familiar places. Passing through Heliopolis, an outer suburb of Cairo where I spent many school holidays, I dig furiously in my memory of the place, but to no avail. I ask about the Roxy Cinema, popular in the 50s. It is still here, says the guide, and so is the statue of the Baron d'Empain, a Belgian industrialist who built Heliopolis at the turn of the century.

Nothing seems familiar. Maybe it's me, maybe I had not paid enough attention when I was a little girl, thinking there would be ample time and opportunities to come back. Nevertheless, although frustrated not to find any identifiable traces of my childhood, I draw comfort from the fact that Cairo was never my city. I was an Alexandrian. Alexandria will not be a stranger, in spite of the long years of separation.

We check into the magnificent Marriott Hotel, situated on a small island on the Nile, called Zamalek. It used to be a palace, built at the time of the inauguration of the Suez Canal, and it welcomed Empress Eugenie, wife of Napoleon III. Portraits of the royal visitor and other dignitaries adorn the walls. Our room overlooks the tennis courts of the prestigious Guezirah Sports Club, where my husband competed in 1954 as a member of the Alexandria Sports Club team.

Not wanting to waste a single minute, we leave for the usual tourist circuit – the Mohammed Ali mosque, the Citadel of Salah-El-Din and the Bazaar of Khan Khalil. As we stroll down the narrow alleys, we are enticed into the shops in such a friendly way that we cannot resist. We chat and joke in English and Arabic with the shopkeepers. They seem so happy to hear us speak our broken Arabic that they nearly forget to push their wares onto us. They offer coffee, cold drinks, wanting to know our story. They are young, they don't know about the past. We rediscover the charm, the hospitality, the gentle nature of the Egyptian people, the flowery language and the flowing compliments. It doesn't matter that they probably don't mean half the things they say. It sounds sincere, and that's enough to warm our hearts.

Early the next morning, we leave with our driver for Alexandria. This is the part of our visit that means the most to us. Not only were we born here, but we want to show off our Alexandria to our daughters. After checking in at the Cecil Hotel – the first stop of this nostalgic pilgrimage – we start our voyage of rediscovery without unpacking. We don't want to miss the sunset from the top of Stanley Beach. We have been warned about the overcrowding, the traffic and the general state of decay, so we are not too surprised. We are too busy trying not to miss any of the sites that have played

such an integral part of our growing up.

My husband navigates with such ease, one would think he had never left. I stay silent, thinking, trying to take it in – the sights, the smell of the sea, the familiar names, Athineos, Trianon, Sidi-Bishr. The Corniche is as I remember, stretching as far as the eye can see, beautiful and alive, the necklace of the Mediterranean. I cannot believe the Casino Chatby is still standing, although it looks unstable – like some of my memories.

We go from place to place, pointing out to our daughters; this is where I caught the tram to school, this is the beach where I spent the summer, this is where we used to buy *falafel* or grilled corn or Turkish cheese, this is my school. Our beloved schools that probably shaped us into what we are. The Lycee Francais, now Lycee El Horreya, where I spent the best years of my life, has not changed much in my eyes, probably because they are full of tears. It looks a little tired, a little worn.

> **We point out the marble columns, the wooden benches still bearing the familiar names of members of a congregation long gone. I feel a shiver running down my spine.**

We knock at the doors of our homes in Camp de Cesar and are welcomed with open arms by strangers - welcome back, come in please, this is your home, *ethaltak, ezesteek*. The visit to the Barda family villa is filled with emotion, especially when Joe recognises most of the furniture and even ornaments that his parents had to leave behind in 1956. Our next stop is the Jewish cemetery where Joe wants to put flowers on his grandparents' grave. As we walk among the graves and magnificent marble mausoleums, we read out the names of the people who once constituted such a vibrant community. We are proud and sad to show our daughters the proof of a world that once was, but is no more and will probably never be again.

The next day is devoted to a visit to the Jewish community office in Rue Nebi Daniel. We want to check family records and dates going back to the 1830s. I need to ask questions related to my research on the Jews of Egypt. The hospitality and cooperation extended by ageing president Joe Harari and Madame Mattatia is touching. They serve the dwindling community with dedication and dignity. Madame Mattatia opens the Nebi Daniel Synagogue for us. We point out to our daughters the magnificent marble columns, the chandeliers, the wooden benches still bearing all the familiar names of members of a congregation long gone. I feel a shiver running down my spine.

Even for us, our life here, with the passing of time, had acquired mythical qualities, but it was no myth. We did not dream it. I remember all the weddings I attended in this very same synagogue, either as a flowergirl or holding one of those tat, tall candles in a fluttering dress. I remember the photos taken with my family on the front porch of the synagogue. I had my bat-mitzvah in this synagogue, which was unusual at the time.

When we return to Cairo, we try to meet Carmen Weinstein, who is doing a wonderful job for the Cairo Jewish community. She is responsible for the restoration of part of the Bassatine Jewish Cemetery, one of the oldest in the Diaspora. She is too busy to see us on such short notice. A gentleman introduces himself as the lawyer for the community. He asks curtly what we want. He is suspicious of our motives and we are taken aback by his reaction. After I explain that I am conducting research on the Jews of Egypt for a PhD and show him my credentials, he mellows. It is the only time during our visit in Egypt that we experience any unpleasantness.

Racheline Barda at the pyramids in Giza with her daughters, Monique and Daniella.

Above: Members of a Jewish youth group on the beach in Alexandria in July 1956, three months before war broke out. Joe and Racheline Barda are in the front row on the left.

Right: In the offices of the Jewish community in Alexandria, back: Joe Barda, his daughter Daniella, the secretary of the community Madame Mattatia, Racheline Barda, her daughter Monique; front congregation president Joe Harari.

We visit the beautiful Adly Street Synagogue and the superbly restored Ben Ezra Synagogue where the famous Cairo Genizah was discovered. I make contact with Samir Raafat, a writer and historian, who tells me about the wonderful Bassatine News website. He indicates his book on the history of the Cairo suburb of Maadi. His research recalls the prominent role played by influential Jewish families in the development of the area.

We end our visit on a high note – a fascinating trip up the Nile from Aswan to Luxor with a side-trip to Abu Simbel. The sophistication of the ancient Pharaonic civilisation is beyond belief. The crew treats us as long-lost family when they discover we were born on Egyptian soil. Every day, the chef cooks some of our favourite dishes – *melokheya* (a green soup), *bamia* (okra), *roz* (rice) and lamb stew. The boat is meticulously clean. Although the heat is unbearable in the middle of the day, we sit on the top deck in the late afternoon and watch the Nile go by. All good things come to an end and it's time to say goodbye, although there is so much to see and do.

Back in Sydney, the place I now call home, I reflect on my visit to what was my first home. I feel richer for having gone back and also liberated. The barrier that stood between me and Egypt for so long has tumbled. I am proud of

our daughters who had the sensitivity to see beyond the dust and the dirt, beyond the years of neglect, and to visualise how we lived. At the same time, they appreciated modern Egypt. The warm welcome we experienced touched me beyond words. Most of all, I was impressed by the level of education attained by our guides, tour operators, drivers, people who would have been illiterate only a couple of decades ago. Even though I know that with the galloping demography of Egypt, a lot remains to be done, I am happy to see how much has been achieved. I look forward to my next visit.

● *Racheline Barda is currently doing a PhD on the Jews of Egypt. Any former Egyptian Jews who would like to contribute to her thesis are invited to contact her on 0419 462 577.*

APPENDIX V

APPENDIX 3. Article by the late Teddy Nahmias, one of the author's interviewees.

THE JEWS FROM EGYPT

The marriage of Doris Nahmias to Sabino Gesua at the Alexandria Synagogue of Eliahou Hanabi in 1941. Teddy Nahmias (see article below) is the little boy in his father's arms in the third row , near the right of the picture. The rabbi (with the white beard) is Haham Maimon Benatar

A LEAVENED PASSOVER

TEDDY NAHMIAS

Following the unfortunate events of 1956 and the Suez Canal Crisis, hundreds of Jewish families packed their belongings and left Egypt, most boarding ships sailing from Alexandria, bound for European Mediterranean ports.

My family chose Italy, my father's dream land. As a Corfiot he felt Venice was his cultural home, so we were on our way to Venice and Trieste. The vessel was the M/S *Enotria* a smaller version of the famous M/S *Esperia* of Adriatica fame, those white luxury liners that rode the Mediterranean with the Lion of Venice watching over from the yellow chimneys.

We took the lift down from our fifth floor flat in Mazarita for the last time. Some of our neighbours opened their front doors and stood in silence on the landings to watch us go. Muhammed, our imposing Sudanese *bawab* (porter) was sobbing like a child. There was no coming back. The emotion was high and my mother could not stop her tears. Dad became tense as we went through

customs and police clearance, but felt more comfortable as he walked the steps to the deck. After all, he was already on Italian soil. As for myself, I was in a daze, feeling that something irreversible was taking place, but too young to realize the implications. I was probably hoping to find another group of youngsters at the other end that would recreate the rock and roll fun-loving crowd I had left behind.

As the ship started to move away from the dock and head for the high seas, we all waved goodbye, and slowly turned our heads from the land that we were not to see again for perhaps half a century.

I noticed a few young people around my age and naturally was drawn to them. My parents by now were in conversation with other Jews who were on their way to Canada. Others were due to catch a ship from Trieste to Australia.

Suddenly, someone said "but tomorrow night is *Pesach*, it's the first *Seder* night. Shouldn't we mark the occasion somehow?" A charming and understanding officer decided we could use a section of the dining room, and I recall about 25 of us sitting around a number of tables assembled to form one big long table. To top it all, as a gift from the Captain, a beautiful cake was placed in the centre of the table with the compliments of the Chef, the crew and the officers. How embarrassing: no *matzah*, no *harosset*, no *maror*, but instead

a massive *chametz* torta to celebrate the festival of the unleavened bread. I remember a discussion on who would officiate. A *Haggadah* was found. I cannot remember whether or not the cake was eaten. We were Jews leaving Egypt, celebrating Jews leaving Egypt. Had we fallen into a mysterious time warp? Although not realizing it at the time, we had gone through a unique experience never to be repeated. This time the bread had risen. ■ *After leaving Egypt Teddy Nahmias lived with his family in Italy and France. In 1971 he came to England where he has worked in the textile industry*

Another 1956 emigrant, Mark Cohen, who now lives in New York

GLOSSARY

Aliyah (literally going up) Immigration to Israel

Ashkenazi (literally German) Jews originating from Central and Eastern Europe

Barmitzvah Religious ceremony to mark a Jewish boy's religious maturity at the age of thirteen

Batmitzvah Religious ceremony to mark a Jewish girl's religious maturity at the age of twelve

Betar Youth organisation of the Zionist Revisionist movement

Bey Turkish governor; title granted to high government officials and public servants

B'nai Brith (literally Sons of the Covenant) International Jewish service organisation

B'nei Akiva (literally Sons of Akiva) Religious Zionist youth movement

Capitulations (chapter) Regime of extraterritorial jurisdiction that shielded foreign nationals from the law of the land

Dhimmi Legal status of Jews and Christians in Muslim lands, denoting the relationship between protector and protected

Diaspora Greek word meaning dispersion, applied to Jewish settlement outside of Israel

Dror Marxist Zionist youth movement

Effendi Title of respect or courtesy in Turkey

Einsatzgruppen (Mobile killing squads) paramilitary units created by Himmler, which operated behind the Nazi Eastern Front

Emigré Emigrant, used in connection with political exile

Fellah Egyptian peasant

Gabbai (literally collector) Communal official

Hagana Underground military organisation of the Yishuv in Palestine

Hara or haret-al-Yahud Separate Jewish quarters

Haret-al-Yahud al-Qara'in Karaites's quarters

Ha Shomer Ha-Tza'ir (literally The Young Guard) Communist Zionist youth movement

Heder (literally room) Religious elementary school

Intifada (literally shudder, awakening) Palestinian uprising

Jizya Poll tax imposed by Muslim rulers on their Jewish and Christian subjects in exchange for protection and freedom of religion

Djihad Holy struggle

Karaite (Readers of the Scriptures) Ancient Jewish sect believed to have coalesced with other Jewish sects in Bagdad in the eighth century. Karaites only follow the Written Law and deny the Rabbinical-Talmudic tradition

Keren Yayesod Palestine Foundation Fund, later United Israel Appeal

Keren Kayemet le-Israel Jewish National Fund

Khawagat Respectful or disdainful Arabic title used to designate Europeans

Khedive Turkish viceroys who ruled Egypt between 1867 and 1914

Ladino or *judesmo* (known also as Judeo-Spanish) Ancient form of Castilian mixed with Hebrew and Turkish words and often written in *Rashi* script

Laissez-passer Travelling permit granted to stateless persons

Madrassah Koranic school

Mamluk (literally slave) Member of military body (originally Circassian slaves) that ruled Egypt from 1254 to 1811

Millet (people or nation) Ottoman Turkish term for a legally protected religious minority

Minyan Quorum of ten male adult Jews required for communal prayer

Misrahim Oriental Jews

Misr al-Fatat (or Young Egypt) Militant nationalist movement founded in 1933

Mukhabarat Egyptian secret police

Nizam jadid (literally new system) New army created by Muhammad Ali

Pasha Turkish officer of high rank, e.g. military commander, governor of province, politician or notable

Pessah Passover, Feast of Unleavened Bread, commemorates the exodus from Egypt

Rabbanites (Rabbinites) Name given by the Karaites to their Rabbininal opponents

Reconquista Reclaiming of Muslim Spain by the Christians

Rehla bodun ragaa (literally journey without return) Egyptian stamp affixed on travelling documents of stateless Jews after the 1956 Suez War

Romaniot Greek Jews

Rosh Hashana (literally Head of the Year) Jewish New Year

Saint-Simonien Disciple of the collectivism doctrine of Saint-Simon, French philosopher and sociologist (1760–1825)

Saraf Moneychanger

Sephardi (literally Spanish) Jews originating from Spain and Portugal, and by extension, from the Old Ottoman Empire and the Orient

Schlecht Derogatory Yiddish term for an Ashkenazi, meaning bad or evil

Sepher Torah Scroll of the Law containing the five Books of Moses

Shari'ah Body of Islamic Law, also known as the Law of Allah, that governs both the secular and religious life of the devout Muslim

Simhat Torah (literally Rejoicing in the law) Holy day on which the annual completion of the reading of the Torah is celebrated

Tarboush fez, Turkish head dress

Umma The community of all Muslims

Wafd Delegation

Yishuv Jewish community in Palestine pre-1948

Yom Kippur Day of Atonement

BIBLIOGRAPHY

Unpublished Jewish Communal Sources

Adelaide Hebrew Congregation, Minutes and Annual Reports, 1945–1960.

Australian Jewish Welfare Society, Sydney, Minutes and Annual Reports, 1956–1960.

Executive Council of Australian Jewry, Correspondence Files, Archive of Australian Judaica, 1955–1962.

NSW Jewish Board of Deputies Files, Correspondence Related to Admission of Sephardi Jews to Australia.

South Australian Jewish Board of Deputies, Minutes and Correspondence, Housed at the AHC, 1950–1960.

South Australian Maccabi, Minutes, 1956–1960.

Government Archives

Statistical Handbook of Middle Eastern Countries (1835–1944), Agence Juive de Palestine, 1945.

National Statistics, Israel Ministry of Immigration, 2002.

Alphabetical File, Marshall Plan B File, United States National Archives and Records Administration, Harry S. Truman Library and Museum.

Australian Archives Office

CA 51, Department of Immigration (1953–1974), Correspondence Files, Annual Single Number with Block Allocations, 1953–, CRS A446, 1972/77857.

CA 12, Prime Minister's Department (1957–1971), Correspondence Files, Annual Single Number series (Classified) 1957–, CRS A1209.

CA 18, Department of External Affairs (II) (1948–1989), Correspondence Files, Multiple Number Series, 1948–1989, CRS A1838.

Books and Chapters

Aaron, Aaron. *The Sephardim of Australia & New Zealand*. Waterloo: A. Aaron, 1979.

Abitbol, Michel. *Le passé d'une discorde: Juifs et Arabes du VIIè siècle à nos jours*. Paris: Perrin, 1999.

Aciman, André. *Out of Egypt: A Memoir*. New York, NY: Farrar, Straus and Giroux, 1994.

———. *Letters of Transit: Reflections on Exile, Identity, Language, and Loss*. New York, NY: The New Press, 1999.

———. *False Papers*. New York, NY: Farrar, Straus and Giroux, 2000.

Aharoni, Ada. *The Second Exodus: A Historical Novel*. Bryn Mawr, PA: Dorrance, 1983.

———. *From the Nile to the Jordan*. Haifa: Michael Lachmann Ltd., 1994.

Aharoni, Ada, Aimée Israel-Pelletier, and Levana Zamir. *History and Culture of the Jews of Egypt in Modern Times*. Tel Aviv: Keness Hafakot, 2008.

Aharoni, Ada, and Thea Wolf. *Not in Vain: An Extraordinary Life*. San Carlos, CA: Ladybug Press, 1998.

Albert, Phyllis Cohen. *The Modernization of French Jewry: Consistory and Community in the Nineteenth Century*. Waltham, MA: Brandeis University Press, 1977.

Alia, Josette. *Quand le soleil était chaud*. Paris: B. Grasset, 1992.

Altabev, Mary. *Judeo-Spanish in the Turkish Social Context: Language Death, Swan Song, Revival or New Arrival?* Istanbul: The Isis Press, 2003.

Andgel, Anne. *Fifty Years of Caring: The History of the Australian Jewish Welfare Society 1936–1986*. Sydney: The Australian Jewish Welfare Society and the Australian Jewish Historical Society, 1988.

Angel, Marc. *The Jews of Rhodes: The History of a Sephardic Community.* New York: Sepher-Hermon Press, 1998.

Appleyard, Reginald T., Alison Ray, and Allan Segal. *The Ten Pound Immigrants,* London: Boxtree, 1988.

Armstrong, Diane. *The Voyage of Their Life: The Story of the SS Derna and Its Passengers.* Pymble: Flamingo, 2001.

Barda, Rachel M. "Les Juifs d'Égypte en Australie et en France: Stratégies d'acculturation". In *History and Culture of the Jews of Egypt in Modern Times,* compiled by Ada Aharoni, Aimé Israel-Pelletier, and Levana Zamir, 278–288. Tel Aviv: Keness Hafakot, 2008.

Babbie, Earl R. *The Practice of Social Research.* Belmont, CA: Wadsworth Publishing Co., 1992.

Bar-Joseph, Uri. *Intelligence Intervention in the Politics of Democratic States: The United States, Israel, and Britain.* University Park, PA: Pennsylvania State University Press, 1995.

Bat Ye'or. *Les Juifs en Égypte: Aperçu sur 3000 ans d'histoire.* Genève, Editions de l'Avenir, 1971.

———. *The Dhimmi: Jews and Christians under Islam.* Rutherford, NJ: Fairleigh Dickinson University Press, 1985.

———. *The Decline of Eastern Christianity under Islam: From Jihad to Dhimmitude.* Madison, NJ: Fairleigh Dickinson University Press, 1996.

Bat Ye'or, Miriam Kochan, and David Littman. *Islam and Dhimmitude: Where Civilizations Collide.* Madison, NJ: Fairleigh Dickinson University Press, 2002.

Beaucour, Fernand Emile, and Noël Dejuine. *La Campagne d'Égypte (1798–1801): D'après les dessins inédits de Noël Dejuine, du 20e Régiment de Dragons.* Levallois: F. E. Beaucour, 1983.

Beinin, Joel. *Was the Red Flag Flying There? Marxist Politics and the Arab-Israeli Conflict in Egypt and Israel, 1948–1965.* Berkeley: University of California Press, 1990.

————. *The Dispersion of Egyptian Jewry: Culture, Politics, and the Formation of a Modern Diaspora.* Berkeley: University of California Press, 1998.

————. *Workers and Peasants in the Modern Middle East.* Cambridge and New York: Cambridge University Press, 2001.

Beinin, Joel, and Joe Stork. *Political Islam: Essays from Middle East Report.* Berkeley: University of California Press, 1997.

Beinin, Joel, and Zachary Lockman. *Workers on the Nile: Nationalism, Communism, Islam, and the Egyptian Working Class, 1882–1954.* Princeton, NJ: Princeton University Press, 1987.

Beki, Avi. *Jewish Communities of the World.* Jerusalem: Institute of the World Jewish Congress, 1998.

Benbassa, Esther. *The Jews of France: A History from Antiquity to the Present.* Princeton, NJ: Princeton University Press, 1999.

Benbassa, Esther, and Aron Rodrigue. *Sephardi Jewry: A History of the Judeo-Spanish Community, 14th–20th Centuries.* Berkeley: University of California Press, 2000.

Ben Sasson, H. H., ed. *A History of the Jewish People.* Cambridge, MA: Harvard University Press, 1976.

Bensimon, Doris, and Sergio Della Pergola. *La Population juive de France: Socio-démographie et identité.* Paris: Centre National de la Recherche Scientif, 1984.

Bernard, Marc. *Sarcellopolis.* Paris: Flammarion, 1964.

Berque, Jacques. *Egypt Imperialism and Revolution.* London: Faber and Faber, 1972.

Blakeney, Michael. *Australia and the Jewish Refugees, 1933–1948.* Sydney: Croom Helm Australia, 1985.

Botton-Bahbout, Renée. *Des Rives du Nil aux berges de la Seine.* Villiers-le-Bel, France: Imprimerie Ras, 2005.

Bradburn, Norman, Seymour Sudman, and Edward Blair. *Improving Interview Method and Questionnaire Design.* San Francisco, CA: Jossey-Bass Publishers, 1980.

Brugger, Suzanne Mary. *Australians and Egypt, 1914–1919.* Carlton: Melbourne University Press, 1980.

Cabasso, Gilbert, et al. *Juifs d'Égypte: Images et Textes.* Paris: Editions du Scribe, 1984.

Carter, B. L. *The Copts in Egyptian Politics, 1918–1952.* Cairo: American University in Cairo Press, 1985.

Casey, Richard G. *Australian Foreign Minister: The Diaries of R.G. Casey, 1951–60.* Edited by T. B. Millar. London: Collins, 1972.

Centre National des Lettres. *Cultures juives méditerranéennes et orientales.* Actes des journées du 12 au 14 septembre 1980 au Centre Georges Pompidou. Paris: Syros, 1982.

Cohen, Lysbeth. *Beginning with Esther.* Sydney: Ayers & James Heritage Books in association with *Australian Jewish Times*, 1987.

Cohen, Amon, and Gabriel Baer, eds. *Egypt and Palestine: A Millennium of Association (868–1948).* New York, NY: St. Martin's Press, 1984.

Cohen, Hayyim J. *The Jews of the Middle East, 1860–1972.* New York, NY: Wiley, 1972.

Cohran, Judith. *Education in Egypt.* London: Croom Helm, 1986.

Combe, Gordon D. *Responsible Government in South Australia.* Adelaide: Government Printer, 1957.

Coxon, Howard, John Playford, and Robert Reid. *Biographical Register of the South Australian Parliament 1857–1957.* Netley, South Australia: Wakefield Press, c1985.

Cromer, Evelyn Baring. *Modern Egypt / by the Earl of Cromer.* London: Macmillan, 1908.

Dammond, Liliane S. *The Lost World of the Egyptian Jews.* New York, NY: iUniverse, Inc., 2007.

Dardaud, Gabriel. *Trente Ans au Bord du Nil.* Paris: Lieu Commun, 1987.

Deshen, Schlomo, and Walter P. Zenner, eds. *Jews among Muslims: Communities in the Precolonial Middle East.* New York: New York University Press, 1996.

Dexter, L. A. *Elite and Specialised Interviewing.* Evanston, IL: Northwestern University Press, 1970.

Devine, Fiona. "Qualitative Analysis", in *Theory and Methods in Political Science,* edited by D. Marsh and G. Stoker. London: Palgrave Macmillan, 1995, 137–152.

Dodwell, Henry. *The Founder of Modern Egypt: A Study of Muhammad Ali.* Cambridge, MA: Cambridge University Press, 1931. 2nd ed. New York, NY: AMS Press, 1977.

Douglas, L., and P. Spearrit. "Talking History: The Use of Oral Sources". In *New History: Studying Australia Today*, edited by G. Osborne and W. Mandle, Sydney, London, and Boston, MA: George Allen and Unwin, 1982, 51–68.

El-Ad, Avri, and James Creech. *Decline of Honour.* Chicago, IL: Henry Regnery, 1976

El-Kodsi, Mourad. *The Karaite Jews of Egypt: From 1882–1986.* Lyons, NY: Wilprint Inc., 1987.

Faivre d'Arcier, Amaury. *Les Agents de Napoléon en Égypte: 1801–1815.* Centre d'Etudes Napoléoniennes, Au Siège de la Société de Sauvegarde du Château Impérial de Pont-de-Briques: Levallois, France, 1990.

Fargeon, Maurice. *Les Juifs en Égypte: depuis les origines jusqu'à ce jour.* Cairo: Paul Barbey, 1938.

———. *Médecins et avocats juifs au service de l'Égypte: histoire génerale depuis l'antiquité nos jours, suivie d'un recueil de biographies des principaux médecins et avocats juifs d'Égypte contemporains*. Cairo: Imprimerie Lencioni, 1939.

―――, ed. *Annuaire des Juifs d'Égypte et du Proche Orient, 1942*. Cairo: La Société des Editions Historiques juives d'Égypte, 1943.

―――, ed. *Annuaire des Juifs d'Égypte et du Proche Orient, 5706/1945–1946*. Cairo: La Société des Editions Historiques juives d'Égypte, 1945.

Felice, Renzo de. *Jews in an Arab Land: Libya 1835–1970*. Translated by Judith Roumani. Austin: University of Texas, 1985.

Finer, Herman. *Dulles over Suez: The Theory and Practice of His Diplomacy*. London: Heinemann, 1964.

Fisher, Marcelle. *Armando*. Tel Aviv: Yeda Sela Ltd., 1982.

―――. *Les Khamsins d'antan: La petite histoire des Juifs d'Égypte*. Tel Aviv: M. Rachlin Ltd., 1990.

Foddy, William. *Constructing Questions for Interviews and Questionnaires: Theory and Practice in Social Research*. Cambridge, MA: Cambridge University Press, 1993.

Foster, John, ed. *Community of Fate: Memoirs of German Jews in Melbourne*. Sydney: Allen & Unwin Australia, 1986.

Fourastié, Jean. *Les Trente Glorieuses ou la révolution invisible de 1946 à 1975*. Paris: Editions Fayard, 1979.

Frankel, Jonathan. *The Damascus Affair: "Ritual Murder", Politics and the Jews in 1840*. Cambridge, MA: Cambridge University Press, 1997.

Gale, Naomi. *The Sephardim of Sydney: Coping with Political Processes and Social Pressures*. Brighton and Portland: Sussex Academic Press, 2005.

Galimidi, Frédéric. *Alexandrie-sur-Seine*. Collection l'Echelle de Jacob IV, Tarascon: Cousins de Salonique Editeurs, 1999.

Gendzier, Irene L. *The Practical Visions of Ya'Qub Sanu'*. Cambridge, MA: Harvard University, MS Monograph XV, 1966.

Gilbert, Martin. *The Jews of Arab Lands: Their History in Maps.* London: World Organisation of Jews from Arab Countries and Board of Deputies of British Jews, 1976.

Goffman, Erving. *The Presentation of Self in Everyday Life.* Edinburgh: University of Edinburgh. 1956.

———. *Encounters: Two Studies in the Sociology of Interaction.* Indianapolis, IN: Bobbs-Merrill, 1961.

Goitein, S. D. *A Mediterranean Society: The Jewish Communities of the Arab World as Portrayed in the Documents of the Cairo Genizah*, Vol. 1: Economic Foundations. Berkeley: University of California Press, 1967–c1993.

Golani, Motti. *Israel in Search of a War: The Sinai Campaign 1955–1956.* Sussex: Sussex Academic Press, 1997.

Golan, Aviezer. *Operation Suzannah: As Told to Aviezer Golan by Marcelle Ninio, Victor Levy, Robert Dassa, and Philip Natanson.* Translated by Peretz Kidron. New York, NY: Harpers and Row, 1978.

Goldberg, Harvey E. *Jewish Life in Muslim Libya: Rivals and Relatives.* Chicago, IN: University of Chicago Press, 1990.

———. *Sephardi and Middle Eastern Jewries: History and Culture in the Modern Era.* Bloomington and Indianapolis: Indiana University Press, 1996.

Gorden, Raymond L. *Interviewing Strategy, Techniques and Tactics.* Homewood, IL: The Dorsey Press, 1969.

Hamouda, Sahar, and Colin Clement, eds. *Victoria College: A History Revealed.* Cairo and New York, NY: American University Press, 2002.

Harari, Meyer. *Second Exodus.* Melbourne: Makor Jewish Community Library, 1999.

Hassoun, Jacques. "De l'Égypte et de Quelques Juifs Égyptiens…," in *Cultures Juives, méditerranéennes et orientales*, 221–231. Paris: Syros, 1982.

———, ed. *Juifs du Nil*. Paris: Le Sycomore, 1981.

Histoire des Juifs du Nil, 2nd ed. Paris: Minerve, 1990.

———. *Alexandries*. Paris: Editions La Découverte, 1985.

———. *Alexandrie et autres récits de Jacques Hassoun*. Paris: Editions L'Harmattan, 2001.

Heilman, Samuel C., and Steven M. Cohen. *The Gate Behind the Wall*. Philadelphia, PA: The Jewish Publication Society, 1984.

———. *Cosmopolitans & Parochials: Modern Orthodox Jews in America*. Chicago, IL: The University of Chicago Press, 1989.

Hudson, W. J. *Blind Loyalty: Australia and the Suez Crisis, 1956*. Melbourne: Melbourne University Press, 1989.

Hyams, Bernard. *Surviving, A History of the Institutions and Organisations of the Adelaide Jewish Community*. Adelaide: Hyde Park Press, 1998.

Hyman, Paula E. *The Jews of Modern France*. Berkeley and Los Angeles: University of California Press, 1998.

Ilbert, Robert, et Ilios Yannakakis, eds., avec la collaboration de Jacques Hassoun. *Alexandrie, 1860–1960*. Paris: Editions Autrement, 1992.

Jacques, Paula. *Lumière de l'oeil*. Paris: Mercure de France, 1980.

———. *Un Baiser froid comme la lune*. Paris: Mercure de France, 1983.

———. *L'Héritage de tante Carlotta*. Paris: Gallimard, 1990.

———. *Déborah et les anges dissipés*. Paris: Mercure de France, 1991.

———. *La Descente au paradis*. Paris: Mercure de France, 1995.

———. *Gilda Stambouli souffre et se plaint*. Paris: Mercure de France, 2002.

Jordens, Ann-Mari. *Redefining Australians*. Sydney: Hale & Iremonger Pty. Ltd., 1995.

————. *Alien to Citizen: Settling Migrants in Australia, 1945–75.* Sydney: Allen & Unwin, 1997.

Jupp, James. *Immigration.* Sydney: Sydney University Press, 1991.

————, ed. *The Australian People.* Cambridge, MA: Cambridge University Press, 2001.

Krämer, Gudrun. *The Jews in Modern Egypt, 1914–1952.* Seattle: University of Washington Press, 1989.

Lagnado, Lucette. *The Man in the White Sharkskin Suit.* New York, NY: Ecco Press, 2007.

Landau, Jacob [Ya'agov]. M. *Jews in Nineteenth Century Egypt.* New York, NY: New York University Press, 1969.

————. *Middle Eastern Themes.* London: Frank Cass, 1973.

Lane, Edward William. *Manners and Customs of the Modern Egyptians 1833–1835.* London: Ward Locker & Co, 1836.

Laskier, Michael M. *The Jews of Egypt, 1920–1970: In the Midst of Zionism, Anti-Semitism and the Middle East Conflict.* New York, NY: New York University Press, 1992.

————. *North African Jewry in the Twentieth Century: The Jews of Morocco, Tunisia and Algeria.* New York: New York University Press, 1994.

Lefebvre, Denis. *L'Affaire de Suez.* Paris: Graffic, Editions Bruno Leprince, 1996.

Levey, Geoffrey Brahm, and Philip Mendes, eds. *Jews and Australian Politics.* Brighton and Portland: Sussex Academic Press, 2004.

Levi, John S. & George F. J. Bergman. *Australian Genesis: Jewish Convicts and Settlers 1788–1860.* Melbourne: Melbourne University Press, 2002. First published by Rigby Limited, 1974.

Lewis, Bernard. *The Jews of Islam.* Princeton, NJ: Princeton University Press, 1984.

———. *Semites and Anti-Semites: An Inquiry into Conflict and Prejudice.* New York, NY: Norton, 1986.

———. *Cultures in Conflict: Christians, Muslims and Jews in the Age of Discovery.* New York, NY: Oxford University Press, 1995.

Lucas, Scott, ed. *Britain and Suez: the Lion's Last Roar.* Manchester; NY: Manchester University Press, 1996.

Luthi, Jean-Jacques. *Introduction à la littérature d'expression française en Égypte: 1798–1945.* Paris: Editions de l'Ecole, 1974.

———. *Égypte, qu'as-tu fait de ton français?* Paris: Synonym, S.O.R., 1987.

———. *L'Égypte des Rois, 1922–1953.* Paris: L'Harmattan, 1997.

———. *En Quête du français d'Égypte: Adoption, évolution, caractères.* Paris: L'Harmattan, 2005.

Mahassen, Réga Noury. *Hier encore, à Alexandrie.* Genève: Rochat-Baumann SA, 1995.

Mallmann, Klaus-Michael, and Martin Cüppers, eds. Translated by Krista Smith. *Nazi Palestine: The Plans for the Extermination of the Jews in Palestine.* New York, NY: Enigma Books, 2010.

Mansfield, Peter. *Nasser's Egypt.* Great Britain: Penguin Books, 1965, revised 1969.

Marsot, Afaf Lutfi Al-Sayyid. *Egypt in the Reign of Muhammad Ali.* Cambridge, MA: Cambridge University Press, 1984.

Maurois, André. *Disraëli.* New York, NY: D. Appleton & Co, 1928.

Matalon, Ronit. *The One Facing Us.* Translated by Marsha Weinstein. New York, NY: Metropolitan Books/Henry Holt, 1998.

Phillip-Matz, Mary Jane. *Verdi: A Biography.* Oxford and NewYork, NY: Oxford University Press, 1993.

Migration Museum (History Trust of S.A.). *From Many Places, the History and Cultural Traditions of South Australian People.* Adelaide: Wakefield Press, 1995.

Mitchell, Timothy. *Colonising Egypt*. Cambridge, MA: Cambridge University Press, 1988.

Mizrahi, Maurice. *l'Égypte et ses Juifs: Le Temps révolu, XIXè et XXè siècle*. Geneva: Presses de Imprimerie Avenir, SA, 1977.

Modrzejewski, Mélèze J. *Les Juifs d'Égypte de Ramsès II à Hadrien*. Paris: Presse Universitaire de France, 1997.

Oudiz, Albert. *Je viens d'un pays qui n'existe plus*. Paris: Editions Nahar Misraïm, 2004.

———. *Une Jeunesse Égyptienne*. Paris: Editions Nahar Misraïm, 2007.

Panich, Catherine. *Sanctuary?: Remembering Post-War Immigration*. Sydney: Allen & Unwin Australia, 1988.

Pardo, Albert. *L'Égypte que j'ai connue*. Paris: Editions Nahar Misraïm, 2003.

Perera, Victor. *The Cross and the Pear Tree: A Sephardic Journey*. London: Flamingo, HarpersCollins, 1995.

Perrault, Gilles. *Un Homme à part*. Paris: Bernard Barrault, 1984.

Peters, Nonja. *Milk and Honey but No Gold: Post-War Migration to Western Australia, 1945–1965*. Nedlands: University of Western Australia Press, 2001.

Polliack, Meira, ed. *Karaite Judaism: A Guide to Its History and Literary Sources*. Leiden; Boston, MA: Brill, 2003.

Price, Charles, Elizabeth Tyler, and Lillian Wilson. *Jewish Settlers in Australia*. Canberra: Australia National University, 1964.

Raafat, Samir W. *Maadi 1904–1962: Society and History in a Cairo Suburb*. Cairo: The Palm Press, 1994.

Rahmani, Moise. *Juifs des pays arabes: L'Exode oublié*. Paris: Editions Raphaël, 2003.

Reich, Chanan. *Australia and Israel: An Ambiguous Relationship*. Melbourne: Melbourne University Press, 2002.

Richards, Alan. *Egypt's Agricultural Development, 1800–1980: Technical and Social Change*. Boulder, CO: Westview Press, 1982.

Riegner, Gerhart M. *Ne jamais désespérer: soixante années au service du peuple juif et des droits de l'homme*. Paris: Les Editions du Cerf, 1998.

Robertson, Beth M. *Oral History Handbook*, 4th ed. Adelaide: Oral History Association of Australia (South Australian Branch), 2000.

Rochefort, Christiane. *Les Petits Enfants du siècle*. Paris: LGF, 1961.

Roden, Claudia. *A Book of Middle Eastern Food*. London: Penguin Book, 1970.

———. *The Book of Jewish Food*. Great Britain: Viking, 1997.

Rodenbeck, Max. *Cairo: The City Victorious*. London: Picador, 1998.

Rodrigue, Aron. *French Jews, Turkish Jews: The Alliance Israélite Universelle and Politics of Jewish Schooling in Turkey, 1860–1925*. Bloomington and Indianapolis: Indiana University Press, 1990.

Rosenblum, Mort. *Mission to Civilize: The French Way*. Orlando, FL: Harcourt Brace Jovanovich, 1986.

Rossant, Colette. *Apricots on the Nile: A Memoir with Recipes*. London: Bloomsbury Publishing, 2002.

Rouchou, Joëlle. *Noites de verão com cheiro de jasmin (Nuits d'été à l'odeur de jasmin)*. Rio de Janeiro: Editoria da Fundação Getulio Vargas (FGV), 2008.

Rubinstein, Hilary L. *Chosen: The Jews in Australia*. Sydney: Allen & Unwin, 1987.

Rubinstein, W. D. *The Jews in Australia*. Victoria: Australian Ethnic Heritage Press, 1986.

———, ed. *Jews in the Sixth Continent*. Sydney: Allen & Unwin, 1987.

Rutland, Suzanne D. *Pages of History*. Sydney: Australian Jewish Press, 1995.

———. *Edge of the Diaspora.* Sydney: Collins Australia, 1988; 2nd edition, Sydney: Brandl & Schlesinger, 1997.

———. *The Jews in Australia.* Cambridge, MA, New York, NY, and Port Melbourne: Cambridge University Press, 2005.

Rutland, Suzanne D., and Sophie Caplan. *With One Voice: A History of the New South Wales Jewish Board of Deputies.* Sydney: Australian Jewish Historical Society Inc., 1998.

Schechtman, Joseph B. *The Refugee in the World: Displacement and Integration.* New York, NY: A.S. Barnes & Co., 1963.

Schur, Nathan. *History of the Karaites.* Frankfurt, Berlin, and New York, NY: Peter Lang Publishing, 1992.

Shamir, Shimon. *Self-Views in Historical Perspective in Egypt and Israel.* Syracuse, NY: Syracuse University Press, 1981.

———, ed. *The Jews of Egypt: A Mediterranean Society in Modern Times.* Boulder, CO, and London: Westview Press, 1987.

———, ed.. *Egypt from Monarchy to Republic: A Reassessment of Revolution and Change.* Boulder, CO: Westview Press, 1995.

Sinoué, Gilbert. *Le Colonel et l'enfant-roi.* Paris: Editions JC Lattès, 2006.

Sluga, Glenda. *Bonegilla: "A Place of No Hope".* Melbourne: University of Melbourne, 1988.

Solé, Robert. *Le Tarbouche.* Paris: Editions du Seuil, 1992.

———. *Le Sémaphore d'Alexandrie.* Paris, Editions du Seuil, 1994.

———. *La Mamelouka.* Paris: Editions du Seuil, 1996.

———. *L'Égypte, passion française.* Paris: Editions du Seuil, 1997.

———. *Les Savants de Bonaparte.* Paris: Editions du Seuil, 1998.

Solé, Robert, et Dominique Valbelle. *La Pierre de Rosette.* Paris: Editions du Seuil, 1999.

Spector, Shmuel, "Karaites". In *Encyclopedia of the Holocaust.* Vol. 2. 785–787. New York, NY: Mac Millan, 1990.

Stanislawski, Michael. *Tsar Nicholas I and the Jews: The Transformation of Jewish Society in Russia, 1825–1855*. Philadelphia, PA: Jewish Publication Society, 1983.

Stillman, Norman A. *The Jews of Arab Lands*. Philadelphia, PA: Jewish Publication Society, 1979.

———. *The Jews of Arab Lands in Modern Times*. Philadelphia, PA: Jewish Publication Society, 1991.

Sudman, Seymour, and Norman M. Bradburn. *Asking Questions: A Practical Guide to Questionnaire Design*. San Francisco, CA: Jossey-Bass Publishers, 1982.

Szulc, Tad. *The Secret Alliance: The Extraordinary Story of the Rescue of the Jews since World War II*. New York, NY: Farrar, Straus & Giroux, 1991.

Tayar, Aline P'nina. *How Shall We Sing? A Mediterranean Journey through a Jewish Family*. Sydney: Picador, Pan Macmillan Australia, 2000.

Teboul, Victor. *Que Dieu vous garde de l'homme silencieux quand il se met soudain à parler*. Montréal: Editions Les Intouchables, 2000.

———. *La Lente Découverte de l'étrangeté*. Montréal: Editions Les Intouchables, 2002.

Teveth, Shabtai. *Ben-Gurion's Spy: The Story of the Political Scandal that Shaped Modern Israel*. New York, NY: Columbia University Press, 1996.

Thomas, Hugh. *The Suez Affair*. London: Weidenfeld &Nicolson, 1967.

Thompson, Charles P., John J. Skowronski, Steen F. Larsen, and Andrew L. Betz. *Autobiographical Memory, Remembering What and Remembering When*. Hillsdale, NJ: Lawrence Erlbaum Associates, 1996.

Thompson-Seton, G. *A Woman Tenderfoot in Egypt*. London: John Lane, 1923.

Thompson, Paul. *The Voice of the Past*. Oxford: Oxford University Press, 1990.

Thompson, Victoria. *Losing Alexandria.* Sydney: Picador Pan Macmillan Australia, 1998.

Trigano, Shmuel, compiled. *La Fin du judaïsme en terres d'Islam.* Paris: Denoël, 2009.

Turnbull, Malcolm J. *Safe Haven: Records of the Jewish Experience in Australia.* Canberra: National Archives of Australia, 1999.

Warburg, Gabriel R., and Uri M. Kupferschmidt, eds. *Islam, Nationalism and Radicalism in Egypt and the Sudan.* New York, NY: Praeger, 1983.

Waskow, Arthur Ocean, and Phyllis Ocean Berman. *A Time for Every Purpose under Heaven.* New York, NY: Farrar, Strauss and Giroux, 2002.

White, Naomi Rosh. *From Darkness to Light: Surviving the Holocaust.* Melbourne: Collins Dove, 1988.

Williams, Ann. *Britain and France in the Middle East and North Africa, 1914-1967.* New York, NY: St. Martin's Press, 1968.

Wilton, Janis, and Richard Bosworth. *Old Worlds and New Australia: The Post-War Migrant Experience.* Ringwood, Victoria: Penguin Books Australia, 1984.

Zuccotti, Susan. *The Holocaust, the French, and the Jews.* New York, NY: BasicBooks, Division of HarperCollins Publishers, 1993.

Journal Articles

Abitbol, Michel, and Alan Astro. "The Integration of North African Jews in France". *Yale French Studies 85* (1994): 248–261.

Barda, Rachel. "A Journey to the 'Edge of the Diaspora': The Jews from Egypt". *AJHS Journal XVIII*, part 3 (June 2007): 372–409.

Ben-Meir, Gad. "The Sephardim of Australia". *AJHS Journal XI,* Part 1 (1990) 20–30.

Bennett, Ralph. "History of the Jews of Egypt". *Avotaynu X*, no. 1 (Spring 1994): 30–32.

Bensimon, Doris. "L'Immigration juive en France, 1945–1999". *Yod, Revue des études hébraïques et juives modernes et contemporaines 6* (1999): 53–66.

Charme, Stuart L. "Varieties of Authenticity in Contemporary Jewish Identity". *Jewish Social Studies 6*, no. 2 (January 2000): 133–155.

Cohen, Mark R. "Islam and the Jews: Myth, Counter-Myth and History". *Jerusalem Quarterly 38* (Spring 1986): 125–137.

———."The Neo-Lachrymose Conception of Jewish-Arab History". *Tikkun 6* (May-June 1991): 55–60.

Della Pergola, Sergio. "World Jewish Population, 2002". *American Jewish Year Book 102* (2002): 601–642.

Evans, M. D. "Immigrant Women in Australia: Resources, Family and Work". *International Migration Review 18*, no. 4 (Winter 1984): 1063–1090.

Foster, Lois, and Ann Seitz. "Applications of Oral History in the Sociology of Ethnic Relations". *Journal of Intercultural Studies 6*, no. 3 (1985): 5–15.

Gale, Naomi. "Sephardim and Sephardic Identity in Sydney". *AJHS Journal XI*, Part 2 (1991): 331–351.

———. "A Case of Double Rejection: The Immigration of Sephardim to Australia". *New Community 20*, no. 2 (January 1994): 269–286.

———. "Religious Involution: Sacred and Secular Conflict among Sephardi Jews in Australia". *Ethnology 36*, no. 3 (1997): 321–334.

———. "Residence, Social Mobility and Practice Theory: The Case of Sephardic Jews of Sydney". *Journal of Sociology 35*, no. 2 (1999): 146–168.

Gitelman, Zvi. "The Decline of the Diaspora Jewish Nation: Boundaries, Content, and Jewish Identity". *Jewish Social Studies 4*, no. 2 (January 31, 1998): 112–122.

Gouttman, Rodney. "A Jew, and Coloured Too! Immigration of 'Jews of Middle East Origin' to Australia 1949–58". *Immigrants & Minorities 12*, no. 1 (March 1993): 75–91.

———. "Prelude to Suez: Australia and the Middle East Command". *Australian Journal of Jewish Studies XIV* (2000): 101–121.

Hassoun, Jacques. "Can Egyptian-Jewish Identity Be Reconstructed in France". *Bulletin of the Israeli Academic Centre in Cairo 23* (June 1998): 8–10.

Hugo, Graeme. "Regional Migration: A New Paradigm of International Migration". Research note no. 56 2003–04, Parliament of Australia, Parliamentary Library: 2.

Kaplan, Marion A. "Tradition and Transition: The Acculturation, Assimilation and Integration of Jews in Imperial Germany". *Leo Beck Institute Yearbook XXVII* (1982): 3–35.

Laskier, Michael M. "France: An Unexpected Centre of Jewish Life". *Judaism XXXIV*, no. 2 (Spring 1985): 231–236.

———. "A Document on Anglo-Jewry's Intervention on Behalf of Egyptian Jews on Trial for Espionage and Sabotage; December 1954". *Michael X* (1986): 143–152.

———. "From War to War: The Jews of Egypt from 1948 to 1970". *Studies in Zionism 7*, no. 1 (1986): 111–147.

———. "From Hafsia to Bizerte: Tunisia's Nationalist Struggle and Tunisian Jewry, 1952–61". *Mediterranean Historical Review 2*, no. 2 (December 1987): 188–222.

———. "Egypt's Jewry in the Post-World War II Period: 1945–1948". *Revue des études juives 148* (July-December 1989): 337–360.

———. "Egyptian Jewry under the Nasser Regime, 1956–1970". *Middle Eastern Studies 31*, no. 3 (July 1995): 573–619.

———. "The Jewish Press in the Inter-War Years: The Journal Israel". *Bulletin of the Israeli Academic Centre in Cairo 23* (June 1998): 11–15.

———. "The Regeneration of French Jewry: The Influx and Integration of North African Jews into France, 1955–1965". *Jewish Political Studies Review 10*, nos. 1–2 (Spring 1998): 37–72.

———. "In the Aftermath of Israel's Sinai Campaign: The Leadership Crisis and Political and Economical decline of Egypt's Jewish Communities during the Late 1950s and 1960s". *Africana Journal XVII* (1998): 289–306.

Lévy, Alain. "Itinéraire d'une famille juive d'Alexandrie de 1900 à 1980; de la tradition ottomane à la modernité". *L'Ethnographie 116* (1994): 71–82.

Lippmann, Walter M. "The Demography of Australian Jewry". *AJHS Journal VI*, Part 5 (1968): 253–265.

Mitsztal, B. A. "Migrant Women in Australia". *Journal of Intercultural Studies 12*, no. 2 (1991): 15–34.

Owen, E. R. J. "Lord Cromer and the Development of Egyptian Industry, 1883–1927". *Middle Eastern Studies 2* (1966): 282–301.

Perret, Françoise. "ICRC Operations in Hungary and the Middle East in 1956". *International Review of the Red Cross 313* (August 31, 1996): 412–437.

Pigott, Leanne. "Lord Casey and the 1939 White Paper: How an Australian British Prime Minister of State Fought to Keep the Jews out of Palestine". *AJHS Journal XIV*, part 2 (1998): 288–321.

Porush, Rabbi, Dr. Israel. "Some Statistical Data on Australian Jewry". *AJHS Journal IV*, part 1 (1953): 1–7.

———. "The 1971 Census: Interesting Data Concerning Jews". *AJHS Journal VIII*, part 1 (1975): 1–5.

———. "Jews in the 1981 Census". *AJHS Journal IX*, part 5 (1983): 325–326.

Rein, Raanan. "Diplomacy, Propaganda, and Humanitarian Gestures: Francoist Spain and Egyptian Jews, 1956–1958". *Iberoamericana 23* (2006): 10–11.

Rodrigue, Aron. "Sephardim and the Holocaust". (Ina Levine Annual Lecture, 19 February 2004). *United States Holocaust Memorial Museum, Center for Advanced Holocaust Studies* (2005).

Rubinstein, W. D. "Australia and the Refugee Jews of Europe, 1933–1954: A Dissenting View". *AJHS Journal 10*, part 6 (1989): 500–523.

Rutland, Suzanne D. "Egyptian Jews in Adelaide: A Case Study in Oral History". *The Oral History Association of Australia Journal 6* (1984): 19–24.

———. "'Are You Jewish?': Post-War Jewish Immigration to Australia, 1945–1954". *The Australian Journal of Jewish Studies 5*, no. 2 (1991): 35–58.

———. "The Honourable Sydney David Einfeld, A. O.: Builder of Australian Jewry". *AJHS Journal XI*, part 2 (1991): 312–330.

———. "Subtle Exclusions: Post-War Jewish Emigration to Australia and the Impact of the IRO Scheme". *The Journal of Holocaust Education 10*, no. 1 (Summer 2001): 50–66.

———. "Post-War Jewish 'Boat People' and Parallels with the Tampa Incident". *Australian Journal of Jewish Studies XVI* (2002): 159–176.

———. "Australian Responses to Jewish Refugee Migration before and after World War II". *Australian Journal of Politics and History 31*, no. 1 (1985): 29–48.

———. "A Changing Community: The Impact of the Refugees on Australian Jewry: New South Wales—A Case Study". *Australian Journal of Politics and History 31*, no. 1 (1985): 90–108.

Sanua, Victor D. "A Study of the Adjustment of Sephardi Jews in the New York Metropolitan Area". *The Jewish Journal of Sociology IX*, no 1 (June 1967): 25–33.

———. "Emigration of Sephardic Jews from Egypt after the Arab-Israeli Wars". *WCJS 11*, B3 (1994): 215–222.

———. "'Egypt for the Egyptians': The Story of Abu Naddara (James Sanua) 1839–1912—A Jewish Egyptian Patriot". *Los Muestros Online 32* (September 1998).

———. "Haim Nahum Effendi (1872–1960), Sephardic Chief Rabbi of Egypt". *Los Muestros Online 46* (March 2002).

Shamir, Shimon. "Notes on Researching the Modern History of Egyptian Jewry". *Bulletin of the Israeli Academic Centre in Cairo 23* (June 1998): 3–7.

Stillman, Norman A. 'Myth, Countermyth and Distortion', *Tikkun 6* (May-June 1991), 60–64.

Whitfield, Stephen J. "Enigmas of Modern Jewish Identity". *Jewish Social Studies* 8, no. 2/3 (Winter/Spring 2002): 162–167.

Newspapers, Periodicals, and Newsletters

Jewish Press:

Australian Jewish Times/News (Sydney)

Sydney Jewish News

AAHA Newsletter

Bassatine News (online)—The Jewish Community of Cairo (JCC) Newsletter

Bulletin du CRPJE, Tel Aviv

Bulletin of the Israeli Academic Centre in Cairo

Goshen, Bulletin des Juifs d'Égypte en Israël, Haifa

IAJE Newsletter, New York

Jewish Renaissance, London

La Lettre Sépharade, Paris

Los Muestros—The Sephardic Voice, Brussels

Nahar Misraim, Bulletin De L'ASPCJE

Nahar Misraim, Bulletin De Liaison de L'ASPCJE

Sephardi Bulletin, Sydney

General Press:

Cairo Times

Egyptian Mail

El-Ahram Weekly

Le Nouvel Observateur

L'Express

Signature

Sydney Morning Herald

The New Yorker

Theses: Unpublished

Barda, Rachel. M. *Les Juifs d'Égypte et la culture française, une perspective socio-romanesque.* BA Honours Diss. University of Sydney, 1987.

Carasso, Ethel. *La Communauté juive d'Égypte de 1948 à 1957.* Maitrise d'Histoire Contemporaine. Université de Paris X, 1982.

Ruth Leftel. *A comunidade sefaradita egipcia de Sào Paulo.* PhD Diss. University of Sào Paulo, May 1997.

Lévy, Alain. *Topologie sociale d'une migration familiale (Égypte, Algérie, France, Grande-Bretagne, Brésil).* PhD Diss. Université de Paris 7, 1994.

Reich, Chanan. *Ethnic Identity and Political Participation: the Jewish and Greek Communities in Melbourne.* PhD Diss. Monash University, 1983.

Rouchou, Joëlle. *Nuits d'été au parfum de jasmin: Souvenirs des Juifs d'Égypte à Rio de Janeiro—1956/57.* PhD Diss. Université de Sao Paulo, 2003.

Rutland, Suzanne D. *The History of Australian Jewry 1945–1960.* PhD Diss. University of Sydney, 1990.

Samra, Myer. *Yisrael Rhammana: Constructions of Identity among Iraqi Jews in Sydney, Australia.* PhD Diss. University of Sydney, 1988.

Saunut, Sophie. *L'Immigration des Juifs d'Égypte vers la France entre 1948 et 1970.* Mémoire. Université Paris I Panthéon Sorbonne, 2004–2006.

Unpublished Sources

Dayan, Freddy E. *Growing Up in Egypt in the Thirties.* Trans. Ian Kenneth Smith.

———. *From the Banks of the Nile to the Shores of the Derwent, 1940–1988.* Trans. Ian Kenneth Smith.

Samra, Myer. *The Founding of Bet Yosef: Conflict and Community among Sephardi Jews.*

Seidman, Talia Clara. *In Every Generation, It Is One's Duty to Regard Himself as though He Personally Had Gone Out Of Egypt: Haggadah.* Sydney: Dr. Hans Kimmel Memorial Prize for Jewish History, Year 10, Moriah College, September 2003.

Encyclopædias

Encyclopaedia Judaica. Jerusalem: Keter Publishing House, 1971.

Encyclopaedia of the Holocaust. New York: Mac Millan, 1990.

The Karaite Encyclopaedia. Frankfurt, 1995.

The Encyclopedia of the Jews in the Islamic World. Leiden, Netherlands: Brill, 2010.

Television Program

Alexandrie: L'autre rive, Kilomètre Delta (main protagonist, Anaël Guéned), 1999.

Radio Broadcast

"Juifs d'Égypte". *Radio communautaire juive,* April 19, 1990.

Quatre émissions de Paula Jacques avec Jacques Hassoun. "Nuits magnétiques, six jours et sept nuits, le temps d'un retour au pays natal". February 2, 1993.

INDEX

Galvin, Patrick, 29, 202, 204–206, 222, 299, 366n571, 367n578, 367n580, 368n583
Gamil, Maurice, 251, 380n683
Geniza, 76, 321n120
Golliger, Alec, 2, 124, 346n374, 366n567, 382n710
Gouttman, Rodney, 28–29, 316n84
Grandes Ecoles, 386n745, 386n747

Hagana, 168, 370n602
Hans Kimmel Memorial Essay, 259, 381n695, 382n707
haret-el-Yahud/hara, 154, 348n395
Harari, Meyer, 46, 214, 324n136, 370n601
Hassoun, Jacques, 14, 16, 37, 123–124, 126, 155, 165, 292–294, 318n106, 318n109, 319n113, 332n229, 334n243, 335n262, 345n366, 345n370, 346n372, 348n395, 348n398, 351n424, 351n431, 353n446, 385n736, 389n776, 390n786, 391n787
Helwan, 118, 343n348
Heyes, Sir Tasman, 203, 317n95, 364n553, 367n576, 367n582
HIAS, 19, 25, 27, 43, 108–109, 194, 198, 207–210, 316n81, 368n588, 375n636
HSJE, 294, 376n653
HLM, 281, 383n722
Huckstep, 18, 188, 214, 312n42, 370n602, 389n772
Hudson, W. J., 35, 365n560, 365n562, 365n565
Hungarian refugees, 31, 210–211, 252, 369n593

Al-Husseini, Mohammed Amin, 97, 337n285

IAJE, 39, 294, 320n117, 391n794
ICRC, 19, 108, 207, 210, 368n586
integration, 1, 3–6, 8–9, 17–19, 27, 29, 41, 43–44, 48, 50, 61–62, 64, 66, 95, 110, 148–149, 170–171, 225, 227, 230–231, 235–236, 238, 244–245, 260, 262–264, 269, 271, 278, 280, 282, 287, 297, 300, 304–305, 308n14, 322n129, 326n163, 375n636, 386n744
intermarriage, 5, 156–157, 164–165, 261, 273, 301–302, 386n740, 386n741
Iraqi/Indian Jews, 32–34, 248–251, 253, 317n93, 317n98, 379n675. *See also* Baghdadi Jews
IRO, 25, 364n552
Islamism/Islamic, 3, 91, 93–95, 97, 100, 104, 109, 169, 195, 298, 339n310

Jacques, Paula, 43, 293, 322n129, 391n790
JDC/AJDC, 18–19, 27, 102, 207, 210, 266, 268–271, 368n587, 369n590–591, 381n698, 385n731
Jewish Agency, 19, 99, 102, 108, 139, 179, 182, 207–208, 268, 337n281, 348n395, 356n472, 368n588, 386n741
Jews of Algeria, 42, 83–85, 115, 122, 127, 210, 267–268, 272, 309n22, 312n40, 333n235

www.ingramcontent.com/pod-product-compliance
Lightning Source LLC
Chambersburg PA
CBHW030855270326
41929CB00008B/435